MAN AND HIS CULTURE:
Psychoanalytic Anthropology after 'Totem and Taboo'

MAN AND HIS CULTURE:

Psychoanalytic Anthropology after 'Totem and Taboo'

Edited by

WARNER MUENSTERBERGER

TAPLINGER PUBLISHING COMPANY
NEW YORK

First Published in the United States in 1970 by
TAPLINGER PUBLISHING CO., INC.
New York, New York

International Standard Book Number 0-8008-5085-8

Library of Congress Catalog Card Number 79-103017

Printed in the United States of America

Contents

5

CONTENTS

Preface

Forewords to books are a curious custom. They sometimes read like apologies. Books like works of art should be self-explanatory. The current volume might be in need of an explanation. The first idea of a book of this kind occurred during many hours of fascinating dialogues with Géza Róheim.

Róheim was a very independent thinker and in some sense a lonely man. Against all odds in the field of anthropology he alone fought for a psychoanalytic approach to the science of man. In 1950, Róheim had been invited by Dr Sandor Lorand to teach at the newly established 'Division for Psychoanalytic Education' at the Downstate Medical Center of the State University of New York. He had taught for many years a course in psychoanalytic anthropology at the New York Psychoanalytic Institute. As he wanted to devote more time to his writing—he had been working on his *Gates of the Dream*—he suggested that I should give the course instead. It was in this connection that we spoke of the necessity for a kind of 'Reader' in applied psychoanalysis.

Conceived and written from different angles and at various times, the essays collected in this volume have proved to be instructive and valuable in teaching and lecturing on psychoanalytic anthropology to candidates in psychoanalytic institutes and residents in psychiatry in the United States, Europe and Asia. The combined knowledge of clinical psychoanalysis and field anthropology has given form and direction to this rather special enclave of the science of man.

Selections are always arbitrary. Some papers were chosen because they seem significant yet not easily accessible. Others focus on particular issues such as the current psychoanalytic view on and critique of the 'Primal Horde Theory' in Freud's *Totem and Taboo*. All contributions, I believe, provide us with new insight into the essential nature of man.

A number of studies had to be omitted. Erik H. Erikson's work with the Sioux and Yurok has been dealt with in various publications, among them his well-known book *Childhood and Society* and is readily available. The extensive field explorations among the

7

Apache by Ruth M. and L. Bryce Boyer, a husband and wife team of psychoanalyst and anthropologist, are very instructive in their detailed observations. Other contributions such as those by William Caudill, Weston LaBarre, Charles Savage and Raymond Prince, Parin and Morgenthaler are closely related to our subject but could not be included. Many works by Margaret Mead, Cora Du Bois, Geoffrey Gorer *et al.* are evidently influenced by psychoanalytic propositions, however sometimes limited to the genetic-adaptive point of view.

I wish to acknowledge the helpful suggestions by many of my former students and the valuable criticism of my friend and colleague Martin H. Stein, M.D. Mr Christopher Nichols kindly provided several additions to the reading list.

Thanks are due to the authors of various papers. Dr Marianne Kris gave me permission to reprint the article co-authored by the late Dr Ernst Kris, and Dr Talcott Parsons allowed me to include his late daughter's excellent study 'Is the Œdipus Complex Universal?'—Dr Alan Fraser's paper is an original contribution to this anthology. Mrs George Devereux was kind enough to condense Dr George Devereux' article on 'Normal and Abnormal'. Drs Parin's and Morgenthaler's paper has not been published before in the English language. Dr Géza Róheim's article (page 31) has been edited for this volume. My introduction 'On the Cultural Determinants of Individual Development' has been especially written for this anthology. All other papers have been reprinted in conformance with their original texts.

I also want to express my gratitude to Dr A. Kagan, President of the International Universities Press, Inc., the Hon. Editor of the *International Journal of Psycho-Analysis*, the editors of the *American Journal of Orthopsychiatry*, the *Psychoanalytic Quarterly*, The Anthropological Society of Washington, D.C. and *Psyche*. Without their co-operation this volume could not have been put together.

March, 1969
State University of New York
Downstate Medical Center   W.M.

1. Theory

1

On the Cultural Determinants of Individual Development

WARNER MUENSTERBERGER

Sixteen years after *Totem and Taboo* (1913)[1] Freud gave his philosophical views on the impact which culture exerts on the life of the individual. In *Civilization and Its Discontents* (1929)[2] he elaborated what in one or the other way had occupied him since the years of his friendship with Wilhelm Fliess and possibly before. In his notes of 1897 we read for example: '. . . civilization consists in [this] progressive renunciation,'[3] a for those days very unusual observation.

The nature and impact of culture—and Freud uses this term when he speaks of the influence and effects of civilization—appears in nearly every work till *An Outline of Psycho-Analysis,*[4] his last comprehensive overview.

Did Freud tell us what culture is? What light can psychoanalysis shed on a question asked by all students of human behaviour?

The range of the phenomenon of culture encompasses the knowledge and findings of many disciplines. The insights gained by psychoanalysis, the revelation of man's inner world and its functions can contribute substantially to the study of man. Here was a new avenue for the understanding of the complexities of individual development in relation to other individuals.

From the standpoint of psychoanalysis it is the control of instinctual demands which is the first requisite of cultural achievement and development. This is partly biologically rooted. For example, non-seasonal sexuality is a fundamental component of human existence and a ubiquitous element of life's essential undercurrent because it enforces the restraint of instinctual demands. Another example is the development from quadrupedality to

---

[1] *Standard Ed.*, 13, London: Hogarth Press, 1955.
[2] *Standard Ed.*, 21, London: Hogarth Press, 1961.
[3] *Standard Ed.*, 1, London: Hogarth Press, 1966, p. 257.
[4] *Standard Ed.*, 23, London: Hogarth Press, 1964.

bipedality. It is a physiological phenomenon which implies in the context of evolutionary capacities a complex variety and different co-ordination of emotion and behavioural mechanisms. Bipedal locomotion developed slowly. According to current hypotheses the transition from quadrupedality of an ape-like fashion to the bipedality of *homo erectus* took not less than 5 million years. This involves, too, the problem of brain function and its relation to motor skills as well as a shift in perceptive abilities and the capacity for organized thinking.[5] Instinct control appears to be the principal condition for any type of organized interaction between individuals. Emotional and physical needs make this interaction indispensable and thus must be considered the initial step towards socialization and enculturation. Even under the simplest conditions interaction between human beings calls for adaptive measures which manifest themselves in cues and responses, in discrete symbolic expressions, in the necessary curtailment of pleasure and gratification. This is the price man must pay for depending on communal existence. Hence Freud spoke of the 'burden of culture'.[6]

Man's inner life and experience, ever since he has lived in any kind of social environment, has thus been under the influence of shared emotions and temporal events. Anthropologists and sociologists attempt to look into and interpret the networks of customs, kinship regulations, social rules and patterns. Psychoanalysts concern themselves with developmental processes and the psychic structure of the individual—the individual, inevitably within his social environment.

The recognition of the influence of external forces on the individual's adaptation has for some time dominated the area of scholarly endeavour which is referred to as 'Personality and Culture'. It is here where the social scientist and the psychoanalyst —though from different angles—recognize the impact as well as the potentialities of societal institutions on individual development. Reason shows that psychoanalytic theory must go beyond therapeutic aims if it is to effectively organize and delineate clinical observations regarding the multidetermined roots of human nature. The exploration of the unconscious has added new and unexpected dimensions to the understanding of behaviour, the uninterrupted

[5] Cf. S. L. Washburn, 'Behaviour and the Origin of Man', *Proc. Roy. Anthropol. Institute Gt. Britain and Ireland*, London, 1968, pp. 21-7.
[6] *The Future of an Illusion* (1927), *Standard Ed.*, 21, p. 42.

process between biopsychological forces, external conditions and the successive moments in the individual's inner life. A fundamental series of signals and responses bring about the delicately maintained balance which forms the substratum for the domestication of the human animal. Man's innate need for survival aids him in his attempts to find an equilibrium between the manifold inner pressures and external demands which are mandatory and often pre-ordained though never strictly identical or stereotyped. The slow development of the human child is largely responsible for the wide range of influences, the intricate interplay between the drives, congenital variations and socio-cultural configurations. The closely knit web of the vicissitudes of early life and the influences stemming from the external situation has been the focal point of psychoanalytic study since the *Studies on Hysteria* (1893-95).[7]

Dealing with the phenomenon of man inevitably calls for a larger view than his biological organism and appetites or the mechanics of overt behaviour. His mammalian needs, his long dependence, his libidinal and aggressive drives and biological functions cannot escape the impact of early directives and invisible operations for man's mere existence depends on the prolonged extra-parasitic life during the formative years.

From the earliest beginning feeling and responses, attitudes and signalling behaviours transmit individual as well as socio-cultural demands. Pleasure and frustration, generosity and harshness, influence the ego's development and affective disposition. The traditional modes of dealing with an infant's needs; the restrictions and restraints as a source of disturbances in the release of aggression; the visual and auditory stimuli the child is exposed to effecting the mode of his cognitive functioning; the culture-bound conditions and moral sentiments which are finally synthesized in ego attitudes and super-ego injunctions—these are some of the many aspects of individual development first clearly seen and understood on the basis of psychoanalytic observations and findings.

When Freud first recognized the roots of neurotic symptoms and became aware of the significance of the environmental influence during childhood and adolescence he began to pay closer attention to certain rules and religious practices, social codes and techniques for educating the young among some pre-literate peoples. It was

---

[7] J. Breuer and S. Freud, *Studies on Hysteria* (1893-95). *Standard Ed.*, 2 London: Hogarth Press, 1955.

his aim to arrive at a clearer understanding of basic phenomena such as the dread of incest and the transmission of a variety of behavioural features from parent to child. In retrospect it is curious to read 'that primitive men . . . are uninhibited: thought passes directly into action. With them it is rather the deed that is a substitute for thought.'[8] There is no evidence that this is so.

The rituals and communal laws with which Freud dealt in the same series of studies reveal, after all, a considerable modification of instinctual expression. Incest taboos, for example, show a collectively organized system of defences and emphasize the capacity for co-ordinated adaptive behaviour. Evidence is not lacking that man's development is determined by phylogenetically based steps which distinctly indicate the progressive mediation between psychophysiological givens and socio-culturally influenced modes of adaptation. The existence of such exchange Freud underlined in *The Ego and the Id* (1923). He then—about ten years after the publication of *Totem and Taboo*—assumed a basically similar psychic structure for *homo sapiens* regardless of the cultural setting:

> The differentiation between ego and id must be attributed not only to primitive man but even to much simpler organisms, for it is the inevitable expression of the influence of the external world. . . . Reflection at once shows us that no external vicissitudes can be experienced or undergone by the id, except by way of the ego, which is the representative of the external world to the id.[9]

The awareness of the impact of the external world on the human mind should not be credited to psychoanalysis. Explorers, historians, travellers of all sorts have described differences in habits and manners, in etiquette and attitudes. Ancient travel logs are full of descriptions of the otherness of others. The tribal names of many pre-literate peoples indicate just that: they call themselves 'people' while all others rank as *kuei* (haunting spirits) as the Chinese used to distinguish foreigners or 'barbarians' as the ancient Greeks described anything not Greek. In the second century A.D. the Roman historian Tacitus was struck by the measured, mono-syllabic response one would receive from those stolid peasants and fishermen along Holland's Northsea shore. '*Frisia non cantat*,' he wrote

[8] *Totem and Taboo* (1913), *Standard Ed.*, 13, p. 161.
[9] *Standard Ed.*, 19, London: Hogarth Press, 1955, p. 38.

in his *Germania*. 'One does not sing in Holland,' was his impression. Tacitus here in referring to a modal personality is in some sense making a general statement about a prevalent reaction formation in a particular cultural environment.

This does not mean that the mere description of culture-rooted habitual responses and predominant adaptive trends sheds any new light on the origin and evolution of behaviour traits nor does it actually tell anything about the correlation between individual modes of thought and characteristics and the developmentally relevant effect the specific environment has on the individual. Again, the anthropologist attempts to classify cultures according to systems and conditions; the psychoanalyst observes the predominant type of ego and super-ego development, the requirements for adequate defences and hence the correlation of shared modes of socially transmitted ways of adaptation.

This is the distinct viewpoint from which to observe the phenomenon of individual development tracing the interaction between endogenous and exogenous stimuli and how they are synthesized in the ego. As one result of psychoanalytic findings the social sciences have turned their attention to the existence and influence of a particular society's ethos and elementary living conditions, on the way a child discovers his macrosphere, in Erikson's descriptive terminology. The answer to this problem is far from simple: the biological parasitism of the human child constitutes the need for a stabilized social condition and thus the predominance of controls which guarantee survival in the service of continued existence. This seems to be a simple requirement. But behavioural regimentation makes imperative demands on the forces of selection, those pathways of discharge of instinctual pressures, in other words the specific ways in which the socio-cultural environment chooses to tame libidinal and aggressive drives and accomplish integrated action between the dual psychic tendencies. It is inherent in the nature of any continually functioning social organism to devise outlets which vouch for an adequate balance between the individual's aggressive and libidinal demands and the object world. This brings man face to face with reality without finding a ready-made single solution. The process can be seen in operation once the child enters the phase of active instinctual expression and social norms tend to provide a matrix for quantitative and qualitative solutions of this conflict. Socio-cultural modes of discharge and restraint work in the service of two masters: the gratification of instinctual appetites and the survival of the individual in communal association.

This constellation and the subsequent elaboration of the resolution of the conflict between the phylogenetically determined potentialities and the conditions to which the child is exposed was one of the early achievements of psychoanalysis. Still, Freud's assumption of the 'uninhibited primitive' is not borne out by the facts. Pre-literate man has his dreams and desires, his prowess as well as his times of despair. There is present too a coherent organization of mental functioning and goal-oriented action and thus, by definition, secondary-process structuralization. Examining the intricate rules of a totemistic society, Freud offered a psychoanalytic interpretation of the highly complex kinship and marriage regulations. As he saw them:

> Taboos, we must suppose, are prohibitions of primaeval antiquity which were at some time externally imposed upon a generation of primitive men. . . . These prohibitions have concerned activities towards which there was strong inclination. . . . Possibly, however, in later generations they may have become 'organized' as an inherited psychical endowment. Who can decide whether such things as 'innate ideas' exist, or whether in the present instance they have operated, either alone or in conjunction with education, to bring about the permanent fixing of taboos?[10]

Does Freud allude to the resolution of these conflicts in favour of the demands of survival and society? Or is it more correct to postulate that reality-oriented, object-seeking forces seek adaptation to a pre-existing conventional pattern? This would ensure a balance between innate drives on one hand and the socio-cultural condition and the representation of external forces in the ego on the other. In assessing the trend towards repression in social and moral development, Freud looked for evidence among peoples about whom there was but scant and barely reliable and systematic knowledge. All the elemental stimuli disclosed by psychoanalysis were believed to appear in much simpler and more rudimentary form among pre-literate peoples.

The route which psychoanalytic search and disclosure took was under the influence of the scientific climate of the time.[11] Thinking

[10] *Totem and Taboo* (1913), *Standard Ed.*, 13, p. 31.
[11] Cf. L. B. Ritvo, 'Darwin as the Source of Freud's Neo-Lamarckianism', *J. Amer. Psychoanal. Assoc.*, 13 (1965), 499 ff.

in terms of a unilateral evolutionary hierarchy of cultural achieve-ments, one would try to find potential trends rather than onto-genetically determined qualities such as the prolonged dependence of the human child. Or one would overlook the consequences of the non-seasonal sexuality of *homo sapiens* for the associative form of social living. One would postulate that the phases of human socio-cultural progress had followed a series of steps from sim-plicity to complexity, from savage brutishness to autonomous mastery and the neurotic internalization of conflict.[12] One would expect, for example, that the intricate institution of totemism would be openly adopted as a phenomenon of a homogeneous native culture but one sees it recede into the barely recognizable and quite fragmentary peculiarities of an excited lady with a mouse phobia or institutionalized taboos of religious faiths once a 'primitive' impulse has not been resolved in a conflict-free manner.

Given Freud's original clinical orientation, he related the primary aspect of a psycho-social phenomenon such as totemism or a magic act to the interplay between the archaic infantile object ties and the restraining factors coming from the object world. The struggle against the drives could not be managed from within. Hence society had to define norms which would control discharge and establish defences imposed by the group. Thus, individuation would be potentially directed by the moral standards and codices of society. Restraining factors would come from without rather than from within. However, the zone-oriented genetic point of view shows convincingly that the gratification of instinctual demands is related to neuro-physiological development and entails intrinsic matura-tional factors independent of socio-cultural conditions.[13]

This viewpoint is a more realistic one, for the interrelationship between instinctual drives and experience is not limited to the object world but relates also to innate sensorimotor releaser mechanisms.[14] In recent years the work in the field of ethology has widened our concept of instinctual development relating the evolu-tion and multidimensional relationships of behavioural and inter-individual manifestations to an intricate variety of biological,

[12] Cf. S. Freud, ' "Civilized" Sexual Morality and Modern Nervous Illness' (1908), *Standard Ed.*, 9, London: Hogarth Press, 1959, pp. 181 ff.
[13] Cf. D. Rapaport, 'Psychoanalysis as a Developmental Psychology' in B. Kaplan and S. Wapner, *Perspectives in Psychological Theory*, New York: International Universities Press, 1960, pp. 209 ff.
[14] Cf. K. Lorenz, *On Aggression*, London: Methuen; New York: Har-court, 1966, pp. 105 ff.

physiological, genetic, ecological, demographical and environmental preconditions. It is logical to conclude that all these forces govern the development of the human individual.[15]

From our psychoanalytic point of view it is the need for structure from within which makes necessary a balance between id and super-ego with the ego mediating. It responds to narcissistic, libidinal and aggressive strivings to be selectively discharged within the confines of one's habitat.[16] Consequently, unconscious drive energy imposes its influence upon thought and action.

Freud chose totemism as one conspicuous institution to show the unconscious roots of adaptive behaviour—in this case the beginnings of social organization and religious concepts—essentially in the light of the synthetic function of the ego. Adaptive endeavours always reflect the essential duality of human nature. But the need for and process of a relationship with the outside world starting with the mother-child dyad indicate the capacity to find devices which will bridge this duality. Indeed, the child *looks* for his adaptive orientation in the object world. Remember our frequently used phrase 'How good to *see* you', or 'Hope to *see* you again soon', or the German 'Auf Wieder*sehen*' and the Dutch 'Tot *ziens*', while the French know the proverb 'voir c'est croire', seeing is believing. In other words the hypercathexis of looking must not be underestimated.

If we may generalize, the trend towards introjection is a basically biological device and the inescapable result of physiological givens influencing the response pattern of the human child under the

---

[15] We must distinguish here between a socio-psychoanalytic and a socio-cultural point of view such as that of C. Lévi-Strauss. It seems reasonable that such a difference does not question the usefulness of either. While Lévi-Strauss considers totemism, for example, as part of a far larger scheme, as an aspect of a universal characteristic of man classifying his natural and situational environment, we might ask for the primary cause which brings about the unique combination of ideas and constructs. 'Far from being an autonomous institution definable by its intrinsic characteristic, totemism, or what is referred to as such, corresponds to certain modalities arbitrarily isolated from a formal system, the function of which is to guarantee the convertibility of ideas between different levels of social reality' (C. Lévi-Strauss, *The Savage Mind*, London: Weidenfeld and Nicolson, 1966, p. 76. See also *Structural Anthropology*, New York: Basic Books, 1963). The concept of structure which holds the interest of current anthropological discussion, is in no way irreconcilable with psychoanalytic hypotheses. The polarity which structural anthropology under Lévi-Strauss's initiative finds to be the predominant underlying concern in man's orientation is by definition an expression of the ego's tendency towards differentiation.
[16] For an illuminating example see now: N. F. Cantor, *The English*, New York: Simon & Schuster, 1967, p. 58.

guidance of the pleasure-unpleasure principle. This is the first step towards setting up mechanisms of defence.

These factors may very well explain the origin of customs, rules, and rational action, in short social life and the emergence of culture.

To understand Freud's first undertaking one must bear in mind that for reasons of conceptualization an attempt was made to develop a system of observation rather than making random discoveries. The evolutionary theories of the nineteenth century were built on the assumption of logical sequences of a developmental programme. Human civilization was part of this programme leading from primordial and rudimentary states to highly differentiated forms of individual life and social organization.

First, neo-Lamarckian views regarding the transmission of acquired characteristics seemed to fit the evolutionary process. But there is no indication that defensive ego attitudes can be transmitted from parent to child. They develop as the outcome of the long dependence of the child. It is apparent that the successive stages of zone-specific development—oral, anal, phallic—in other words the diphasic sexuality allows for gradual adaptation and co-operative behaviour. Referring to the visual experience we see increasingly efficient introjection, identification and the gradual capacity to form mental representations, a long process which serves for man's humanization. Luckily we have some clear and conclusive information about certain organismic reactions to environmental conditions.[17] According to these and various other studies an animal is born with innate fears. Genetic and developmental factors determine the emotional response pattern on the basis of hereditary endowment.

We thus see a distinct relation between internal and external givens. But the pattern is not easily charted. Adaptive and defensive measures must be understood in their function within the individual's environment. They have an integrative and co-ordinative effect. In essence then the ego is supposed to act as a stabilizer responding to the currents of events, to pulls and counterpulls, to bribes and subterfuge.

The study of man encompasses the study of the stabilizing or

[17] See for example: R. Melzack, 'The Genesis of Emotional Behaviour: An Experimental Study of the Dog', *J. Comp. Physiol. Psychol.*, 47 (1954), 166ff.; W. R. Thompson and W. Heron, 'The Effects of Early Restrictions on Activity in Dogs', ibid., pp. 77ff.

synthetic and differentiating functions of the ego. There can be little doubt about the environmental interference with the direction of impulses, the kind and quality of restrictions, of order and frustrations and the hierarchy of values. We are dealing with a set of conditions which concern the relationship between the social organism and individual character formation. Man is born into a society, i.e. a system of culturally prescribed and defined relationships. He has but little choice: he is required to cope with a pre-existing reality of which he is part once past his infancy. From then on every functioning relationship is influenced and refined by the ego's ability to respond within a spectrum of the conceptually possible.

Many examples from trans-cultural analyses illustrate this point. The manifest dream content of an Australian native may deal with a certain experience in a *cave*, while a New Yorker may use the *subway* or a Londoner the *underground* in a similar connection. The subway is conceptually closer to consciousness in the case of the New Yorker, an image an Australian aborigine could not possibly create. The latent meaning is not necessarily fundamentally different and might be related to uterus or birth fantasies. Man's vital experiences are much alike. Phenomena like birth, hunger, helplessness, or pain are inherent in the basic mechanisms of living. The need to defecate is physiological but the way one goes about relieving oneself is influenced by ego and super-ego, and various cultural settings have devised habitual norms and practices to comply with these needs. Some cultures build a major part of their moral edifice on guilt and purification, a step towards internalization of conscience. Here is a visible effect of the transformation of bodily features into emotional ones under the guidance of socio-cultural norms. Thus, the ego has an aim relative to internal pressures and external demands. 'It is in keeping with the course of human development that external coercion gradually becomes internalized,' Freud pointed out. '. . . the degree of this internalization differs greatly between various instinctual prohibitions'.[18]

The word coercion is decisive here because it gives us to understand in how far the individual development is influenced by the emotional climate of the child's microsphere as well as by the dominant trends and traditions of his macrosphere.

For a comprehensive theory of culture one must take the

[18] *The Future of an Illusion* (1927), *Standard Ed.*, 21, p. 11.

combined insight of psychoanalysis and the social sciences into consideration. As the primary visible criterion we may think of certain regularities in various basic response mechanisms. They can be designated as pre-cultural or proto-cultural such as the ones mentioned above or the reaction to lack of sleep or imminent danger. They can be understood as part of a functional prerequisite to multiple stimuli of different empirical determinants. However, there is no civilization of man which does not attempt to modulate these elemental reactions.

The prolonged dependence of the human child makes this gradual tuning-in possible. As infant care is a universal necessity the child is subjected to internal influences and innate maturational agents as well as external coercion. These circumstances suggest that the young child gets attuned to the particular way the mother interacts with him, holding him, feeding him, gauging his needs, responding in her fashion to his demands as well as achieving her own need gratification. The mother as the primary social agent sets an effective basic theme for the subsequent course of her child's development.

Conceptually, psychoanalytic anthropology bases its approach on the evidence of unconscious impulses, the existence and necessity of repression and hence of conflicts and on the developmental sequences of the libidinal and aggressive drives. Behaviour, then, is not exclusively dependent on the variable conditions of one's socio-cultural environment. The zone-determined chronological unfolding of intrapsychic differentiation, the progressive shift of emphasis from oral to anal and phallic stimuli, is instrumental for the domestication of the 'animal in man'. These genetic determinants help us co-ordinate internal conditions with demands coming from the object world. We see a gradual development from complete helplessness and vulnerability to eventual physical, mental and social maturation. Secondary-process functioning and a state of relative self-reliance are inherent aims under suitable conditions. Again, how this step towards individuation is taken, depends to a large extent on the range of genetically determined potentials. Physically there is no differentiation of the kind one finds among insects and animals. What is peculiar to man is the specific and complex growth process and consequently the intricate social fabric which is so much in contrast to even those animals which have developed an integrated social response system.

It is logical to conclude that individual development is linked with the human child's parasitism. The initial parasitic mode of existence has been observed in considerable detail. Internal dispositions and biological forces corresponding to the developmental route meet external stimuli and barriers. The co-existence of two or more generations invariably effects the interplay between genetic conditions, the transmission of dominant environmental modes of conduct, and those subtle vicissitudes which are the source of individual character formation. As one example I may refer to the immediacy of instinctual gratification. While we know that postponement of satisfaction or relief acts as an impetus for the development of mental representations, it influences thought processes, the recognition of inside and outside and the modification of drive energy. Hence, in trying to understand the various roots for subsequent emotional maturity, details of this quality must not be put aside as the simplifying method of some psychologically oriented anthropologists tries to demonstrate. It is such combinations which lend colour and texture to individual differences even within a simple homogeneous culture. It points, too, towards the duality in man, his unconscious instinctual demands and the necessary need for socialization and enculturation if he is to live in an associative social way. The inescapable interaction of these multicoloured strands makes the individual, i.e. tends to cultivate a basic condition for character differentiation.

We assume that the child's learning potentials are influenced and effectively modified by his individual experience as well as by the particular environmental mould.[19] The sequential pattern, the step-by-step chain reaction, is biophysiologically and thus chronologically predetermined. In this overall classification human infants have equal underlying cognitive capacities. Yet the increasing communal participation and correspondingly the object-related evolution bear the imprint of those unique combinations which lead to the individual's distinct personality.

Socialization under any human condition anticipates the child's gradual cognitive assessment of his surrounding as one of the most basic functions in the process of enculturation. The experience of the object world brings with it the awareness of the average expect-

[19] See for example: J. S. Bruner, R. R. Olver and P. M. Greenfield, *Studies in Cognitive Growth*, New York: John Wiley & Sons, 1966; also my 'Psyche and Environment: Sociocultural Variations in Separation and Individuation', *Psychoanal. Quart.*, 38 (1969).

able: one learns the rules of the game. This helps us to explain why an Ibo behaves like an Ibo and not like a Yoruba or an Eskimo; why certain exogenous factors effectively influence ego and super-ego and aid man in his capacity for flexible adaptive functioning. The physical and emotional need to belong generates the integrative properties and fosters the domestication of the human animal. Self-preservation dictates the control of aggressive and libidinal strivings.

And yet we cannot disregard those distinct signs in man's emotional make-up which involve the counterpart of the wish to belong. There is sufficient evidence to assume that it is predominantly rivalry and self-indulgent attitudes which are equally instrumental in the adaptive behaviour throughout man's history. They too help man to erect defences against the conflicting interests of instinctual drives and the imperative demand for social learning. Ultimately every act between two or more people, even in its most rudimentary form, is characterized by some manifestation of man's assimilative mode of functioning. Communication between two people inevitably leads to a kind of regimentation of drive activity and hence to the curbing of immediate and outright drive discharge. Loving others for the sake of self-love and living with others for the sake of self-preservation have a libidinal as well as a social function. One can see how these conditions must put a damper on innate aggressive strivings and deserve close attention. They are rooted in man's biological make-up, the unalterable need for prolonged care. These circumstances in all their individual and socio-cultural nuances lead inevitably to a 'social contract'. They, too, must be credited with the recomposition of man's 'instinctual budget' and influencing the social fabric.

The necessity for management of continued drive control is evident. The symbiotic existence over a comparatively long period of one's life creates a particular bond which patterns and often ritualizes forms of behaviour. This entails pre-conscious and non-verbal elements which carry the mark of intergenerational transmission. Dynamically, the child accepts a pattern first experienced in the dyadic relationship with his mother. Hence, the core of the socio-cultural adaptive process is the re-establishment of the mother-child situation in disguise. The triad of the Oedipal constellation can be understood as an extension of the need for protection and hence as a biological as well as cultural and societal necessity.

In order to maintain the dual unity it is the father or his substitute who carries part of the burden to protect the young. We may notice that adaptive mechanisms can function in the service of archaic needs. Róheim saw in the institution of marriage a basic form of the dual unity restored. Friendship, particularly among many pre-literate people who know the institution of the 'best friend', is another pertinent example of man's incessant search and longing for someone who listens to you and whom you can trust.[20] Forms of greeting and bidding farewell are often revealed to be extensions of the same continuing desire. The hope and need for libidinally founded substitute relationships—substitutes of the archaic symbiosis—influence ego and super-ego manifestations and function as one essential vehicle for drive modification. It seems conceivable that every cultural act shows elements of both, the object-seeking tendency as a manifestation of man's innermost fear of being left alone—the fear of death is a telling example[21]—and, on the other hand, the establishment of self, that search for individuation which Róheim has called the 'away-from-the-mother trend'. From this point of view individuation can be understood as an innate defence against the archaic desire for prolonged dependence and unity with the mother. Freud hinted at the fact that the abandonment of this powerful bond and the move towards narcissistic endeavours entails a desexualization of one's regressive tie to the mother. We realize that the child's eventual insistence on feeding himself or, as the Chinese put it, 'to wean himself from the breast' creates instinct modifications in the service of adaptation. Here progression in terms of individuation and enculturation go hand in hand: by feeding himself the child identifies with the giving mother and demonstrates a certain degree of motor control and self-sufficiency. Similar illustrations could be given with respect to bowel training, to cleanliness, to play as trial activity and hence organizing and adaptive capacities can be correlated with cultural origins from the individual's point of view.

By examining child-rearing practices as part of the developmental processes within the boundaries of a given society we study the early steps towards enculturation or the outline of predominant

[20] Cf. L. Rangell, 'On Friendship', *J. Amer. Psychoanal. Assoc.*, 11 (1963), 3-54.
[21] Cf. W. Muensterberger, 'Vom Ursprung des Todes. Eine Psychoanalytisch-ethnologische Untersuchung zur Todesangst' in *Psyche*, 17, (1963), 169-84.

defences and the range of alternatives. Since physical separation from the mother is the beginning of psychic separation from infantile bonds, the awareness of and subsequent capacity for separateness is the pre-condition for individuation.[22] This process aided by introjections and identifications fosters the recognition of the 'me' and the 'you'.

This, I take it, is a major reason for the universality of cultural evolution: anxiety at being left alone is one of the prime movers for adaptability and the sense of self. The subtle transformation from infantile dependence to the achievement of communal existence, from symbiosis to associative living entails the acceptance of those obligatory conditions and privations which the individual is potentially supposed to bear. He must navigate between the Scylla of instinctual forces and the Charybdis of external restrictions. The 'proper' use of the culturally provided defences facilitates normative behaviour though it does not necessarily eliminate the possibility of conflict as, for example, the institution of rites or taboo regulations proves.

In view of this struggle for maintenance, it is not surprising to find all possible combinations of social orders and individual adaptations in an attempt to create a safeguard for pleasure and need satisfaction.

Against this background psychoanalytic anthropology studies the adaptive evolution of individual characteristics under divergent conditions of social order. But it also attempts to explain the rise and persistence of distinct phenomena within a certain culture.

It must be spelled out that when the psychoanalyst turns his attention to social phenomena he is overstepping the clinical situation in which the strict psychoanalytic method has been developed and established. The intimacy of the two-person relationship is the pre-condition for the therapeutic application of psychoanalytic technique. The relationship of psychoanalyst-psychoanalysand is unusual in its confinement, in its relative one-sidedness, in its purpose and insistence on verbalization. This goes far beyond the basic rule of free association as the indispensable technical instrument of the psychoanalytic process.

[22] Cf. M. S. Mahler, 'Thoughts About Development and Individuation', *The Psychoanalytic Study of the Child*, 18, New York: International Universities Press; London: Hogarth Press, 1963, pp. 307-24 and other works by the same author.

Psychoanalysis observes individual behaviour, normal and pathological, from a specific dynamic-phenomenological point of view. It studies mental processes of individual man, drawing conclusions about unconscious and preconscious mechanisms, the vicissitudes of drive energy, the particular defence organization, in other words the arrangement and function of psychic forces. This allows us to gain deeper insight into the pre-conditions of behaviour, unconscious fantasies, emotional responses, the particular conflict situation as related to the prevalent defences. There are many other issues, in fact too many to enumerate here.

What concerns us is the problem of the *technique* of psychoanalytic work outside of the therapeutic relationship. Once one expands the original frame of reference and singles out for attention and research phenomena which have no immediate empirical connection with the therapeutic situation, differential degrees for investigation must be developed. The deficiency of the application of psychoanalytic theory to certain social institutions such as the existence of the primal horde has been shown in relevant inquiries. New approaches had to be found. Only on the basis of extensive field observation was Róheim in the position to refute the early psychoanalytic speculations regarding the prehistory of human social life. It became evident that the many variations of human behaviour cannot be interpreted on the basis of a hypothetical event in primeval times.

This brings us to the important point of the problem of extra-clinical psychoanalytic research methods. In applying psychoanalysis to work in the social sciences new techniques must be developed. The transference relationship between analysand and clinician cannot be applied in the field. However, it is the only approach for creating that multifaceted interchange which produces continually useful and relevant data, making it possible to draw conclusions of the profundity psychoanalysis may claim. The transference situation cannot be duplicated or repeated unless the analysand is willing to co-operate with the basic rule of minimal thought control, i.e. free association. This method cannot be transplanted into the social research field. One is thus bound to abandon this kind of communicative relationship. There is a reversal of roles since it is the psychoanalyst who seeks information from his informant who is not a patient. It modifies the entire tenor of the relationship.

Yet our clinical experience allows us to apply certain procedures to field exploration. While working with the Pomo Indians of the Ukiah region in Northern California my main informant was an elderly lady who had served in the same capacity before to other anthropologists. My first contact was deliberately casual in order to establish a relationship which might develop certain transference elements. One day she told me about a dream in which I appeared. Clinical experience has taught us that when the psychoanalyst appears in the analysand's dream one may count on the transference. Keeping this strategical knowledge in mind I then dared ask questions which otherwise might have elicited a negative response and interfered with the early fragile relationship. Now the old woman was co-operative and responded laughingly and with a certain glee: 'You are funny man. Everybody else asks me from belly button up and you ask me from belly button down. . . .'

This vignette in itself is not, in its specific aspect, necessarily conclusive. Other methods have been applied such as Erikson's intensive collaboration with experienced anthropologists, or Parin's and Morgenthaler's multiple interviews on a limited interpretive basis eliciting certain transference reactions.[23] But all variations of field technique are dependent on and modelled after clinical experience. It is only on this basis that we collect psychoanalytically relevant data or in turn are in the position to validate psychoanalytic hypotheses.

In the light of these considerations it seems evident that there is a reciprocal relationship between practice and theory. 'In anthropology,' Anne Parsons observed, 'field work is the *pièce de resistance*. We make particular kinds of observation in the field because we have asked particular theoretical questions and in turn it is because of new field observations that we come to ask new theoretical questions'.[24]

If we are to attempt to apply psychoanalysis to research outside of the clinical setting we must be aware of the limitations. Yet the

[23] In the case of the study by Parin and Morgenthaler the transference was considerably modified because the 'patients' were remunerated for their willingness to co-operate. A re-direction of the relationship between the psychoanalyst and the patient-informant appears unavoidable under such conditions. In an unpublished paper Robert A. LeVine explored the range of methods applicable ('The Couch and the Field: Toward a Psychoanalytic Ethnography', 1968).
[24] 'The Growing Demand for Behavioral Science in Government', *Human Organization*, 23 (1964), 93.

theoretical edifice of psychoanalysis makes it possible to utilize our knowledge under different observational conditions, to ask questions which have not and could not have been asked before; to recognize the covert meaning of overt behaviour; to better comprehend the meaning of symbolic acts. Psychoanalytic concepts of psychic structure, of drives and conflict, of primary process and secondary elaboration, of reaction formation and mechanisms of defence—all provide us with a distinct theoretical equipment which we hold in the service of the science of man.

Dr Róheim was the first trained psychoanalyst who studied pre-literate peoples directly. He worked with the Aranda, Lurittya and Pitjentara in Central Australia among whom he did his most comprehensive field work. One of the results of his direct observation was his ontogenetic theory of culture which questions—on psychoanalytic grounds—the earlier assumption of the primal horde theory.

Róheim was a pioneer, an outspoken individualist whose very personal style is also expressed in his writings. It was his opinion that man's relatively prolonged infancy necessitates the need for object-directedness and consequently the development of defence mechanisms. It is to be noted that he assumed the differentiation of cultures on the basis of the infantile trauma customary in a specific environment. Disillusionment forces man to become realistic even though the mechanisms of denial and overcompensation try to overcome the frustrations of reality in favour of fantasy and the hope for wishfulfilment.

2

The Psychoanalytic Interpretation of Culture[1]

GÉZA RÓHEIM

1. THE PRIMAL HORDE

The first psychoanalytic interpretation of culture as a whole was given by Freud in *Totem and Taboo*. After having killed the primal father, the sons of the primal horde identified themselves with him and forbade themselves the very things which he had forbidden them to do. Society and culture were thus erected on the basis of the *post mortem* obedience of the victorious sons.[2] An implicit assumption in this theory is that of a collective unconscious. If we accept this assumption we are justified in interpreting group activities of succeeding generations as if they were performed by the same individual. Is it probable that mankind ever lived in the 'Cyclopean family'[3] type of social organization? Since the publication of *Totem and Taboo* we have had corroborative evidence on the life of higher monkeys and apes and we know that what has been described as the dominance type of society[4] is very similar to the picture so familiar to us from the immortal pages of *Totem and Taboo*. Moreover in many myths of primitive people we find certain traits which strongly suggest the 'primal horde' as opposed to the pure 'Oedipus' explanation.[5]

We find a certain radical contrast between the victorious brothers (sons) and the father; the latter may be a supernatural being or an animal or a demon, while the young heroes of the story are

[1] This paper first appeared in the *International Journal of Psycho-Analysis*, 22 (1941). For the purposes of this volume it has been slightly abridged by the Editor.
[2] S. Freud, *Totem and Taboo* (1913), *Standard Ed.*, 13, London: Hogarth Press, 1955.
[3] A. Lang and J. J. Atkinson, *Social Origins and Primal Law*, London: Longmans, 1903.
[4] S. Zuckerman, *The Social Life of Monkeys and Apes*, London: Kegan Paul, 1931.
[5] G. Róheim, *The Riddle of the Sphinx*, London: Hogarth Press, 1934, Ch. 4.

alone human in our sense of the word. Freud's assumption of the primal father's psychological attitude as being fundamentally different from that of the young males[6] might be regarded as an explanation. In these myths we find an individual as opposed to a group and we find that the myths are placed at the beginning of human evolution. Institutions of human culture are derived from the tragic event, just as described in *Totem and Taboo*.

Let us assume for the moment that mankind actually lived, or the forerunners of mankind actually lived, in the 'dominance' or 'primal horde' type of social organization;[7] so far as the evidence regarding the higher apes goes there are other observers who describe monogamous forms of the family, and, as for the myths, it is quite possible to explain them as based on the Oedipus complex and projected into the past. In other words, they are not necessarily records of phylogenesis, they may also represent an attempt to explain phylogenesis on the lines of ontogenesis.

However, if we make the initial assumption of a primal horde period in the past, the next difficulty that confronts us is to explain how such a period could have survived in traditional forms. If we accept the collective unconscious this difficulty does not arise. But there are weighty arguments against this assumption. It is one thing to accept inherited dispositions and quite another to assume the latent memory of an event or even of a series of events in the dim past.

If then we try to do without this assumption, there are two ways to explain the survival of the primal horde tragedy from pre-human to human days. I have argued in favour of both possibilities. In the baboon horde described by Zuckerman there are real battles for supremacy in the horde when the 'overlord' begins to show signs of decreasing strength or potency. Besides these, however, there are sham fights which partake of the characteristic features of the real struggle. Hardly a day goes by without an uproar among the bachelors. This usually begins with one animal adopting a threatening attitude, opening his mouth and baring his teeth. The disturbance spreads through the whole group. The riot becomes general and spreads to the married groups. 'The more aggressive animal seems to be unaffected by the increase in the number of enemies he

[6] S. Freud, *Group Psychology and the Analysis of the Ego* (1921), *Standard Ed.*, 18, London: Hogarth Press, 1955, p. 123.
[7] Cf. also R. Linton, *The Study of Man*, New York: Appleton-Century, 1936, p. 140.

has called upon himself and thus a baboon fight assumes its peculiar character—*a single animal defending himself against a group*. Usually a group retreats whenever the single animal advances.'[8] The sham fights are probably abreactions of the real primal horde tragedy—play repetitions revealing their origin in the formal element (one against many). We may regard them as halfway between real repetition and repetition in the drama. Central Australian ritual as performed today purports to be a repetition not of the sexual battles fought by the ancestry, but of rites performed by these ancestors. These sham battles may have survived after the real primal horde battles had disappeared and may have been handed down from one generation to the other by imitation, traditionally, before human speech was evolved. The myth is a narrative of ancestral drama not of grim reality. For the growing generation these traditional dramatic performances had a functional value as a socialized sublimation of their own ontogenetically formed Oedipus complex.[9]

The other solution assumes that the primal horde type of organization was a significant feature of human prehistory but not the *fons et origo* of human culture in general. In this case the periodic killings of the leader may have survived in some modified form in human conditions and the myth could be a narrative of one of these latter events.[10] 'Actually we know that primitive kings perform incest and are ritually killed at the end of a certain period. No Baja king may live for more than fourteen years and his son and successor is also his murderer'.[11]

2. THE ONTOGENETIC THEORY OF CULTURE

The theory of a collective unconscious would be an assumption we might be compelled to make if we had no other way to explain the phenomenon of human culture. I believe, however, that psychoanalysis has another contribution to offer and that this second suggestion is safer and easier to prove. The second suggestion is that the specific features of mankind were developed in the same

---

[8] S. Zuckerman, op. cit., pp. 228, 250.
[9] G. Róheim, op. cit., pp. 234f.
[10] idem, 'Primitive High Gods', *Psychoanal. Quart.*, 3 (Suppl.) (1934), 123.
[11] idem, *Animism, Magic and the Divine King*, London: Kegan Paul, 1930, p. 254.

way as they are acquired today in every human individual as a sublimation or reaction-formation to infantile conflicts. This is what I have called the ontogenetic theory of culture. I found a society in which the infant was exposed to libidinal trauma on the part of the mother and have shown that this predominantly male society was based on the repression of that trauma. In the same way I have shown that in a matrilineal society the libidinal trauma consisted in the father playing at devouring the child's genital and that this society was based on the fiction that there are no fathers.[12]

If we remember some significant passages in Freud's writings, we notice that Freud also holds this second view of culture. If culture consists in the sum total of efforts which we make to avoid being unhappy, this amounts to an individualistic and therefore, from the psychoanalytic point of view, to the ontogenetic explanation of culture. If culture is based on the renunciation of instinctual gratification, this means that it is based on the super-ego, and hence also explained by the fact that we acquire a super-ego.[13]

Or if we take Freud's papers in which he explains not culture as a whole, but certain elements of culture, we find that these interpretations are individualistic and psychological,[14] and not based on a hypothetical phylogenesis. Finally, if we consider especially the interpretations given by Melanie Klein and in general by the English school of psychoanalysts,[15] it is quite evident that all these interpretations of individual evolution also imply an interpretation of human culture as based on the infantile situation. Thus, if Melanie Klein regards symbolism as a necessary consequence of the infant's aggressive trends and the mechanisms mobilized against these trends and also as the basic elements in the subject's relation to the outside world and in sublimation, this implies an explanation of culture in terms of the infantile situation. If demons are explained as projections of the super-ego, if the functions of a

---

[12] idem, 'Psycho-Analysis of Primitive Cultural Types', *Internat. J. Psycho-Anal.*, 13 (1932).
[13] S. Freud, *Civilization and its Discontents* (1930), *Standard Ed.*, 21, London: Hogarth Press, 1961.
[14] Cf., for instance, 'The Taboo of Virginity' (1918), *Standard Ed.*, 11, London: Hogarth Press, 1957; 'A Seventeenth-Century Demonological Neurosis' (1923), *Standard Ed.*, 19, London: Hogarth Press, 1955; 'The Theme of the Three Caskets' (1913), *Standard Ed.*, 12, London: Hogarth Press, 1958.
[15] Cf. M. Klein, 'The Importance of Symbol-Formation in the Development of the Ego', *Internat. J. Psycho-Anal.*, 11 (1930), 26.

medicine man are explained by the assumption that the help of an external object is sought against the introjected object, or if introversion or extraversion in an individual or a group are due to the flight of the internal or external object, these and many others are obviously explanations based on the infantile situation.[16]

3. PROLONGATION OF INFANCY

In the preceding paragraph I have discussed what may be regarded as two distinct types of interpretation. It might be argued that the psychoanalytic interpretation of literature or art or magic is one thing and the interpretation of one specific culture as based on a specific infantile situation is another. I suppose most anthropologists would admit that some sort of correlation must exist between infantile experience and culture, but they might be inclined to favour the opposite view of cause and effect and say that the cultural pattern determines among other things also the type of infantile experience. It is quite true of course that the infancy of an individual is the origin of his behaviour as an adult but then again this infancy is determined by the behaviour of other adults, the infant's mother and father. If we go one step further and again interpret what the parents have done in terms of their infancy, we see that we are moving in a vicious circle and that we have here the old problem of the priority of the hen or the egg.

Culture is taken in its broadest possible sense in this paper and is equivalent to all those features which distinguish man from his brethren in the animal world. If we can find a distinctive feature in the biological make-up of mankind which is also a variation in the infantile situation and does not depend on cultural tradition, we are likely to have found the key that will unlock many locks. The idea that over-prolonged infancy is the decisive feature in human evolution is not new, and a variety of ways have been indicated in which the prolongation of infancy may have determined human evolution. Herbert Spencer explains maternal love as a useful variation in a species characterized by the prolonged helplessness of the infant,[17] and Westermarck explains the duration of the

---

[16] M. Schmideberg, 'The Role of Psychotic Mechanisms in Cultural Development', *Internat. J. Psycho-Anal.*, 11 (1930), 389, 397, 414.
[17] H. Spencer, *Principles of Psychology*, vol. 2, p. 623.

marital tie in the human species on the same basis.[18] That man has surpassed the ape by passing on his experience to the next generation is obvious,[19] and prolonged infancy is a necessary condition for the existence of tradition. Briffault has given full weight to the significance of our prolonged immaturity. Below writes:

> I have found that among animals that bring forth their young in a condition of helplessness, such as man, the dog, cat, rat, mouse, rabbit, the development of ganglion cells is incomplete at the time of birth and even soon after; whereas the horse, calf, sheep, guinea-pig show completely developed ganglion foetal life, invariably before birth.[20]

This incomplete development is much more pronounced in the human baby than in any other young.

> The retarding of the rate of growth, the bringing into the world of the young mammal, as a helpless being before its full development, makes, then, so far as regards its anatomical structure, but the trifling difference represented by those microscopic filaments in the substance of the brain. But upon these almost impalpable cobwebs, a new world of being depends. Let the connections which they effect be completely established in the darkness and seclusion of the womb; the new-born creature is almost as well fitted for life as the parent; it can look after itself, feed, outdistance a man in a race.[21]

In proportion to its perfection, 'in proportion to the specialization of its nervous interconnections, it is fixed, rigid, unalterable'. If, however, the connecting paths between inherent trends and environment are not completely formed before birth, we have a creature in which instinct is superseded by tuition. Hence, it is in exact proportion as the immaturity of the offspring is prolonged that the mammalian animal is superior in intelligence, in power of learning from experience and of adapting himself by modifications in its behaviour.[22] Our adaptation to reality is therefore conditioned by our retarded maturation in so far as this process manifests itself

[18] E. Westermarck, *The Origin and Development of the Moral Ideas*, London: Macmillan, 1908, vol. 2, p. 191. Linton explains group formation similarly. R. Linton, op. cit., p. 141.
[19] R. H. Lowie, *Are We Civilized?*, London: Routledge, 1929, pp. 293f.
[20] Below, 'Die Ganglienzellen des Gehirnes bei verschiedenen neugeborenen Tieren', *Arch. Anat. Physiol.* (Physiol. Abt.) (1888), 188.
[21] R. Briffault, *The Mothers: The Origins of Sentiments and Institutions*, London: Allen & Unwin, 1927, vol. 1, p. 102.
[22] ibid. Cf. also F. H. Allen, 'The Dilemma of Growth', *Arch. Neurol. Psychiat.*, 37 (1937), 859.

in brain structure. Another way in which our prolonged infancy must be regarded as a basic element in our adaptation to reality has been followed up by Bally. He says that in their preying activities the lower animals show rigidity in the form of their behaviour; whereas the animals which remain for a long period under the care of their parents show variability in these actions. In the latter case the parents are putting their behaviour at the service of their young for the purpose of enabling them to obtain oral satisfaction and to keep off their enemies. But the behaviour of the young themselves is phylogenetically determined and thus becomes undeliberate behaviour, without an object or with a substitute object; in this way play arises.[23] As the oral needs are gratified by the parents the young animal or pre-human being can withdraw cathexis from the purely practical aim of eating to playful observation, to perception or introjection of environment; and this would be what K. Gross has called the practice value *(Übungswert)* of our play activity. We have here some basis for regarding the reality principle, that is the capacity to tolerate delay, as being based on the pleasure value of play. An important difference between human beings and animals is conditioned by the retardation in our dentition and the capacity to move about. Whereas all animals effect a direct transition from mother's milk to adult food, the delay in dentition makes it necessary for human beings to have an interim period in which food of a milk-like consistency and quality is given to the infant.[24] A relative independence of motor reactions from the acquisition of food is thus developed and this independent play activity is the basic element of our culture. Apes are capable of trial activity, that is of an activity which is not rigidly riveted to the goal. And thinking is reduced trial activity.[25]

If we follow the argument put forward by Bolk we see another series of steps that leads from animal to human life. Bolk finds that through retardation structural properties or relations that are only temporary in other primates have become stabilized in the human species.[26] Bolk attributes the slowing down of our growth to the endocrine system, to hormonal products that have inhibited

[23] G. Bally, 'Die frühkindliche Motorik im Vergleich mit der Motorik der Tiere', *Imago*, 19 (1933), 341ff.
[24] In primitive communities the situation is different. The suckling period is much longer and this transition period less significant.
[25] G. Bally, op. cit., p. 357.
[26] L. Bolk, *Das Problem der Menschwerdung*, Jena: Gustav Fischer, 1926, p. 7.

maturation. Our troubles arise not only from the prolonged infancy of the species, but also from the discrepancy between the development of the soma and the germ plasm. The soma is relatively retarded as compared to the germ plasm, which means that humans are beings with a relatively prolonged infancy (compared to the total duration of life) and a relatively precocious sexual development. It is quite clear that we have here the biological foundation for early object relations, for the Oedipus complex. The ties between child and mother last longer than in any other species and the sexual impulse has already attained a measure of object-directedness when the only available object is the mother. On the other hand it is also clear why a relatively undeveloped soma would necessitate the development of defence mechanisms,[27] that is, of an ego, as a superorganic soma as protection against a premature inundation of libido.[28] Our relative immaturity would therefore explain the traumatic character of early sex experience.

We know that Freud has pointed out how human nature is conditioned by three factors. The biological factor is the relative helplessness of the infant, the phylogenetic factor is the break in the development of human sexuality and the psychological factor is the differentiation in our physical structure.[29] The second, or phylogenetic factor, is a specialized instance of the first, while the third is also a consequence of our relative immaturity. This amounts to the statement that human nature in general (or, what amounts to the same thing, that culture) is due to our prolonged infancy.

If, as Freud has shown, neurosis is an archaism or infantilism,[30] and if obsessional neurosis is but an exaggerated instance of the normal super-ego formation of the latency period,[31] this amounts to the statement that neurosis is but an exaggerated form of culture,[32] or that human nature as differentiated from animal nature is based on the conservation of the infantile situation. Finally, if we

[27] 'We have reason to believe that the Oedipus complex and the castration fears that spring out of it are themselves consequences of the fact that in human beings the period of childhood is so prolonged.' T. M. French, 'Defense and Synthesis in the Function of the Ego', *Psychoanal. Quart.*, 7 (1938), 547.

[28] Cf. Anna Freud, *The Ego and the Mechanisms of Defence*, London: Hogarth Press, 1937.

[29] S. Freud, *Inhibitions, Symptoms and Anxiety* (1926), *Standard Ed.*, 20, London: Hogarth Press, 1959, pp. 154-6.

[30] ibid., p. 148.

[31] ibid., pp. 115-18.

[32] G. Róheim, *The Riddle of the Sphinx*, London: Hogarth Press, 1934.

consider the facts revealed by the London school of psychoanalysts and their theoretical viewpoint, we see that here again the delay in maturation is the key to the whole system. For although Joan Riviere emphasizes the viewpoint that the helplessness of the infant when faced with its own *thanatos* is the primary, and the dependence on the mother only a secondary factor, one might well ask what this helplessness means if not an incapacity to bear even the smallest amount of frustration—that is, a state of absolute dependence on the mother? This psychological experience seems to be one of the peculiarities in man to which his evolutionary development has led. It is part of the same phenomenon as the long physical helplessness and dependence which the human child goes through, as compared with other animals.[33]

In following one line of argument we are explaining the origin of defence mechanisms against libidinal strivings as due to our retarded soma and relatively precocious germ plasm development (Bolk and Róheim). Then again it seems that the development of our brain (Briffault) and that of our capacity to tolerate suspense (reality principle) can be explained from the relative immaturity of the human infant (Bally). The differentiation of self and non-self, the mechanisms of introjection and projection, are due to the infant's capacity to deal with its own aggressiveness and its dependence on its mother as a source of reassurance (Klein and Riviere). Finally, neurosis itself is an infantilism (Freud) and in a sense only an exaggeration of the essential feature of human development (Freud).

We may therefore accept the conclusion that psychoanalysis as a psychology is in harmony with a biological theory that would attempt to explain human nature on the basis of a specific infantile situation. But how is this to lead to the assumed differentiation of cultures on the basis of a differentiation in the infantile situation, i.e. in the infantile trauma customary in a particular human group?

If we see that in one society the nipple is given or withdrawn in a certain way, or that sleeping habits, or the way the adults play with the children, provoke certain libidinal reactions, we still do not see clearly how these specific situations could have evolved from the universal fact of delayed human infancy. The same question might be asked in every individual case. Why was A. subject

[33] J. Riviere, 'Hate, Greed and Aggression', in M. Klein and J. Riviere, *Love, Hate and Reparation*, London: Hogarth Press, 1937, p. 9.

to a specific trauma, why was a certain situation traumatic for B. and not for C? These are questions that are very difficult to answer —in these cases we invoke constitution as our *ultima ratio*. In the case of human groups we must probably do the same. For one thing, we have the fact of the unequal retardation of various races,[34] which in itself must have some effect on the interaction of id, ego and super-ego, and hence on the human psyche in general.[35] As for the variations in the mother-child situation, these may be compared to the variations in the coitus position or in the male-female situation. We know that the European or ventro-ventral position is not the characteristic position of some primitive races,[36] and that it is the position in which only immature apes copulate.[37] We might conjecture for instance that the absolute dominance of the male in Australian society leaves the women without an outlet for the male elements in their make-up and that these have to manifest themselves in the mother-child situation. At any rate, we must admit that such variations in the infantile situation exist and that they are probably based on constitutional variations of human groups.

On the other hand, I do not intend this theory to be taken too rigidly as a final determination of group character which will henceforth run on eternally in the same groove in a circle of infantile traumas, adult sublimations or reaction-formations and repetition of the same infantile traumas.[38] Even in a primitive group we must assume variations in the infantile situation and in the personality of its members. As the group grows larger[39] the range of these variations increases not only on account of the number of the individuals but also because they are in a decreasing ratio subject to identical introjection-formations.[40] Culture has authorized and

---

[34] L. Bolk, op. cit., p. 37.

[35] G. Róheim, 'Racial Differences in the Neurosis and Psychosis', *Psychiatry*, 2 (1939), 375 ff.

[36] Cf. G. Róheim, 'Psycho-Analysis of Primitive Cultural Types', *Internat. J. Psycho-Anal.*, 13 (1932), 41, 205; *Riddle of the Sphinx*, p. 253.

[37] Cf. S. Zuckerman, op. cit., p. 285; C. F. Jacobsen, *Development of an Infant Chimpanzee during Her First Year, Comp. Psychol. Monog.*, 9, University of California Press, 1932, p. 316. See Derek Freeman, 'Totem and Taboo: A Reappraisal', now in this volume.

[38] Cf. R. Money-Kyrle, *Superstition and Society*, London: Hogarth Press, 1939, p. 146.

[39] Cf. R. Lowie, op. cit., p. 293. (The savage solves his simple problem; we fall short of solving a more intricate one.)

[40] We might compare primitive societies to the *family neurosis* emphasized by some psychoanalysts: R. Spitz, 'Familienneurose und neurotische Familie', *Internat. Z. Psychoanal.*, 23 (1937), 548.

socialized a specific sublimation of reaction-formation and can therefore canalize the latent conflicts of its members in a decreasing proportion. Those who have other emotional needs will introduce cultural modifications.[41] As all human beings consist of a bundle of id-trends and defence mechanisms and as culture provides a sub-limation for only some of these, the others, not being thus satiated, will grow in momentum and provide the psychic background in the group which makes the reform movement possible. The sugges-tion made by Cora Du Bois of an individual introducing a variation in a culture should therefore certainly be taken into consideration.[42]

4. EARLY OBJECT RELATIONS

The effects of prolonged infancy have been commented upon by various non-psychoanalytic authors. Jevons writes:

> Now, as regards the family affections there can be no possibility of doubt; the infancy of man is longer than that of any of the animals, most of which can walk and take care of themselves almost, if not quite, as soon as they are born. Man's infancy, on the other hand, is so long that the human race could not have survived in the struggle for existence, had not the parental instincts and family affections been strong in primitive man.[43]

Social animals nurture their young and nurtured animals tend to be social. The social disposition seems to be a modified continuance of the infant's need for the nurtural parent's presence, and the infant is born with a simple attachment-to-mother tendency. Attachment to the mother is the sole source of food and protection. When the trend to retain the mother is thwarted, this naturally produces the utmost extreme of terror and rage.[44] The question

[41] The fact that in very primitive societies these modifications are based on dreams is a further proof for the decisive role played by the unconscious in culture formation.

[42] C. Du Bois, 'Some Anthropological Perspectives on Psychoanalysis', *Psychoanal. Rev.*, 24, (1937), 254. *Editor's Note:* See now David Rapaport, 'Psychoanalysis as a Developmental Psychology', in B. Kaplan and S. Wapner (eds.), *Perspectives in Psychological Theory*, New York: Interna-tional Universities Press, 1960, pp. 209ff.; and W. Muensterberger, 'On the Biopsychological Determinants of Social Life', now in this volume.

[43] F. B. Jevons, *An Introduction to the History of Religion*, London: Methuens, 1902, p. 46.

[44] I. Suttie, *The Origins of Love and Hate*, London: Kegan Paul, 1935, pp. 15f.

of early object relations is a topic much discussed by various analytical schools. According to Fenichel the new-born infant has no ego. 'The human child is born in a far more helpless state than the majority of other mammals. It cannot survive unless it is cared for.'[45] The organism can get rid of tensions only through another organism and therefore in a biological sense the infant is anaclitic; but this does not mean that it is also anaclitic psychologically, for it has no concept of the object. The tension is hunger. When it has been satisfied by the mother, the infant goes to sleep.[46] Thus the first acceptance of environment is only an intermediary aim on the path of withdrawal from it.[47]

Joan Riviere, as representing the London school of psycho-analytic thought, agrees with Fenichel in describing the attitude of the infant as narcissistic, but she regards this as a narcissism which is dependent on introjection; i.e. on object relations.[48] Finally we have the Hungarian school of psychoanalysis which emphasizes the passive object love (Ferenczi) of the infant, its insatiable desire for the care and nurture of the mother.[49] This psychic attitude is a state in which the independent existence of the object is not yet recognized and might be called primary (archaic) object love and cannot as yet be differentiated from the egoistic sentiments. The Hungarian language describes the child's relations to the mother by the term, *ragaszkodás* ('clinging or sticking to'),[50] and it is just this grasping or clinging attitude of the infant that Hermann has described as a primary attribute of our libidinal and ego-development.[51] It seems to me that Fenichel's objection to empha-sizing the object-directedness of this early phase of development on the ground that the concept of the object has not yet appeared in the infantile mind would be more in keeping with the point of view of a psychology that identifies the psyche with consciousness than

[45] O. Fenichel, 'Frühe Entwicklungsstadien des Ichs', *Imago*, 23 (1937), 245. *Editor's note:* For English translations of Fenichel's papers see now *The Collected Papers of Otto Fenichel*, 2 vols., New York: W. W. Norton, 1954; London, Routledge, 1955.
[46] S. Bernfeld, *The Psychology of the Infant*, London: Kegan Paul, 1929.
[47] O. Fenichel, art. cit., p. 247.
[48] J. Riviere, 'On the Genesis of Psychical Conflict in Earliest Infancy', *Internat. J. Psycho-Anal.*, 17 (1936), 400.
[49] M. Balint, 'Early Developmental Stages of the Ego', *Internat. J. Psycho-Anal.*, 30 (1949), 265-73.
[50] A. Balint, 'Love for the Mother and Mother love', *Internat. J. Psycho-Anal.*, 30 (1949), 251-59.
[51] I. Hermann, 'Sich-Anklammern, Auf-Suche-Gehen', *Internat. Z. Psycho-anal.*, 22 (1936), 349.

with the psychoanalytic attitude. After all, we are dealing with a phase of existence in which the clear-cut frontier between conscious and unconscious does not exist and in which the first elements of the psyche are emerging from the physiological situation. The characterization given by Freud leaves nothing to add to the description:

> Childhood love is boundless; it demands exclusive possession, it is not content with less than all. But it has a second characteristic: it has, in point of fact, no aim and is incapable of obtaining complete satisfaction; and principally for that reason it is doomed to end in disappointment and to give place to a hostile attitude.[52]

Every little child in Normanby Island is *gewana*, i.e. always desirous or demanding too much. One frequently hears mothers scolding their children: *'gewana arena ojo!'* ('oh, you supreme pesterer!'). The child is born in a state of relative immaturity, it needs more love than it can get.

In publications on the rites of covenant, or speaking more generally of union, I have tried to show how eternally infantile mankind continues to repeat the mother-child situation with the fundamental pattern of separation (anxiety, aggression) followed by union. In most cases the union is based on an oral introjection. If only one party eats the food, that party will depend on the other, but if both eat of the same substance, or both drink each other's blood, the tie and the obligation are mutual. The former situation is especially prominent in love magic. Girls will mix menstrual blood, their perspiration, or axillary hair into a man's food, and he then becomes completely infatuated.[53] In the area of Szatmar girls sieve mother's milk through the lower part of their shirt (the part that touches the vagina) and give cake prepared with this milk to their lovers.[54] The love potion is dangerous, as a marriage based on this oral introjection may easily turn into hatred, and in this case the outcome might be death.[55] The pattern is the

---

[52] S. Freud, *Female Sexuality* (1931), *Standard Ed.*, 21, London: Hogarth Press, 1961, p. 231. Cf. also idem, *New Introductory Lectures* (1933), *Standard Ed.*, 22, London: Hogarth Press, 1964.
[53] C. Wuttke, *Der deutsche Volksaberglaube der Gegenwart*, Berlin, 1900, pp. 365f.
[54] G. Róheim, *Magyar Néphit és Népszokasok*, Budapest: Atheneum, 1925, p. 59.
[55] Cf. B. Gutmann, 'Die Frau bei den Wadschagga', *Globus*, 92 (1907); L. Strackerjan, *Aberglaube und Sagen aus dem Herzogtum Oldenburg*, Oldenburg, 1867, vol. 1, p. 115.

child-mother situation, the reaction to absence or frustration is aggression and anxiety. In some rites of the covenant type, i.e. in the case of those based on a mutual introjection or mother-child situation, the first phase of the ritual consists in slaughtering an animal. The Wadschagga kill a goat. The hide is cut off the animal when it is still alive and both parties spit on the hide. They are thus united through the saliva of both and through the blood of the animal.[56] The animal slaughtered on the threshold when an honoured guest is expected[57] represents the aggression based on the separation and followed by the bond, covenant or union. The security of the house as a mother symbol is a reparation because it is based on the previous sacrifice of a mother or child symbol.[58] Crawley explains all human relations as based on a mutual inoculation,[59] or, as we should call it, mutual introjection. He quotes the Narrinyeri custom of *ngia-ngiampe*. The barter between the tribes on the Murray river and those near the sea was carried on by agents who were mutually in the relation of *ngia-ngiampe* to each other. When a man has a child born to him he preserves its umbilical cord by tying it up in the middle of a bunch of feathers. This is called a *kalduke*. He then gives this to the father of children belonging to another tribe and those children are henceforth *ngia-ngiampe* to the child from whom the *kalduke* was procured and that child is *ngia-ngiampe* to them.[60] This means that they are in avoidance situations to each other. Evidently the *kalduke* is the bond upon which the relationship of mutual trust is based. But the *kalduke* is a navel string and the people who enter upon similar bonds are frequently called brothers or blood brothers.[61] The navel string is the bond that unites mother and child; the parties of the ceremonial union are called brothers,[62] which means that

[56] J. Raum, 'Blut-und Speichelbünde bei den Wadschagga', *Arch. für Religionswiss.*, 10 (1907), 265, 275.
[57] H. C. Trumbull, *The Threshold Covenant*, London: T. & T. Clark, 1896, p. 5.
[58] G. Róheim, 'The Covenant of Abraham', *Internat. J. Psycho-Anal.*, 20 (1939), 452.
[59] E. Crawley, *The Mystic Rose*, London: Methuen, 1927 ed., vol. 1, p. 285.
[60] G. Taplin, 'The Narrinyeri', *The Native Tribes of South Australia*, London: Low, 1879, pp. 32ff.
[61] E. Crawley, op. cit., vol. 1, pp. 288ff.
[62] As early as in 1918 the ceremonial blood-brotherhoods were explained by Jellinek as repetitions of the mother-child situation. ('Ethnologische Beiträge zur Psychologie der Freundschaft', Budapest Psycho-Analytical Congress.)

man is a social animal because he is continually striving to overcome the primal separation trauma and to establish new mother-child situations.

An important difference between the animal and the human or infantile being is that while for the animal environment is nature, a stabilized world in which he is perfectly well adapted on account of his inherited reactions, for a human being at the dawn of life environment is essentially another human being—the mother—and the reactions of this environment are, from the point of view of the infant, highly labile. Recent work in animal psychology has shown that if gratification of a tension becomes uncertain, the result is a behaviour disorder in the animal, which is the prototype of a neurosis or psychosis.[63] In some cases which I have analysed I have found that the infant lives in an insecure environment, that he is bewildered by what for him is a confusing succession of tension and gratification, of 'bad' and 'good' mother-imagos.[64] In mankind the situation that is induced by the experimenter is the initial situation of his life provided by nature, that is, by our relative immaturity.

5. EGO DEVELOPMENT AND CULTURE

The task of psychoanalysis is 'to strengthen the ego, to make it more independent of the super-ego, to widen its field of perception and enlarge its organization, so that it can appropriate fresh portions of the id. Where id was, there ego shall be. It is a work of culture—not unlike the draining of the Zuider Zee'.[65] 'We need scarcely look for a justification of the view that the ego is that portion of the id which was modified by the proximity and influence of the external world, which is adapted for the reception of stimuli and as a

[63] Cf. Stuart W. Cook, 'The Production of Experimental Neurosis in the White Rat', Psychosom. Med., 1 (1939), 293. Editor's Note: Cf. now L. Reingold (ed.), Maternal Behavior in Mammals, New York: Wiley, 1963.

[64] I do not believe there is a 'misunderstanding between adult and infant' in the sense that the sadism of the adult frightens the infant, who only desires tenderness. Cf. S. Ferenczi, 'Sprachverwirrung zwischen den Erwachsenen und dem Kinde', Internat. Z. Psychoanal., 19 (1933), 5. The 'misunderstanding' or confusion is between the pure pleasure principle of the infant and the dawn of reality called forth by the alternately tension-creating and tension-dispelling behaviour of the mother.

[65] S. Freud, New Introductory Lectures (1933), Standard Ed., 22, p. 80.

protective shield against stimuli, comparable to the cortical layer by which a small piece of living substance is surrounded.'[66]

The development of the ego and that of culture must be closely related to each other and the ego is simply the *extroverted* part of the id. In his culture, or rather in a considerable part of his culture, man's face is turned towards his environment.

For example: I draw a distinction between food-gatherers and food-producers. It may be 'natural', that is, phylogenetically predetermined, for man to kill and eat animals or gather and eat berries, but it is certainly not 'natural' for primitive man to plant a garden or to domesticate animals. If we analyse the 'professions', apart from those of the hunter, the fisher, and the gatherer of wild plants, we find that the most ancient of all professions is that of the medicine man. This is followed by trade and later by primitive agriculture, then the domestication of animals and finally plough culture. All these can only be explained as based on sublimations of specific aspects of the infantile situation. It shows very little insight into the mental processes of primitive man to believe that he is likely to plant yams because he has come to the conclusion that they will bring him a plentiful crop in the future, or that he keeps dogs because they are useful in hunting kangaroos. The carefree children of the jungle or desert never think of the morrow in pre-agricultural societies. But if they have associated fantasies of destroying the body with taking the yams out of Mother Earth, it would be easy to see how the reparation aspect of those fantasies might lead to a replanting, that this in turn might lead to an observation of the crop, and so secondarily to a practical result from the endopsychically conditioned activity. Or, if man extended the mother-child situation to the puppy of the wild dog, these dogs, brought up in human society, might prove useful in the chase; but this was a result of play activity which nobody could have foreseen. My view, therefore, is that the bulk of human culture, even in its adaptational or ego-aspects, arises out of play or ritual activities. The reason for these activities lies in the infantile situation, and they acquire survival value secondarily by assimilating a part of the environment to man's needs. This is the way of culture—the transformation of id into ego.

There are two ways of facing environment: the way animals face it and the way humans face it.

[66] ibid., p. 75.

In unconditioned reflexes the path of the impulse from receptor to effector is already established when the individual is hatched or born. The link-up of the elements within the reflex-arc is hereditary like any other part of the individual's physical structure. In conditioned reflexes the path of the impulse from receptor to effector is not determined at birth. The link-up of the elements within the reflex-arc comes as a result of selection and routing of impulses within the reflex centres, coupled with the gradual wearing of a path through the synapses. The unconditioned reflex is the foundation of automatic or instinctive behaviour, the conditioned reflex the foundation of learned behaviour.[67]

I suppose it would be generally admitted that in the course of evolution the part played by the unconditioned reflex in adaptation tends to decrease and the part played by the conditioned reflex (that is, learning) tends to increase. What psychoanalysis has to add to this would be that the reflexes are conditioned in infancy and that learning is introjection; *therefore in the development of human adaptations the tendency is for adaptations that are based on the infantile situation to replace in an ever decreasing degree those based on the stimulus-reaction pattern.* Although, in the paper quoted above, I have dealt chiefly with man's adaptations or professions above the food-gathering level, there can be no doubt that the effects on the infantile situation have already been shaping man's destiny in the world for ages when he advances to the food-producing level. Language is born when the mother understands the babbling of her baby. Our tools are the projections of our body and we owe the art of making fire to a displaced play repetition of the genital act or of masturbation. In the venture called human life environment supplies the opportunity, the id supplies the capital, while the ego is the intermediary between the inside and the outside world.

It is, therefore, clear that, whatever economic or social systems man has created, man is the measure of all things, and that we must explain human institutions as based on human nature and not human nature as based on human institutions.[68] In a secondary sense, of course, the nature of the individual is modified by the institutions he has to live up to, but these institutions themselves

[67] R. Linton, op. cit., p. 64.
[68] A paper by Fenichel himself (if I understand it correctly) fulfils these requirements, because it explains social class on the basis of infantile omnipotence and the displacement of this omnipotence to the parents: O. Fenichel, 'Über Trophäe und Triumph', *Internat. Z. Psychoanal. Imago*, 24 (1939), 258.

only represent the petrified strivings of past generations of human beings. Thus our infancy, that is our dependence on other human beings, is prolonged not only in our own life, but also into the past of our species. We have innumerable parents who condition our individual lives, not so much by biological heritage, as by the social institutions that represent their conflict situations. It may be added in this connection that this transformation of id forces into ego forces explains what we call human progress. It has often been remarked that human progress consists in the conquest of nature, whereas it is doubtful whether there is any progress in the conquest of our endopsychic world. We may leave the second half of the sentence a moot point for the present, but I think we can explain the conquest of nature. It is due to the fundamental function of the ego, which consists in attaining a synthesis. It is by means of this ever-increasing synthesis of our infantile fantasies and our environment that we are gradually transforming nature and re-creating it in our own image.

The synthesizing function of the ego may also manifest itself in another way. A situation is imposed upon the individual by the environment and this is secondarily libidinized by the ego. That is, the situation is supplied by the environment, but the capital for dealing with this situation is derived from the id. This situation, showing the pure 'environment-id' contrast, is probably more characteristic of early phases of evolution. It would also apply to the later phases, if we regard human-made environment (society) as equivalent to geographical environment, and this would be the process envisaged by Fenichel. But there is this important difference: that the social environment situation is really an inter-action with other human beings and therefore determined more decisively by the infantile (pre-Oedipus or Oedipus) situation.

Finally, we probably accomplish our conquest of reality through another channel. We may here take the views of English psycho-analysts as our starting point, according to which the psyche is originally an organ for falsifying perception, for modifying reality till it becomes acceptable to the ego. However, we must assume an increasing tendency to be disillusioned by our illusions and con-sequently an increasing development of reality testing. The satis-faction derived from hallucination is after all different from a real satisfaction of a need, and this something that is missing will act as *vis a tergo* to induce a flight to reality. We become realists because our ideals are not realized. Although this waning faith in our fantasies is always bolstered up again and again in denials and over-compensations, we are gradually driven towards reality and we can enjoy our fantasies only when they appear in the disguise of realities. And thus we have created a fantastic reality in which our fantasies survive.

6. INDIVIDUAL ANALYSIS AND CULTURE ANALYSIS

The question might be asked whether, if we have found the latent significance of a social phenomenon in the analysis of a single individual, we are justified in assuming that this latent meaning was also the origin of the institution. In analysing patients who have seen the ceremony of the *kapparah* fowl (the modern Jewish form of the ancient scapegoat) performed in their childhood, we often find that the sin transmitted to the fowl is sexuality or that the ceremony itself represents the primal scene. Here, for instance, is the dream of a bank employee undergoing a character analysis. *The patient sees a series of minute photographs. They are dancing girls—one big photograph looks like the director of his bank. He has various erotic fantasies; finally a red-headed girl with only one leg, then a woman with legs drawn up, very thin, like the legs of a chicken.* He remembers buying the *kapparah* chicken for the Day of Atonement, the woman who sold the chicken, and his desire to look under the woman's skirt, how at the age of ten he opened a door once when staying with his cousin and found her in intercourse with her boy friend. Then he talks again about the *kapparah* ceremony and says that the head of the rooster when cut off looks just like that of his bank manager.

Similar primal scene dreams or projections of the libidinal strivings to the *kapparah* cock or hen occur in the dreams of other patients. In a dream published by Weiss a big *kapparah* cock symbolized the father, a small one the son, and beside the big cock there was seminal fluid.[69] I have shown that the scapegoat sent to Azazel in the desert represented the penis, just like the cock which took his place afterwards.[70] In this case, therefore, as also

[69] E. Weiss, 'Totemmaterial in einem Traume', *Internat. Z. Psychoanal.*, 2, (1914), 163.
[70] G. Róheim, *Animism, Magic and the Divine King*, p. 334.

in the case of the phylacteries, it can be shown that the latent meaning today is the same as the latent meaning several thousand years ago.[71] In carrying out an analytical investigation of an initiation ceremony in Central Australia I have used this method extensively. The dreams of the initiators contained valuable hints regarding the latent meaning of the ceremony.[72] In one case we have individuals who are actually living in a ceremonial world, in the other only persons who have seen the last survivals of the ritual in their childhood. The result is much the same. However, this need not be the case. In a paper on the dragon myth I have been able to show that the latent content of the myth has also a history: new wine has been poured into old bottles. Yet the old wine also remains in the bottle, and in a case of dragon phobia which I have analysed, I found in this single person in modern life all the latent elements that are stratified in the secular evolution of the myth.[73] On the other hand I can also show that totemism may mean one thing in a given area (Normanby Island) but that the totem animal in a certain dream of a given individual may mean something different. The analysis of the individual helps to understand the culture he lives in, but, in order to attain certainty, it must go hand in hand with the analysis of non-individual data.

7. SUMMARY

The argument of the present paper may be summarized as follows:

(i) Culture or sublimation in a group are evolved through the same process as in the individual.

(ii) Cultural areas are conditioned by the typical infantile situation in each area.

(iii) Human culture as a whole is the consequence of our prolonged infancy.

(iv) Typically human forms of adjustment are derived from the infantile situation.

[71] Cf. M. D. Eder, 'The Jewish Phylacteries and Other Jewish Ritual Observances', *Internat. J. Psycho-Anal.*, 14 (1933), 341-75.
[72] G. Róheim, *The Riddle of the Sphinx*, pp. 112, 116.
[73] idem, 'The Dragon and the Hero', *Amer. Imago*, 1 (1940), 40-69.

(v) Our conquest of nature is due to the synthetic function of the ego.

(vi) Psychoanalytic interpretations of culture should always be ego plus id interpretations.

(vii) The interpretations of cultural elements through individual analysis is probably correct, but should be combined with the analysis of anthropological data.

The ontogenetic theory of culture explains the relation of human culture to the delay of biological maturity of 'homo sapiens', *thus replacing Freud's neo-Lamarckian phylogenetic theory (see also Lucille B. Ritvo, 'Darwin as the Source of Freud's Neo-Lamarckianism', in* J. Amer. Psychoanal. Assoc. *13 (1965), 499-517). Freud insisted on the neo-Lamarckian views almost against his better knowledge (see Ernest Jones,* The Life and Work of Sigmund Freud, *vol. 3, New York: Basic Books, 1957, pp. 312 f.). Dr Freeman's paper takes a twofold approach. It discusses the questionable hypothesis in terms of recent ethological findings and then ventures the psychoanalytic interpretation of Freud's theory of the* 'primal murder' *and comes to the conclusion that it is based on the strong ambivalence the founder of psychoanalysis had towards his own father.*

3

Totem and Taboo: A Reappraisal[1]

DEREK FREEMAN

Freud himself regarded *Totem and Taboo* as one of his major achievements.[2] Undoubtedly, it is a study containing many brilliant insights; yet, it is also a work which has been largely dismissed by anthropologists.

Kroeber published his first criticism of *Totem and Taboo* in the *American Anthropologist*.[3] In a second paper entitled '*Totem and Taboo* in Retrospect', published in 1939,[4] he remarked:

> There is no indication that the consensus of anthropologists during these twenty years have moved even an inch nearer the acceptance of Freud's central thesis.

Jones[5] and others have attributed this kind of response to unconscious as well as other forms of resistance. These processes have certainly occurred, but they are not the whole explanation, for there are, in fact, some virtually insuperable scientific objections to the precise formulations finally reached by Freud, and, on the basis of these objections it has been all too easy for anthropologists to dismiss from consideration the rest of Freud's writings.

This is a regrettable state of affairs, for anthropology, as the science of man and his behaviour, has an immense amount to learn from psychoanalysis. But at the same time, psychoanalysis, if it is to remain a science and not become a closed system of discourse,

---

[1] This paper first appeared in *The Psychoanalytic Study of Society*, 4, ed. by W. Muensterberger and S. Axelrad, New York: International Universities Press, 1967.
[2] E. Jones, 'The Inception of *Totem and Taboo*', *Internat. J. Psycho-Anal.*, 37 (1956), 34-5.
[3] A. L. Kroeber, '*Totem and Taboo:* An Ethnologic Psychoanalysis', *Amer. Anthropologist*, 22 (1920), 48-55.
[4] *Amer. J. Sociol.*, 45 (1939), 446-51.
[5] See article cited above, and *Sigmund Freud: Life and Work*, 3 vols., London: Hogarth Press, 1956.

must constantly adjust to the course of discovery in cognate sciences.

Thus, in this paper I shall attempt to identify the scientifically untenable elements in Freud's hypothesis about the origin of totemism, and to advocate that these elements ought now to be abandoned.

In what follows, I shall necessarily have occasion to be critical of some of Freud's theorizing. Let me say, then, that this criticism is joined with a high appreciation of Freud's remarkable powers of scientific creativity, as well as his rare human qualities of exceptional honesty and courage.

I propose to direct my attention to the final chapter of *Totem and Taboo*, for this, as everyone (including Freud himself) seems to agree, is the crucial chapter of the book.

The first twenty-five pages of the final chapter of *Totem and Taboo* are devoted to a critical survey of the theories of Frazer, Lang, Durkheim, Wilken, and others. These I shall not consider. Freud's presentation of his own case begins (p. 125 of the *Standard Edition*, vol. 13) with a discussion of the first of the three elements on which his theory is based. These elements are (as Freud notes on p. 141):

(i) Darwin's hypothesis about 'the social state of primitive men';

(ii) psychoanalytic discoveries about totemistic fantasies in children;

(iii) Robertson Smith's hypothesis about the totemic meal.

I shall discuss each of these briefly in turn.

(i) Darwin's views about the probable nature of the social state of primitive man were stated in his book *The Descent of Man* (first published in 1871). Darwin placed great emphasis on the 'strength of the feeling of jealousy all through the animal kingdom', and he argued that

> from what we know of the jealousy of all male quadrupeds, armed as many of them are, with special weapons for battling with their rivals, that promiscuous intercourse in a state of nature is extremely improbable. . . . Therefore [continues Darwin], looking far enough back in the stream of time, and judging from the social habits of man as he now exists, the most probable view is that he aboriginally lived in small communities, each with a single wife, or, if powerful, with several, whom he jealously guarded

against all other men. Or, he may not have been a social animal, and yet lived with several wives like a gorilla. . . .[6]

And here, Darwin quotes a paper by Dr Savage,[7] appearing in the *Boston Journal of Natural History* as his authority for asserting, with reference to gorillas, that all the natives:

'agree that but one adult male is seen in a band; when the young male grows up, a contest takes place for mastery, and the strongest, by killing and driving out the others establishes himself as the head of the community.' The younger males [Darwin continues]. being thus expelled and wandering about, would, when at last successful in finding a partner, prevent too close interbreeding within the limits of the same family.[8]

Freud cites almost the whole of this passage from Darwin (in addition to the Cyclopean family theory of Atkinson),[9] and, as he notes, his own theory is 'based upon' the conclusions reached by Darwin and Atkinson.

The first point to be noted is that Darwin and Atkinson (as well as Freud) in reaching these conclusions were arguing deductively and with tenuous contact with empirical reality.

This was the first of the criticisms made against *Totem and Taboo* by Kroeber.[10] The Darwin-Atkinson supposition, Kroeber pointed out, is 'only hypothetical'. 'It is a mere guess,' Kroeber continues 'that the earliest organization of man resembled that of the gorilla rather than the trooping monkeys.'

When Darwin and Atkinson were thinking about human origins there was almost a complete absence of reliable observational data about infra-human primates. The sole authority cited by Darwin was in fact Savage, who together with Wyman, discovered the lowland gorilla. The statements made by Savage about gorilla social behaviour in his paper of 1847 (which Darwin relied upon so heavily) were based on the hearsay evidence of native informants.

[6] *The Descent of Man and Selection in Relation to Sex*, London: John Murray, 1901, p. 900.
[7] T. S. Savage and J. Wyman, 'Notice of the External Characters and Habits of *Troglodytes Gorilla* a New Species of Orang from the Gaboon River; Osteology of the Same', *Boston, J. Nat. Hist.*, 5 (1847), 417-43.
[8] Darwin, op. cit., p. 901.
[9] J. J. Atkinson's concept was of 'the original Cyclopean form of family, with its solitary male head'. See *Primal Law*, London: Longmans, 1903, p. 24.
[10] '*Totem and Taboo:* An Ethnologic Psychoanalysis', loc. cit.

In recent years, primatology has become a science, and we now have in Dr George Schaller's book, *The Mountain Gorilla*,[11] a brilliantly accomplished study of gorilla behaviour in the wild, based on intensive first-hand observation.

It emerges that the native testimony recorded by Savage, and relied upon by Darwin and Freud, is inaccurate—so inaccurate, indeed, that it must now be classed as a projected fantasy.

In the first place, it is not true that there is *always* only one adult male in a band. About 70 per cent of the bands for which Schaller gives details had only one fully mature, silver-backed male; but there were two cases of bands containing four fully mature males. Moreover, the composition of bands changes a good deal. Thus, one group (No. IV), which Schaller had under intermittent observation for a year, and the composition of which he checked on nine different occasions, had seven different silver-backed males as members during this period.

More importantly, there is no evidence in Schaller's materials for the occurrence of contests within gorilla groups in which the strongest animal establishes dominance either by killing or driving away other males.

Dominance hierarchies within gorilla groups there certainly are, but dominance is commonly exercised without the infliction of severe or fatal injury. This, as modern ethological research indicates, is because of the innate inhibitory mechanisms present in the members of those species existing within social groups based on dominance. That is, a submissive display by one of the animals engaged in a dominance contest commonly inhibits the impulsive aggression of the other animal, in whose favour the contest is thus settled. Konrad Lorenz[12] has given an excellent descriptive analysis of this process in wolves, and it has also been studied in many other species, including primates. I would add that, in evolutionary terms, it was imperative that some such inhibitory mechanism as this should have been evolved, for otherwise species with highly efficient natural weapons, such as the wolf and the baboon, would be in danger of self-extermination. Thus, while Schaller[13] did observe gorillas quarrelling violently on several occasions, 'the

[11] G. B. Schaller, *The Mountain Gorilla: Ecology and Behaviour*, Chicago: University of Chicago Press, 1963.
[12] *King Solomon's Ring: New Light on Animal Ways* (with an Introduction by W. H. Thorpe), London: Methuen, 1961, p. 181.
[13] op. cit., p. 291.

grappling, screaming and mock-biting never resulted in discernible injury.'

Schaller's observations also fail to confirm the existence in gorillas of the intense sexual jealousy postulated by Darwin.

Schaller observed copulatory behaviour in gorillas on two different occasions. Both were in Group IV, which, it will be remembered, contained, during the period of observation, four mature silver-backed males, organized in a clear dominance hierarchy, and three occasional visitors, all of whom were also mature males.

The first copulation, witnessed on the 4th September, 1959, involved the silver-backed male second in the dominance hierarchy, and one of the ten females of the group.[14] It continued for fifteen minutes during which period the two animals advanced forty feet down a steep slope, until they came to rest against a tree trunk; there was much noisy vocalization both preceding and accompanying orgasm. During the whole procedure, the dominant male lay on a knoll which initially was only ten feet away from the copulating pair, and although they were, throughout, plainly in sight, he paid them no obvious attention.

The second copulation, observed nineteen days later, was between a peripheral male (i.e. a visitor) and (in Schaller's judgment) the same female. On this occasion the group was scattered over a steep hill-side. The female approached the male, clasped him round the waist, mounted him and made about twenty pelvic thrusts. Initially, the male paid little attention to these overtures, but then, he turned to the female and they began to copulate. At this, the dominant male, who had been resting fifteen feet away, slowly arose and advanced towards the pair. In response to this gesture, the copulating male immediately withdrew and ambled ten feet uphill. The dominant male sat by the female for about a minute before moving off to a spot, again about fifteen feet distant from her. The other male then reoccupied his former position, and the copulation was resumed. Soon after orgasm the female moved off. The dominant male who during the prolonged copulation had been without apparent response, arose again from his spot and began once more to advance towards the remaining male, who at this made off uphill again.

In this second case there was a slight show of dominance

[14] ibid., p. 283.

behaviour, which might be interpreted as arising from sexual jealousy, but there is, in Schaller's data, no evidence to support the intense jealousy and consequent aggressive behaviour postulated by Darwin (and accepted by Freud). Indeed, Schaller has concluded on the basis of 'the infrequency of observed copulations, together with the lack of sex play, homosexual behaviour and other forms of sexual expression' that gorillas have 'a high threshold of sex arousal'.[15]

Schaller's observations do indicate some slight evidence for promiscuous sexual behaviour, in that the same female, apparently, had sexual connection with different males within the space of nineteen days. Promiscuous behaviour has also been reported for other primate species. For example, Bolwig[16] in a recent study of the chacma baboon *(Papio ursinus)* has reported that 'on one occasion, an amiable old superior male allowed the other five mature males of the troop to cover the same female in turn, after he had satisfied himself, and subsequently turned to food.'

This is not to argue that jealousy, or aggressive behaviour arising from sexual rivalry, is absent or negligible in primates. There is abundant evidence of its existence as, for example, in Zuckerman's observations on 'sexual fighting' among hamadryas baboons.[17] However, the comparative evidence does suggest that aggressive behaviour arising from sexual rivalry is highly situational, and that such behaviour is more common and intense with the human animal than with other primates.

What we can also say from our inquiries so far is that there is no adequate anthropological evidence for the Darwin-Atkinson postulate that human social groups originally consisted of Cyclopean families. Indeed, recent research in this field points in very much an opposite direction. Thus many palaeoanthropologists would be in agreement with the recent conclusion of Hall that:

if the accounts of Dart and Oakley for the predatory behaviour of baboons in South Africa can be systematically reinforced in long-term field-studies, we have one more line of evidence to support the view, long ago put forward by Garveth Read, that the pre-hominids may have had many of the characteristics of a

---

[15] ibid., p. 286.
[16] N. Bolwig, 'A Study of the Behaviour of the Chacma Baboon, *Papio ursinus', Behaviour*, 14 (1959), 138.
[17] S. Zuckerman, *The Social Life of Monkeys and Apes*, London: Kegan Paul, 1932.

wolf-like primate, the nearest contemporary parallel to which is the baboon.[18]

Baboon troops, as the recent researches of Washburn and DeVore[19] have shown, range in size from 9 to 185 members. The commonest size is between 30 and 50, and is composed of approximately 5-10 adult males, 10-20 adult females, and juveniles equal to the number of adults.

Recent estimates of group size for pre-hominids and for early human groups have been offered by Chance and by Washburn and DeVore. Chance's estimate[20] for pre-hominids of the Pliocene is groups of 20-200 individuals 'arranged around a hierarchical core of males'; and that of Washburn and DeVore[21] for 'preagricultural humans' is groups of 50-60 individuals.

In the light of modern anthropological knowledge, then, there are major, if not insuperable, objections to the first of Freud's assumptions[22] that 'men originally lived in hordes, each under the domination of a single, powerful, and jealous male.'

(ii) The second of Freud's starting-points was the psychoanalytic discovery that in some instances boys having Oedipal neuroses identified their fathers with animals (usually domestic) on to which they displaced aggressive and other fantasies, with occasional acting out.

The three cases cited by Freud are those of:

(a) Little Hans (studied by Freud himself and first published in 1909),[23] a five-year-old boy, who identified his father with a horse;

(b) a nine-year-old boy (studied by Wulff and first published in 1912),[24] who identified his father with a dog;

[18] K. R. L. Hall, 'Aggression in Monkey and Ape Societies', in J. D. Carthy and F. J. Eblings (eds.), *The Natural History of Aggression*, London and New York: Academic Press, 1964, p. 63. References to Dart, Oakley and Read in this quotation are to R. A. Dart, 'Carnivorous Propensity of Baboons', *Symp. Zool. Soc. London*, No. 10, 49-56; K. P. Oakley, 'A Definition of Man', *Science News*, 20 (1951), 69-81, published by Penguin Books; G. Read, *The Origin of Man*, Cambridge University Press, 1917.
[19] S. L. Washburn and I. DeVore, 'Social Behaviour of Baboons and Early Man' in S. L. Washburn (ed.), *Social Life of Early Man*, London: Methuen, 1962, p. 91.
[20] M. R. A. Chance, 'The Nature and Special Features of the Instinctive Social Bond of Primates', ibid., p. 31.
[21] op. cit., p. 102.
[22] S. Freud, *An Autobiographical Study* (1925), *Standard Ed.*, 20, London: Hogarth Press, 1959, p. 67.
[23] S. Freud, 'Analysis of a Phobia in a Five-Year-Old Boy', (1909) *Standard Ed.*, 10, London: Hogarth Press, 1955.
[24] M. Wulff, 'Beitrage zur Infantilen Sexualitat', *Zbl. Psychoanal.*, 2 (1912).

(c) the five-year-old Apard (studied by Ferenczi and first published in 1913),[25] who identified both his father and his mother with domestic fowls.

To this 'starting-point' there can be, as far as I can see, no valid objection. Kroeber[26] wanted to know in what percentage of cases such displacements occurred. But this is a minor point, for such identifications are certainly common, and in so far as the shared beliefs of a group are concerned, a symbolic displacement can spread rapidly from one member to others by identificatory processes.

I shall later return to the discussion of these Oedipal fantasies which, as Freud discerned, are of crucial importance for the explanation of totemism.

(iii) Finally, there is the assumption of the basic significance of the totemic meal which Freud derived from his study of Robertson Smith's scholarly and perspicacious book, *The Religion of the Semites.*

'I propose,' writes Freud, 'that we should adopt Robertson Smith's hypothesis that the sacramental killing and communal eating of the totem animal, whose consumption was forbidden on all other occasions, was an important feature of totemic religion.'[27]

In support of this proposal, Freud cites three examples from Robertson Smith (the Aztec and the Otawa, both of North America, and the Ainu of Japan), and three from Frazer (the Zuni of California, the aborigines of Central Australia, and the Bini of West Africa) of the ritualistic devouring of sacred animals.

This, to the ethnographically uninformed reader, may seem an impressive list. What is not mentioned is that this list virtually exhausts the universe of possible instances, and that, in fact, there are very numerous other instances of totemism in which the sacramental meal is entirely absent.

Furthermore, the status of some of the instances cited by Freud is open to question. I do not, however, propose to examine these issues in any detail. I shall merely report the conclusion reached by Frazer at the end of his extensive survey of the ethnographical

[25] S. Ferenczi, 'A Little Chanticleer', (1913), in *First Contributions to Psycho-Analysis*, London: Hogarth Press, 1932, pp. 240-52.
[26] A. L. Kroeber, '*Totem and Taboo*: An Ethnologic Psychoanalysis', loc. cit.
[27] S. Freud, *Totem and Taboo* (1913), *Standard Ed.*, 13, London: Hogarth Press, 1955, p. 139.

literature, and recorded in the fourth volume of *Totemism and Exogamy* that the only two examples of 'what may be called a totem sacrament' were those found among the tribes of Central Australia and among the Bini of West Africa.[28]

The exact incidence of the totemic sacrament has never, to my knowledge, been established, but whatever the precise number of instances may be, the fact remains that when the total ethnographic record is considered, the sacramental totemic meal is a rare phenomenon.

Hence, the anthropologist tends to regard as unduly restrictive Freud's acceptance of the sacramental meal as a *sine qua non* of totemism.

Much more common are the prohibitions, and often severe prohibitions, against the eating of the totem animal (or plant) regardless of the circumstances. These forms of totemism are also of great interest. I will quote one example from ancient Samoa.

In ancient Samoa it was usual for families *('āiga)* to have their own particular gods who were identified both with the ruling chief of the family and with one or more animals. One of these gods, for example, called Salevao,[29] was identified with the turtle and the eel. Should any member of the family eat of these creatures, even inadvertently, he was at once taken ill, and before death the god would be heard saying from within the body of the stricken individual (that is, in the tones of his dissociated utterances): 'He ate me and I am eating him.'

Instances of totemism such as this are not easily subsumed under Freud's explanatory hypothesis which is at the phallic level of development, but they none the less call for psychoanalytic interpretation; and the example from Samoa, which I have just given, is clearly amenable to analysis in terms of introjective identification.

At this juncture, let me draw attention to Freud's almost total neglect of the mother in his discussion of totemism, and this, despite the fact that it was *specifically* a dish of 'potted mother' that little Arpad wanted to eat. This is something to which Abraham indirectly drew attention, in discussing Freud's interpretation of the totem-feast, when he wrote: 'What I must here point out is

[28] J. G. Frazer, *Totemism and Exogamy*, London: Macmillan, 1910, vol. 4, p. 232.
[29] G. Turner, *Samoa a Hundred Years Ago and Long Before*, London: Macmillan, 1884, p. 50.

that the criminal phantasies of the manic patient are for the most part directed against his mother.'[30]

There is, I would suggest, good cause to seek the mother as well as the father in totemic fantasies and rituals, in terms of both introjective and projective identifications.

Having now considered briefly the three principal assumptions of Freud's theory, let us return to his main argument.

> One day [writes Freud], the brothers who had been driven out came together, killed and devoured their father and so made an end of the patriarchal horde . . . the totem meal . . . would thus be a repetition and a commemoration of this memorable and criminal deed, which was the beginning of so many things—of social organization, of moral restrictions and of religion.[31]

But, continues Freud, the sons had feelings of love as well as hate for their father, and having got rid of him, the affection which had all this time been pushed under, made itself felt again in the form of remorse.

> They revoked their deed by forbidding the killing of the totem, the substitute for their father; and they renounced its fruits by resigning their claim to the women who had now been set free. They thus created out of their filial sense of guilt, the two fundamental taboos of totemism. . . .[32]

It will be noted that in this formulation the killing and devouring of the father is held to have been an *actual and finite historical event*. Furthermore, implicit in Freud's whole argument is the notion that the consequences of this event have had a persisting effect on the brain and behaviour of the human animal *by some process of genetic inheritance*.

That this is his position Freud himself fully recognizes, and he discusses both of these 'difficulties' (as he calls them) in the last

[30] K. Abraham, 'A Short Study of the Development of the Libido, Viewed in the Light of Mental Disorders' (1924), in *Selected Papers of Karl Abraham, M.D.*, London: Hogarth Press, 1950.
J. W. M. Whiting, in his interesting paper, *Totem and Taboo—a Reevaluation* (Duplicated copy from the Laboratory of Human Development, Harvard University) states that the 'clinical evidence *certainly* suggests that cannibalistic wishes are more often directed toward the mother than the father', and advances the hypothesis that totemism may well be 'a culturally provided defence' against a child's 'hostile cannibalistic wishes towards his mother rather than against his oedipal rivalry with his father'. Whiting's final comment is 'that the mother-child diad may have to take its place along with the oedipal triad as an important determinant of personality development'.
[31] *Totem and Taboo* (1913), *Standard Ed.*, 13, pp. 141-2.
[32] ibid., p. 143.

five pages of *Totem and Taboo*, dealing first with what I shall call 'the phylogenetic issue', and secondly, with what I shall call 'the fact or fantasy issue'.

(i) *The Phylogenetic Issue*

Before concluding his essay Freud says:

> No one can have failed to observe, . . . that I have taken as the basis of my whole position the existence of a collective mind, in which mental processes occur just as they do in the mind of an individual. In particular, I have supposed that the sense of guilt for an action has persisted for many thousands of years and has remained operative in generations which can have had no knowledge of that action. I have supposed that an emotional process, such as might have developed in generations of some who were ill-treated by their father, has extended to new generations which were exempt from such treatment for the very reason that their father had been eliminated. It must be admitted that these are grave difficulties; and any explanation that could avoid presumptions of such a kind would seem to be preferable.[33]

None the less, on the general grounds that the 'continuity of the mental life of successive generations' must somehow be explained, Freud postulates a process which he terms 'the inheritance of psychical dispositions'.[34]

This postulate is fundamental to Freud's whole position. Stated in abstract terms it may appear, to some, unexceptional; but, a moment's reflection will establish that what, in fact, is involved is the belief that following the committal of a finite historical act (namely the killing and eating of the father), the consequent 'sense of guilt' has persisted by process of genetic inheritance. In short, we are here presented with an extreme example of the inheritance of an acquired character.[35]

At the time Freud was working on *Totem and Taboo* (from 1910

[33] ibid., pp. 157-8.   [34] ibid., p. 158.
[35] Freud's Lamarckian cast of thought is also revealed in his letter to Abraham dated Vienna, 11 November 1917 (H. C. Abraham and E. Freud (eds.), *A Psycho-Analytic Dialogue: The Letters of Sigmund Freud and Karl Abraham 1907–1926*, London: Hogarth Press, 1965, p. 261), in which he wrote: 'Have I really not told you anything about the Lamarck idea? It rose between Ferenczi and me, but neither of us has the time or spirit to tackle it at present. The idea is to put Lamarck entirely on our ground and to show that the "necessity" that, according to him, creates and transforms organs, is nothing but the power of unconscious ideas over one's own body, (of which we see remnants in hysteria) in short, the "omnipotence of thoughts". This would actually supply a psychoanalytic explanation of adaptation; it would put the coping stone on psychoanalysis.'

to 1913) the science of genetics was still in its infancy. It is true that as early as 1885 Weismann had established the important concept of the independence of the germ plasm from the body proper, and, following the rediscovery, at the turn of the century, of Mendel's historic paper of 1866, there was much significant research done by Sutton (1903) and Boveri (1904), who formulated the chromosome theory, and Bateson, who introduced the term genetics in 1906.

Nonetheless, by 1910, the chromosome theory was still uncon-firmed by experimental evidence, and there was no scientifically established theory of genetical inheritance to which Freud might have turned. In the years immediately following the publication of *Totem and Taboo*, however, major advances in genetical science were made by Morgan and his co-workers, Bridges, Sturtevant and Muller, whose elaborate researches on the fruit-fly *Drosophila*, provided strong confirmation of the chomosome theory of heredity. Experimental proof of the chromosome theory was finally furnished independently by Stern and McClintock in 1931.[36] From then on the science of genetics has made remarkable progress through the work of such men as Beadle, Avery and Hersbey and the brilliant researches of Wilkins, Crick and Watson on the structure of deoxyribose nucleic acid, in the complex molecules of which, genetical information is coded for transmission from one genera-tion to another.

I have presented this brief outline of the history of genetics to indicate two things. The first of these is that Freud happened to write *Totem and Taboo* (and commit himself on the inheritance of acquired characters) just prior to the making of fundamental dis-coveries in transmission genetics; and the second is that genetics is now a highly developed and exact science.

What then has the science of genetics to say about the notion of the inheritance of acquired characters? I can best answer this question by citing the judgments of some leading geneticists and evolutionary zoologists.

Simpson writes:

> Experiments in heredity in the present century . . . not only have failed to corroborate that there is such a process, but also have shown that it is highly improbable, if not impossible.[37]

[36] See V. Grant, 'Genetics', *Encyclopedia Americana*, 12 (1960), 391-7.
[37] G. G. Simpson, *The Major Features of Evolution*, New York: Columbia University Press, 1953; London: Oxford University Press, 1954, p. 133.

Etkin notes that:

> ... the development of modern genetics has given us clear insights into the mechanisms of inheritance, and, as these are now understood, they do not provide any way in which environmentally induced modifications in the body could influence the genes.[38]

And Dobzhansky states:

> Experimental evidence has shown unambiguously . . . that environmentally induced change in the phenotype, so called acquired traits, are not inherited.[39]

Here, of course, Dobzhansky is referring to the genetical transmission of any acquired change in the phenotype; the notion that a psychic state, such as guilt, might be transmitted to the molecules in the reproductive cells is one which receives no support at all from modern genetics.

In short, Freud's notion that acquired psychical dispositions, such as a sense of guilt, are genetically transmitted has been shown by the 'reality testing' of genetics to be without scientific basis.

(ii) *The Fact or Fantasy Issue*

The second 'difficulty' considered by Freud is one which, he remarked 'might actually be brought forward from psychoanalytical quarters'.[40]

When we inquire into the behaviour of neurotics, Freud notes:

> We find no deeds, but only impulses and emotions, set upon evil ends, but held back from their achievement. What lie behind the sense of guilt of neurotics are always *psychical* realities and never *factual* ones. What characterizes neurotics is that they prefer psychical to factual reality and react just as seriously to thoughts as normal people do to realities.
>
> May not the same have been true of primitive men? We are justified in believing that, as one of the phenomena of their narcissistic organization they overvalued their psychical acts to an extraordinary degree. Accordingly the mere hostile *impulse* against the father, the mere existence of a wishful *phantasy* of killing and devouring him, would have been enough to produce the moral reaction that created totem and taboo.[41]

[38] W. Etkin (ed.), *Social Behaviour and Organization Among Vertebrates*, Chicago: University of Chicago Press, 1964, p. 3.
[39] T. Dobzhansky, *Mankind Evolving: The Evolution of the Human Species*, New Haven: Yale University Press, 1962, p. 16.
[40] *Totem and Taboo* (1913), *Standard Ed.*, 13, p. 159.
[41] ibid., p. 159.

C

Here, I would suggest, we have the statement of a theory that is fully tenable in the light of modern knowledge. (I would, however, like to see the epithets 'mere' deleted, for impulse and fantasy are forces which are neither slight nor insubstantial; and again, I would prefer to talk of a reaction that both created and *sustains* totem and taboo.)

This theory, it will be seen, avoids all difficulties over the inheritance of acquired characters, for it begins with the phylogenetically given impulses and the symbolizing brain of the human animal, which have evolved by the processes of natural selection.

Moreover, it is a theory which accords well with modern psychoanalytic and anthropological knowledge.

Psychoanalytic research in recent years has indicated how intimately fantasy is related to instinctual drive, and how very varied, depending on situational factors, fantasies may be. These are findings consistent with the rich variation actually encountered in primitive myth and ritual.

Again, it is a theory consistent with anthropological observations of the sociogenesis of primitive myth and ritual. At present, I have in preparation a paper based on my researches among the Iban of Borneo, to which I am giving the title 'Myth and Ritual in *Statu Nascendi*'. The paper includes description and analysis of a number of cases in which I was able to observe the establishment of myths and rituals by identificatory processes, within a group, from the dreams and fantasies of one or more of its members.

Finally, it is a theory which makes no narrow assumptions about the structure of social groups; instead, this question is left open for empirical documentation. All that the theory implies is that whatever the nature of the groups concerned we are likely to find myths and rituals that have arisen from the impulses and fantasies of the resulting Oedipal situations.

There is then, from a scientific point of view, great merit in the first of the two theories propounded by Freud in his last chapter of *Totem and Taboo*. The choice between them—i.e. between 'the fantasy hypothesis' and 'the actual event hypothesis'[42]—was, Freud

---

[42] It is of interest to note the previous occasion on which Freud made a decisive choice between fantasy and reality. Up to the spring of 1897, as Jones records (op. cit., vol. 1, p. 292) 'so strong was Charcot's teaching on traumatic experiences and so surely did the analysis of the patients' associations reproduce them', that Freud held firmly to his conviction of the reality of childhood traumas (of premature sexual experience). Then in a letter to Fliess dated 21 September 1897, he wrote of the 'great secret'

says 'indeed no easy one', but his predilection for the theory of the actual event is, in fact, very apparent throughout the whole of his essay, and one feels it was an integral part of the 'vision' of which he writes in *An Autobiographical Study*.[43]

The reasons that Freud[44] gives for his choice of 'the actual event hypothesis' are, moreover, of no great weight when objectively examined.

The first of these reasons is the argument that a change in the form of society 'from a patriarchal horde to a fraternal clan did actually take place'.[45] This argument, however, we may dismiss, for, as we have seen, there is no adequate anthropological evidence that human societies ever consisted of isolated Cyclopean families as Darwin, Atkinson and Freud supposed.

The other main argument advanced by Freud runs as follows: while it is true that obsessional neurotics in their symptomatic behaviour are 'defending themselves against *psychical* reality' it is also true that in their childhood they had 'evil impulses, pure and simple' which they turned into acts 'so far as the impotence of childhood allowed'.

Primitive people, the argument continues, are in this same respect, like children. Thus, while 'neurotics are above all *inhibited* in their actions: with them the thought is a complete substitute for the deed', primitive people 'are *uninhibited*: thought passes directly into action'.[46]

Once again, the anthropological evidence fails to support Freud's reasoning. Thus, although primitive people, like all other humans, may, on occasion, lose control of themselves and act impulsively, their behaviour, in general, as demonstrated by anthropological evidence is not like that of uninhibited and impulsive infants. On the contrary, their behaviour is, to a marked degree, inhibited by customary observances, taboos and avoidances of all kinds.

that had been dawning on him 'in recent months'. 'It was the awful truth that most—not all—of the seductions in childhood which his patients had revealed, and about which he had built his whole theory of hysteria, had never occurred.' 'It was,' as Jones comments, 'a turning point in his scientific career, and it tested his integrity, courage and psychological insight to the full. Now he had to prove whether his psychological method on which he had founded everything was trustworthy or not. It was at this moment that Freud rose to his full stature.'

[43] *An Autobiographical Study* (1925), *Standard Ed.*, 20, p. 68.
[44] *Totem and Taboo* (1913), *Standard Ed.*, 13.
[45] ibid., p. 160.
[46] ibid., pp. 160-61.

In these respects, custom-ridden primitives are, in cardinal ways like obsessionals. It is precisely this comparison which Freud himself so ably established in the long and important second chapter of *Totem and Taboo*, in which he directs attention to the behaviour of obsessional neurotics who have 'created for themselves individual taboo prohibitions' which they obey 'just as strictly as savages obey the communal taboos of their tribe or society'.[47]

It is, therefore, somewhat strange to find Freud suddenly asserting in the final paragraph of his essay, quite contrary to the evidence he presents in the second chapter, that primitive people, in sharp contrast to neurotics, are *'uninhibited'* in their actions. It is so strange, indeed, that at this point in my appraisal of *Totem and Taboo*, I found myself faced with the question: What was it that impelled Freud to maintain with such conviction, in the absence of convincing evidence, his belief in the historical actuality of the primal deed?

It will be noted that Freud's theory of the primal deed bears a marked resemblance to the doctrine of original sin, for it would attribute the origin of Oedipal guilt to the primeval father-killing, father-devouring sons, just as the origin of sin is attributed to the actions of Adam and Eve in the Garden of Eden.

Any such theory of finite origins is, in the light of modern evolutionary theory, untenable, for it is now plain that human nature is the outcome of many millions of years of evolution, and that such basic elements of our behaviour as our sexual, aggressive and fear impulses (all of which are of decisive importance in the Oedipal situation) can be traced back to our remote primate ancestors.

What then can have been the basis of the special attraction which the theory of the primal deed had for Freud?

We have already seen that one of the effects of this theory has been to displace guilt from the living on to the parricides of long ago. Moreover, it was from these parricides, so Freud would have it, that our guilt has been inherited. In other words, our guilt is really not our own but rather that of our remote parricidal progenitors.

One of the results of belief in this theory then, is a diminution in the guilt of the believer, and it may perhaps have been possible that Freud was, in making his difficult choice, unconsciously attracted to the theory of the primal deed because its acceptance

[47] ibid., p. 26.

had the effect of reducing his own Oedipal guilt by projecting it on to the imagined parricidal sons of the primeval Cyclopean family.

Let us then, glance briefly at the evidence for this hypothesis.

We know from his letters and from Ernest Jones' informative paper on its 'inception',[48] that *Totem and Taboo* was a work which had a very deep significance for Freud. This especially applied to the last chapter which was written with 'certainty and elation' and with the feeling that it was his 'greatest' and 'best' work.

However, soon after the completion of the manuscript, Freud became depressed and began to have serious doubts about what he had written. 'It is too uncertain', he wrote to Ferenczi, 'it would be too beautiful'.[49] He also wrote anxiously to Jones, seeking his opinion as the only other analyst with some knowledge of the subject.

> When I answered that letter, I told him that his doubts must have a subjective origin. I suggested he had in his imagination lived through the experiences he had described, that his elation represented the excitement of killing and eating the father, and that his doubts were only the reaction to this. When I saw him a few days later on a visit to Vienna, I asked him how it was that the man who had discovered the Oedipus complex should be so disturbed at the idea of its having been operative in primitive man. He wisely answered: 'Then I described the wish to kill one's father, and now I have been describing the actual killing; after all there is a big step from a wish to a deed.'[50]

Here, plainly enough, we are dealing with an aspect of Freud's own Oedipus complex, and it is revealing, I would suggest, to compare the depression he experienced after writing *Totem and Taboo* with the depression he experienced in Trieste some years before, on 29th April 1904. He had gone there to meet his brother, Alexander, with the intention of vacationing in Corfu.

Quite unexpectedly Freud and his brother were suddenly presented with the opportunity of visiting Athens instead. Despite the fact that to see Athens was one of Freud's dearest wishes, the imminent realization of his desires produced in him 'remarkably depressed spirits',[51] and initially he could think of nothing but

[48] E. Jones, 'The Inception of *Totem and Taboo*', loc. cit.
[49] ibid., p. 35.　　　　　　[50] ibid., p. 35.
[51] S. Freud, 'A Disturbance of Memory on the Acropolis', (1936), *Standard Ed.*, 22, London: Hogarth Press, 1964, p. 240.

obstacles which would prevent these new plans from materializing. Later, on the Acropolis, he underwent a curious psychological experience. 'It was peculiar disbelief in the reality of what was before his eyes, and he puzzled his brother by asking him if it was true that they really were on the Acropolis'.[52]

This experience was analyzed by Freud over thirty years later, with great honesty and sureness of touch, in a letter to Romain Rolland. The very theme of Athens and the Acropolis, Freud notes,[53] contained evidence of the son's superiority over his father, for whereas Freud's father, a businessman, had had no secondary education, and, therefore, little realization of the significance of Athens and the Acropolis, Freud, in contrast, had become a University Professor with a passionate interest in and knowledge of classical antiquity and 'the prehistoric in all its human forms'.[54]

In other words, it was guilt at triumph over his father which interfered with the enjoyment of Freud's journey to Athens, and which produced the defensive denial of the realization of his ascendency when Freud had finally climbed to the renowned Acropolis. As Freud himself puts it : 'It seems as though the essence of success was to have got further than one's father, as though to excel one's father was still something forbidden';[55] and, in comparison, he cites the behaviour of Napoleon, who, during his coronation as Emperor in Notre Dame, turned to his brother and remarked, 'What would Monsieur notre Père have said to this, if he could have been here today.'[56]

Our theme then, is triumph over the father and the way in which the feelings of elation at such a triumph conflict with the feelings of piety and submissive dutifulness proper in a son.

One is at once reminded of Freud's bravely frank account[57] of how, as a lad of seven or eight years, he was severely reprimanded by his father (for having 'obeyed the calls of nature' in his parent's

---

[52] E. Jones, op. cit., vol. 2, p. 27.

[53] S. Freud, 'A Disturbance of Memory on the Acropolis', (1936), *Standard Ed.*, 22, p. 247.

[54] idem, *The Origins of Psycho-Analysis: Letters to Wilhelm Fliess. Drafts and Notes 1887–1902*, London : Imago, 1954, p. 275.

[55] idem, 'A Disturbance of Memory on the Acropolis' (1936), *Standard Ed.*, 22, p. 247.

[56] As Strachey notes (cf. S. Freud, 'A Disturbance of Memory on the Acropolis', p. 247), this story is usually told of Napoleon's assumption of the Iron Crown of Lombardy in Milan.

[57] S. Freud, *The Interpretation of Dreams* (1900), *Standard Ed.*, 4, London : Hogarth Press, 1953, p. 216.

bedroom, when they were present) with the words: 'The boy will come to nothing!'

This occurrence, Freud remarks, 'must have been a frightful blow to my ambition, for references to this scene are still constantly recurring in my dreams and are always linked with an enumeration of my achievements and successes, as though I wanted to say: "You see, I *have* come to something".'

This constellation of feelings, it will be noted, is the same as that which underlay Freud's disturbance of memory on the Acropolis.

On comparative grounds, we can be reasonably sure that Freud's feelings at the sharp reprimand of his father were of an intense kind, and that they were associated with an impulse to retaliate, to reduce his father to nothing.

This interpretation is largely substantiated by Freud's own interpretation of part of his Count Thun dream.[58]

In the last episode of this dream Freud was in front of a station with an old man. The old man appeared to be blind, at all events in one eye, and Freud (the dreamer) handed to him a male glass urinal, which the old man used. In his analysis of this section of his dream Freud identifies the old man with his father (who had unilateral glaucoma) who was, says Freud, 'micturating in front of me, just as I had in front of him in my childhood'. In other words, the roles were reversed, a state of affairs which was, as Freud notes, 'in revenge' for the father's cutting remark of over thirty years before.[59]

In 1885, Freud had greatly helped his father by arranging what was a successful operation for his glaucoma, and there is abundant evidence that Freud had, for his father, a profound regard. We know that his father's death in October, 1896, affected Freud deeply; he wrote to Fliess that he felt as if he had been 'torn up by the roots'. In the Introduction to the second edition of *The Interpretation of Dreams* he describes the father's death as 'the most important event, the most poignant loss, of a man's life', and he

[58] ibid., p. 209.

[59] In a footnote to this dream, Freud remarks (ibid., p. 217) that 'the whole rebellious content' of his dream 'with its *lèse-majesté* and its derision of the higher authorities' went back to rebellion against his father, and he says of the male urinal, that 'it was associated with a bohemian party in Vienna at which a poisoned chalice belonging to Lucrezia Borgia had been exhibited', its central and principal constituent 'being a male urinal of the type used in hospitals'.

refers to *The Interpretation of Dreams* as 'a portion of my own analysis, my reaction to my father's death.'

It is also in *The Interpretation of Dreams* that Freud discusses his boyhood identification with the Semitic general, Hannibal, and links this with an event of his youth which moved him most deeply.[60] It was an account, given by his father, of how when a Gentile had arrogantly knocked a new fur cap from his head, with insulting words, he had humbly submitted instead of making any show of retaliation.

This struck the young Freud as being 'unheroic conduct', and he contrasted his father's behaviour with that of Hannibal's father, who had made his son swear, before the household altar, to take vengeance on the Romans.

It is of particular significance, for our present purposes, that in the first edition of *The Interpretation of Dreams*, Freud incorrectly gave Hasdrubal (instead of Hamilcar Barca) as the name of Hannibal's father. This was an error that especially annoyed Freud who was, from prolonged study, very well acquainted with the history of the House of Barca.

Freud convincingly accounts for his mistake in *The Psychopathology of Everyday Life*,[61] by showing that Hasdrubal, who was in fact, Hannibal's brother, was unconsciously identified with Freud's own half-brother Emanuel, who was twenty-four years older than Freud, and whom Freud preferred to his own father, to the extent that he used often to fantasy that he was Emanuel's son, in which case his situation in life would, he thought, be much improved.

In this material we are given clear insight into the profound ambivalence of Freud's feelings towards his father. There is also evidence that he feared him. This is to be found, I would suggest, in Freud's intense guilt at the prospect of surpassing his father in any way, as well as in the inhibition which, for many years, prevented him from visiting Rome.

In a letter to Fliess (dated 3 December 1896) Freud wrote: 'my longing for Rome is deeply neurotic. It is connected with my schoolboy hero-worship of the Semitic Hannibal, and, in fact, this year I have no more reached Rome than he did from Lake Trasimene.'

---

[60] ibid., p. 196.
[61] S. Freud, *The Psychopathology of Everyday Life* (1901), *Standard Ed.*, 6, London: Hogarth Press, 1960, p. 219.

Ernest Jones[62] has illumined this matter. He identifies Rome as the Mother of Cities, and notes Freud's acceptance of this in *The Interpretation of Dreams* where he cites the oracle given to the Tarquins that 'the conquest of Rome would fall to that one of them who should first kiss his mother'[63] as one of the variants of the Oedipus legend. It is evidently, states Jones, a reversal of the under-lying idea that in order to sleep with one's mother one has first to conquer an enemy.

It would follow that one of the determinants of Freud's inhibition against entering Rome was fear of his father, and it is significant that it was not until the late summer of 1901, almost five years after the death of his father and the self-analysis that culminated in the publication of *The Interpretation of Dreams*, that Freud was able to bring himself to visit Rome.

Finally, I would like to direct attention to the third of the three parapraxes concerning his father that occurred in the first edition of *The Interpretation of Dreams*, and which Freud himself discusses in *The Psychopathology of Everyday Life*.[64] This is the Zeus para-praxis, which I consider to be important additional evidence of Freud's fear and guilt with regard to his father.

The error in question occurred in the fifth chapter of *The Inter-pretation of Dreams*, just at the point where Freud is discussing the unpleasing picture, in mythology and legend, of the father's 'despotic power' and the 'ruthlessness' with which he makes use of it, while also pointing out the way in which filial piety is wont to give way to other interests. As an example of this Freud cites the behaviour of Zeus, 'who emasculated his father and made him-self ruler in his place.'

Now, as Freud acknowledges in *The Psychopathology of Every-day Life* he had, in citing this incident, erroneously carried the atrocity a generation forward, for in Greek mythology it was Cronus who castrated his father, Uranus.

Freud attributes this error to the influence of his half-brother, Emanuel, one of whose admonitions had lingered long in Freud's memory. 'One thing', Emanuel had said to his younger brother, 'that you must not forget is that as far as the conduct of your life is concerned you really belong not to the second but to the third generation in relation to your father.'

[62] E. Jones, op. cit., vol. 2, p. 21.
[63] *Standard Ed.*, 4, p. 398.   [64] *Standard Ed.*, 6, p. 218.

In other words, if Jakob Freud (b. 1815) be classed as belonging to the first generation, then Emanuel (b. 1832) belonged to the second, and Sigmund (b. 1856) to the third. The arrangement, it will be remembered, accords with Freud's youthful fantasy in which his brother Emanuel became his father in preference to Jakob, whose son he really was. It is also an arrangement whereby Jakob becomes identified with Uranus, Emanuel and the real Sigmund with Cronus, and the fantasied Sigmund (the 'son' of Emanuel) with Zeus.

The motivation of Freud's parapraxis now becomes apparent. If the fact that it was Cronus who castrated his father is mentioned, this is too threateningly close to the realization that a real son might think of inflicting comparable damage on his own father—a wish, that were it discovered, would surely lead to some terrible form of retaliation.

In this situation, therefore, the act of castration is displaced on to Zeus, who is unconsciously identified with the fantasied Sigmund, the 'son' of Emanuel. In this way the threat of an action grossly inconsistent with filial piety is much lessened, for the action has now been transferred to the realm of fantasy, and the fantasied father is the much more benign and less feared Emanuel.

There is thus substantial evidence for the view that in making his 'difficult' choice between 'the fantasy hypothesis' and the 'actual event hypothesis', Freud may have been unconsciously influenced in the way that has been indicated.

While fully admitting the difficulty of his decision, Freud, it may be noted, clung to the belief that 'the primal deed' was an actual event, to the end of his life. 'To this day', he wrote in *Moses and Monotheism*, 'I hold firmly to this construction'.[65] And the last sentence of *Totem and Taboo* reads: 'And that is why, without laying claim to any finality of judgment, I think that in the case before us it may be safely assumed that "in the beginning was the Deed".' Let me now, therefore, return to my appraisal of this particular theory of the primal deed which was, for whatever reasons, the final formulation reached by Freud.

As a result of this appraisal, Freud's theory, in the precise form that he stated it, has been found deficient on three main grounds:

(i) the anthropological and zoological evidence gives no support

[65] *Moses and Monotheism* (1939), *Standard Ed.*, 23, London: Hogarth Press, 1964, p. 131.

for Freud's basic assumption that human social groups originally took the form of Cyclopean families;

(ii) basic discoveries in the science of genetics since the time that Freud formulated his theory, have made scientifically untenable the notion of the genetical inheritance of acquired characters (and especially of acquired psychical dispositions), a notion which is integral to Freud's theory;

(iii) a range of evidence, both psychoanalytic and anthropological, indicates that the rituals of primitive peoples arise from dreams and fantasies (a view which adequately accounts for their adaptive value), rather than from the repetitive performance of actual deeds.

My general conclusion then, is that the scientific objections to Freud's theory of the primal deed are of a kind which make this theory no longer tenable in the precise form in which Freud stated it in the last two paragraphs of his essay. This, however, is in no sense to suggest that the rest of *Totem and Taboo* ought to be abandoned, for it is an essay full of brilliant insights. As I have already remarked, in his alternative theory,[66] namely, that 'the mere hostile *impulse* against the father, the mere existence of wishful *fantasy* of killing and devouring him, would have been enough to produce the moral reaction that created totem and taboo', Freud has provided us with the basis of an hypothesis which is fully tenable in the light of modern scientific knowledge, and which is, at the same time, entirely consistent with classical Oedipal theory.

It will be recollected that Freud took as the 'starting-point' of his attempt to explain totemism, the three cases in which young boys had displaced on to animals, their ambivalent Oedipal feeling towards their parents, and especially their fathers. And, Freud goes on to argue, it is 'probable that the totemic system—like little Hans' animal phobia and little Arpad's poultry aversion—was a product of the conditions involved in the Oedipus Complex'.[67]

In other words, as Róheim has observed 'people who have beliefs or customs comparable to those of these children . . . have an Oedipus complex'.[68] With this conclusion we can agree; it stands

[66] *Totem and Taboo* (1913), *Standard Ed.*, 13, p. 159.
[67] ibid., p. 132.
[68] G. Róheim, 'The Oedipus Complex, Magic and Culture,' *Psychoanalysis and the Social Sciences*, 2, New York: International Universities Press; London: Hogarth Press, 1950, p. 190.

even though the theory of the primal deed (which, as Róheim remarks, has 'little to do with the findings of clinical analysis') is to be entirely abandoned.[69]

Let us then glance briefly at the Oedipus complex in the light of anthropological evidence.

Fenichel has defined the Oedipus complex in these terms: 'the Oedipus complex signifies the combination of genital love for the parent of the opposite sex and jealous death wishes for the parent of the same sex'.[70]

The sexuality of human infants has now been established by the researches of Halverson, Kinsey, and many others; comparable observations are available for infra-human primates. For example, Boelkins,[71] of the Primate Laboratory, University of Wisconsin, has reported that infant rhesus monkeys (who are usually mature at about four years of age) commonly mount their mothers, with phallic thrusts, at an age of about fifty days. Zuckerman[72] has described the case of an infant male pig-tailed monkey (Macaca nemestrina) who, at the age of six to seven months, mounted his mother with erections and pelvic thrusts. Moreover, this mother, who was still nursing her infant, regularly presented to him.

It must be added, however, that in both of these cases we are dealing with behaviour from which almost all inhibitory social forces had been removed. In other words, in both cases mature males were excluded.

This brings us to the second part of Fenichel's definition: 'the jealous death wishes for the parent of the same sex'. In studying this subject a fundamental question at once presents itself: What is the phylogenetic basis of the 'jealous death wishes' that characterize the Oedipus complex?

The answer, I would suggest, lies in the phenomena of rivalry,

[69] Editor's Note: Cf. also Róheim's views expressed in Psychoanalysis and Anthropology (New York: International Universities Press, 1950, p. 424): '. . . it is evident that the Oedipus complex must be universal. I do not assume that the Oedipus complex is universal because we inherit our Oedipus complexes from hypothetical events that may have taken place in primeval mankind (Freud, Primal Horde theory). This ultra-Lamarckian point of view is untenable. But it is evident that the Oedipus complex is a direct derivative of our partly premature, partly conservative (prolonged or retarded) rate of growing up.'

[70] O. Fenichel, The Psychoanalytic Theory of Neurosis, New York: Norton, 1945, p. 97.

[71] R. C. Boelkins, 'Seminar on the Behaviour of the Rhesus Monkey', Zoological Society of London, 6.12.63.

[72] S. Zuckerman, op. cit., p. 272.

contention, and dominance which are intrinsic to the behaviour of most animals.

A contention situation arises when two animals become rivals for the possession of the same object. Such a situation is commonly resolved by the more powerful animal getting his way, and by the other animal, who has submitted to the threats of the dominant animal, more or less inhibiting his impulse to retaliate aggressively. Here in essence, I would suggest, we have a basic aspect of the Oedipal situation, and its elements, the evidence indicates, are phylogenetically very old.

We have seen from Schaller's observations how a slow movement forward by the dominant male of a gorilla group was sufficiently threatening to cause a less dominant male to immediately terminate his sexual activity.

Zuckerman reports that when the young pig-tailed monkey, whose behaviour I have already noted, mounted his mother, his powerful father, who was in an adjoining cage, expressed his displeasure 'in the form of violent lunges at the intervening wire partition.' In discussing the inhibitory effect of the presence of the father, Zuckerman notes that according to Lashley and Watson:

> their young monkey showed extreme fear when introduced with his mother, at the age of four months, into a cage containing two males, one of whom was his father. The degree of relative independence that he had displayed when confined alone with his mother, was now greatly reduced, and he seemed 'in constant fear of his life'. . . .[73]

Again, Phyllis Jay,[74] in a recently published account of her research on the behaviour of free-ranging Langur monkeys in India, has described how, when a female enters estrous and recommences copulation before having weaned a previous infant, this infant may direct its aggression toward the copulating male, even though in part afraid, by trying to slap or bite him.

I would argue then, that the essential elements of the Oedipal situation—the sexual drive, dominance, aggression, and fear—are phylogenetically given, and that they are basic to the nature of the

---

[73] ibid. The original reference is to K. S. Lashley and J. B. Watson, 'Notes on the Development of a Young Monkey', J. Animal Behaviour, 3 (1913), 114-39.

[74] P. Jay, Mother-Infant Relations in Langurs', in L. Rheingold (ed.), Maternal Behaviour in Mammals, New York: John Wiley & Sons, 1963, p. 300.

human animal and to human behaviour in all known kinds of family or procreative groups.

This is not to say, of course, that there is a universal form of the Oedipus complex. Psychoanalytic research has indicated that even under the same family system the Oedipus complex may take significantly different forms. Where there is marked variation in the structure of the family from one society to another, we may expect to find marked variations in the form of the Oedipus complex, and it is the discovery and analysis of these variant forms which is one of the important future tasks of psychoanalytic anthropology.

This paper was first written in memory of Géza Róheim. For the purposes of this volume it was selected because it elaborates on and summarizes one of Róheim's pioneering contributions to psychoanalysis and the social sciences. The essay examines the psychoanalytically relevant problem of man's delayed infancy and differential infantilism which call for the functional necessity of defence mechanisms and controlled behaviour. In this connection the paper draws attention to those consequences of the ontogenetically determined separation anxiety which can be considered a moving factor in the individual's effort to internalize aggression and communicate through identification. Pair-formation is born out of man's need to cling and non-seasonal sexuality. Moral bonds are an adaptive achievement of desexualized libido.

The basic childhood conditions are biologically determined and universal. Their subsequent elaboration is under the influence of external interventions and certain developmental trends as exemplified on the basis of anthropological data.

4

On the Biopsychological Determinants of Social Life[1]

WARNER MUENSTERBERGER

In 'The Individual, the Group and Mankind', a paper that I found among Róheim's numerous unpublished manuscripts, he summarized his ideas thus:

> Owing to the biological fact of our prolonged and never-quite overcome juvenile way of life, sex has become independent of its original goal of procreation. Dependency has been prolonged far beyond its natural limits. Fantasy and memory (which means: the past) determine our actions and we have become a very confused kind of primate. In these anxieties, and the measures our psyche takes to counterbalance them, we find the explanation of man's greatness, achievements, and of all our woes and conflicts.

To understand this line of thinking one must be aware of the significance that fantasy and emotion have in cultural processes as well as in maladjustment. Róheim's concept of the nature of human behaviour and the motivation of social actions, it is true, was influenced by Freud, by the research of the Dutch anatomist Bolk and to some extent by the theories of Melanie Klein. It was in merging the two fields of science—psychoanalysis and anthropology—that he developed his ontogenetic theory of culture.

The ontogenetic interpretation of cultural behaviour was perhaps first suggested by Stanley Hall, and then taken up by the sociologist William I. Thomas, who pointed out that

> . . . the characteristic helplessness of the child, which at first thought appears to be a disadvantage, is in fact the source of human superiority, since the design of nature in providing this condition of helplessness is to afford a lapse of time sufficient for the growth of the very complex mechanism, the human brain, which, along with free hands, is the medium through which man

[1] This paper first appeared in *Psychoanalysis and the Social Sciences*, 4, ed. by W. Muensterberger and S. Axelrad, New York: International Universities Press, 1955.

begins that reaction on his environment—inventing, exterminating, cultivating, domesticating, organizing—which ends in his supremacy.[2]

Since Freud's original observations, it has often been stated that the super-ego developed along the same biological and historical lines—that is, the prolonged childhood period of helplessness and dependence and the Oedipus complex, the repression of which (as Freud pointed out) was connected with the interruption of libidinal development by the latency period and, consequently, with the beginnings of activity characteristic of man's sexual life. It was with these ideas of Thomas and Freud that Róheim prefaced his book *The Riddle of the Sphinx*.[3]

It was Bolk[4] who termed the slowing down of the development of higher mammals, and in particular of apes and man, *retardation*. The knowledge of this retardation of growth and the inferiority of the human constitution appeared to be highly significant for the understanding of the great differences among men as well as among human groups—that is, society. Inevitably, he felt, the unique degree of individualization in man stems from the duration of the growth process. The slow post-natal development leads to the intensity of the mother-child relationship. But this is only one cause of the wide variation in human behaviour, since the retardation of the growth process permits a confluence of events to contribute to the moulding of the individual.

In looking for the origin of human individuality we must go beyond the complicated network of society and beyond the countless variations of diverse cultural, economic, and geographical conditions. Largely because of the propositions made by psychoanalysis, students have been able to separate the elements of human existence that are adaptive from those elements that are ever present in the core of explicitly human needs and biological predispositions, regardless of culture and social environment. To be sure, the multiplicity of environments tends to obscure our view, but the variety and complexity of adaptations and reaction formations have led students of human behaviour to confuse these with basic human characteristics. This is the way I understand Anna Freud's remarks:

[2] W. I. Thomas, *Sex and Society*, Chicago: University of Chicago Press, 1907, p. 226.
[3] London: Hogarth Press, 1934.
[4] L. Bolk, *Das Problem der Menschwerdung*, Jena: Gustav Fischer, 1926.

A man's id remains the same at all times. It is true that instinctual impulses are capable of transformation when they push toward the ego and have to meet the demands of the outside world. But within the id itself little or no change takes place, apart from the advances made from pregenital to the genital instinctual aims.[5]

The broader implications of these considerations can be shown when we take the trouble to sift this great variety of cultural material and information. In Róheim's work, the Oedipus complex is but one of the points in question, but he considered it to be of infinite importance as one aspect of our being—virtually, as one of the cornerstones of human civilization.

To his reservoir of evidence of the immense importance of the child-mother-father relationship (the Oedipus situation, as we have learned to call it in Western culture), Freud added the role and pattern of the inter-individual relationship in non-Western—that is, primitive—societies. People living at great distance from one another showed surprising similarities, not so much from the standpoint of social structure as in the realm of human interaction. Hence the varieties of the Oedipal situation ought to be seen as superstructures built upon the first vital experiences of the individual.

In observing the diversity of cultural elements, anthropologists formerly were impressed by the similarities found among people in quite different areas. Frazer, who was among the anthropological pioneers, presented us with voluminous studies of mythology, custom, and ritual that showed impressive similarities. Today anthropologists and sociologists have a number of theories concerning the similarity of these cultural features, some explaining them on the basis of ancient relationships, migrations, and mutual influences, and others explaining them by involved systems of exchange. And yet so many questions remain unanswered. Why did a tribe in the jungles of Africa have institutions, beliefs, and even objects similar to those of a tribe in a remote island of Oceania? Why was there a similarity of tools and weapons, of signs and symbols, despite insuperable geographic barriers? Here the contributions of psychoanalytic research have provided an answer.

[5] The above quotation is retranslated from *Das Ich und die Abwehrmechanismen* (London: Imago, 1936, p. 161), because the English translation, *The Ego and the Mechanisms of Defense* (New York: International Universities Press, 1946, p. 152) differs in several respects from the original German text.

The concept that man's ego is a device of man's psychic apparatus, which enables him to surrender his impulses to the demands of mutual interests and survival, has a valid application in an area beyond the clinical understanding of the individual. Would it not be cynical to believe that man only *once* was able to invent a hammer, a house, or the story of Adam and Eve? We find tools even among the most primitive tribes—because all people try to make their lives endurable. And we find creation myths among every culture—wherever children want to know from whence they come. The ability to channel mobile energy into bound energy is inherent in every human being and is the mainspring of civilization; it is the unconscious gratification of needs and demands through a socially accepted form—in a sense it is a fender against injury. Man tries to give himself a chance to survive and thus arranges for substitutes—imagined and real—to gratify impulses that often, if not renounced, would result in the devastation of the community which, in turn, acts as his protector. Hence a ritual serving this end does not have to be invented only once and then carried from people to people. (A symptom does not appear in one individual to be copied by other neurotics).

Freud's interest in the earliest libidinal tendencies led him to look for elements that evolve around the roots of man's relation to the external world, especially his love objects—in other words, the omnipresence of the Oedipal constellation. The Oedipus complex as the basis of social order seemed a disillusionment to people who had profound belief in man's religious and ethical aims or in the practical necessity of some form of social arrangement as the guiding feature of our modes of life. The parallels that Freud showed between the horse phobia of little Hans and the totemistic institutions of primitive tribes were not convincing to the social scientists. They saw no more validity to his argument than they did to Atkinson's attempt to see traces of the primal horde (as described by Darwin) in a primitive society. The training of the anthropologists was sufficient to enable them legitimately to reject the purely evolutionary biological theories of Darwin as applied to primitives, and their resistance to psychoanalytic hypotheses made it impossible for them to interpret completely Freud's concepts in terms of verified field observations. And yet, despite all such resistance, certain evidence made their acceptance of some psychoanalytic propositions inescapable.

Most conspicuous was the fact that no known tribe has ever permitted incest or, more specifically, that every known tribe has had one or another regulation concerning incest, particularly with regard to the mother-son relationship. The existence of this universal element brought psychoanalysis and the social sciences closer together and the anthropologist Murdock went so far as to state that Freud's theory 'provides the only available explanation of the peculiar emotional intensity of incest taboos'.[6] Pointing out that it did not help us to understand why all cultures have institutionalized incest taboos, he nevertheless felt that it does 'provide a basis for assuming that all people have the essential behavioural ingredients out of which taboos can be fashioned.'

The incest taboo is one of the significant 'by-products of man's basic uniqueness', we might answer Murdock in the words of Julian Huxley.[7] Incest taboos belong to the uniqueness of man because all humans have a basically identical experience. Here psychoanalytic considerations aid us in understanding specific aspects of man in society, and we owe it to Róheim that today we understand culture and cultural elements as derivatives of or reaction formations to the specifically human infantile situations— in Róheim's words: 'as defence mechanisms against certain libidinal strivings'.[8]

One might claim that *Totem and Taboo* was conceived under the influence of evolutionary ideology which had led Freud to extend his inquiries to the anthropoids and primitive man.

> Psycho-analysis has revealed that the totem animal is in reality a substitute for the father. . . . If, now, we bring together the psycho-analytic translation of the totem with the fact of the totem meal and with Darwin's theories of the earliest state of human society, the possibility of a deeper understanding emerges. . . . There is, of course, no place for the beginnings of totemism in Darwin's primal horde. All we find there is a violent and jealous father who keeps all the females for himself and drives away his sons as they grow up. This earliest state of society has never been an object of observation. The most primitive kind of organization

[6] G. P. Murdock, *Social Structure*, New York: Macmillan, 1949, p. 293.
[7] J. Huxley, *Man in the Modern World*, New York: Mentor Book, 1948, p. 26; London: Chatto, 1950, p. 19.
[8] G. Róheim, *The Origin and Function of Culture*, New York: Nervous Disease Monographs, 1943, p. 10. See also W. Muensterberger, 'Ueber einige psychologische Fundamente der menschlichen Gesellschaftsbildung', *Psyche*, 6 (1953), 683, and D. Freeman, 'Totem and Taboo: A Reappraisal', now in this volume.

that we actually come across—and one that is in force to this day in certain tribes—consists of bands of males; these bands are composed of members with equal rights and are subject to the restrictions of the totemic system, including inheritance through the mother.[9]

Freud then gives his well-known description of the brother horde and the cannibalistic celebration of the father's death with its following remorse, a sense of guilt that led to the 'subsequent obedience'.

We are confronted then with three questions: Do we have any additional proof for the existence of the primal horde? Can anthropology establish the universality of the Oedipus complex? And, do we actually need the phylogenetic theory in order to explain the phenomenon of the Oedipus complex?

Alone among the anthropologists, Róheim set out to clarify the apparent conflicts that existed between the two sciences. He pointed out[10] that Freud's thinking was highly influenced by the theories of his time, by Lamarck's, Haeckel's, and Darwin's concepts of evolution or, more precisely, by a specific trend in evolution, namely, the unilateral tendency of progress with modern man as the highest living creature. And this concept, so Simpson tells us, was linked with the assumption of an ever-increasing tendency for perfection whereby 'acquired characters, those induced by environment and habit, are inherited in kind'.[11]

As we know today, the combined attempts of genetics, anatomy, biology and paleontology show no evidence for this working hypothesis. Acquired characters cannot be inherited. The postulate of the primal horde was built, in Freud's words, on the assumption that:

. . . the sense of guilt for an action has persisted for many thousands of years and has remained operative in generations which can have no knowledge of that action. I have supposed that an emotional process, such as might have developed in generations of sons who were ill-treated by their father, has extended to new generations which were exempt from such treatment for the very reason that their father had been eliminated.[12]

[9] S. Freud, *Totem and Taboo* (1913), *Standard Ed.*, 13, London: Hogarth Press, 1955, p. 141.
[10] G. Róheim, *The Riddle of the Sphinx*, London: Hogarth Press, 1934.
[11] G. G. Simpson, *The Meaning of Evolution*, New Haven: Yale University Press, 1950, pp. 270f.
[12] *Totem and Taboo* (1913), *Standard Ed.*, 13, p. 158.

But this reasoning does not satisfy our present-day understanding of evolutionary processes. It would imply that a specific event or set of events had been recorded and continually transmitted by the mneme over hundreds of generations. As Róheim pointed out, there are valid objections to this hypothesis. One might ask why this event in particular should be phylogenetically inherited while others left no mark? Why should this event have left a scar of guilt through thousands of years of social mutations and an ever-increasing complexity of communal living? One could point to many other circumstances and pressures to which man has been subjected, to a variety of demands made on the human mind, that left no traces on the individual. Therefore, in re-examining this aspect of the primal horde theory, we must assess the essential findings of biology and anatomy in conjunction with the genetic approach that psychoanalysis has taught from the beginning. Observable facts do not seem to support the theory.

But, in re-evaluating the theory of the primal horde, do we have to abandon the concept of the Oedipus complex? The anthropologists thought that we did. On the basis of Linton's field observations, Kardiner[13] concluded that the Marquesans are free from any hostile feelings against their father (although their mythology tells of an attempt to castrate their hero Tiki after a couple of his fingers had been cut off). Another example frequently referred to in analytical and anthropological literature are the Trobriands, a Melanesian tribe organized along matriarchal lines. They were described by Bronislaw Malinowski, the English anthropologist, who perhaps was the first field worker to pay serious attention to psychological issues.[14]

If one accepts the theory of the Oedipus complex for a patriarchal society according to Freud's description of a jealous and violent father who would resemble the primal overlord, how then can it work in a matriarchal setting, which presumably provides a different framework for personality development? According to Thompson, 'anthropological research has clearly shown that the Oedipus complex as it is described by Freud is not universal but is a product of monogamous patriarchal society'.[15] (There seems

[13] A. Kardiner, *The Individual and His Society*, New York: Columbia University Press, 1939, p. 197.
[14] Cf. A. Parsons, 'Is the Oedipus Complex Universal?', now in this volume.
[15] C. Thompson, *Psychoanalysis: Evolution and Development*, New York: Hermitage Press, 1950; London: Allen & Unwin, 1952.

to be some misunderstanding here about Freud's concept, because the society depicted in *Totem and Taboo* is certainly anything but monogamous.) She continues with a reference to *Sex and Repression in Savage Society* wherein Malinowski says:

> . . . law and constraint are represented by quite another person than the father, by mother's brother, the male head of the family in a matriarchal society. He it is who actually wields the *potestas* and who indeed makes ample use of it . . . (The) *kada* (mother's brother) is always held up to (the boy) as the real authority behind the rules.[16]

Can there be an Oedipus complex where the uncle's authority is substituted for the father's? Was Freud's picture derived merely from Victorian doctrine as Fromm[17] believes, seeing in the idea of the Oedipus complex the child's reaction to the pressure of parental authority in the patriarchal society? Would it not be better to throw out the entire libido concept (as Thompson does) and see instead the individual's development in terms of 'growth and human relation'?[18] These questions were asked by social scientists to illustrate the futility and onesidedness of the Oedipus theory and to reduce it at best to a grandiose fantasy of the founder of psychoanalysis—as if Oedipus were a particularly Viennese invention. What the opponents of Freudian theory seem to undervalue is the biological basis of human needs and drives. But for everybody who has studied without bias human psychosexual development, there cannot be any doubt about the sexual nature of the child's impulses towards its parents.

In the light of these questions, the following description of the Mentaweians, a tribe in the most remote region of Indonesia, should prove valuable. Among the Mentaweians certain institutions and modes of behaviour were conditioned by an elaborate and highly compulsive taboo system.[19] These taboos were so all-pervading that for the greater part of the year the Mentaweians abstained from everything they considered 'activity'—from certain ritual foods,

[16] B. Malinowski, *Sex and Repression in Savage Society*, London: Routledge, 1937, p. 44.
[17] E. Fromm, *Man for Himself*, New York: Holt, Rinehart, 1947; London: Routledge, 1949, p. 157.
[18] C. Thompson, op. cit., p. 42.
[19] W. Muensterberger, 'Oral Trauma and Taboo: A Psychoanalytic Study of an Indonesian Tribe', *Psychoanalysis and the Social Sciences*, 2, New York: International Universities Press; London: Hogarth Press, 1950, p. 129.

from sexual intercourse, from hunting and fishing. Their social structure shows some traces of a class system according to marital status of the members but, in contrast to the situation existing in human society, it is the young men who enjoy the greatest freedom. The higher a man's social position, the more he is restricted by a complicated network of laws and taboos.

Anthropologists found it difficult to explain this unusual system, yet from an analytic point of view this cultural configuration is largely explained by the early childhood experiences of these people. They have a peculiar marriage arrangement in that the official marriage does not take place until several children have been born. Premarital relationships are never steady or lasting, and a young woman may have children from several men before she decides to marry. The children of these premarital contacts officially belong to her clan, of which her father is head. After the marriage her husband becomes the official father of her children. As infants the children are neglected by the mother and left to the care of other members of her family. Separation anxiety, fear of object loss, and lack of maternal care seem to bring about an early hostility against the mother as well as against the man who deprives the child of maternal protection. The anxiety that the child feels at being abandoned and starved or treated roughly is a frequently recurring theme in Mentaweian mythology. Two myths—and members of the tribe believe them to be their true history—will show the connection between the people's real experiences and their reactions beyond the manifest behaviour.

According to the first myth, there once lived a father and a mother and their two children, an older girl and her young brother. One day the father came home and gave his wife some fish for a meal. The mother put the fish in a pan and filled another pan with bananas. She then left the hut for a moment. Her little son took advantage of her absence to throw out the fish and put snakes in the pan in their place, and for the bananas he substituted their skins. Upon her return the unsuspecting mother put the pans on the fire and let them cook until their contents were done. When she served the food, a quarrel arose between the mother and the father. He accused her of wanting to feed him banana skins and she insisted that he had wanted to feed her snakes instead of fish. Their anger rose to fury, and finally the father left. Soon afterwards the mother went down to the river to fish and instead of returning to her children went into the woods. The next day the children went in search of her, and when finally they found her the three sat down and the mother nursed the little boy. But as soon as the children fell asleep, the mother got up and disappeared again. When the brother and sister awoke, they again went in search of her. They called her and wandered through the woods, but in vain. When they at last found her, she appeared in the form of a deer. They begged her to return home but she refused. Then the daughter met a man whom she married and the new couple took care of the little boy. Meanwhile the father looked for his wife, and on his walk through the woods saw a deer. Not recognizing his wife, he shot the deer for food.

Besides the rather obvious symbolic meaning of this myth, several features express an actual experience projected into the mythological past. We recognize that the boy's wish for his mother is linked with his separation fantasies directed against the father. Not long after birth, usually a month or so, the Mentaweian child plays a minor role as the recipient of his mother's attention. She leaves him with others—or as the myth declares, in the care of an older sister—and it is easy for the child to interpret his mother's rejection as the result of the attention she is paying to her lover, after all a stranger who is keeping the mother from him. And since these premarital love relationships are quite unstable, the insecurity of the children is even more significant. Conversely, the instability of love relationships stems from the instability of maternal care and attention. This is illustrated in the tribe's wedding ceremony. Before marriage sexual relationships are permitted but the two lovers are not allowed to eat together. The ritual of the wedding ceremony consists merely of the partners sharing a meal, which is being united on an oral level. Completely lacking are the genital symbols of the wedding ceremonies which we find amongst most other people. There is no divorce. The strictness of the marital laws and the freedom of premarital relationships seem to complement each other.

The second myth illustrates the point from another angle. It tells of the origin of man. In the beginning the earth was a dreary waste with no human beings, only powerful evil demons. The most powerful of the demons was looking for a good weapon. He selected a strong tree trunk, but when he split it, out came four human beings, two men and two women. As soon as they saw the demon they fled into the depth of the forest. There they tried without success to raise some crops. It was in this desperate situation that the evil spirit discovered them. He pitied them and promised help. Thereafter matters improved until monkeys and field mice ravaged the fields, and stole the fruit. The four then decided to go hunting while the demon, who had turned into their protector, guarded the crops. When the people had left, their guardian spirit transformed himself into an iguana the better to keep an eye on their property. Shortly afterwards an enormous number of monkeys arrived, pressed upon him from all sides, destroyed the crops and stole the fruit, but left the iguana where he was. When the four people returned from the hunt to find their fields in ruin and their crop stolen, they naturally assumed that no other than the iguana was the culprit. Without recognizing him as their benefactor, two of the people threw themselves upon the iguana, killed, and consumed him. Very shortly afterwards they died in great pain and fear, as if they had been poisoned. The other couple, in great anxiety, fled in haste. They became man's first ancestors.

I do not intend to go into the anthropological details of this particular culture, nor does it seem necessary to interpret the myths other than to stress the preoccupation with oral fears and desires. In the second myth the couple that 'eats' the iguana (or father) is killed (and killing can be understood as castration); in the first myth the mother leaves the children, but then the father eats the mother. The myths tell of the children's struggle for food and protection. The symbolic situation with which each individual's life starts is well expressed in these stories. The Oedipal conflict does not appear as rivalry on a genital level but as the ultimate consequence of the oral needs of the infant.

We can recognize a number of obvious symbols and themes in the two tales that might be interpreted as convincing evidence for the existence of the primal horde. But when we analyze the myths and consider the social organization of the Mentaweians, we cannot overlook Róheim's definition that 'myth always represents as projected into the past whatever conflicts exist in the present'.[20] These tales clearly express the oral mechanisms contained in the precursors of the Oedipal situation. The ontogenetic, individual experience is the basis for these projections. We do not have to seek explanations in an occurrence in some remote era. An extremely traumatic

[20] G. Róheim, 'Oedipus Complex, Magic and Culture', ibid., p. 194.

experience of early infancy is retold in mythological form and reacted to in the ritual doctrine of these people. The anxiety that the infant feels about the mother's availability and (what is largely identical) about self-preservation is revealed in both myths. In the first one we learn about a primal scene: the child's wish to separate the parents and the mother's retaliation. In the end the father slays the deer (which is the mother) and consumes her (confusion of oral and genital demands). The man-woman relationship then appears as a murderous and cannibalistic act. The real picture is being distorted. What was traumatically experienced on an oral level is repeated during the phallic phase. The hostility once felt for the careless mother is displaced to the father. The monkeys in the second myth destroy the crops (which should be understood as the destruction of the mother). The people then slay their benefactor (the father).

Among the Mentaweians there is an important ritual that expresses just this mechanism. Upon the death of the chief the young men mutilate his body and destroy his property. But the release of the hostile feelings creates talion anxiety, and as a result the people punish themselves by becoming entirely abstinent. After almost any act of aggression—hunting, fishing, working, etc.— they abstain from all procreative and productive activity. They continually vacillate between the temptation to kill and eat the animal, on the one hand, and the ensuing taboo as a repetition of self-approach and remorse, on the other. One might venture to say that after the killing of an animal and the eating it—that is, the oral introjection—a form of oral regression follows.[21] After each act of aggression follows a period of inertia and abstinence that bears the mark of depressive neurosis.

Anthropological data make it evident that the multitude of ego structures and reality systems does not influence the *fact* of the Oedipal situation, since this is explained on the basis of the inevitable ontogenetically defined dependence of man. The Oedipal situation may vary or differ in degree and in kind. The attitude of the parents towards the child or of the child towards the parents may be modified in the view of social demands or of individual sentiments, but this can be interpreted only as one or the other way of adaptation to inner and outer controls.

[21] Cf. S. Freud, *The Ego and the Id* (1923), *Standard Ed.*, 19, London: Hogarth Press, 1961, p. 29, fn. 2.

Among the Chinese the traditional rules of filial piety carefully prescribe the child-parent relationship and especially the son-father relationship. No son 'belongs to himself'; instead he is responsible to the generations and is supposed to live up to such expectations. The famous book of *The Twenty-four Examples of Filial Piety* defines how an obedient son should behave: Lao Lai-tze was seventy when he put on a child's dress and played with toys to amuse his parents; Wu Mang let himself be eaten by mosquitoes to keep them away from his parents; a Chinese patient in his middle thirties would make no important decision without consulting his older brother, inevitably feeling compelled to follow his brother's advice although the brother had frequently misled him. The outer conformity, however, leads to tensions and a reservoir of hostility that is directed mainly against the self. The Chinese male is prepared by an early, rather undisturbed and yet involved mother-son tie. Babies are fed at all possible times, cared for, and rarely left without company. This condition makes a fixation on an oral level easy and equips the man with the mechanisms needed to alleviate Oedipal tensions through oral regression.[22]

Thus reminded of the infant's libidinal tendencies, his wish for immediate gratification, his identification with the mother, and his low frustration tolerance,[23] we must ask what precedes this specific constellation that, according to our present knowledge, is exclusively human. So far as the overt mechanics are concerned, we have reason to assume that there is no living creature so dependent on maternal care for such an extended period of time as is the human.

Once having established these facts, Róheim drew attention to psychological and biological phenomena. Man's exceedingly slow development as compared with that of any other animal has been stressed by biologists and anatomists for many decades. We know that man's development from ovum to birth takes approximately 280 days while the same development in the chimpanzee requires only 251 days. The period of human pregnancy is about 266 days, but the period of gestation for the chimpanzee is 231 days and for

[22] Cf. W. Muensterberger, 'Orality and Dependence: Characteristics of Southern Chinese', now in this volume.

[23] Cf. H. Hartmann, R. M. Loewenstein and E. Kris, 'Comments on the Formation of the Psychic Structure', *The Psychoanalytic Study of the Child*, 2, New York: International Universities Press; London: Hogarth Press, 1946, p. 11.

the lower monkeys, between 150 and 160 days. When we compare the relative growth rate of humans with the higher primates, we learn from Schultz[24] that the duration of postnatal growth in man is 27 times the prenatal growth, whereas in the macaque, for instance, it is only 15 times greater than the prenatal growth; for the chimpanzee it is 15·7 times. There is no reliable data for the orangutan and no gorilla has been born in captivity, but Hooton[25] feels that we can deduce that growth takes place in the chimpanzee and orangutan at a moderate rate until about the seventh or eighth year, when the apes begin their pre-adolescent spurts, and that they grow very much more rapidly than does man. Therefore, when man reaches a state of genital maturity, he has put behind him a fifth or a quarter of his entire life, whereas other mammals arrive at this point in a much shorter time, a tenth, a twelfth, or even less of their entire life span.

There would seem to be a correlation between mental limitation and fast development and comparatively higher organization and slow development. As pointed out before, it is this slowing down of the development of higher mammals, especially of apes and man, that we have learned to call *retardation* according to Bolk's findings.

This retardation is a facet of human development that needs the psychoanalyst's full consideration, because it is this very fact that makes man's early postnatal period so elemental and vital from the standpoint of differentiation and conditioning. Man not only spends a comparatively long time in the endoparasitic period, the psychological importance of which we are just discovering, but he also passes through a much prolonged ectoparasitic phase, which, as Freud pointed out,[26] accounts for the intensified influence of the external environment. The actual dependence on the environment, of course, varies from individual to individual, as well as from culture to culture. But the facts speak for themselves: human babies advance much slower than do mammalian ones after leaving the maternal womb.

A major implication of man's retardation, then, in the light of

[24] A. H. Schultz, 'Growth and Development in the Chimpanzee', *Contrib. Embryol.*, 28 (1940), Carnegie Institute, 1-63.
[25] E. A. Hooton, *Up from the Ape*, New York: Macmillan, 1947, p. 237. See now: G. B. Schaller, *The Mountain Gorilla: Ecology and Behaviour*, Chicago: University of Chicago Press, 1963.
[26] S. Freud, *Inhibitions, Symptoms, and Anxiety* (1926), *Standard Ed.*, 20, London: Hogarth Press, 1959, pp. 77-175.

comparative morphology, is that the human individual shows many signs of arrested infantilisms—of *fetalization*, in Bolk's expression —and a few random examples will show that this unique element is at the base of our being human. One instance is our comparatively rudimentary hair growth. It was Huxley[27] who pointed out that the distribution of hair on man is closely similar to that of the late fetus of the chimpanzee, and he felt that there is little doubt that this 'represents an extension of this temporary anthropoid into permanence'. But we have to remember that the human fetal body is covered with a fine down or lanugo from the sixth to the eighth month, which it loses during its last endoparasitic month. Excessive hairiness (hypertrychosis) is considered a pathological symptom *only* in man. Many other features of our physic are fetalized: the form of the earshell; the orthognathy—that is, the supposition of the jaw under the forehead; and increasing brachycephalization are evidence of fetalization still in progress. The labia majora of the adult chimpanzee, as Ford and Beach point out,[28] are rudimentary, but at one stage of the chimpanzee fetal development they are present in much the same form as they assume in the human female. These and other constitutional characteristics are in essence typical for certain fetal stadia of higher mammals and primates. In other words, characteristics typical for the fetus in other mammals are stabilized in the human. What for the primate is a step in his development becomes permanent in *homo sapiens*.

Another aspect of human development is the comparative reduction and limitation in the production of large litters. It is easy to see the inter-relationship between the dependence of the primate (and again especially of the human infant) and the number of offspring. Notable among the conditions for reduction of offspring is the mammalian way of providing nourishment for the fetus in the uterus and the suckling under more or less protective conditions. Hooton concludes that:

> With the further prolongation of foetal development, the number of offspring produced at birth is still further diminished, because the continued intra-uterine growth of the foetus demands more and more space in the maternal womb, the expansion of which is strictly limited. . . . The long prenatal period and the protracted helpless infancy of man and the anthropoid apes are

[27] J. Huxley, op. cit., p. 15.
[28] C. S. Ford and F. A. Beach, *Patterns of Sexual Behaviour*, New York: Harper, 1951; London: Eyre & Spottiswoode, 1952, p. 21.

prerequisites for the ultimately high development of the nervous system and of the mental powers of these families.[29]

One other example of man's retardation is worth noting. Much work has been done in comparative dentition to give us genetic evidence for decisive psychological consequences. Among the higher apes, the eruption of the milk teeth starts almost immediately after birth, and shortly after the second milk molar the first permanent one appears. By the time of the first permanent molar's eruption the ape loses his milk incisivi and the permanent teeth arrive. This rather rapid change demands an equally rapid growth of the jaw as well as of the entire skull. In man, however, we observe two intervals that mean retardation. His milk teeth are fully grown only towards the end of the second year, so that the human child depends on sucking—rather than on biting—for a much longer phase. (The psychological effect of teething with its emphasis on pain has not been stressed clearly enough in psychoanalytic case studies. There is much reason to assume that the inevitable and often painful though transitory period of teething has a significant influence on disillusionment and is a step in the direction of the acceptance of reality and the renunciation of insinctual demands. Erikson[30] feels that it is of 'prototypal significance', 'a model for the masochistic tendency to assure cruel comfort by enjoying one's hurt'.) After the second year there is an interval of about four years before the first permanent molar comes through.[31]

Psychoanalysis has always stressed the fundamental relationship between our prolonged dependence and our psychological development. There is no doubt that man's biological and physical condition lays the foundation for his elaborate and intricate reaction pattern. It is, as Simpson[32] points out, an 'inescapable biological fact that no individual is fully self-sufficient'. We cannot be fully self-reliant and, of necessity, seek other people's help, assistance, and understanding. Concomitant with the psychological retardation and delayed infancy arise man's ego functions.

To return to the original problem, the precursors of the Oedipus

[29] E. A. Hooton, op. cit., p. 264.
[30] E. H. Erikson, *Childhood and Society*, New York: Norton, 1950; London: Hogarth Press, rev. ed., 1964.
[31] Cf. A. Gehlen, *Der Mensch*, Bonn: Athenäum Verlag, 1950, p. 110.
[32] G. G. Simpson, op. cit., p. 323.

complex as well as the Oedipus complex itself are uniquely human. The biological determinants make it necessary for the human infant to rely on the mother's body, on nourishment and protection provided by an external agency. Whether or not this agency is the biological mother seems irrelevant for the further existence of the infant. The child needs this object for his physiological development and gratification but does not seem able to distinguish in her or him a separate entity.[33] The bond built through the physiological necessity becomes also a psychological necessity. The predominant part that this bond of *dual unity* plays has been discussed extensively among psychoanalysts. It lays the groundwork for any form of social cohesion and communication as it is; in its negative aspect it is the source of feelings of separation, anxiety, and helplessness (castration fear) created by the experience of solitude and dependence.

Róheim described the ultimate effect of man's delayed infancy thus:

> The child discovers the non-self in a frustration situation and then it discovers the same object as relieving this frustration. Since the infant is still in a stage of dual unity (that is), it oscillates between regarding itself as part of the mother and as an independent human being. . . .[34]

It is the phase of infantile experience to which Freud referred in his observation about the child's demands for exclusive possession. The first object cathexis contains the nucleus for human socialization, the need for psychic and physical contact, and in particular for that kind of contact which eventually gives the young human being the capacity to cope with frustrations.

This fundamental characteristic of human experience has long been obscured. It is true that it has two sides, because the unavaila-

---

[33] Cf. A. Balint, 'Love for the Mother and Mother-Love', *Internat. J. Psycho-Anal.*, 30 (1949), 251; M. Balint, 'Early Developmental States of the Ego. Primary Object Love', ibid., p. 265; H. Hartmann and E. Kris, 'The Genetic Approach in Psychoanalysis', *The Psychoanalytic Study of the Child*, 1, New York: International Universities Press; London: Hogarth Press, 1945; H. Hartmann, 'Comments on the Psychoanalytic Theory of Instinctual Drives', *Psychoanal. Quart.*, 17 (1948), 368, and idem, 'Comments on the Psychoanalytic Theory of the Ego', *The Psychoanalytic Study of the Child*, 5, New York: International Universities Press; London: Hogarth Press, 1950, p. 74.

[34] G. Róheim, 'Oedipus Complex, Magic and Culture', *Psychoanalysis and the Social Sciences*, 2, New York: International Universities Press; London: Hogarth Press, 1950, p. 20.

bility of immediate gratification forces the child to turn to substitutes. As early as 1905, in *Three Essays on the Theory of Sexuality*,[35] Freud described how the infant turns to autoerotic and substitute gratifications in order to satisfy his needs for attachment. How can we interpret this in the light of Oedipal strivings? The infant's love—or shall we say his need for libidinal contact?—is biologically conditioned, but what started (or was experienced) as a unit or dual unity became separated. We do not know just when the infant is actually able to distinguish between inner and outer world, between subject and object, and when he perceives the object as a foreign body, a source of pleasure and pain, but reactions to objects have been proved to exist at the age of five days and during the second and third month the infant's pleasure responses can be recognized. At this point, when we recall the biological necessity for prolonged dependence, it becomes evident that separation anxiety is one of the fundamental elements of our being human, of our being social and co-operative creatures. We do not dare to give up our inborn need for maternal gratification. We cling to each other as if we were mothers to each other, while every third person appears as a disturber of this union and, consequently, as the target of our—often unconscious—hostile fantasies. This union is the *primary group* in which the members identify themselves with one another in their ego. In Róheim's opinion, our retardation and prolonged period of helplessness make out of our attachments 'repeat performances' of the child-mother union, linked with the necessary sequence of separation—fear of object loss—aggressive feelings—reunion.[36]

These are the specific aspects of human cohesion. The prolonged infancy of man never enables him to overcome certain infantile features. Our id remains the same. The Oedipal myths that I quoted show how powerful is the tendency to keep mother for oneself, and, consequently, to experience every third person—be it a sibling, father, or (as we know theoretically) even the 'bad' mother—as a potential enemy. What was conceived as a unity on an oral, or, in the case of many people, an oral-tactile-kinaesthetic level is later repeated as genital reunion and satisfaction, so that the groundwork for the Oedipal—that is, genital—reaction, is laid on in infancy. The

[35] *Three Essays on the Theory of Sexuality* (1905), *Standard Ed.*, 7; London: Hogarth Press, 1953, pp. 125ff.
[36] G. Róheim, 'The Psychoanalytic Interpretation of Culture', now in this volume.

gratification of the originally passive desires, the anxiety caused by helplessness and the awareness of separation, the avoidance of frustration—all are based on retardation and prolonged infancy, and the eventual step towards individuality. They are the ingredients for social organization, for adequate restraint and self-control, and for the institution of human marriage as a permissible repetition of the original union, because we never overcome our desire for permanent company whether we are Viennese, Chinese, or Alorese. In fact, the Alorese Fantan, one of Du Bois's informants, knew all this without having gone through analysis.

> Wives are like our mothers. When we were small our mothers fed us. When we are grown our wives cook for us. If there is anything good, they keep it in the pot until we come home. When we were small we slept with our mothers: when we are grown we sleep with our wives. Sometimes when we are grown we wake in the night and call our wives 'mother'.[37]

To find conclusive observations such as these in anthropological field studies is to reveal a new level of scrutiny, involving a point of view that leans heavily on psychoanalytic sophistication. There is no denial that such external criteria as climate, economics, tradition, and history are also active in shaping or modifying the particular type of societal and individual relationships. Yet the fundamental incentives stem from the fact that we are human— which means that the parasitic way in which we started out has a primary impact on all that follows. It imposes on man the necessity to love and to be loved, to be a social being, to be a 'joiner' and seek security. By applying what we have learned from psychoanalysis to the study of society, we demonstrate how the various ingredients of man's biopsychological composition sow the seeds for human action, human conflicts, and human love.

[37] C. Du Bois, *The People of Alor*, Minneapolis: University of Minnesota Press, 1944, p. 90.

The two following papers discuss the problem of normality and abnormality in different perspectives. They both aim at clarifying certain psychological pre-conditions. Dr Fraser elaborates the structural point of view and recognizes the socio-cultural influence on ego and super-ego. Acts and attitudes supported or subdued by one's cultural matrix influence the ego ideal. Both papers examine how the spectrum of culturally condoned or promoted defences directs the particular channelization of instinctual demands.

5

Concepts of Normal Behaviour in the Light of Psychoanalysis

Ideas about normal and abnormal behaviour are indispensable to everyday life, where they are used subjectively without much regard for definitions. In the social sciences, definitions of these concepts is a perennial problem. There seems to be a durable urge to construct permanent definitions, but the attempts do not feel satisfying and have to be repeated. I quote from the concluding paragraphs of a recently reprinted paper[1] by way of illustration:

> The confusion arises, of course, from subsuming different types of abnormalities under one heading, 'abnormality', and speaking of them as if they were homogeneous entities. Obviously abnormal behaviour is *called* abnormal because it deviates from the behaviour of the general group. It is not, however, the *fact* of deviation which makes it abnormal, but its causal background. That is why the hallucinations of the Plains Indians are not abnormal, while those of the schizophrenic are. It is not the fact of social sanction in Plains Indian society which makes that bit of behaviour normal, but the fact that it does not have the background of a symptomatic resolution of an inner conflict such as produce that phenomenon in the schizophrenic. The 'abnormal' behaviour of the Indian is analogous to the behaviour of the psychotic, *but not homologous.* Just because it is analogous, the confusion has arisen of identifying the two . . . we could state the quintessence of abnormality as *the* tendency to choose a type of reaction which represents *an escape from a conflict-producing situation instead of a facing of the problem.* . . . It is obvious, for example, that masturbation *per se* is not abnormal and represents a quite normal, i.e. usual growing-up phenomenon. In certain

[1] II. J. Wegrocki, 'A Critique of Cultural and Statistical Concepts of Abnormality', in *Personality in Nature, Society, and Culture*, ed. by C. Kluckhohn and H. A. Murray, New York: Knopf, 1967, pp. 696-701. First printed in *J. Abnorm. Soc. Psychol.*, 34 (1939), 166-78.

instances, however, its great frequency or its inappropriateness point to the use of it as an escape mechanism. What holds true for masturbation is true of all 'abnormal mechanisms'. *It is not the mechanism that is abnormal; it is its functions which determine its abnormality.* It is precisely for this reason that the institutionalized 'abnormal' traits in various cultures are not properly called 'abnormal' entities. Because this distinction is not kept in mind and because a primarily statistico-relative conception of abnormality is adhered to, the unwarranted conclusion is drawn that standards of 'abnormality' differ with cultures and are culturally determined.

The psychoanalyst will find in these passages much with which he cannot agree. He will find it difficult to be convinced that the Plains Indian who goes through a process of fasting, exercise, suggestion, and hallucination is not at the time working towards the mitigation of some inner conflict. The analyst will tend to think that the ego functions of the Plains Indian are simply selecting a culturally standardized way of trying to restore inner psychic harmony which he would experience subjectively as increased comfort. The analyst will surmise that, if such an Indian were to be analyzed, or even drawn into conversation with someone he trusted, his inner conflict could be outlined fairly well and comprehended in terms of universal human strivings. The Indian's behaviour might not be descriptively schizophrenic in the sense of being autistic, progressing, and malignant, but these qualities are by no means necessary to psychic conflict nor to its resolution through symptom formation. Some symptoms are benign and brief, but function exactly like more burdensome ones which presumably are formed by similar mechanisms. Moreover, to say that the Indian's hallucination is analogous to but not homologous with the hallucinations of a schizophrenic implies that we can describe the psychic mechanism of hallucination formation in fully detailed terms. Even if we could do that, and had enough data to differentiate all degrees of mechanistic dissimilarity, we might lack reason to designate the one as a symptom and the other as something else. A symptom is, after all, nothing more than a compromise formation representing the best available solution for an intrapsychic conflict, and there is no value in bestowing the term symptom on behaviour according to an hypothetical 'homology' with something else. Only the details of mechanism should determine the designation symptom.

Again, in appraising Wegrocki's 'quintessence of abnormality', it will occur to the analyst that the italicized portion of the statement is only a value judgment. As such, it is better to subsume it under assumptions about adaptation, rather than about abnormality: if an ego can 'face' a problem rather than having to 'escape' from it, it will be more fruitful to say that that ego has at its disposal sufficient resources in the form of neutralized energies[2] so that it can observe correctly and think about the conflict. It may, possibly, then act according to the understanding it achieves and according to the decrease of anxiety which that understanding gives. It is, therefore, performing a task of adaptation. If this ego is analyzed, it may also be able to utilize data from its genetic past in understanding and hence in facing the conflict, and as such it will be more adapted than the non-analyzed ego. But, while ideas of 'facing' and 'escaping' can be placed in an appropriate locus in psychoanalytic theory, there is nothing to be gained by trying to make the concepts 'normal' and 'adapted' equivalent.

In Wegrocki's paragraph on masturbation, we also find things which are difficult. We will find it hard to define 'inappropriateness' and 'escape mechanism' in unequivocal terms; and, as to his last sentence, most people will observe that standards of 'abnormality' *do* differ with cultures. By placing the word abnormal in quotes here, Wegrocki means to eliminate it altogether in favour of defining abnormal in terms of the function of a mechanism (as in his italicized sentence). In other words, what is abnormal is to be connected with mechanisms which are to be assigned to categories of 'escape', 'inappropriateness', or 'facing up'. This is, again, a value judgment which reduces normal and abnormal to good and evil. This is an appropriate result, but it has been accomplished entirely on philosophical grounds. It has neither scientific basis nor scientifically useful derivatives.

None of these considerations get us nearer to the goal which many writers want: an objective, lasting, cross-cultural definition of normal behaviour. My thesis is that we do not reach this goal because the project is formulated incorrectly, and, as ordinarily put, is not part of the proper business of any behavioural science. I find that the problem can be reposed and the dissatisfactions

---

[2] H. Hartmann, 'Comments on the Psychoanalytic Theory of the Ego' (1950), in H. Hartmann, *Essays in Ego Psychology*, New York: International Universities Press, 1964, pp. 113-41.

resolved, by rethinking it in terms of Freud's structural theory.[3] What we would like to know is, first, how the mind uses these ideas of normal and abnormal and, second, what is a scientifically fruitful way of regarding this use.

We will find it helpful to concentrate our attention on the noun 'norm' rather than on its various derivatives. All formal, non-specialized definitions of this noun include the idea of expectability. Introspection and clinical experience find no inconsistencies with the formal definition. Now, let us observe that the construction, acceptance, and manipulation of norms is a part of the perceptive-cognitive-integrative functions of the ego. By 'integrative' in this connection I mean that the ego finds it expedient to maintain a catalogue of impressions about expectability which it may then connect in various ways with its executive tasks of directing the musculature, discharging the drives, and avoiding pain. These norms are of great economic advantage to the ego because, through repeatability, the norms make it unnecessary for the ego to be burdened with a sense of newness or strangeness. For example, the ego makes observations concerning the norms of the properties of the physical world. It establishes the expectation that objects which are unsupported will move in a consistent direction called 'down'. It integrates this norm into countless situations in an unconscious, highly efficient fashion which conserves energy for more complicated functions. Again, using its adaptive capacities, the ego can learn to allow for new situations where old norms must be abandoned— as in an orbiting space capsule, where unsupported objects do not fall.

Likewise, in the much more complex realm of reacting to other persons[4], every ego is equipped with ideas about norms. Life with-

[3] The term structural theory is preferable to 'ego psychology' because it is more accurately inclusive. The structural theory seeks to describe the interaction of three psychic structures which are construed from their functions and called id, ego, and super-ego. See S. Freud, *The Ego and the Id* (1923), *Standard Ed.*, 19, London: Hogarth Press, 1961, pp. 3-68; A. Freud, *The Ego and the Mechanisms of Defense* (1936), New York: International Universities Press, 1946; H. Hartmann, E. Kris and R. Loewenstein, 'Comments on the Formation of Psychic Structure', *The Psychoanalytic Study of the Child*, 2, New York: International Universities Press, 1946; London: Hogarth Press, pp. 11-38; J. Arlow and C. Brenner, *Psychoanalytic Concepts and the Structural Theory*, New York: International Universities Press, 1964.

[4] I shall use the words person, individual, and self as essentially equivalent and in their ordinary senses. The term ego should be reserved for the specific meaning established by Freud, confusing it neither with these nor with mind and psyche. The ego is a part of the psyche, which is a part of the individual.

out such value judgments is unimaginable. Let us take a more extended example: in most societies, people expect some degree of body covering in public. The degree to which this norm is consistent, and the kinds of ego, id, and super-ego reactions when it is abandoned, will vary greatly from person to person, from culture to culture, and from time to time. Moreover, and this is the crucial point, every ego has the option of reacting to this norm for its own purposes in a variety of ways. Let us make some assumptions, based upon clinical experiences, about a man on a certain European beach, where disrobing in public to change clothes is culturally accepted and therefore potentially conflict-free. By this act, he may achieve certain narcissistic emotional gratifications as well as a change of clothing. However, a few yards removed in space, in the shopping district of the beach town, the norm is different. The culture has arranged it so. If our man disrobes there, the culture decrees that the act is exhibitionistic—i.e. not culturally accepted. This presents the ego with a different set of possibilities. One would assume, if our man chose to disrobe there, that his impulse represented an unconscious conflict which made demands sufficiently strongly to overcome his adherence to the norm. A typical configuration of such a conflict might be this: as a child, he had felt in danger of castration (because of sexual impulses which were forbidden by his super-ego and by his culture) and the idea had been repressed. Some recent event, say an attack of urethritis, when added to the total of his past experience, threatens to disturb the repression and thereby destroy his psychic harmony. Under these circumstances, the ego attempts to avoid the anxiety which would be produced by remembering the childhood fear of castration. It does this by performing an act which it can take unconsciously to indicate that no body injury has occurred. This reassurance can be found in the reaction of the spectators to exhibition of his penis. They react in a way which he can translate: 'You see my penis; therefore, it exists.' This example illustrates how an individual requires a culturally determined extrapsychic matrix for the expression (which is an attempt at resolution) of intrapsychic conflict. In certain other cultures, where custom or legislation had not connected the shopping place with a norm for clothing, the psyche needing an exhibitionistic symptom would have to find some other style in which to express it.

Let us consider the situation of another individual who is observing this exhibitor. Provided that this second ego is acculturated to the same norm, then it is suddenly confronted with a reversal of a norm, and has several possibilities for reacting to the unexpected. Perhaps it will be 'traumatized', which is a word we use to describe a situation in which a life event (sometimes even a trivial one) stirs up profound emotional or other types of reaction because it forms connections with repressed materials. This person, dreading a return of the repressed, might have to develop some drastic symptom such as hysterical blindness in order to feel: 'I have seen nothing'. On the other hand, the reaction might be quite different. Determined by previous experiences, including experiences with the norms of this culture (and perhaps others as well), he might feel some sort of uncomplicated gratification, expressable in the thought 'my penis is bigger than his'. True, this gratification might in time give rise to anxiety, or guilt feelings, and become quite the reverse of gratification, but here we are concerned only with the immediate range of possibilities for an ego confronted with a permutation of a norm. This range includes, from the subjective point of view, possibilities for both tragedy and triumph. But, whether the event is anxiously or happily coloured, all that is shown is that the ego has used culturally determined details, both from the past and present, in an attempt at solution of conflicts between itself and its associated id and super-ego. In so doing, it has not established anything about a permanent definition of 'normal behaviour', but has only taken the departures from norms as either pains or pleasures depending on the determinants of the moment. We may conclude that 'normal' does not stabilize within the operation of an ego in ordinary circumstances.

Here is a clinical example from an analysis. A middle-aged bachelor called at a lady's home to take her out. As they were leaving, she gave him the key, requesting that he lock the door, which he did. This episode made him mysteriously uneasy and soon formed the nucleus of a brief obsessional reaction. In analysis he spent much time heaping criticism upon women for not 'sticking to the rules of courtesy', and for 'suddenly doing things unexpectedly contrary to custom'. Considerable work was necessary in order to make clear to both analyst and analysand the several structural implications of this event. The analytic work succeeded in lifting this episode from some descriptive plane—where it would be called 'abnormal fussiness'—and disclosing the complicated interactions of the psychic structures beneath the surface. First, his associations soon convinced him that he had taken her request as a sexual proposition. From the side of the ego structures, it was found that he had observed earlier the seductive hints by this lady, which had set off a signal of anxiety. She reminded him of his seductive mother. In childhood he had been the darling of a mother who considered him her sole love object. He had responded in kind. This circumstance was connected in turn with fantasies of being the victim of his mother, and also with guilty fantasies in which he was punished by his father for his desires towards his mother. Against this guilt he had had to erect strong prohibitions of conscience. Attached to these super-ego counterforces, developing over the years, was a whole string of norms for behaviour, showing on the surface as 'fussiness'. By feeling duly righteous when his lady departed from his norm, my patient could appease his super-ego by the use of a defensive projection: 'It is not my impulse, but hers, which draws us together.'

This little regressive defensive episode also included some drive discharge: structually speaking, it succeeded in expressing an id impulse in a form which was acceptable to both ego and super-ego. Some slight gratification came from inserting the key in an outwardly bold, masculine fashion. Beyond that safe substitutive act, he had to take defensive steps against his wish to take up the lady's sexual invitation. This defence was in two principal parts: (i) not immediately consciously perceiving the invitation, and, (ii) splitting off the aggressive component of his sexual wish and discharging that, with gratification, in the form of 'reasonable male criticalness'. This example shows the simpler defensive operations of the ego, operations which warded off some anxiety and restored sufficient inner harmony to make any more lasting symptom formation unnecessary. It is an example of a miniature traumatic event based on departure from a norm. By rejecting her norm and reaffirming his own, with all the unconscious ego actions in this framework, he temporarily resolved a complicated inner conflict.

It is interesting to note that the issue of cultural differences also appeared in the course of analyzing this episode. The patient remarked in his associations: 'In France, if a girl says "I'm hot", it means something quite different from what it means here.' He had been taught early in life that all French women were sexually predatory. He had, without awareness of his purpose, taken steps to protect himself against this danger to which his culture had conditioned him. During the years when he was developing his genital sexuality, he learned French with astonishing rapidity, retaining the skill carefully 'for use in social situations'. He had armed himself against the frightening possibilities of another culture by making sure he could speedily interpret the danger signals coming from the women of that culture.

It would be easy to extend these examples, with similar results, into other defensive operations of the ego. We might suspect that the defences of rationalization and denial would be closely connected with a use of norms, and that norm use would be seen in various degrees of complexity in certain syndromes such as adolescence, obsessional character disorders, criminality, and perversion. But, irrespective of the factor of complexity, I think that the thesis could best be stated in this way: manipulations of norms is an ego function carried out within the norm possibilities presented by a given culture.

Now, having illustrated some uses of norms within the psychic structure, I wish to maintain that among the tasks of the social scientist, and of the psychoanalyst, is that of observing, describing, and interpreting the ego function of norm manipulation, and that this is the only responsibility of these scientists towards norms. They will have quite enough to do without attempting to assume responsibility for defining them. That task is assigned by society to moralists and to legislators, who promulgate their assumptions in terms of behaviour requirements which represent their best estimate of what is congenial to the prosperity of the group plus what is consistent with their own unconscious needs and fears. Their work, while necessary for all cultures in the present stage of evolution, is not, nor can it yet be, scientific. Legislators may be influenced by knowledge derived from science as to what is conducive to health, but the definition of normal as inherent in law must remain both subjective and changing. Legislators, if they maintain perspective about their work, will admit that norms which they declare socially indispensable today may appear quite differently to their posterity. Even within their own time they will encounter the mutability of norms when prohibitions on murder are reversed in war. It is also evident that several of the institutions of government are designed to deal with the extreme mutability of norms by giving them a practical degree of stability while also providing for their gradual change.

The reader may object that I have absolved the scientist from defining normal but have left him with the duty of defining healthy and that nothing has been accomplished. Some will see in this a 'semantic' problem. Like many problems so designated, this is a *conceptual* one. Health is a much broader concept than normalcy, implying as it does the totality of a longitudinal process rather than a cross-sectional assessment of a phase of a process. Health is the more abstract concept. People tend to feel rather vaguely about health, often puzzling over questions of what is healthy for themselves, but rarely do they show any hesitation over the relatively concrete, though subjective, notion 'normal'. Scientific definitions of health will vary with the state of our understanding of mind and body, and, to a lesser extent, will vary with the kind of society in which we are picturing an hypothetical 'healthy' man. 'Healthy' is not equivalent to 'adapted' any more than it is to 'normal', or to 'moral'. Hartmann, in several papers,[5] has lead in clarifying this complicated problem.

What I have done is to differentiate two aspects within the concept of normal behaviour. The one is its position in everyday life, where it is endowed with an arbitrary stability. This stability varies in degree according to whether a given idea of normal is being shared by a group in the form of law or custom or whether it is being put to use by an individual psyche. But the stability is always illusory and contrasts sharply with the uses to which ideas of normal are put intrapsychically. Here, ideas of normal are not defined stably but are changed freely for their value in carrying out the defensive operations of the ego. Accordingly, the defining of the concept normal should be left in everyday life and the scientist should rest content with observing the fate of these definitions within the psyche. Nobody can define normal once and for all because there is an inescapable need in the mind to establish fluid concepts of it in a subjectively determined way.

I will summarize the main points which I have asserted: (i) Ideas about normal behaviour, conveniently referred to as norms, are formed in individual minds. (ii) Norms are formally projected onto society through the mechanisms of law and the accretion of custom. (iii) Norms are variable in both individuals and in cultures, though

[5] For example, H. Hartmann, 'Psychoanalysis and the Concept of Health' (1939), in H. Hartmann, *Essays in Ego Psychology*, New York: International Universities Press, 1964, pp. 1-18.

more sluggishly so in cultures. (iv) The egos of all individuals are continually reacting to cultural norms. (v) The super-ego, as the seat of conscience, ideals, and standards, is particularly likely to require some manipulation of norms in playing its role in the efforts of the whole psyche to avoid anxiety. (vi) The id recognizes nothing of norms, but only presses for the discharge of instinctual pressure. (vii) Manœuvres with norms are used in the resolution of conflicts arising among the three psychic structures, either by contributing to simple defences or by being used in symptom formation. (viii) Scientists should study the vicissitudes of norms within the psychic structure and the culture structure. (ix) The *defining* of norms is a reciprocal process between individuals and their cultures, and is not a subject for scientific solution. (x) Attempts at rigid definition of normal behaviour inevitably result in failure because all egos must use concepts of normal in a fluid, non-rigid fashion.

Some potentially interesting results of this application of structural theory immediately suggest themselves:

The structural view of the place of norms in mental life is capable of defining more clearly a meeting ground for anthropologists and psychoanalysts. It is a point at which their fields neatly coincide. The manipulation of norms is an individual intrapsychic process, but the formation of norms requires an additional factor of group action and their use requires a relatedness of the individual to the group. These reciprocal processes provide an opportunity for mutually developing observations. The group-oriented anthropologist will have many observations on norm formation, retention, and alteration by the group, while the psychoanalyst will be able to observe and report the contributions of individual psychic needs to this particular group process.

It would be correct to say, I think, that all ideas of normal are put to use by the unconscious portion of the ego only for their permutation potential. The fluidity of norms is seized upon by the ego in adaptation, in art, in dreams, and in neurosis in its struggle against the immutability of the id. The ego tries to offset the power of the implacable, unvarying demands of the id by means of a nimble employment of everything inside and outside of itself which is mutable. It might be useful to consider the structure of the analytical situation from this point of view. In the analytic situation two persons establish mutually a number of norms which they think of as expected behaviour having certain practical advantages for the work they are trying to do. Foremost among these is the norm which says that the analysand will communicate his thoughts freely and fully to the analyst. From that point on, the work of any analysis relies heavily on observing and understanding the ways in which the analysand abrogates this norm. In customary terminology, the analysis works upon resistances. The resistances are conspicuous for their ingenious variability, drawing into their service all manner of details, including culturally determined ones. It might be fruitful to follow up the idea that to this variability the analyst opposes a certain relentless stability. He stands for the immutable idea 'there shall be no secrets here'. This apposition of the immutable to the variable is similar to the situation between id and ego, and it is likely that the similarity contains a useful point.

We cannot fail to notice that, in contrast to the mutability of the norms in the unconscious portion of the ego, the definitions of normal in everyday life are strongly defended and made to appear unchanging. We may speculate, guided by certain clinical impressions, that the tenacious urge to define normal in a final way is based upon unconscious super-ego demands. It is likely that 'normal' always evokes feelings about what the parents expected, and this is why discussions of it tend to run in value judgment channels until dislodged by broader structural consideration.

As stated in the introductory note to the previous chapter Dr Devereux' paper is also concerned with the problem of normality and abnormality and the clarification of certain psychological pre-conditions. Dr Devereux' proposition is more daring than Dr Fraser's. His assumption of two types of unconscious seems relevant to the study of socio-cultural variations in personality development. His notion of an ethnic unconscious as distinct from an individual one is not related to the Jungian idea of a collective unconscious. It is true that the cultural climate creates scales of value which provide a certain range of 'ready-made' defences and adaptive measures.

6

Normal and Abnormal: The Key Concepts of Ethnopsychiatry[1]

GEORGE DEVEREUX

INTRODUCTION

The interdisciplinary science of ethnopsychiatry cannot come into being through a mere borrowing of techniques. It requires the cross-fertilization—though not the blending—of two sets of basic concepts: those of psychological and those of socio-cultural science, since psychological and socio-cultural explanations stand in a complementary relationship to each other.[2]

THE PROBLEM OF ADJUSTMENT

The illegitimate blending of psychological and of ethnological concepts leads to a confusion between adjustment and normality; the former, which is a purely sociological concept, is often treated as though it were a psychological concept. This crucial difficulty can best be disposed of by analyzing the paradigmatic problem of the shaman's normality or abnormality. In so doing, one must bear in mind Reider's[3] finding that both the need to be adjusted and the pretence of being adjusted *may* be neurotic.

Ackerknecht[4] claims that the 'adjusted' shaman is 'autonormal but heteropathological'. Others simply equate adjustment with normality, never once inquiring either into the psychological cost or

[1] Abridged by Mrs George Devereux from *Some Uses of Anthropology*, Anthropological Society of Washington, 1956. A greatly expanded French version will appear in George Devereux, *Essais d'Ethnopsychiatrie Générale* (provisional title) to be published by Gallimard, Paris.
[2] G. Devereux, *Essais d'Ethnopsychiatrie Générale*.
[3] N. Reider, 'The Concept of Normality', *Psychoanal. Quart.*, 19 (1950), 43-51.
[4] E. H. Ackerknecht, 'Psychopathology, Primitive Medicine and Primitive Culture', *Bull. Hist. Med.*, 14 (1943), 30-67.

into the psychodynamics of such an 'adjustment', nor ascertaining too precisely to what segment of his culture the shaman adjusts himself. This approach reduces diagnosis to a determination of degrees of adjustment. It leads one to say that in April, 1945 a German psychiatrist's task was completed the day his patient joined the Nazi party, while in May, 1945 it was finished the day the patient joined, in Frankfurt am Main, the Christian-Democratic party, or, in Frankfurt an der Oder, the Communist party.[5] This theory disregards the fact that a society can be so 'sick' that only abnormal people can adjust to it.[6] In saying this, I do not seek to revive Benedict's[7] controversial psychiatric diagnosis of cultures; I have in mind only phenomena which traditionally form the subject-matter of social pathology. In addition, I hold that some societies are so enmeshed in the vicious circle of their pathology, that everything they do to save themselves only causes them to sink further into the quicksand. Thus, the Tonkawa clung so tenaciously to cannibalism that, in the end, nearly all of their neighbours waged a war of extermination against them. This forced them to become scouts for the U.S. Cavalry, which they could also do only at the cost of giving up cannibalism.[8] In seeking to uproot imaginary internal enemies and to avoid encirclement, Nazi Germany created for itself both internal enemies and a worldwide alliance pledged to destroy it.[9] The social self-destructiveness of both ancient Sparta[10] and of the segregationist South,[11] which undermined the psychological health of both the dominant and the oppressed groups is, in some ways, an even better example of this process. Moreover, if adjustment is the real criterion of sanity, Fromm's[12] cogent distinction between adjustment and sado-masochistic conformism becomes meaningless.

In short, one must differentiate between external (overt) and internal adjustment and also between rigid (stationary) adjustment

[5] G. Devereux, *Reality and Dream: the Psychotherapy of a Plains Indian*, New York: International Universities Press, 1951.
[6] idem, *Essais d'Ethnopsychiatrie Générale*.
[7] R. Benedict, *Patterns of Culture*, Boston: Houghton Mifflin; London: Routledge, 1934.
[8] R. Linton, Personal Communication.
[9] G. Devereux, *Essais d'Ethnopsychiatrie Générale*.
[10] ibid.
[11] J. Dollard, *Caste and Class in a Southern Town*, New Haven: Yale University Press, 1937.
[12] E. Fromm, *Escape from Freedom*, New York: Holt, 1941; London: Routledge, 1942.

and continuous *re*adjustment. Some overt adjustment is required by every society. In a healthy society the normal person can introject healthy norms in the form of a subsidiary ego ideal; in a sick society he cannot introject the norms without becoming a neurotic or worse.[13] Moreover, if a man is rational enough to adjust overtly to a sick society, though without introjecting its norms, he must eventually escape from this double life, either by engaging in an ill-timed, ineffectual and self-destructive rebellion, or else by forcing himself to introject dereistic norms, thereby becoming a fanatic.

TWO TYPES OF UNCONSCIOUS

The unconscious contains that which never was conscious (the psychic representations of the instincts)[14] and that which was formerly conscious but was subsequently repressed (memory traces of experiences, emotions, fantasies, body states, the defences and most of the super-ego).

From the cultural point of view, repressed material can be divided into: (i) the unconscious segment of the ethnic personality and (ii) the individual unconscious.

(i) *The Ethnic Unconscious*
The ethnic unconscious is a psycho-cultural, not a bio-racial (Jungian), unconscious. It is that portion of the individual unconscious which is shared by most members of the group, and which each generation teaches the next one to repress. It changes as culture itself changes; it is acquired the way the ethnic personality is acquired.[15]

Ethnic character has both a conscious and an unconscious phase,

---

[13] G. Devereux, *Essais d'Ethnopsychiatrie Générale.*
[14] Cf., however, modern theories of the undifferentiated infantile ego (H. Hartmann, 'Comments on the Psychoanalytic Theory of the Ego', *The Psychoanalytic Study of the Child*, 5, New York: International Universities Press, 1950; and H. Hartmann, E. Kris and R. Loewenstein, 'Comments on the Formation of Psychic Structure', *The Psychoanalytic Study of the Child*, 2, New York: International Universities Press, 1947; London: Hogarth Press) and the view that it is the id that splits off from the infantile ego and not vice-versa. (W. R. D. Fairbairn, *An Object-Relations Theory of the Personality*, New York: Basic Books, 1954; London: Tavistock, 1952 under the title *Psychoanalytical Studies of the Personality*). Animals seem to have no id in this sense.
[15] It does not matter in this context to whose theory of ethnic personality formation one subscribes.

and the latter is complementary to the former. Each culture permits certain impulses, etc., to become and to remain conscious, while requiring others to be repressed. Hence, all members of a group have certain unconscious problems in common.

The ethnic unconscious is repressed by defence mechanisms, which are usually supplemented by cultural pressures. The latter tend to be inadequate whenever numerous persons have suffered a particular kind of *atypical* cultural traumata. When that happens, culture also provides a marginal and halfhearted implementation for the resulting needs. Thus, though the transvestite deviated from the 'heroic' self-definition of the Plains Indian, culture sanctioned the inevitable by implementing transvestism marginally.[16] This does not make transvestism either culture syntonic or ego syntonic. A culturally regular, but subjectively motivated, vision instructed a Plains Indian to become a transvestite. Rather than comply with this 'command', he killed himself.[17] Conversely, though the Mohave extensively implement transvestism, they ridicule and despise the transvestite.[18] Even if most members of a tribe are involved in some way in the cultural implementation of an impulse emanating from the ethnic unconscious, their psychic state and overt behaviour must be held to be abnormal. Thus, in witch epidemics, the laity's 'low grade paranoia'[19] is the counterpart of the witches' personal psychopathology.

My basic position is at variance with the traditional anthropological outlook, which pays too much attention to such complexly elaborated items as witchcraft, shamanism and ritualism. The high degree of institutionalization of a cultural item is no proof of its nuclearity and importance. Earning a living or getting married are far more nuclear in any culture than are complicated rituals. This thesis goes far beyond Kardiner's[20] classification of institutions into 'primary' and 'secondary'; it rank orders cultural items in terms of their importance for the individual. Indeed, while everyone works and gets married, hardly anyone is a shaman on a full-time

---

[16] G. Devereux, *Reality and Dream.*

[17] R. H. Lowie, *Primitive Religion*, New York: Boni & Liveright, 1924; London: Peter Owen, 1960.

[18] G. Devereux, 'Institutionalized Homosexuality of the Mohave Indians', *Human Biology*, 9 (1937), 498-527.

[19] A. L. Kroeber, *The Nature of Culture*, Chicago: University of Chicago Press, 1952.

[20] A. Kardiner and R. Linton, *The Individual and His Society*, New York: Columbia University Press, 1939.

basis. With respect to such over-implemented but marginal activities, the majority of the population function only as 'consumers' or spectators. The Mohave crowds which accompany a transvestite on some scurrilous venture only seek to gratify vicariously their unconscious homosexual impulses, while reinforcing their defences against such impulses by watching the transvestite's discomfiture.[21]

These considerations apply also to the shaman, *whose dominant conflicts are rooted in his ethnic unconscious.* In many cultures the budding shamans' psychic experiences are so painful that they reject the 'power', the way a Plains Indian rejected the vision which commanded him to become a berdache. A Sedang may drink his own urine so as to disgust the spirits which offer him unwanted power.[22] A Mohave shaman may refuse to practise his art and become psychotic as a result.[23] Even those who accept the 'call' find their situation so ego dystonic that they incite the kinsmen of their victims to kill them.[24] One such reluctant Mohave shaman was hospitalized with the (questionable) diagnosis: manic-depressive psychosis.[25] There is no real difference between such vicarious suicides and the suicide of the Plains Indian, whose vision commanded him to become a transvestite. Such findings prove that the shaman is a neurotic or a psychotic in remission.

Shamanism is also culture dystonic: the shaman is a 'trouble-unit'.[26] The Mohave call the shaman crazy and cowardly; the Sedang dislike the rapacity of their shamans. The Siberian shaman is usually wretchedly poor and not highly regarded.[27] Even higher religions treat their saints as trouble-makers: Joan of Arc was burned at the stake. The opposition of primitive priesthood to shamans is conspicuous and chronic.[28]

[21] G. Devereux, 'Institutionalized Homosexuality of the Mohave Indians', loc. cit.
[22] G. Devereux, MS. Sedang Field Notes, 1933-5.
[23] G. Devereux, 'L'Envoûtement chez les Indians Mohave', *J. de la Société des Américanistes de Paris*, N.S. 29 (1937), 405-12; idem, *Mohave Ethnopsychiatry and Suicide*, Bureau of American Ethnology, Bulletin 175, Washington, D.C., 1961.
[24] G. Devereux, 'L'Envoûtement chez les Indians Mohave', loc. cit.; idem, *Mohave Ethnopsychiatry and Suicide*; A. L. Kroeber, *Handbook of the Indians of California*, Bureau of American Ethnology, Bulletin 78, Washington, 1925.
[25] G. Devereux, *Mohave Ethnopsychiatry and Suicide.*
[26] idem, 'Functioning Units in Há(rhn)de:a(ng) Society', *Primitive Man*, 10 (1937), 1-7.
[27] M. A. Czaplicka, *Aboriginal Siberia*, Oxford: Clarendon Press, 1914.
[28] R. Linton, *Culture and Mental Disorders*, ed. George Devereux, Springfield, Ill.: Charles C. Thomas, 1956; London: Blackwell, 1956.

Like Kroeber[29] and Linton[30] I hold that the shaman is psychologically ill. Boyer's finding[31] that the Apache shaman is less disturbed than the non-shaman, is due to the fact that in a severely disorganized tribe in transition, the shaman can continue to organize his personality around an obsolete and dereistic nucleus, whereas the non-shaman can no longer pattern his on any cultural model. Ackerknecht holds, however, that the shaman is 'autonormal' (though 'heteropathological'), because he is adjusted. In so doing, he confuses, as do many others, adjustment with sanity; he also disregards that the shaman is adjusted to a marginal segment of his culture and that his position, though institutionalized, is both culture and ego dystonic. He is also less realistic than are other people: what is only a *belief* to others is for him a *real experience*. It is one thing to *believe* in a guardian angel; it is another to *see* (hallucinate) him.

Kroeber[32], too, holds that the shaman is *less* deranged than the recognized psychotic, but fails to explain what he means by this. He cannot mean that the symptoms of the latter are more florid than those of the former: the symptoms of many shamans are notoriously dramatic. Psychiatrically, this is unimportant: the symptoms of the hysteric are dramatic, but curable; the character neurotic is usually almost symptom-free, but often almost incurable. Possibly Kroeber meant to contrast the shaman with the recognized psychotic in terms of the malignancy of their respective disorders. If so, his statement is too general to be of practical use.

Linton,[33] too, holds that the shaman is 'less crazy' than the recognized psychotic and thinks that the former is usually a hysteric. His theory takes into account the malignancy of the underlying disorder and suggests a definite psychodynamic configuration. He places the relatively quiet shaman of certain groups and the violently disturbed Siberian shaman in the same continuum, since extremes of hysteria verge on a psychosis, and account for the florid symptomatology of many shamans.

Clinically, Linton's diagnosis is probably correct, but it does not explain why, in a given culture, certain hysterics become shamans while others do not.

[29] A. L. Kroeber, *The Nature of Culture.*
[30] R. Linton, op. cit.
[31] L. B. Boyer, 'Further Remarks Concerning Shamans and Shamanism', *Israel Ann. Psychiat. Rel. Discipl.*, 2 (1964), 235-57.
[32] A. L. Kroeber, *The Nature of Culture.*
[33] R. Linton, op. cit.

The crucial difference between the shaman and the 'private' neurotic (or psychotic) is that *the shaman's conflicts are located in his ethnic, rather than in his idiosyncratic, unconscious*. Unlike the 'private' abnormal, he need not devise his symptoms: he can utilize (usually ritualized) devices which culture provides for those whose conflicts are of a conventional type. The shaman is ill for conventional reasons and in a conventional way; his conflicts are simply unusually intense; he is like everyone else, only more so. His normal fellow-citizens therefore echo his conflicts and find his defensive manœuvres (symptoms, rituals) reassuring.[34] Shamans and shamanism strike the normal as uncanny in Freud's sense,[35] his unconscious experiences it as 'disturbingly and unexpectedly familiar'. The patient feels relief when the shaman provides him with ethnopsychologically suitable, congenial and culturally sanctioned defences against his idiosyncratic problems. This is not a 'psychiatric cure', but simply a 'corrective emotional experience', which does not lead to insight. Thus, Apache shamans cure tics, which are notoriously resistant to psychotherapy, by substituting for them a personal taboo; when the tic disappears, the taboo is removed.[36] In some tribes the shaman is a successfully 'treated' former patient.[37] In all such instances there is simply a changeover from an idiosyncratic conflict producing idiosyncratic symptoms, to conventional and/or ritualized symptoms—but without curative insight.[38]

It is the conventional patterning of the shaman's problems which differentiates him from the 'private' abnormal. The delusions of all Sedang shamans and of a certain Sedang psychotic were made up of the same elements; only their patterning was different. The difference between certain socially approved abnormal personality types and hospitalized psychotics is of the same type. This difference is of great diagnostic significance. The conventional patterning of a shaman's delusions—be he a Sedang or something else—results from a 'secondary elaboration' comparable to that which

---

[34] Cf. Kroeber's remark on the 'low grade paranoia' of the laity during witch epidemics in *The Nature of Culture*.

[35] S. Freud, 'The "Uncanny" ' (1919), *Standard Ed.*, 17, London: Hogarth Press, 1955.

[36] M. E. Opler, 'Some Points of Comparison and Contrast between the Treatment of Functional Disorders by Apache Shamans and Modern Psychiatric Practice', *Amer. J. Psychiat.*, 92 (1936), 1371-87.

[37] K. Stewart, *Pygmies and Dream Giants*, New York: Norton, 1954; London: Gollancz, 1955.

[38] See the halfbreed Indian's case below.

occurs unwittingly in the recall and the retelling of dreams.[39] A sanctioned pattern is impressed upon (sometimes subverbal) material, as it emerges from the unconscious, though this happens only where 'social negativism'[40] is not excessive and where there is still a residual need to remain integrated with society. What matters here is, of course, what the ego does with the unconscious material, which is much the same in every individual.[41]

I have always stressed that the patient who—perhaps after being treated by a shaman—'recovers' and becomes a shaman, lacks insight. Ackerknecht,[42] too, says that the shaman is 'cured without insight' yet attacks me for having said the same thing before he did and more precisely than he did.[43] Also, it is inadmissible to speak of a *cure* without insights; a remission is not a cure and the patient remains vulnerable.[44] No shaman is 'cured' in this sense; he is in remission. When subjected to further stress, he does not evolve a new neurosis: he simply elaborates further his old one. At other times he replaces defences that have gone stale with new ones.[45] Black Elk, a conflict-ridden Sioux, had a shamanistic vision which received enough social approval to enable him to function 'normally' for a while. After a few years he felt, however, impelled to perform publicly the ritual he had learned through a vision.[46] In short, rumination was replaced by acting out and compulsive ritual. This is the typical *vicious circle* of psychopathology: the initial symptoms create new difficulties, which must be warded off by additional symptoms. This does not happen where there is a cure with insight and sublimation.[47] The shaman's basic problem is aggression; his healing activities are therefore simply 'reaction formations'. When these defences become stale, he becomes a witch, and may, later on, provoke others into killing him.[48] This

[39] G Devereux, *Reality and Dream*.
[40] idem, *Essais d'Ethnopsychiatrie Générale*.
[41] idem, 'Belief, Superstition and Symptom', *Samiksa, J. Indian Psychoanal. Soc.*, 8 (1954), 210-15; idem, *Essais d'Ethnopsychiatrie Générale*.
[42] E. H. Ackerknecht, 'Psychopathology, Primitive Medicine and Primitive Culture', *Bull. Hist. Med.*, 14 (1943), 30-67.
[43] G. Devereux, *Essais d'Ethnopsychiatrie Générale*.
[44] A syphilitic is *cured* when he can contract a new case of syphilis.
[45] An incomplete treatment may suppress a syphilitic's primary lesions, but does not prevent the appearance of secondary and tertiary ones.
[46] J. G. Neihardt, *Black Elk Speaks*, New York: Morrow, 1932.
[47] R. H. Jokl, 'Psychic Determinism and Preservation of Sublimation in Classical Psychoanalytic Procedure', *Bull. Menninger Clinic*, 14 (1950), 207-19.
[48] G. Devereux, *Mohave Ethnopsychiatry and Suicide*; A. L. Kroeber, *Handbook of the Indians of California*.

proves that 'remission without insight' only exacerbates the underlying psychopathology.

(ii) *The Individual Unconscious*
The shaman's psychopathology is rooted in his ethnic unconscious.
As a rule, his idiosyncratic conflicts are repatterned in the course
of a healing vision or dream. By contrast, the 'private' abnormal's
conflicts are not so repatterned and remain permanently rooted in
his idiosyncratic unconscious. Moreover, the shaman's main problem is a culturally typical stress, while that of the 'private' abnormal
is a culturally atypical one: it is different in nature, or is overly
intense, or has been experienced prematurely. I therefore hold that
the term 'trauma' should be reserved for culturally atypical experiences, against which culture does not provide ready-made
defences. Indeed, not the force of the stress but the lack of defences
against it causes an experience to be a trauma.[49] Falling into water
is no trauma for the Polynesian, who learns to swim early in life;
if, however, a Bedouin falls into water, he is traumatized and must
improvise ways of getting out of his predicament: he must churn
the water and shout for help.

PREMATURE TRAUMA AND UNAVAILABLE DEFENCE

I must now differentiate between psychological defence mechanisms
(e.g. projection) and the cultural materials (e.g. scapegoating)
implementing and reinforcing them. Culture also establishes a preferential hierarchy of the defences and patterns them; the chief
product of this process is the ethnic personality. The same patterning can also influence social processes. Identification with the enemy
is a psychological defence, culturally implemented by means of
'antagonistic acculturation': thus, one may borrow the enemy's
means, the better to defeat his ends.[50]
    This distinction is important for an understanding of the concept
of 'premature trauma', which is not simply a chronologically early
one, but one which occurs before the infant is able to use, or is
given access to, the appropriate cultural defences. For a small child,

[49] G. Devereux, *Essais d'Ethnopsychiatrie Générale.*
[50] idem, and E. M. Loeb, 'Antagonistic Acculturation', *Amer. Sociol. Rev.*,
7 (1943), 133-47, now reprinted in *Essais d'Ethnopsychiatrie Générale.*

the death of his parents is a premature trauma, since culture only provides it with *external* protection (orphanages), but not with *internal* defences, such as a sudden, culturally fostered, maturity, which abolishes infantile dependent needs.[51] This theory explains why true psychoses are caused by very early (usually: oral) traumata. At that stage of development the infant does not experience the impact of cultural materials, but that of the ethos ('cultural pattern') only, as reflected in parental, etc., attitudes. It must therefore improvise defences, which are necessarily strictly intrapsychic—i.e. affective-attitudinal—since that is all a (still unenculturated) child can evolve.[52] This implies that psychosis, as distinct from neurosis, always involves a severe impairment of the ethnic personality, which is produced by the impact of the culture pattern, rather than by that of culture traits (child rearing techniques), upon the immature psyche.[53] It also explains the stability of the ethnic personality, even when culture changes.[54] This disproves the allegedly paramount importance of mere child rearing techniques,[55] subsequently partly repudiated by Linton.[56] Neurotic parents traumatize the child even if they utilize all standard child rearing techniques, because their atypical affects mediate to the child a distorted ethos, instead of the affective equivalent of an undistorted one.

[51] The early diffusion of affective ties over the whole lineage or tribe in primitive society (G. Devereux, 'Social Structure and the Economy of Affective Bonds', *Psychoanal. Rev.*, 29 (1942), 303-14) may be an unconsciously evolved cultural defence against the trauma of being orphaned, in a group where the predictable life-span of parents is relatively short. The loss of the mother is less traumatic where a classificatory kinship system provides for each child several, functionally equivalent 'mothers'. This theory may even account for character types, since in 'modern' society the diffusion of the libido is discouraged (G. Devereux, *Essais d'Ethnopsychiatrie Générale*) and children are forced to remain immature for a long time (G. Devereux, *Therapeutic Education*, New York: Harper, 1956; idem, *Essais d'Ethnopsychiatrie Générale*). Hence the appalling psychological situation of the orphan in modern society.
[52] G. Devereux, *Reality and Dream*; idem, *Essais d'Ethnopsychiatrie Générale*.
[53] idem. *Reality and Dream*; idem, *Therapeutic Education*; M. Mead, 'The Swaddling Hypothesis: its Reception', *Amer. Anthropologist*, 56 (1934), 395-409.
[54] G. Devereux, *Reality and Dream*; A. I. Hallowell, 'Some Psychological Characteristics of the North-eastern Indians', in F. Johnson (ed.), *Man in Northeastern North America*, Papers of the Robert S. Peabody Foundation of Anthropology, Andover, Mass., 1946.
[55] A. Kardiner and R. Linton, *The Individual and His Society*, New York: Columbia University Press, 1939; London: Oxford University Press, 1939.
[56] R. Linton, *Culture and Mental Disorders*.

These considerations explain both the harmfulness of premature traumata and the impairment of the ethnic personality of the psychotic, which finds an expression in a severe 'social negativism'.[57]

Premature traumata can also occur after infancy, i.e. at a time when the child or adolescent is either still too young to be able to use cultural defences or when, as in Samoa,[58] he is denied access to them because he must not 'presume above his age'. The equivalent of a 'premature trauma' is also experienced by the oppressed. Their characterological defects and immaturities[59] are due to their being denied access to many important cultural defences: self-respect, having 'honour', etc., which are available to the privileged. The oppressed are therefore psychologically as vulnerable and as easily dominated as are strangers, who have not yet learned, nor strongly cathected, the most important cultural defences of their new environment. In short, the achievement of maturity and of objective normality requires free access to culturally provided defences.

Some cultural items—such as myths, etc.—may even serve as a kind of impersonal 'cold storage' for individual fantasies resulting from inner conflicts. Such fantasies are laden with too much affect to be repressed, but are also too ego dystonic to be recognized as subjective and self-relevant. By putting them into the 'cold storage' of culture, one gives them a formal and generalized expression within the (impersonal) culture, while keeping them out of an idiosyncratic 'private circulation'. Partly because the psychotherapist, too, knows and uses these cultural cold storages, such fantasies emerge in an idiosyncratic form and are recognized as self-relevant only at the end of a successful analysis; until then, they remain projections supported by the culture. In the case of the shaman culturalized fantasies emerge in the form of semi-subjective 'experiences', in which myths and fantasies, rituals and idiosyncratic compulsions, etc., are inextricably interwoven. This view fits what was said about the culturally standardized 'type conflicts' and 'type solutions' of the shaman.

[57] G. Devereux, 'Belief, Superstition and Symptom', loc. cit., and idem, *Essais d'Ethnopsychiarie Générale*.
[58] M. Mead, *Coming of Age in Samoa*, New York: Morrow, 1928; London: Cape, 1929.
[59] J. Dollard, *Caste and Class in a Southern Town*.

The traumatized individual usually seeks to escape his difficulties through the *misuse of cultural material.*

THE ETHNIC PSYCHOSES

Sometimes culture practically provides directives for its misuse in situations of atypical stress, for example in the form of Lintonian[60] 'patterns of misconduct', in which culture seems to say: 'Don't do it—but if you do, proceed as follows. . . .'

The relevant directive here is: 'Don't become insane, but if you do, you must behave as follows. . . .' During funerals the Nyakyusa pretend to be psychotic, in the prescribed manner, so as to protect themselves against becoming truly psychotic.[61] Various American Indian tribes say that 'the insane mention the names of the dead' and many Indian psychotics seem to do just that: such acts seem to be 'signal symptoms', which inform the group that the speaker is insane—but also that he is *not* sacrilegious or criminal.[62] Occidentals expect psychotics to grimace, to babble, and to say 'Brrr' or 'B-B-B'. Slightly more sophisticated, but still wholly cultural notions of what is 'insane behaviour' are embedded in our laws. Hence, the courts often force psychiatrists to answer psychiatrically senseless questions. In one instance the prosecutor urged that the accused was sane and simply grossly selfish because, after killing his wife and then shooting off a corner of his own skull, when he recovered consciousness he called to his dead wife to help *him.* My testimony, that this proved that he had murdered his wife during an epileptic fugue blanketed by amnesia, was rejected, because it did not fit 'legal commonsense'. The man was sentenced and shortly thereafter confirmed my predictions by making a genuine suicidal attempt. Last but not least, hospitalized psychotics seldom behave as the layman expects them to behave.

Cultural preconceptions regarding the 'proper way of being insane' are, by contrast, mirrored in the behaviour of malingerers and it is this that enables the psychiatrist to show them up as

[60] R. Linton, *The Study of Man*, New York: Appleton-Century, 1936; London: Peter Owen, 1965.

[61] M. Wilson, 'Nyakyusa Ritual and Symbolism', *Amer. Anthropologist*, 56 (1954), 228-41.

[62] G. Devereux, *Mohave Ethnopsychiatry and Suicide*; idem, *Essais d'Ethnopsychiatrie Générale.*

frauds.[63] At the same time, the impulse to malinger is, in itself, pathological. This may explain why one of the Esposito brothers tried to simulate psychosis by *eating* paper; he must have been sufficiently abnormal to sense that oral traumata underlies many severe psychoses. Equally interesting are culturally required transitory eruptions of abnormality. Linton[64] felt that we might never know whether Mohammed was truly epileptic, since the convulsive seizure was the Arab abnormality *par excellence* and was so consistently interpreted as a token of divine backing that many Arab chiefs faked a 'fit' before a battle in order to encourage their followers. Odysseus faked the Greek collective representation of psychosis when trying to avoid being drafted for the Trojan war, and that of senile psychosis when spying on the suitors. Saul acted out the Judaic conception of insanity—letting his saliva dribble on his beard—when he was fleeing from David.

Ordinarily, the idiosyncratic psychotic's symptomatology is not only at variance with cultural expectations, but also deliberately provocative, in that it expresses his social negativism.[65]

Those disturbed persons whose ethnic unconscious is not sufficiently disorganized to incite them to a wholesale rebellion against all social norms (including 'patterns of (psychotic) misbehaviour'), borrow from culture the *means* for the *conventional* implementation of their idiosyncratic disorder. This enables them to develop *ethnic psychoses*, such as amok, latah, imu, windigo, koro, etc., which are not found in our society. Thus, Aberle[66] ingeniously proved that even though the Siberian myriachit resembles Gilles de la Tourette's disease, it is not identical with it. Likewise, both newspapers and psychiatrists erred in saying that the psychotic mass-murderer of Camden, N. J. ran amok. Indeed, a genuine Malay amok seizure

[63] The situation is somewhat more complex. Ganser's syndrome, observed chiefly amongst imprisoned persons (who have a 'good reason' for malingering) is often mistaken for malingering, because such patients tend to behave as culture expects the psychotic to behave. Since a detailed analysis of this syndrome is beyond the scope of this study, I simply suggest that it is something like an 'ethnic psychosis' of persons in prison.

[64] R. Linton, Personal Communication.

[65] G. Devereux, 'Belief, Superstition and Symptom', loc. cit.; idem, *Essais d'Ethnopsychiatrie Générale*. Four years after the publication of my relevant article R. L. Jenkins and L. Hewitt independently emphasized the *variable* role of pure rebelliousness in psychiatric disorders ('Types of Personality Structure Encountered in Child Guidance Clinics', *Amer. J. Orthopsychiat.* 14 (1944), 84-95).

[66] D. F. Aberle, 'Arctic Hysteria and Latah in Mongolia', *Trans. New York Acad. Sciences*, Series II, 14 (1952), 291-7.

can not only be self-induced,[67] but may even occur in response to a formal order.[68] Premeditation also plays a decisive role in the Crow Crazy-dog-wishes-to-die syndrome.[69] In short, the behaviour of the ethnic psychotic fits the expectations of his own culture, but not those of other cultures, our own included.[70]

The symptomatology of ethnic psychoses fits cultural expectations mainly because both reflect the type conflicts of a culture and its cultural defences against such conflicts. Given the nature of Crow (or Malay) culture, the traumatized Crow (or Malay) can, because of his distinctive ethnic makeup find relief in 'going crazy' (Crazy-dog-wishes-to-die; amok) in a culturally expected way. The cultural conformism of ethnic psychotics sometimes causes psychiatrists to minimize the seriousness of their basic derangement.[71]

Case 1: An ambitious and educated white woman married a fairly primitive American-Indian on the rebound, but, as a means of compensating, wanted her gifted son to be successful by American standards. However, the son, who consciously rejected everything Indian, unconsciously identified himself with his father and frustrated his mother's ambitions. He did well in college, but dropped out rather than accept financial help from a well-to-do 'lousy Indian' aunt. He married a white girl, but one as primitive as any 'blanket squaw'. He refused to become a foreman, fearing that his white colleagues, whom he would have to entertain, would consider his home a 'wigwam'. His race prejudice also enabled him to deny his Oedipal conflicts. He did not hate his father—he only loathed Indians; he recognized his father's right to cohabit with his mother, but was revolted by 'miscegenation'—though not by his own relations with his white wife. He exploited the fact that race prejudice is a culturally provided defence in our society and used it to ward off insight into his Oedipal problems. This function of prejudice was more obvious in a halfbreed than it would have been in a

---

[67] H. Fauconnier, *Malaisie*, Paris: Librairie Stock, 1930.
[68] Anonymous, *Hikayat Hang Tuah*, 3 vols., Weltevreden, 1930 (German translation by H. Overbeck, 2 vols., Munich, 1922).
[69] R. H. Lowie, 'Takes-the-Pipe, A Crow Warrior', in E. C. Parsons (ed), *American Indian Life*, New York: B. W. Huebsch, 1922; R. H. Lowie, *The Crow Indians*, New York: Holt, Rinehart, 1935.
[70] Lay ideas of 'how the insane behave' may be derived from the symptomatology of *formerly* prevalent psychoses, or symptoms. Cf. the popular belief that there are still psychotics who think they are Napoleon.
[71] Thus our schizoid culture (see R. Bain, 'Our Schizoid Culture', *Sociol. Soc. Res.*, 19 (1935), 266-76) underestimates the abnormality of the 'beatnik' particularly if he is 'well adjusted' to a beatnik group.

white Anglo-Saxon from the South: it revealed how dual cultural allegiances can be fitted into the series: Conflict—defence—secondary conflict—secondary defence, etc.[72] A study of acculturation in terms of this scheme is likely to prove rewarding.

Thus, both ethnic psychoses and shamanistic derangements use defences and symptoms which culture provides for just that purpose.[73] However, ethnic psychoses draw upon one segment, and shamanistic derangements upon another segment of culture. In the ethnic psychoses the underlying conflicts are not rooted in the ethnic unconscious, but in certain idiosyncratic traumata so prevalent in a culture that it must evolve defences against them. I.e. only recurrent stresses, which culture itself considers to be 'traumatic', lead to ethnic, non-idiosyncratic disorders. It therefore places at the disposal of persons so traumatized prepatterned symptoms, representing a 'pattern of misconduct'.

The warlike Plains Indian cultures kept the men in line by rewarding foolhardy heroes and by glorifying death in combat. Yet, in such a society fear of death must have been universal, and culture therefore provided, for those whom even such 'cultural bromides'[74] could not make brave, the traditional transvestite 'pattern of misconduct'. In Tanala culture, which ridiculed sexually inadequate men, the transvestite pattern of misconduct provided a refuge for men of dubious potency.[75]

Culture itself must specify what is, and what is not, a 'genuine' trauma. That which Crow culture defines as 'unendurable disappointment'[76] leads to the Crazy-dog-wishes-to-die syndrome. What Northern Algonquian culture views as 'excessive deprivation' causes the windigo psychosis.[77] A culturally specified degree of 'fascination with the kris' and a culturally defined 'unendurable humiliation' triggers off the amok seizure.[78] What culture calls a

[72] F. Alexander (Personal Communication) observed a similar exploitation of dual cultural allegiances in a Hawaiian-born Japanese.
[73] Cultural items not evolved for this purpose can also serve as symptoms and defences (cf. below).
[74] G. Devereux, Essais d'Ethnopsychiatrie Générale.
[75] A. Kardiner and R. Linton, The Individual and His Society, New York: Columbia University Press, 1939.
[76] R. H. Lowie, 'Takes-the-Pipe, A Crow Warrior', loc. cit., and The Crow Indians.
[77] R. Landes, 'The Ojibwa Woman', Columbia University Contributions to Anthropology, Vol. XXXI, New York, 1938; M. I. Teicher, 'Windigo Psychosis', Proc Amer. Ethnolo. Soc., Seattle, 1960.
[78] H. Fauconnier, Malaisie; and F. H. G. van Loon, 'Amok and Lattah', J. Abnorm. Soc. Psychol., 21 (1926), 434-44.

'frightening experience'—the word 'snake' among the Ainu,[79] or a sharp command among the Malays[80]—induces an imu, that is a latah, seizure. I have explained elsewhere[81] why the idiosyncratic trauma experienced by old men deserted by a young wife produces the Mohave heartbreak syndrome, and also why old Mohave women deserted by a young husband do *not* experience this extreme mourning reaction. I was even able to link these observations with the fact that only Mohave women try to throw themselves on the funeral pyre of a dead spouse.[82]

In short, in ethnic psychoses the etiological factor is an *idiosyncratic but statistically prevalent* type of culturally recognized trauma, which causes the afflicted person to mobilize certain atypical, though culturally provided, defences. This explains why all amok runners behave alike, regardless of whether they are running amok for subjective reasons, or because they have decided to become (militarily valuable) juramentados,[83] or because they have been ordered by an official to run amok,[84] or simply because they are ill and delirious.[85] Moreover, in nearly all ethnic psychoses, observed behaviour fits cultural expectations. Hence, e.g. every description of latah behaviour, regardless of its authorship, is a so-called 'textbook case'. This proves that powerful cultural forces pattern certain types of abnormal behaviour. By contrast, idiosyncratic ('non-ethnic') deranged behaviour is so variable, that in clinical experience, the 'textbook case' is the exception rather than the rule.

Our culture, too, has its ethnic psychoses: genuine schizophrenia, character-disorders and especially psychopathy seem to be the modern ethnic derangement.[86]

[79] W. Winiarz and J. Wielawski, 'Imu—A Psychoneurosis Occurring among the Ainus', *Psychoanal. Rev.*, 23 (1936), 181-6.

[80] P. M. Yap, 'The Latah Reaction: its Pathodynamics and Nosological Position', *J. Mental Science*, 98 (1952), 515-64.

[81] G. Devereux, *Mohave Ethnopsychiatry and Suicide*.

[82] ibid., pp. 457-9. The only Mohave man who tried to commit funeral suicide threw himself on the pyre of his son, whom he himself had driven to despair.

[83] J. F. Ewing, 'Juramentado', *Anthropol. Quart.*, 28 (1955), 148-55; V. Hurley, *The Swish of the Kris*, New York: Dutton, 1936.

[84] Anonymous, *Hikayat Hang Tuah* (cited at n. 68).

[85] P. Van Wulfften-Palthe, 'Psychiatry and Neurology in the Tropics', in A. Liechtenstein (ed.), *A Clinical Textbook of Tropical Medicine*, Batavia, 1936.

[86] G. Devereux, *The Psychotherapy of the Ethnic Psychoses*. Paper read before the Annual Meeting of the American Sociological Society, 1955; idem, *Essais d'Ethnopsychiatrie Générale*.

My theory of ethnic neuroses and psychoses does not imply that they cannot be classified also in terms of current psychiatric nosology. The Mohave 'heartbreak' syndrome is obviously akin to a mourning depression; imu, latah and myriachit are almost certainly hysterias, etc. This is to be expected, since basic psychodynamics and pathodynamics are universal. Both the normal and the abnormal members of a culture utilize the same defence mechanisms. They differ from each other the way the Eskimo differs from the Bedouin: not in terms of the presence or absence of certain defence mechanisms, but in terms of the culturally patterned hierarchization of the various defences. This patterning does not presuppose a deliberate act; it is simply a byproduct of the prevailing cultural climate.

Where culture does not single out for special notice certain idiosyncratic, but statistically prevalent, traumata, or where a certain trauma is even statistically exceptional, culture provides no anxiety-binding defences against them. The individuals so traumatized therefore evolve 'ordinary' (non-ethnic) disorders; they improvise symptoms and defences, usually by distorting certain cultural items whose primary purpose is not that of serving as defences.

I have shown elsewhere[87] that 'ordinary' derangements can best be analyzed in terms of the manner in which, and of the extent to which, cultural material is misunderstood, mismanaged and distorted.

(i) The infantile, fixated or regressed person's handling of culture reflects a cultural-psychological lag. He is an anachronism, living psychologically in his childhood and culturally in the past. His boss is primarily a father figure and he believes in charismatic leadership.

(ii) The neurotic recognizes that a given item is cultural in origin, but assigns a subjective meaning to it. A Plains Indian woman assigned an oral significance to a genital rite of her tribe. She also envied men who, under the pretence of cohabitation, gained access to their partner's breasts.

(iii) The psychotic completely deculturalizes culture. He uses speech as a means of expression, rather than of communication. For him, a scalpel is *mainly* a dagger and a throne *mainly* a chamber-pot.

(iv) The psychopath is culturally sophisticated, but has no cul-

[87] idem, *Essais d'Ethnopsychiatrie Générale.*

E

129

tural loyalties. He does not rob women; he exploits their cultural loyalties for his anti-cultural ends: He marries them (a cultural act) and then absconds with their money. Samuel Johnson's dictum: 'Patriotism is the last refuge of the scoundrel' obviously applies only to patrioteering: to the criminal exploitation of the loyalties *of others.*

CLINICAL APPLICATIONS

The psychiatrist increasingly asks the anthropologist to help him diagnose culturally atypical or marginal patients. Far too often the anthropologist says only: 'Among the Bonga-Bonga such behaviour is normal, such a personality is well adjusted, such a belief is culturally standardized.' Though often true, such statements are psychiatrically insufficient. I have often had occasion to correct mistaken diagnoses of Indian patients, by stressing, for example, the difference between a delusion and a belief.[88]

Case 2: An Indian, mistakenly diagnosed in a certain hospital as schizophrenic, was subjected repeatedly to electric shock treatment, which only made him completely unmanageable. When he was transferred to the hospital which employed me, I was able to prove that he was only neurotic. A colleague therefore gave him supportive psychotherapy, with the result that, within six weeks, the patient was able to leave the hospital and to function adequately in the community.

It is, however, usually not enough to differentiate between delusion and belief, etc. Indeed, the standard underlying this diagnostic procedure might prevent one from giving psychiatric help to an Indian who goes into remission and defines himself as a shaman.[89] Such a patient is not even 'culturally normal' and still needs psychiatric help. He is, moreover, *in social remission only with reference to a particular social setting:* his own tribe. *He is not adaptable and, above all, not readaptable.* By contrast, a normal Indian, who is not a shaman, may also be well adjusted to his culture, but retains the capacity to adjust also to other cultures.[90]

The cultural essence of normality is not adjustment, but the capacity for constant readjustment. Indeed, certain 'model patients' are

[88] idem, *Reality and Dream.*
[89] idem, 'Mental Hygiene of the American Indian', *Mental Hygiene,* 26 (1942), 71-84.
[90] idem, *Reality and Dream.*

perfectly adjusted to the hospital; they seem rational, co-operative and well-behaved, but promptly 'crack up' when they are discharged.[91]

The psychiatric treatment of a shaman need not de-Indianize and acculturate him, especially since Indians are handicapped when they try to live in a white American setting.[92] It is not even culturally expedient to de-Indianize him, since every culture benefits from contacts with different cultures: the Indian in the United States is a 'cultural yeast'. The psychotherapy of a shaman must simply de-shamanize him, without destroying his ethnic character structure. It must remobilize his capacity for readjustment, by breaking down his pathologically rigid, marginal and dereistic adjustment to only one segment of his own culture.

It may be objected that Indian tribes need shamans and that, if one de-shamanizes the patient, one deprives his tribe of something it needs. This objection is untenable. The *bona fide* (abnormal) shaman's role can be adequately performed also by adaptable normal persons *posing* as shamans.

Case 3: When I practised first aid medicine among the Sedang Moi, I soon discovered that even though my patients asked for and dutifully swallowed Occidental drugs, they also desired psychocultural support. Hence, after I had urged a patient with a mild bronchitis to stay indoors and keep warm, he also proceeded to call in a shaman, who usually dragged him out into the rainy night in order to perform a curing ritual, thereby aggravating the patient's bronchitis. Finally, I simply claimed to be also a shaman,[93] and thereafter not only handed out aspirin or quinine, but also performed the traditional curing rite—needless to say, indoors. This performance gave my patients the ritual, psycho-cultural support they needed, even though *I* did not believe in the supernatural efficiency of these rites, but viewed them as supportive 'first aid psychotherapy'.

Though useful in practice, the traditional adjustment-oriented outlook 'among the Bonga-Bonga this is normal' continues to inspire

[91] I am indebted to R. L. Jenkins, M.D., for citing this example in support of my theory that normality presupposes the capacity for readjustment.
[92] G. Devereux, *Reality and Dream.*
[93] My claim was believed because I disappeared for one night from the village and pretended to have been taken to the land of the Thundergods. Moreover, shortly thereafter I found two neolithic axes, which only shamans are supposed to be able to find. ('Indochina's Moi Medicine Men', *Tomorrow*, 4 (1955), 95-104.)

even the diagnosing of the shaman as a psychotic in remission, adjusted exclusively to a marginal segment of his culture, and the diagnosing of the ethnic psychotic as a genuine psychotic, adjusted to a 'pattern of misconduct'. One risks, in both instances, mistaking a belief for a delusion. I thought for a long time that these refinements of diagnostic technique were sufficient. A somewhat dramatic occurrence showed me the need for a radically different approach.

Case 4: Two Acoma Indian half-brothers, already sentenced to the electric chair, were sent to the Medical Center for Federal Prisoners for a final psychiatric diagnosis. The prison psychiatrist, being culturally sufficiently sophisticated not to mistake Indianness for psychosis, and finding no *culturally neutral* evidence of psychosis, was obliged to declare them 'legally sane'. Nonetheless, he continued to be disturbed by the feeling that there was more to these men than met the eye, and therefore asked me at a moment's notice to interview them.

The two half-brothers—who could not communicate with each other, being confined to maximum security cells for prisoners under sentence of death—were seen separately, in the presence of the prison psychiatrist. To my amazement, each of them poured out, in less than ten minutes, information on witchcraft and on personal experiences with witches which fitted (as I discovered later) Acoma belief, but puzzled me, because, as an experienced field-worker, I am accustomed to have to work long and hard for such information. Moreover, it was particularly surprising to have traditionally suspicious Pueblo Indians pour out such material to a perfect stranger. This behaviour was culturally as irrational as would be that of a cryptographer, who discussed the Navy's secret code with a chance-met stranger in a bar. When this clue was followed up, it became evident that:

(i) These men had ceased to experience these beliefs as cultural material. They had de-culturalized them (see above) and had begun to experience them in a subjective, delusional manner.

(ii) They reacted in a culturally atypical manner when they felt threatened by witchcraft. They menaced the witch with guns, instead of trying to get rid of him, in the traditional manner, by asking the competent Acoma ritual society to help them.

A fictitious case will show what I mean by the statement that these men experienced cultural beliefs as though they were private delusions.

Case 5: A (fictitious) electronics engineer believes himself persecuted by radar. He makes a blueprint of this device which even contains real improvements over existing radar devices. His machine will do everything any radar device can do and may even do it better—but, *whatever* it does, it cannot *persecute* him. In this instance, cultural (scientific) material is handled efficiently, but in a delusional manner, in that this new radar device is detached from the domain of physics and assigned to that of supernatural persecutory devices.

Returning to *Case 4*, once I ascertained how these men distorted their culture, it was easy to elicit also the idiosyncratic hallucinations—completely at variance with tribal belief—which had caused them to murder a state police officer. Hence, long before the end of the interview, both I and the prison psychiatrist diagnosed one of these men as a paranoid schizophrenic and his half-brother as a psychotically tinged psychopath. The idiosyncratic core of these psychoses was concealed by an outer layer of half shamanistic, half ethno-psychotic material. This and related observations suggest that the following problems deserve close study:

(i) Is a shamanistic and/or ethnic psychosis the opening gambit of an idiosyncratic psychosis?

(ii) Do shamanistic and/or ethnic psychoses mask, at a later stage, an underlying idiosyncratic psychosis, the way a seemingly benign monosymptomatic hysteria sometimes masks a schizophrenia?

(iii) Are some shamanistic and/or ethnic psychoses the terminal, restitutional manifestations of fundamentally idiosyncratic psychoses?

These three alternatives need not be mutually exclusive: they may occur either separately, or else in combinations of two or three, in a variety of idiosyncratic derangements. This hypothesis fits the observation that a neurosis is sometimes the opening gambit in the development of a psychosis, that neurotic traits can also be found in psychotics and vice versa, that neuroses sometimes mask psychoses and that, in the course of a recovery or of a simple remission, a psychotic may become temporarily a neurotic or possibly a psychopath.

In the initial diagnosis of these Acoma Indians it was not—as so often happens—a belief which was mistaken for a delusion; it was a delusion which, because of its traditional *content*, was mistaken for a belief. What suggested a delusion was the culturally deviant manner in which these men experienced and handled cultural items. They did not even handle them in terms of some culturally permissible 'alternative',[94] or in terms of their secondary cultural meaning, i.e. in the sense in which a rolling pin is not only a kitchen implement, but also a traditional device for punishing erring husbands.[95] In fact, these cultural items were not even handled in accordance with some marginal pattern of misconduct. Traditional beliefs about witches were handled in an arbitrary, idiosyncratic manner; cultural items were deculturalized in a characteristically psychotic way.

Not wishing to leave this case history suspended in midair, I add that the psychiatrist presented our findings so competently to the court, that the men escaped the electric chair and were confined to the Medical Center for Federal Prisoners.

THE PRACTICALITY OF THEORY

Since the psychiatrist cannot become an expert on the culture of each of his patients, he cannot practise the kind of 'cross-cultural psychiatry' I practised in treating a 'Wolf Indian' *after* studying carefully the customs and beliefs of his tribe.[96] I therefore cast about for a new device which would enable the psychiatrist to diagnose and to treat patients belonging to cultures of which he knows little or nothing.

Failing to find a purely psychiatric or ethnographic solution, I tackled the problem not in terms of *cultures*, but in terms of the *concept* of *Culture*. I began to analyze Culture as an experience and the manner in which the individual *experiences* and *handles* Culture when he is normal and when he is abnormal. This theoretically correct solution soon proved its efficacy. It enabled me to diagnose the Acoma Indians, of whose culture I knew practically nothing, since I had no time in which to prepare myself for the interview by reading an ethnography of the Acoma tribe. I had at my disposal only my general knowledge of world ethnography, some field experience with another Pueblo group—the Hopi—and an under-

[94] R. Linton, *The Study of Man*.
[95] G. Devereux, *Essais d'Ethnopsychiatrie Générale*.
[96] idem, *Reality and Dream*.

standing of the function of Culture and of the nature of the 'universal culture pattern'.[97] Hence, when I was told that these men went after a witch with guns, I did not know how the Acoma dealt with witches; I simply knew that most cultures deal with witches collectively and in a traditional way. Hence, my diagnosis was not made in terms of Acoma culture, but in terms of Culture. This suggests that the analysis of Culture, and of the 'universal culture pattern', as well as the specification of their nature, requires also a psychiatric approach to Culture, because the 'experience of having a culture' is a universal trait and man functions everywhere and in the same way as 'creator, creature, manipulator and transmitter of culture.[98]

This means, for instance, that my fictitious electronics engineer's blueprint was *ethnographically* correct, but culturally (=anthropologically) delusional. Similarly, a real paranoid patient, while so delusional as to mutilate himself, contributed articles to the Oxford Dictionary. However, in stressing the objective quality of this patient's scientific performance, Kempf[99] failed to ask what *subjective significance* this (ethnographically) 'scientific' performance had for the patient. I therefore hold, with Dodds,[100] that Pythagoras was a shaman, since his mathematical discoveries were not inspired by mathematical, but by mystical, interests.

I now call this approach to psychiatric problems 'metacultural' or 'meta-ethnographic'.[101] I hold that it is more than a mere palliative for the psychiatrist's inability to become a universal ethnographer. The metacultural approach to psychiatry is clinically the most effective one and theoretically much superior to any other approach, in that it provides a genuinely deep insight into psychodynamics which, in turn, leads to deeper insights into the nature of Culture. It also disproves the currently fashionable allegation that the so-called 'culturalistic' schools of psychiatry are culturally more sophisticated and also more useful to the anthropologist than is classical Freudian psychoanalysis.

[97] C. Wissler, *Man and Culture*, New York: Crowell, 1923.
[98] L. W. Simmons, *Sun Chief*, New Haven: Yale University Press, 1942.
[99] E. J. Kempf, *Psychopathology*, St. Louis: Mosby, 1920.
[100] E. R. Dodds, *The Greeks and the Irrational*, Berkeley: University of California Press, 1951.
[101] I had originally called it 'transcultural' (see *Reality and Dream*) as contrasted with 'cross-cultural', but changed my terminology because today my original technical term is indiscriminately applied by others to all types of ethnopsychiatry.

The anthropologist cannot make a real contribution to psychiatry if he only acquires its jargon and contents himself with trotting out his little museum of cultural curiosa. He must remain a student of Culture, defined as a patterned way of experiencing both social and extra-social reality. This disposes of Kroeber's[102] biased assertion that the ethnopsychiatrist is not a *bona fide* anthropologist, because he does not study Culture. I hold that he does nothing else but study Culture, and the manner in which the individual experiences it. In so doing, he is a more genuine student of Culture than are the so-called 'culturologists', who study Culture as though man did not really exist.

[102] A. L. Kroeber, *The Nature of Culture.*

II. Field Work

All men dream but their dreams have different meaning to them. Dream interpretation in preliterate cultures is common practice. The first anthropologists saw a connection between animism and the natives' belief in the manifest dream content. In 1924, Charles G. Seligman in his Presidential address to the Royal Anthropological Institute of Great Britain and Ireland dealt largely with the problem of dreams and dreaming 'among people of diverse race'.

Due to his psychoanalytic interest Róheim paid particular attention to the dreams he was able to collect in Australia and Normanby Island in Melanesia. He was the first field worker who not only collected dreams but applied the clinically derived method of asking for free associations. Only on the basis of associations is one in the position to come to distinct interpretive conclusions. In this sense the following paper is of methodological significance. It shows that dream interpretation must take the culture and the culture-defined symbolism into consideration in order to understand the secondary elaboration. On the other hand it is Róheim's feeling that the latent content of a dream can be understood without knowing the cultural background of the dreamer. Both aspects are justified. Some anthropologists will claim that certain dream elements are affected by the culture. It was Róheim's contention that id-analytical interpretations go beyond cultural boundaries since environmental conditions provide only a manifest frame of reference.

7

Dream Analysis and Field Work in Anthropology[1]

GÉZA RÓHEIM

Ever since Tylor based his theory of animism on dream life or primitive man's interpretation of dream life[2] anthropologists have been interested in what primitive man believes about his dreams. In his now well-nigh forgotten attempt to achieve a synthesis of anthropological data and build a *Völkerpsychologie*, Wundt discusses the role of dreams in animistic and demon beliefs from several points of view.[3] Anthropologists of the old school have therefore always recorded two things: dreams as evidence of animistic beliefs and dream interpretation given by the primitives themselves. Howitt, for instance, tells us what the Dieri believe about the dead visiting them in their dreams or their own soul leaving their body and going to the other world.[4] The animistic meaning was emphasized by anthropological theory. The dream interpretation was offered by the primitives themselves.[5]

A new chapter in dream research opens with psychoanalysis or rather with anthropology becoming aware of psychoanalysis. The fourteenth volume of the *Journal of the Royal Anthropological Institute* contains the Presidential address by C. G. Seligman, 'Anthropology and Psychology'. The section on 'Type Dreams' discusses both the tooth-losing dream, the flying dream and the climbing dream. Seligman comes to the conclusion that *'the essential mechanisms of non-Europeans, including savage and barbaric people, appear to be the same as in ourselves'*, and that 'dreams with the same manifest content to which identical (latent) meanings

[1] This paper first appeared in *Psychoanalysis and the Social Sciences*, 1, ed. by G. Róheim, New York: International Universities Press; London: Hogarth Press, 1947.
[2] E. B. Tylor, *Primitive Culture*, London: J. Murray, 1903, vol. 1, p. 428.
[3] W. Wundt, *Völkerspychologie*, Leipzig; W. Engelmann, 1906, vol. 2, p. 98. 'Wachvision und Traumvision', p. 109, 'Angstraum und Krankheitsanfall', p. 114. 'Der Fratzentraum', p. 118, 'Der Alptraum', and so forth.
[4] A. W. Howitt, *The Native Tribes of Southeast Australia*, London: Macmillans, 1904, pp. 434-5. Cf. R. H. Codrington, *The Melanesians*, Oxford: Clarendon Press, 1891, p. 249.
[5] Cf. for instance, Ch. Keysser, 'Aus dem Leben der Kaileute', in R. Neuhauss (ed.), *Deutsch-Neu-Guinea*, Berlin: D. Reimer, 1911, pp. 109-11.

are attached (type dreams) occur, not only in cognatic groups but among people of diverse race and in every stage of culture'.[6] Seligman's papers resulted[7] in an increased interest in dreams. The data collected confirm our knowledge of dream symbolism[8] but there are no individual dreams and of course no associations. Seligman also wrote the introduction to Lincoln's book.[9] This book contains unpublished dream material partly collected by the author (Navaho) partly by Blackwood (Solomon Islands) and also by Radin (Eastern Woodlands). Whenever the author has association material he analyzes the dreams correctly, but in most cases no associations are given. Looking back at what I had to say on this subject after my field work, I find that the 'transference' aspect of the situation is adequately discussed,[10] but a few remarks might be added on external circumstances. Most of the work was done with an interpreter. Both in Central Australia and in Normanby Island, I was very lucky in the choice of my interpreters. They were natives (or half-castes) of exceptional intelligence and a perfect understanding of English. It would probably have been very difficult even when I knew the language to explain to an average native what was meant by 'interpretation'. This is pretty obvious since the difficulty arises even with the most intelligent representatives of our own culture. What I mean by association was first explained to the interpreter (in one case using his own dreams). He could then make the informants understand what I was driving at. My first field publication contains also the first series of analyzed dreams from one native informant.[11]

[6] C. G. Seligman, Presidential Address, *J. Roy. Anthropol. Inst.*, 14 (1924), 46 (my italics).

[7] C. G. Seligman, 'Notes on Dreams', *Man*, 23 (1923), 186-8.

[8] 'To dream of a flood—wife commencing her period'. 'To dream of an ant heap—wife is pregnant by another man'. A. G. O. Hodgson 'Dreams of Central Africa', *Man*, 26 (1926), 67-8. In Tikopia 'a woman dreams that she goes to the stream, fills her water-bottles and puts them in a kit on her back—she will conceive'. R. Firth, 'The Meaning of Dreams in Tikopia', in *Essays Presented to C. G. Seligman*, London: Kegan Paul, 1934, p. 68. To dream that one's hand is smeared with faeces means that one will haul up a shark, ibid., p. 70 (the equation is: faeces equals plenty as in our culture faeces equals money). Among the Dazomba and Moshi, to dream of a snake biting one's wife's right side means that she will soon have a child. A. W. Cardinall, 'Notes on Dreams among the Dazomba and Moshi', *Man*, 27 (1927), 88.

[9] T. S. Lincoln, *The Dream in Primitive Cultures*, London: The Cresset Press, 1935.

[10] G. Róheim, 'Psycho-Analytic Technique and Field Anthropology', *Internat. J. Psycho-Anal.*, 13 (1932), 8-15.

[11] idem, 'Doketa', ibid., pp. 150-79.

DREAM ANALYSIS AND FIELD WORK IN ANTHROPOLOGY

If the anthropologist in the field is also trained as a psychoanalyst, he will find that dreams, *providing he can get some associations*[12] can be used for three distinct purposes:

(i) The associations reveal ethnological data that might otherwise escape notice. Obviously, there are two ways of finding something out about the life of a tribe: a. By asking questions; b. by observing events.

The first method has the drawback that if the culture is not already very well known one does not know what questions to ask. The second method is more reliable than any other, and would be perfect if the time spent in the field were not limited. The gathering of free associations to the dreams supplements both methods because the informants relate life situations and customs which otherwise might have escaped our notice.

(ii) The second aim was what I had in mind in my field work[13] and that is that the unconscious meaning of an institution, or belief or the like, can be obtained by analyzing the dream in which it occurs. Instances of this method are my interpretation of the *alknarintja* on basis of the dreams of Yirramba banga[14] or of the latent meaning of the dogma of totemic incarnation on the basis of the dreams of women in Central Australia.[15]

Some anthropologists or non-Freudian psychoanalysts may object at this juncture. Dreams have to be analyzed only 'in cultural context'.[16]

The question, of course, is what is meant by this. If it means that in order to analyze a dream it is necessary to know what the dreamer is talking about—then this is quite obvious. On the other hand, anyone who really knows what a dream is will agree that there cannot be several 'culturally determined' ways of dreaming just as there are no two ways of sleeping.

It is true, of course, that I am in a better position to understand a dream in which a baseball scene occurs if I know what baseball is. But as long as the dreamer is willing to explain matters this

---

[12] I do not see much use in collecting dreams without associations.
[13] G. Róheim, 'Psychoanalysis of Primitive Cultural Types', *Internat. J. Psycho-Anal.*, 13 (1933), parts 1, 2.
[14] idem, 'Sexual Life in Central Australia', *Internat. J. Psycho-Anal.*, 13 (1932), 48, 49.
[15] idem, 'Women and their Life in Central Australia', *J. Roy. Anthropol. Inst.*, 63 (1933), 241-50.
[16] Cf. L. Gottschalk, C. Kluckhohn and R. Angell, *The Use of Personal Documents in History, Anthropology and Sociology.* Social Science Research Council Bulletin 53, 1945, pp. 105, 106.

only means a delay or loss of time. Everyday experience shows that if a patient brings a dream for the first hour of analysis and associates, I can understand that dream[17] even before I know anything about the patient. The dream work is the same for everybody although there are differences in the degree and technique of secondary elaboration.

(iii) A third aim is an approximation to the real psychoanalytic situation. In the work of Cora Du Bois and Kardiner this has been attempted.[18] The biography is really a substitute for an analysis but the difficulty here, apart from all other obstacles, lies in the duality of workers. If I give an analysis of a patient on the basis of what another observer reports, it would hardly be the same as if the analyst is doing the work himself. Another weakness of the Du Bois-Kardiner work is that few dreams are given with associations. Notwithstanding all this, the book represents a great step forward in the direction of a regular analytic conceptualization.

There is one record of an analysis of a native medicine man. The trouble is that it is published like a novel without the dreams and interpretation. Incidentally, we have here the proof of my contention that dreams can be interpreted and correctly interpreted without knowing the cultural background or rather without asserting that each culture gives a specific frame of reference in which the dream should be understood.[19]

Working in the field (1929-31) I was only aiming at what I have now called the second possible aim of dream analysis in field work. I did not devote enough time to each informant as an informant *per se* to give them an hour every day as was done by Cora Du Bois. If I had stayed a second year, both in Central Australia and on Normanby Island, I suppose I would have done this. As it is, the dreams obtained do give some data of this type. Following are two such dream series, obtained in Normanby Island.

I. RAMORAMO

Ramoramo is a man of about thirty-five, an energetic, manly

[17] 'Understand' here means: to be able to formulate the latent dream content.
[18] Cora Du Bois, *The People of Alor*, Minneapolis: University of Minnesota Press, 1944. (*Editor's note:* Since the publication of Róheim's article other anthropologists and psychoanalysts have worked along the lines suggested by clinical psychoanalysis.)
[19] W. Sachs, *Black Hamlet. The Mind of an African Negro Revealed by Psychoanalysis*, London: Geoffrey Bles, 1937, p. 11.

type. His name means *making a new garden*; it is a Missima word, the name of a man there. His parents were

Subukwaijega (father)	Rikeke (mother)
of Wejoko of the *gewara* (small parrot) totem. (Subukwaijega =he came down and hid.)	of the *magisub* (eagle) totem, born in a Tubetube village. (Rikeke=eagle hunting pigs.)

He is therefore a *magisub* (eagle). His wife is Sadaramo of Kebebeku; she is the *toni-kasa* or owner of the village, a woman of the *gewara* totem. Her original village is Nedukarena (plenty of grass), a Sipupu village further inland. *Sadaramo* is a Dobu word meaning 'breadfruit'. They have the following children :

1. Sadaramo or Mwanigia, a boy of about sixteen.
2. Dehuroro, a girl of ten (the name is the name of a canoe in Tubetube).
3. Kewona (bird song), a boy of about eight.
4. Rabeodani (two stand up together = name of Ramoramo's friend in Tubetube) a girl, age about two.

At present (i.e. 1930) they live in Kebebeku, but they are also making a house in Duruha where a *sagari* (food distribution ceremony) will be given next year.

Ramoramo is friendly, outspoken, independent, easy to get on with. He is not such a nuisance as most of them are, not so much a *gewana karena* (trunk of asking); that is, he is not continually asking for various things. He has the same tendencies as all the others but keeps up a manly front and does not want to look childish. But he is really an *ose* (stingy) and not the generous *esa-esa* (great man, leader) he impersonates. When my boys cut off a few trees from a wood that was supposed to belong to him, he demanded immediate payment although I had been giving him piles of things for months when this happened. He brought me a few turkey eggs as a present, and immediately demanded payment for it. That would be in accordance with their customs, for a gift has to be met by a counter-gift. But he was decidedly going too far when he kept asking for things afterwards with the petulant exclamation, 'Well, didn't I bring you the eggs?' quite disregarding the fact that he had asked and received payment for the eggs.

Dream 1

Last night I dreamt they were trying to *barau* [kill by magic] me. I ran, I jumped into a small canoe [*kewou*] and paddled out to a white man's boat. I said to the white man, 'I will sail with you', and 'I will work for you'. Then I woke.

Associations

The white man was one for whom he had worked before, a friend of his. The man who is trying to kill him by magic is *his son* (really his brother's son) Kuhuwa, who is mourning for *his little son* who was drowned recently. As a young boy Ramoramo mourned for his *nibina* (cross-cousin) and before that *for his father*. The reason for going to the white man is quite clear in this dream. It is the conscious or unconscious anxiety in the family circle. The father who mourns for his son and who is a son to Ramoramo stands for the dead father he mourned for in the past.

Dream 2

I dreamt that they buried yams in the ground. I went with Kwadiura and we took some out of the earth oven. Many women were there, carrying yams and a *sagari* pig. There was a feast [*sagari*]; we got presents. A man called Keweso from Lomitawa speared me with a spear in the breast. I took an axe and cut his nose. He died.

Associations

Kwadiura had his yams in an earth oven like this when he was getting ready for a *sagari*. Kwadiura married Ramoramo's sister. He used to have his ground here and Ramoramo now gets the money for it from the Mission *(Bwaruada)*.

He made a *sagari* for Kwadiura's uncle (that is, he went to the *sagari* as *muri*, married relation). They give each other presents and they are *kune* (trade) partners. He, Ramoramo, got his first *kune* from his uncle.

The *sagari* scene is like a *sagari* at Kasakoja, a Widiwidi hill village (*kasakoja* means 'village hill'). He was there with his classificatory brother To Diweta. To Diweta beat his wife Mwedidi because she had flirted with his nephew. This was also Ramoramo's nephew and he is just now getting ready to help the nephew who is a good boy for his *sagari*. When his uncle died, he told Ramoramo to take care of all the women in the family; Kwadiura's wife (Ramoramo's sister), his niece Matanogi, his mother, Taniore's (his clan 'son', same totem) wife, his own wife—all these he has to take care of.

Keweso is his hereditary enemy, a Lomitawa man. Keweso was put into jail recently by the government for killing a man. His mother used to tell him about fights with Lomitawa. Her uncle, Moketa, killed a Lomitawa man called Tarabunama like he kills the man in his dream, by hitting him on the nose. One of his opponents he killed by a hit on the nose, another by spearing him through the breast.

Ramoramo had been feeling sick before this dream. He thought he might die before he could make the big *sagari* for his 'old people'.

Moketa was an angry man, a great war leader, and he killed many of the Lomitawa. That was because his aunt was crying after his father's death. Moketa's father committed the suicide that is typical of Normanby Island. He quarrelled with his wife, he was jealous. Then he went to a Lomitawa village and said, 'Come and kill me!' They speared him through the breast and ate him.

His son 'paid back by killing' two men; he hit one of them on the nose, the other he speared through the breast. He brought them to his father's clansfolk to be eaten.

Interpretation

Ramoramo is thinking of making a *sagari* in honour of his dead 'uncles', the old men of his clan. He is now the old man of his clan who has to take care of all the women of the clan. In the list of women he includes his wife. Legally this is, of course, wrong; she is not a member of his totem group. But whether a society be matrilineal or patrilineal or in any form of social organization, it is obvious that his own wife is one of the women he is taking care of and it is also obvious that she is one of the 'mothers' (the women of the clan are called mothers), that emotions are displaced from the mother to the wife. The *sagari* with its presents and counter-presents expresses and cements the psychological unity of the clan, the identification with its male members and the sublimated owner-ship of the women of the clan. Through the women these bonds of identification go beyond the frontiers of the clan. Ramoramo's sister is Kwadiura's wife; he has a 'share' in her and in her lands.

In the fight he represents his clan against the arch-enemy; Moketa, his ideal, killed one man by hitting him on the nose, one by spearing him through the breast. Ramoramo acts like Moketa but is also wounded like Moketa's opponent. Every ideal formation is ambivalent; he *is* both Moketa and Moketa's enemy.

Who is this Moketa? The avenger of his father. It is therefore quite possible that the ambivalence was first connected with the father image and hence displaced to the uncle or mother's uncle.

Dream 3

A pig chased me and I climbed up a tree.

Associations

The place was his own garden. The pig was like his own pig which he is growing now for the *sagari* in honour of his mother and mother's brother. But it was also like a bush pig; it had tusks. His mother was very good to him. She always told him and his brother not to leave her because the *barau* (sorcerer) would get them. He dreams this very often; once it is a black pig, then a red pig that chases him.

Before telling me his dream, he was talking about the *bawe garegara*, a mythical pig who is or which is sent by the *barau* to carry the man away whom they want to kill. After what are ostensibly the associations to the dream, he talks about *people who married their own relations* and tells the story of the Tauhau who married his sisters. In the love magic derived from this story, *Tauhau's pig* is his sister. Then he talks about his love life as a young man, how he slept with every woman he wanted and how he fought for his present wife with a rival.

Interpretation

It is evident that the pig with tusks (male) represents his guilt feelings. He has disobeyed his mother and he had desired his own relations, the women of his own maternal clan.

Dream 4

I dreamt that I saw a big bird. I ran, I went to the village; it came after me to kill me. I shouted to the people. The bird ran away and the people held me.

Associations

The bird is like his totem bird, the *magisub* (eagle), and to see the *magisub* in the dream means the *rara*. The *rara* is a disease people get by eating food in a village that was hostile to their father's clan. It amounts symbolically to eating their fathers and the blood kills them. Taisanina died recently of *rara* in Kebebeku; or rather, he was buried alive as is the custom in these cases. If such people are not disposed of, they run to the members of their own clan, catch them, and then they can die because they pass over their disease and their life to the other clan member.

The night before he had this dream they were talking about old times and other cases of *rara*. In his life, one was especially signifi- cant, his mother's real brother, the uncle who taught him every- thing. Everybody ran away, but he stayed with his uncle. This time he is certain that the dead man has been coming out of the grave and throwing stones at him. 'By chance', he sings a song in which a man wants to have intercourse with his sister, but she refuses. A day before he told the origin myth of his totem. The interesting thing in this myth is that, in contrast to the other totem myths of this area, the symbol is derived not from the ancestress but from the man who marries her, i.e. not from the mother but from the father.

Interpretation

This dream conforms completely to the pattern described by Malinowski;[20] the ambivalent conflict is with the uncle who wields the authority in the clan, the incestuous desire is for the sister. However, the totem bird is the mother's (or sister's) *husband*, not her brother.

Dream 5

On the 21st day of May the event with the *rara* reappears in another dream. The dead man, i.e. 'blood' (he uses the word for the disease instead of the name), they went to his grave, they buried him, saying, 'You stay here, we go away'. But the dead man said, 'You go away, I stay in my house [grave].' Later he

[20] *Editor's note:* Reference is made to Malinowski's proposition that the Oedipus complex is explained on the basis of the social moralities in a patriarchal society. Psychoanalysts like Róheim, Jones, etc. have shown that, in a matriarchal setting, the mother's brother takes the corresponding role of the father-frustrator. See Anne Parsons' chapter now in this volume.

came out and the people ran away from him. He said, 'You have bewitched me.' Then he went to another village and became an owl.

Associations

This time he goes back to an earlier case of *rara* in his life. It was his *tubuna* (matrilineal grandfather) who died of the *rara*. When that happened he dreamt of a red man who looked like a red flower with red eyebrows and eyelids, who threw stones at him. Then he talks about a *sasara*, that is, a fight that breaks out at a *sagari* (food distribution). The *sasara* in question happened at Nuadubu; a Donakija (name of village) man was attacked by the Lomitawa. This man was the husband of his cross-cousin. He looked after him and Ramoramo as a young boy lived in his house. First he lived with father, and mother, then he went to his uncle; then when his uncle died he went back to his mother and then his cousin's husband took him because he liked him. It was there that he grew up to a man's estate. Boys do not always grow up at their uncle's house; some stay with father or go to other relations of the mother. Sometimes the parents are dead and there are members of their clan who will then function after the marriage in the role of the uncle—that is, they will get the presents. An old woman happens to pass; he says this is his cross-cousin, the one he was just talking about. She was really his mother's cross-cousin, and is about his mother's age. Therefore she calls him '*natugu*' (my son). The event at Nuadubu was the continuation of an old feud which is commemorated in the following song:

> *Dajaru   kana   mudu   taga*
> Dajaru   her   pudenda   drip
>
> *Mwanena   kainega   inao*
> His wife over the legs   goes
>
> *Tamana   quajaquaja   ina*
> Father   dead   his [his penis]
>
> *Kaheguja   jaragunaja*
> In my mouth I put it

Dajaru's husband was a man from Lomitawa. The people from Donakija had tied him up and laid him on a mat in order to roast him. They did not wish to lose a single drop of blood for it was *mebu* (blood revenge). Therefore they had put him on the mat. His wife was from Boasitoroba and Boasitoroba sided with them, so they did not hurt her. She had to go to urinate and in doing so she stepped over her husband's legs as he was stretched out ready for roasting. In the second part of the song Dajaru identifies herself with her father's people—they are going to eat her husband ('In my mouth I place'). Moreover the husband's body is identified with the father's penis.

Interpretation

The cross-cousin's husband represents the father. The song as association shows the desire to castrate the father.

Dream 6

Nekelesi, a woman from Bunama came and she stayed in Donakija. My cousin Nasimua went up to her and said, 'What about it?' 'You show me' he said to me, 'how to have intercourse with her.' So I showed him how to make a cigarette. He gave it to her and they had intercourse.

Associations

He explains how this magic is made. Before they had tobacco, they would do the same with the betel-nut. 'We make a spell, we light the cigarette, we stop the fire, we light it again and then we go to sleep with it. Then we tell our own shadow: "You go and wake the woman and give her the cigarette". Next day she comes and says, "I dreamt of you last night. You came and gave me a cigarette." Then they have intercourse and their body gets soft.'

Interpretation

He gave no more associations that day. Before telling the dream he said: 'I remember the dream and when I see your face I forget everything,' which shows that repression is at work and that it is somewhat of an analytical situation. The cousin in the dream corresponds to the shadow in the magic.

After awhile he observes, 'My father had very long hair. I lost him when I was quite young. My mother wanted to make my hair grow with oil and a root (*bwayawe* i.e. magic) but I said: "No, if you oil it, it will get white quickly and they will say he is an old man".'

As the cross-cousin is often called 'father' in their terminology, I conjecture that the dream in which he sees his cross-cousin having intercourse with Nekelesi, the *sine-bwaina* of Bunama, is really a *primal scene dream*. The latent anxiety is shown by his rejection of the father role (in the associations) while the manifest anxiety is economized by putting him in the position of the experienced man who *teaches* the other elements of love magic.

When Ramoramo talks about his wandering from one relative to the other after his father's early death, he left out an event which must be significant in his life. Next day he told the story of his conflict with Dujero, his brother. When his uncle died, Ramoramo made a clearing and Dujero came behind him. Ramoramo put his sticks into the ground to mark the territory he claimed. Then Dujero came and threw them out. Dujero said: 'Who picked that ground out for a *sagari* garden?' Ramoramo said, 'I did'. Dujero said, 'It is my garden'. So Ramoramo challenged him to meet him there next day and fight. Dujero did not accept this challenge so Ramoramo kept his share. As Dujero had not wanted to give him anything, so, when Dujero died, Ramoramo kept it all for himself and nobody got anything. If he had killed his brother he would have had to make a new village on another ground because of the *rara* or 'blood' for then he would have been forbidden to take fruit, food or fire from his old village.

The *rara* spirit who wants to kill him represents his elder brother or uncle, originally his father, and he will be killed because it was he who wanted to kill.

Dream 7

I was carrying my daughter. My wife's first husband [he is dead now] came and threw the child away. I was crying.

Associations

This man had first married Ramoramo's wife's sister. Then when she died he married Ramoramo's present wife. The dead man was his (classificatory) *tabuna*; that is, he had the same totem as Ramoramo's paternal grandfather. But they belonged to the same group; they used to talk about their lovers and to go to girls together. In the dream the spirit appears as he used to be in real life when he was getting ready for a *sagari* with a club and sweet-smelling flowers. Everybody is getting ready now for Sawaitoja's *sagari* at Boasitoroba and Sipupu. When he got as far as this with the associations he seems to have finished the topic and says, 'Now what shall I tell you? The story of Tokedukeketai? But, of course, you know that.'

At the *sagari* in question, there was a fight between a Sipupu man (Ramorama's *wahana*, i.e. uncle or nephew) and the Boasi-toroba people. His *wahana* and the people of Sipupu were justified in their resentment; a pig was due to them and they did not get it. So he attacked his own people. This is a recognized form of show-ing the Boasitoroba people that they are wrong.[21]

The uncle for whom the feast was held was a great singer. One of his songs was about a widow. Her relations could not pay a pig to her deceased husband's relations, so the new suitor had to send the widow back. The second is about a deserted wife whose former husband says he cannot give her anything more because he has a new wife.

Interpretation

Ramoramo and the other husband, his friend, both stand for the dreamer himself. One of them kills the child; the other cries for it. In the scene of the *sagari* at Boasitoroba we see the same ambi-valence; he attacks his own side to show that they are in the right.

The song shows something else—a love object is relinquished, a desire is unfulfilled. The ambivalence of a father and a love object lost—when we add to this the chance associations of the myth of the cannibal ogre, the Oedipal theme is quite evident. For in this myth the Duau Oedipus Matakapotaiataia[22] kills the cannibal ogre and in another version the cannibal eats his own sons. The feast is in honour of a deceased uncle and here we have the ambivalent fight—the conflict is displaced from father to uncle.

Dream 8

I went up a big hill. I went, I stayed. It kept turning around quicker and quicker. From the moving hill I jumped across to a house. This house was on the top of a coconut tree. A white man

[21] Cf. G. Róheim, 'War, Crime and the Covenant', *J. Clin. Psychopath.*, Mono. Series, No. 1, p. 75 (also on the *ruru*).
[22] Cf. on this myth Géza Róheim, *The Riddle of the Sphinx*, London: Hogarth Press, 1934.

came and I asked, 'Where did I come from?' He raised his hand: 'You came from my hand', and I came down to the earth.

Associations

The white man looked like Usubeni, a missionary, who lived at Giligili. He was a very good man; Booki used to look after his pigs. He used to ask Booki, *'Did the boar fuck the sow?'* If Booki said no, Usubeni would threaten to shoot him.

The place where the dream occurred looked like the whole earth.

The hill was like a hill at Bwebwesco called Sabedi. This is a witch's hill. Kaiaraj of Murua told him that the *werabana*'s hill always turns around. This was a strong man, a young man, his friend. The *werabana* told him: 'Inside the earth there is a trunk that makes the whole world turn around.' The *werabana* went down to the land of the *numu* (spirits of the underworld and of fertility) to see this *arena* (trunk) *gidarina* (small) *gidemusa* (like) *sijaru* (needle).

From the hill he saw the house on the tree. They build houses like that on the mainland to protect them from enemies, for instance, from the white police.

People came from Bunama yesterday. They were going on an *une* (trade-exchange expedition).[23] They told Bebe: 'Why do you tell the white man everything? The government will make our tax big! Then all the white people will come. They will take our ground and wives!' But he replied: 'For ourselves we tell the story because the white think we are only kangaroo.' Then without any apparent reason he remarks: 'If women ask me to have intercourse, my eyes get red like blood from desire.' Then he says: 'Everybody is afraid of a storm because famine is the consequence of a storm.' In such a situation he would exchange his children with other parents and each would eat the other's child.

His maternal grandmother told him all about this. A fire may come from Kelologea and it will burn everything from Kelologea to Duau. If a famine comes again she would say: 'Your mother will give you away in exchange for another child and you will be eaten.'

But since the white people are here, the storm is afraid of the gun and it is finished.

[23] Cf. R. F. Fortune, *Sorcerers of Dobu*, New York: Dutton, 1931; London: Routledge, 1932, p. 200; G. Róheim, *The Origin and Function of Culture*. Nervous and Mental Disease Monograph Series, 1943, p. 31.

Interpretation

What is the role of the white man in this dream? He is a sort of intermediary between the white man's god and the dreamer. 'Where did I come from?' is the question asked by children of all races. 'From my hand,' the missionary replies—that is, he represents the father in the dream. And he came from the sky where the Creator God of the white man lives. The day-stimulus of the dream was the talk with the people of Bunama; the white man will come into the country and take their land and wives. The white man's government is also a powerful protector. The storm does not dare to put in an appearance since the white man has been here. A storm means for the child that their parents are going to eat them or let them be eaten. The association before this theme was his sexual desire and before that we have again the 'white man' anxiety of the natives. The white man will come and take their women.

The whole dream is about the theme, 'Where did I come from?' i.e. about parental coitus. If this is the case we have the explanation in the association as to how the missionary Usubeni enters the dream as a father symbol. He used to ask: 'Has the boar fucked the sow?' Anxiety in connection with the primal scene comes into the picture; he threatens to shoot Booki if he does not help to bring about the 'primal scene' which is the very thing the child does not want to do. On the other hand, the representative of the benevolent Christian Creator God as a father-image allays anxiety in connection with the primal scene.

The piece of Woodlark (Marua) mythology fits well into this setting. The trunk or needle that makes the world turn round is the father's penis in the mother. The witches see this in the nether world where all mysterious things take place. The child saw the father's penis (raised hand) the movement that followed ('hill turning round', i.e. primal scene) and jumps into the protecting house (fantasy of uterine regression). The 'raised hand' (erect penis), originally the source of anxiety, is transformed by the dream work into reassurance and protection.

Dream 9

I dreamt that I caught a fish with a round net. I called my uncle; he came, he ran to me and he took the fish. We went ashore to divide it. Qualeilej [his sister, wife of Tubujaj] was there, Matanogi [daughter of Qualeilej], Booki, Maibogi, Bakira, Dokija. I divided to them. I got angry. I threw fish down and when I looked, the fish was chasing them. I shouted: 'You catch my fish!' Then I jumped up and I was awake.

Associations

The man in the dream is Mwarahusa, Gabebe's father. This was the uncle with whom he stayed and who taught him everything. His sons are now preparing to make a *bwabware* (mortuary ceremony) for him. When this uncle grew old Ramoramo had to help him in the garden. The uncle used to go away and climb a breadfruit tree and Ramoramo used to tell him: 'I have a share in the *une* now, so it throws a bad light on me if you have to climb for fruit. I will give you food if you ask for it!' And then he would send his wife to the garden to fetch food for him. Qualeilej is his sister, Tubujaj's wife. There is great *oboboma* (love) between them. They are always giving things to each other. She 'pets' his pigs (i.e. strokes them or feeds them) and always keeps some yams for him for the hunger month if she has many. He fishes for her and her husband fishes for him. If nobody has any tobacco and she has just one stick of tobacco or one betel-nut he gets it. Matanogi, her daughter, is just like her mother. She obeys only her father and she will only give people things if her father tells her to do it. With regard to Maibogi, he remarks that if one gives him hard words he won't eat. After the death of the man who died recently (the *rara* case) Bakira scolded the others: 'Why don't you get ready for the *basa* (mortuary ceremony: farewell to the dead)? If Tubujaj dies, you will be like that too.' 'If a stranger marries into our village, we have to take good care of him because he loses his life in our village.' Dokija is a man who came back recently from the white people. He is a good worker but he gets angry very easily and goes away.

Then he related episodes in his life in which he behaves the way he behaved in the dream. 'Once when I was young at Donakija I smashed the yam pots. This was because my wife reproached me that I don't work enough, so I smashed the fish, yam, and everything. Some days ago I was waiting for the food in the garden. They were rather slow in bringing it and I wanted to chew (i.e. betel-nuts) but I could not because I had not eaten. So when Deororo brought it I threw all the yams into the bush. Deororo cried'. Then they picked the yams up, washed them and he ate it. Now he is preparing for a *sagari* for Tahabo, his *madiana* ('son', step-son). He appears at that *sagari* as *muri* (follower, i.e. in-law relation).

Interpretation

In this dream we see that he is thoroughly fed up with gifts, uncles, and other social obligations. The uncle deprives him, he does not give it voluntarily. The day-stimulus is the mortuary ceremony they are preparing for this uncle. Although according to the social fiction he is the one to receive gifts, the day-stimulus revives the whole ambivalent 'gift complex' (the fish attacks those who receive). Ultimately, it does not make much difference whether he is to give gifts or receive them, because he must reciprocate them. The remark about his uncle climbing a tree is significant. A *barau* (sorcerer) makes people climb trees to kill them. People would therefore suspect that he wants to kill his uncle. And they would be right. Now he talks about gifts, counter-gifts and love in relationship to his sister. The ambivalent nature of this relationship is perfectly evident. Then comes the theme of 'super-ego', i.e. reproaches and reactions to reproaches either depressive or aggressive. Finally we have the reproach and reaction theme in the husband-wife situation and the oral sources of his aggression (slow in bringing him his food, chewing). I suspect that the fish which the uncle wants to take and which attacks those who are to receive the gift (sister, wife) is a phallic symbol.

Dream 10

My brother came, he embraced me and said, 'You come and we go! I have built a house for you. I am feeding a pig and a hog for you. My body is tired.' He said it and I cried. 'I came to fetch you, we go', he said. 'You go and I stay,' I said. 'I am going to make a *sagari*.' 'I, too,' he said, 'I am sounding the drums for you and later I will make the *sagari*.' 'No, you are dead, and I make the *sagari*,' I replied.

Associations

His younger brother was a good man. He could kill his pig in his absence and if Ramoramo made a feast he would catch a bush pig for him. They helped each other.

His brother ate of the fish called *mweura* which is *borausa* (poison) and died.

The dream is like an event that took place before. His people *(igu susu)* came from Soburasi to fetch him. But he said: 'No, I wait for a *sagari*'. They said, 'Come with us. You will come in a *madawa* (a big Tubetube canoe) with your seeds' (the garden does not count). He replied to his uncle Ta Besa: 'If you had taken me as a child, yes! But now, No!' He could take all his things, they said. But he was afraid that one of them might send him up a tree and he might fall.

Then he describes the preparation for the *sagari* which will be next year. This younger brother of his always used to spear the boys, him too, in play. But he would obey him in everything.

Then he goes back to the people of Soburasi. The way his younger brother speaks in the dream is like the people of Soburasi when they came to fetch him. 'Come with your mother', they said.

Then he thinks, what stories would he tell me? The first that comes to his mind he has told already. It is about a man who runs away from a woman because he thinks that her pubic hair is her belly hanging out. The next story is about a man who comes out of a stone and has intercourse with two sisters every night till finally the mother-in-law catches him and he marries the two sisters. The third story is about To Kedu Keketaj, the Man Eater who marries a woman and whenever a child is born he eats it, until she hides the children and they grow up in hiding and go to a human village.

Interpretation

The first thing that we see from the dream and the association is that making a *sagari* is connected with guilt. The ghost has come to fetch him and the consolation in the dream is: 'No, you are dead and I am alive'. Although he gives the conventional praise to his younger brother, the relation of the two was not without an underlying current of hostility for he mentions that the boy would throw spears at everybody, including him. To go to Soburasi would have been a kind of death; the anxiety is quite manifest when he says that he might have been told to go up a tree and then he would fall, which means that he would have been killed by *barau* (sorcery). The key to the whole anxiety and guilt is contained in the stories. In one story a hidden man has intercourse at night; in the other the father eats all his children except those who have been hidden by the mother.

At the bottom of the guilt and anxiety we find the Oedipus complex; the boy who is afraid that the father will kill him for his hidden incestuous desires.

Dream 11

I was gathering yam, there were many women. I dug the yam out of the ground and many women carried it. We filled up a house with the yam. Matanogi was there and my wife and Deuroro and Majowa.

Associations

He remarks that he has three houses, one in his wife's village, one in his own village and one in the gardens. The house that is being 'filled up' is in his wife's village; he is in the role of an 'in-law relation'.

The scene reminds him of his mother's *sagari* when he was a child. Father and mother sung the *baita* (incantations). 'My mother and my uncles were proud; then we paid them back.' The point in this is (i) that his wife's *sagari* is a repetition of his mother's *sagari*, (ii) that he, quite against custom, identifies himself with his father's clan, 'later we paid them back'.

Then he gives the following songs:

Their leaves get crumpled
Young girls of Rabiaj
Cousin, talk to me first!
The story gets home first.

A young man went to a girl at Rabiaj, a village in Bijawa. 'Talk to me first,' she said, 'then you will get what you want!' i.e. intercourse. The mat they were lying on got crumpled, i.e. they had intercourse, and the news of what happened travelled faster than the young man; by the time he got home to his village they knew all about it.

The next song is about the people of Lomitawa; whatever they do they do it wrong.

Then he gives a dirge about the death of a chief at Soburata and then an incantation which derives the origin of yam from a woman's blood which poured forth when she was cut by her jealous husband.

Interpretation

A *sagari* is for fame; the song about the boy and his mistress emphasizes how fast fame travels. There is a genital element in the *sagari*; filling up the house is filling up a woman. We know that the *sagari* in the dream is a repetition of the one given by his father for his mother. Now he is giving it for his wife and he is taking his father's place. The death of the great chief and the motive of jealousy follow naturally since the latent content is evidently the Oedipus complex (compare dream no. 10. *Ed.*).

Dream 12

I climbed a big hill on a ladder. I went to a *sagari* wanting to get a present. I found a woman; she gave me ripe bananas and said: 'Come and sleep with me.' 'I did not come to make love; I came for the *sagari*,' I replied. Then we went and we had intercourse. My wife was jealous and I beat her. Then we went to court. The Government said I had to pay one pound of paper money. I paid.

Associations

The woman was like Nivano, a very old woman near Panajati. This is an island near Samarai. He chewed betel-nuts with this old woman and she gave the policemen betel-nuts. She was their friend. The *sagari* was like the one for his first wife at Kebebeku. The *toni-kasa* (owners of village) people, Inois and Tanusiani said: 'To-morrow we pay back'. But Booki and Tabujaj replied: 'Oh, no, you can't pay back.'

The woman in the dream is also like Naomi. She was his *rawer-awe* (mistress). He had To Poru (the round or nice one: name of a *mwari*, the white armshell of the *une exchange*) and passed it on to Tubuduau at Dobu. The woman in the dream was really like Naomi. She roasted some pork for him before they slept. She gave him a bunch of bananas; that is the general custom before sleeping together. Once a woman sent a big bunch of bananas to him through her nephew. The bananas were wanted by her husband who was sick. He wanted to send them to his in-laws. The house where he has intercourse with the woman is a house in Tubetube. Tabesa, a young woman, sent by Tabesa's mother (whom he also calls mother in the narrative) came and took him by the hand. She took him away from some young girls who wanted to have intercourse with him, but would have killed him by their witchcraft *(werabana)*.

The scene before the court: Tau Didimajero, his *wahana* (nephew) went to court like that. He wanted to have intercourse with a woman, this was Mwagarea's wife. She made a fuss about it and they put him in prison for three months. He dreamt this the night after he wanted to 'make court' for his ground. This refers to the ground we had built our house on. He says that some of the men who were clearing the jungle for us cut down some trees on his land; it should be taken out of their pay.

He tells some more amorous adventures, how he fought for his girl with her lover, and says, 'I would have fought for my ground with those men today if there had been no government'. Then he sings a song about a young woman who walked on the shore with her little son. She saw a young man and said to her mother: 'You carry your grandson. I go for shells, i.e. for coitus.'

Interpretation

Climbing the ladder is a symbolic coitus. The interpretation of the *sagari's* genital significance is confirmed here. The woman in the dream reminds him of several of his lovers, of an old woman and of the dreaded *werabana*, the witches who are always called 'our mothers'. The day-stimulus is the conflict about the ground inherited in the maternal clan, Mother Earth.

Ramoramo is the son in the song, whom his mother leaves to go to her lover. He has always fought for his women and his land (Oedipus situation).

Dream 13

> I cut a man with a club and he got angry and cut me. I caught his club and we pulled it one way and the other. Then he said: 'Stop! you pay me a *bagi*, [Shell string in the *une*].' I stopped, and I gave him a *bagi*.

Associations

He had a fight like this with Diaiki. Diaiki is his *manua tasina*, i.e. totem brother. They fought because of the girls. Diaiki also had an affair with Ramoramo's wife. Ramoramo cut him and then made peace by giving him *mwari* and a pig. The way the fight is stopped in the dream corresponds to custom in general, if somebody says this fight cannot go on.

The man with whom he fights in the dream, however, does not look like Diaiki. He looks like Suaratega, Ramoramo's uncle, who was the leading personage of Kebelogwari. Suaratega told him how he handled the problem of courtship when he was a young man.

This is how the *gwari* took place: 'We went together to every village and one went up to the girl. I always let the others go first and I went last. This is the way of a good man. He will say, "No, don't take me; take my friend".'

The point in this narrative is what the speaker does not say. That he got the girls nevertheless, that they wanted him more than anybody else. Suaratega was eventually killed by the *barau* because of his success in gardens and *sagaris*.

The way they put the club *(wepasi)* between them is a scene that took place at a *sagari* between Talokapu and Mogej.

When the war was finished between Sipupu and Lomitawa, Lomitawa gave a *bagi* to Sipupu; Sipupu gave a *mwari* to Lomitawa. Ramoramo's maternal grandfather was killed in this war.

The fight also reminds him of a fight he had with his real uncle. He tried to cut his uncle with a knife. Ramoramo gave his uncle a pig; his uncle gave him a dog.

Interpretation

He fights with his 'brother'. Sociologically they are rivals, enemies. But behind the brother we find the uncle, the man who represents authority, as his opponent. Moreover the man who represents authority is also the one who knows how to manage love affairs. The casual remark about the *gwari* (courtship) and the polite gesture in letting the other man have the girl shows the emphasis on over-compensation.

Suaratega was the great man of the village. He had everything—fame, women, gardens—and Ramoramo challenges him as he challenged his uncle. He remarks perhaps the whole thing took place in the *numu world* (spirit world, i.e. in the unconscious). Then in a disconnected fashion: 'Our mothers are not witches. They don't kill us,' i.e. our mothers *are* witches, they *do* kill us. Witches are always descending to the *numu* world to have intercourse with the chief of the underworld (Tau Mudurere), i.e. the fight is the consequence of the primal scene.

Dream 14

(Dreamt the night before Dream 13, but told afterwards.)
    We pulled out a boat, we sailed, we ran; it went off a reef.
They put handcuffs on me, and they said: 'You kill a pig; then
we shall let you go.'

Associations

The boat was like a big steamer with many white people. The
place where it goes on the reef is like Bwaruada. They handcuffed
Notura like that because of Bebe's wife. Mr Rich *lokapu* Lemwasaj
like that because of his affair with a married woman.

Then he relates a story in which he worked on a white man's
boat and was beaten by a white man.

Interpretation

. The associations do not give us very deep insight. Bwaruada is
the place where I live and I am the only white man with whom he
is in contact at the time of the dream, so one would suspect his
aggressions are now directed against me and that he is being 'locked
up' or *lokapu* in its Duau form in the dream for these aggressions.

Conclusions

The first dream reveals the Oedipus complex. His classificatory
son who is mourning for his real son is trying to kill him i.e. the
Kuhua whom Ramoramo calls 'son' is in mourning. The dead
person is a child, Kuhua's son. Mourner and sorcerer are closely
related, guilt is the connecting link. In the second dream we discover that although sociologically making a *sagari* can only mean
succeeding to his mother's brother's dignity (since the organization
is matrilineal) psychologically it means replacing his father. The
third dream spells incest and guilt with the mother's brother as
avenger and the next dream follows the same lines. In the fifth
dream the father is again revealed as the real enemy of the son.
The sixth dream is clearly a primal scene dream in which the
dreamer makes the transition from the passive (voyeur) to the
active (exhibitionist) role. The seventh is an anxiety dream, the
father figure threatens to deprive him of his daughter (girl). The
eighth is a primal scene dream and throws some light on witch
beliefs. The ninth dream deals with the ambivalence underlying all

F   *161* relationships. The next dreams (10, 11, 12), give the key to the understanding of the *sagari*: filling up a house is making mother pregnant. The thirteenth and fourteenth dreams reveal his ambivalent attitude both to his uncle and to the white man who wants his dreams.

2. KAUANAMO

Kauanamo is certainly a typical representative of his culture. If there is one thing that characterizes this old man it is his incessant greed or demanding things. Doketa characterizes him as *taubada gejogejoj*, an ugly or mean old man. If he sees a single betel-nut in the basket of a young girl or boy, he will ask for it although he has many betel-nuts and nobody dares to refuse because they are so afraid of his powers as a *barau*. Doketa also told us that the old man was not giving us the real incantations for the *barau* art. 'Why not?' I asked. 'What is missing?' 'The text is all right,' he said, 'but he does not spit when he says it.' 'Spitting' is not an exact translation; he really means emitting the saliva through his teeth, sort of withholding it and emitting it at the same time. 'If Kauanamo did this a cloud would arise from his mouth and we who listen to him and all the people in the neighbourhood would be killed.' I had to accept this as a valid reason for ethnographical inaccuracy and take the words without the saliva.

Whatever gifts he received he accepted with utmost stoicism— or asked for more. In contrast to others like Bebe or Seguragura or Jarekeni he could never say that he was pleased or smile when he got a gift. Once when we had to go to Samarai, we decided that we would bring a really magnificent gift from the white man's stores to see whether we could break through his wall of indifference. We got him whatever we could think of: that is all the white man's goods a native coveted. There was an undershirt, a bush-knife, tobacco, calico, a pipe, sugar, and I don't know what else. He accepted the gifts, and took them home to his house without a word or gesture of 'thank you'.

Next day, however, when he came to see me, he made the terse comment: *'Be sopi nigeia,'*—'But there was no soap'. It took him the whole day to think of something that was not included in his bundle. Perhaps the old saying *nomen est omen* is valid here for his name Kauanamo means, 'mouth-only'.

These are his *ipsissima verba* about his childhood and life:

'I was a young boy when the people of Panamosi[24] took me. I left mother and father behind and while I was at Panamosi father died. We went to Murua (Woodlark) and came back again and went again.

'When I grew up a little I heard a talk (i.e. I understood what was said to me). My mother said to me: "You look out how your father does! How he gets his *bagi* from Tubetube, his *mwari* from Dobu. Don't be *uwauwa* (mad, or doing things the wrong way) and don't steal from the gardens and don't make love to married women." I grew somewhat[25] and I made a little *sagari* with yams which I got from my own little garden. My playfellows are all dead now. *Some boys were of the aggressive type—these we chased back to their mothers.* These were the boys who when we made a play *sagari* always wanted to be the *toni-butu* (master of fame, giver of the ceremony). *If prevented he would get a stick and smash all the yams* (he is talking about a certain boy now). This boy was *wahagu* (i.e. my uncle—classificatory), a little older than I was. He died very soon; the *barau* killed him because he was too wild.

'They take a *sumwana* (particle of garment, saliva, blood, nail, hair, or the like) and they fry it with pepper and they make magic and call his name and then that man will die. Our body becomes soft. If a *barau* eats something (like sugar-cane) they take his saliva and also put it into the bundle. Some *barau* will do this against a bad *barau*.[26]

'People learn *barau* from their father or uncle. When I came back there was nobody to teach me since my father was dead.'[27]

The following statements are comments on what ought to be and have nothing to do with reality.

'Our old people told us not to go near the girls because if we did we would later have intercourse with them. Our ancestors did that and so they made their sisters pregnant. Therefore they stopped it.

'If we live with father and mother, the first thing they tell us is not to go to the grave and not to eat fruit from father's village;

---

[24] An island not far from Duau. The people belonged to his mother's clan.
[25] The word used is *esa-esa sara*; *esa-esa* means chief or rich man. *Esa-esa sara* also means to play.
[26] The latter remark is a colossal piece of *hypocrisy* for the benefit of the white man. There is no such thing as a good *barau*.
[27] Another outstanding lie. He is well known as a great *barau*.

it would give us *togutogura* (coughing sickness). Don't walk alone but with friends! If you go alone the *barau* or the *werebana* will kill you!'

Dream 1

I dreamt this before I came to you [middle of April, 1930].

I heard the voice of a witch calling, 'Kauanamo, don't walk about. The sorcerers or the witches will kill you.' I woke up frightened.

Associations

'Once I went for a *bagi* (string of shells obtained in the *kune*) and the people offered me food too, and said, "You cook your food." But I was afraid to eat and I went home to my wife although I was very hungry. My wife cooked food for me and I ate that.

'I heard only a voice, but that was exactly what my mother used to tell me when I was a little child.

'I saw a gully in the dream, a hole. The witch in the dream wanted to put me in the hole. The gully was like the gully of Majawa *where Matakapotaiataia was born'*.

He does not know that he is still 'free-associating' to the dream,[28] but he now chooses to relate a myth.

'A woman was pregnant and she was delivered of a pig. The pig mated with a bush pig and was delivered of twins, a boy and a girl. The sow went into the garden and people speared and ate the animal. *The children cried for their dead mother and got the belly.* They took the belly to the water to clean it, and they opened it. They found *bagi* and *mwari* and a *dona* and a *somwakupwas* and a *mwau*[29] and earrings and a stone axe in the belly. So they took all this out, cleaned it in the water and then they cleaned themselves and made themselves flash and they went to their father. Their father said, "Who is this?" They replied, "You killed our mother and ate her[30] and these things we have got out of her belly." He got

---

[28] That is, I have stopped asking about the dream and he thinks that theme is finished. It is left to him to choose a theme.

[29] *Bagi* and *mwari* are the red shell strings and the white arm-shells respectively. They circulate in opposite directions. The *somwakupwa* is an inferior kind of *bagi*. The *dona* is a string-shell with a disc. The *mwau* is a white shell rose pin. All these including the earrings and the stone axes are *kune* objects.

[30] Here the myth explains that the father was the owner of the spear that killed the pig.

all the people to come to see all the things the children had got out. Then the children had a talk with their father and they gave names to the *bagi*, calling them Pretty Snake, Fine Weather Bird, Red Tongue. The *mwari* they called Ginger-man, We-go-to-bathe-at-Quaraiuwa, Dirty Skin, and so forth. They decided that the *mwari* should go round to the east and the *bagi* to the west and this is how the *kune* was started. The children wanted to wash the excrements out of the belly but instead of excrement they found these things.'

Interpretation

The identity of witch and mother is perfectly clear. The wish in the dream is to go into the mother's hole, i.e. the hole where the mythical hero was born. This uterine regression is transformed into anxiety by the super-ego (as represented by the voice). Mataka-potaiataia is the Oedipus hero. The uterine regression is the regressive equivalent of this Oedipus wish.

One of the associations of the dream was about *bagi* and food anxiety. The myth told as an association relates the origin of the *kune*—in terms of a body destruction fantasy of the orphaned children (as demonstrated by the theoretical propositions of Melanie Klein). The father appears in the role of the cannibal ogre who eats the mother (sow).

Dream 2

I dreamt of a person with a big belly. It was a witch who had died of the *rara* (blood). They said: 'Stay at home, or we will kill you. Your brother has been sick for a long time and you go to Bwaruada. If he has eaten his yams and his time is finished then you can leave him.'

Associations

His wife had said the night before: 'Don't stay at Bwaruada, tell the doctor I am sick'. The witch was the spirit of his dead *tubuna* (grandmother). *Rara* is a disease that afflicts those who have eaten food in an enemy village. He adds a detail to the dream. The witch in the dream cut him and made his navel bleed.

Interpretation

The witch is his wife. The facts that she has a big belly (preg-

165

nancy) and cuts his navel make it very likely that she stands also for his mother. He is really afraid to leave home because of his wife (mother). That is what every child is told: don't go far, the sorcerers or witches might catch you. The detail about the bleeding indicates castration anxiety. The other dream factor is his guilt feeling about his brother who was actually sick and died while we were living there.

Dream 3

I dreamt that a child had died and there were many mourners. There were two *tokwatokway*, Sine Mweire [Woman Round] and Sine Gaurejana [Woman from Cave]. The second was the older one. They cried and danced and said 'Kauanamo! you are asleep and we came to see you. Rise and give us a present [of the *iwara* type], yams and coconuts. Many a time we have come to wail for you and you have not given us our pig or our yams. We look after your village and if the *barau* makes incantations against you we stop it; if the witches do the same, we stop it. You are Kauanamo, our child and if we left you the witches would kill you!'

Associations

There is very little in the way of day-stimulus except his eternal complaints about being here (in Sipupu) and about wanting to go back to his village. The spirits who appear in the dream as mourners came to the burial of Monadijero, his sister's daughter.

He enumerates the mourners and then talks about the spirits:

'These *tokwatokway* near the village are like our people. If we cry they come and cry and if we go for an *une* they go with us. My mother used to say, 'Sine Mweire and Sine Gaureja are your mothers. They will always protect you against witches and sorcerers.'

The associations are too meagre for an interpretation.[31]

Dream 4

We went for a *sagari* to Mwaruquasia. They were beating a man called Rugujamwej. He asked for our help and we came to the rescue. His enemy again ran at him and told us to desist from helping the man; then he can kill him: 'Why do you want to kill him?' I asked. 'For a pig!' he said. 'Why do you help my enemies,

[31] *Editor's note:* Since we know from the previous dream that his wife is pregnant, Kauanamo refers here to his ambivalence regarding his as yet unborn child.

the people of the Quanaura?' he said. He threw a spear at us and the missionary of Soburata said: 'Don't do that. This is the time of Christianity. Stop it.' We refused the food they gave us.

Associations

The man in the dream is called Rugujamwej (went in waiting). He is a good man but weak, *taj nadigega waine* (a man like a woman).

To the *sagari* at Mwaruquasia he remarks: 'Kedarakija had a *sagari* there once (relation of his father)'. At the dance they sang this song.

> Virgins their dirt
> In the district of Joho, I bathe naked
> Cloud of Jaibweuri [plain at Kelologeia]
> Standing it covers me.

A Kelologeia man went to a girl to make love. He bathed at Joho. But he was homesick for Kelologeia.

A man called Wijawija attacked another one called Laseni at a Soburata *sagari*, saying that he had not been repaid for his pig. He cut the other man's neck with a knife. The result was that Laseni, the injured party, received a whole pig to 'make peace'. One of the men who helped him was his cousin Waramaija. He has just sent his wife to ask Waramaija for food. His other helper was a man called Nupa-ura, his *wari-esa* (a man who has the same name that he has). He is an *esa-esa*; another word for *esa-esa* is *masura kadi kasau* = where food accumulates. By the way, he says to me, 'give me my rice!'

The missionary's words were actually spoken at a *sagari* at Soburata by the missionary Wasselo, his cross-cousin.

Interpretation

We cannot get very far on the basis of these associations. One element we can see, Kauanamo is aiding a 'woman' (man like a woman) against an 'angry man'. Also, that the 'dispenser of food', the chief, is essentially a female ideal and that they go to the *sagari* oscillating between aggression (male) and the desire to be an *esa-esa* (female). Moreover, that going to a *sagari* in a foreign village is an ambivalent matter, they want to go yet they are home-sick to return as soon as possible. But all this does not disclose the latent dream content.

Dream 5

We sailed and we caught a fish near an island called Sarupaj [means island-vegetable; good water there] and then we sailed to another island called Bunora [sea shell; no water to drink there] and *a ghost said*: 'Kauanamo, you bring our net.' The name of that net was *Pasikeda* and we fished and we caught a man. He said: 'I am not a fish but a man. My name is Utau [You man]. Take me to my sister Kedebwejara [Road ripe].' Kedebwejara said, 'You caught my brother. If you give me a basket full of *mwari* and *bagi* you can kill him and eat him.'

She then made a *mona* [pudding; taro and coconut oil]. This brother and sister are from the same grandmother.

Associations

The Ghost: The voice was the voice of a man called Qualieli, his *ejena* (in-law relation). This was a man from Panamosi. The fishermen of Panamosi used to come to sell fish at Duau. This Qualieli was an important man in the *une*. His *gumagi* (i.e. *une* partner), a man called Tapa Ruruana stole his wife. (The wife was Kauanamo's *nuhuna*, class sister). They had a quarrel. Qualieli said: 'Why do you take my wife?' The other man said, 'What are you going to do to me?'

The Net: The net Pasikeda was owned by Bisari. Bisari was his *kana gwara's* (mother's sister) son, his *tasina* (ortho-cousin). This is the man who took him to Panamosi because Nisari's mother wanted him. During his stay in Panamosi his father died. (He has told me this several times). 'Bisari would say to me, "Take whatever you like from my basket. Then you will go to the women, offer it to them and you will have intercourse".' Bisari reminds him of his own father. He was a great giver. He used to say: 'There is my wife, there are my children. They will all gather round me and cover me (i.e. love me).'

The name of the net is Pasikeda (Grown on Road). If you say that to a man that is equivalent to calling him a 'son of a bitch'. Somebody said this to Bisari and therefore he called the next net that he made Pasikeda. (This is according to custom. They are always consoling themselves for what they have suffered.) About the man called Utau (You Man) whom they catch in the net, he has the following observations, 'I got five *bagi* from Utau Didijara mwedujena, Gomakarakedakeda, Siboigaj, Mwaraurau, Senubeta.' The names mean 'Thorn of the Grass Didijara', 'Lizard on the

Road', 'Their own Thing', 'Walker', 'Cough'. From the two islands mentioned in the dream he used to bring many fish as *pokara*, i.e. presents to elicit *bagi*.

The man whom they catch is therefore his *une* partner. Now, *une* partner means *gu magi* (my betel-nut), i.e. something to *chew*. The idea of catching a man takes him back to the pre-white days with cannibal raids.

A man called Enoeno (Sleeping) was caught by his sister's husband. This was in revenge for a brother of Kauanamo who had been caught and eaten by the enemy. A woman called Bukau said, as in the dream: 'Pass it on for *bagi*'. He was bought and eaten by the people of Wewekona, a village in Majawa.

Interpretation

The voices in the dream represent the super-ego. In Dream 1 the super-ego is the mother, here it is the father. But beside the father two other images are superimposed—(i) that of a man whose wife was stolen, (ii) that of his adoptive father at Panamosi.

The overtly all too giving behaviour of his father and his adoptive father increases his guilt feelings, for there can be scarcely any doubt about it, the name of Utau (You Man) is not chosen by accident but represents Kauanamo himself. This great eater (Mouth only) whom everybody characterizes as a greedy child was a spoilt child, a fact which increased his greediness and also his guilt feelings. The great eater is going to be eaten. The associations lead to a man who was caught and eaten on a revenge expedition for Kauanamo's brother. Therefore sibling rivalry has evidently something to do with the guilt feelings. Then there is the man whose wife was stolen and whom he identifies with his father and the adoptive father who urged him to take his things and use them in winning women—clearly showing the Oedipus sources of his guilt feeling.

And he finishes the session by a *gau* (hiding incantation) against witches, i.e. the mother who has been transformed into an object of dread, both on account of pre-Oedipal (oral) and of Oedipal feelings. This is the incantation:

Sine	*Kuku*	*Maijero*
Woman	Sound	Come to us
Kaua	*bwaga*	*jagauli*
Her	ocean	I hide [i.e. cover with fog]

Igu	*kasa*	*jagauli*
My	village	I hide
Igu	*waga*	*jagauli*
My	boat	I hide
Jagau	*jagau*	*kausi*
I hide	I hide	cover
Jarujaruagu	*makamakajaugu*	
My soul	my shadow	
Jagau,	*jagau*	*kausi*
I hide,	I hide,	I shut
Jagau,	*jagau*	*bodej*
I hide,	I hide	close

While saying this incantation they hit a tree with a ceremonial axe. He shows how they do it with his hand, representing the axe and my hand as the tree.

The witch who is a sound is a witch at Dutuna Point. There used to be an echo there. The choice of this incantation is not accidental; the voice is the super-ego. He hides (i.e. regresses into the womb), because he chops the tree (mother) with his axe (tooth, penis).

Dream 6

A person from Bwebweso called Dibwajaore [their magic, meaning magic leaves, *bwajawe*] came and said: 'You get up and we go! Bwebweso dance we dance.' My soul got up and said: 'Didwajaore! Where are we to go to dance?' He said, 'We go to Bwebweso and on their dancing place we dance.' We were there and he started the dance with the following song:

Bwebweso	*goma*	*keseba*
Bwebweso	young	girls
Tau	*wae lemaej*	
Man	you take from each other	

They danced and then they sang the second half of the song:

'Jaita	*kami*	*sibonu*
Who is	your	young boy
Nuana	*wagenonaya*	
His mind you turn around		
Nekite		*idoudou*
[name of his daughter]		cries

Jaira	*be*	*jagebeg*
I go back and I see her		
Tau	*wae*	*lemae*
Men	you go on taking from each other.	

Associations

When he dreamt this dream he was sick. They came for his soul to fetch him to a dance at Bwebweso.

Once before, his friends woke him for a dance and then they made this song at Quauaura:

Wainari	*iwari*	
Wainari	sings	
Weyagana	*bwebwejana*	
Weyagana	pretty	
[name of a flower]		
Gwama	*katuna*	*wejej*
child	push	back
To	*kawe*	*radiradina*
What	tree	its colour
Tabadi	*gejojowej*	
We stick in hanging from the side		

The song is based on the following event: A man came to make love to a woman but she had her child with her. He said: 'Push the child away. I have brought a pretty flower *(ane)*. It may stick out and hurt the child.' She replies: 'It won't hurt the child.'

The women of Bwebweso wanted to have intercourse with Negita's father (i.e. Kauanamo) but he says: 'No, I am going back to my daughter.'

This Dibwajaore was a man he never knew, but when he was a little boy his ancestors used to talk about him as a great dancer.

Interpretation

A sick man is afraid of death. The spirit comes to fetch him. But it is for a dance and for love-making with the young girls of Bwebweso. For him these mythical beings mean his own daughter towards whom the old man's libido is directed. The song reflects the Oedipus situation. The child is pushed aside when the adults are having intercourse. The flower that sticks out symbolizes the penis.

Dream 7

I walked about in the bush and the people of Guj chased me. 'Why did you come?' they asked me. 'I came for betel-nuts,' I replied. A man called Napijeni led them. They chased me and I ran. I jumped into a gully. They wanted to kill me. I said: 'Now you beat me for nothing. I came for betel-nuts.' They said: 'We planted our betel-nuts. They are ours. You can take what is in the bush.' We went to a house. They cooked food and put it down beside me, saying: 'You eat.' I refused, saying: 'I came for betel-nuts and you hit me. Now it is up to you. If you want to, you can kill me.' I came away with betel-nuts and food. 'You go,' they said, 'and never come back.'

Associations

Napijeni is his *rabaraba*, his brother's son. Napijeni calls him 'my father'. He looks ugly. He has a lot of fun. If he sees a woman he will say: 'My wife, I had intercourse with her before.' He comes from the inland village with yams for which he gets coconuts. He is Kauanamo's son. The place is a village called Sumarawe. He goes there quite often to Napijeni for his betel-nuts. He would call and Napijeni would come down from the garden on the hill to bring him this betel-nut. Napijeni is just like his son. The gully into which he jumps is Kekura gully, the place of Matakapotaiataia. Matakapotaiataia's footstep is visible there. It is his place of *gagasa* (pride). Matakapotaiataia is *tau tokumalina* (a bad man) *Gamwasoara arena* (the root of anger). He was really chased like that once. This was at Kebelugua (his uncle's bush village). He was on a perfectly innocent visit to his uncle. They thought he came to get *sumwana* (left-overs of food, spittle, blood, clothing, and the like) to *barau* them. They chased him and he ran away. This uncle's name was Selilo (he was not a real uncle, only an older member of the same totem-clan).

This uncle was held by the young people the way he is held in the dream. The words: 'You beat me for nothing' were said by this uncle. 'I came for the single girls.' He was in the village and asleep when the shouts woke him. The men shouted. 'We caught Selilo. We thought he came for married women or *barau*.' They will all rally against any stranger; he is supposed to *come for barau or to steal their wives*. But a light is enough to drive them away. Then they will all run away for *omaiamaia* (shame).

The words: 'We planted our betel-nuts; they are ours. You can take what is in the bush,' are what old men always say to the young men who walk about at night. He often says it himself to the young men in his village (Kebelugua). 'What I planted is mine! Let me chew it and when I die it will be yours!' The young men want the betel-nuts so that they can give them as presents to the girls to whom they go for *gwari*.

When he was young, Mwajtagili said the same thing to him. Mwajtagili was his sister's husband. He protested and said: 'I did not come to steal betel-nuts, I came for the girls.' They thought he came for *barau* or stealing.

The words in which he refuses to take the food were said by some people of Quanaura who were chased by the Guj people. 'Next time they come with their yams for coconuts, we shall refuse the exchange and beat them.' Taweroga said this, his *tasina* (brother) of Quanaura. This is a quiet man, a good gardener, and a great singer.

Interpretation

Another dream that is dominated by his guilt feelings. His main opponent or persecutor is a man whom he calls 'son', and who calls him 'father'. We often find in analyzing our patients that the son plays the role of the reincarnated father, in the sense of the Uranos-Kronos-Zeus myth; the deed demands retribution to fit the crime.

Actually we find the younger man in the role that is typical of old men, while he, Kauanamo, is a young Kauanamo, once more out to kill the old men and to steal their wives. The intimate link in the associations between girls, stealing, sorcery and betel-nuts makes this quite clear. Of course Kauanamo protests his innocence. He uses the words of the 'quiet man', his brother, yet these very words were spoken in a mood of fighting.

But more important than all this is the gully into which he jumps. It looks like Kekura gully, the place in which the mother of Mata-kapotaiataia hides when she is afraid of the man-eating giant Tokedukeketai and is pregnant with Matakapotaiataia, the Papuan Oedipus[32] (cf. Dream 1). Kaunamo jumps into his mother's vulva, the gully, *for like every barau he is Matakapotaiataia*. This is the latent wish fulfilment in the dream: the *gwari* and the betel-nuts are symbolic representatives of the same. For the old man, the

[32] Cf. G. Róheim, *The Riddle of the Sphinx*, p. 182.

young men represent the father image and the rest of the dream is dictated by the super-ego.

Conclusions

In the first dream the witch is revealed as the mother and the trading expedition as the move 'away from the mother'. Father murders mother (primal scene) the sons take the 'good body content' out of mother and make peace with father on basis of the *kune*. The second dream reveals his anxiety about not being at home; the voice of the super-ego in the dream is again the mother's voice. In the fifth dream we again have the voice of conscience; this time it is the father's voice. The father is identified with a man whose wife he has stolen. The associations point to the Oedipus complex. They show us the effect the 'good father' of a matrilineal society has on the formation of a personality. The goodness of the father increases the guilt feelings. Moreover we can also see how the fact that they are 'spoiling' the child most of the time[33] while at the same time traumatizing it orally, creates the 'oral aggressive' character type described by Bergler. Siblings are not wanted; guilt for these death wishes is dealt with in the cannibal raid. The spirits are coming to fetch him in the sixth dream but Eros transforms death into coitus with his own daughter. The last dream is again an anxiety dream. Kauanamo, the great *barau* is guilty and his guilt is based on the Oedipus complex. His 'son' who now has the woman appears in the role of a father. We can definitely see from all this that the great sorcerer is no less afraid of people than they are of him.

What follows from these two cases?

(i) From the point of view of institutions and beliefs:

The dreams of Kauanamo give us a hypothetical clue to the meaning of the great ceremonial trade and barter institution or *kune*. It is really the body destruction fantasy of a thwarted child projected beyond the boundaries and represented as a restitution instead of a destruction. If this hypothesis helps us to understand the details of ritual myth and magic we shall assume it is a valid one.

Surely the analysis of a *barau* (evil sorcerer) must have some

---

[33] It is true that they beat the child sometimes and therefore, compared to Australian aborigines they are severe. But on the whole the children are spoilt little tyrants whose *gewana* (demanding) they often indulge.

bearing on the psychology of black magic. We see from these dreams that Kauanamo has strong guilt feelings (the voice = super-ego) and anxiety (his narrative practically starts with how the *barau* got people). Nor can there be any doubt about the oral sources of Kauanamo's ever-demanding character, which is just what the people themselves regard as typical of their own 'ethos'. If somebody would, however, deduce the conclusion from these facts that in this matrilineal society personality is based on the pre-Oedipal situation, we would be justified in calling attention to the dreams in which the voice (super-ego) is paternal and to the references to the Oedipus myth of Matakapotaiataia.

Then we have Ramoramo, a less typical and more virile personality. We know that he is this way through my personal contact. In a difficulty, he is more likely to use his spear than his knowledge of sorcery. The dreams confirm this, as Oedipus and genital motives dominate the scene. In Dreams 1 and 2 we have guilt connected with the father-son situation. The cannibal orgre (Toke-dukeketai) is a projection of the father image. Then, again we find Ramoramo chased by his totem-bird or in an open fight with his elder brother. Even the *sagari* (food distribution ceremony) with its obvious oral symbolism becomes genital and Oedipal.

(ii) From the point of view of the personalities:

I said that Ramoramo was less typical than Kauanamo. By that I mean less like the projected type, less like they appear to be. But whether he is also less like the way they are—that is quite a different question. It should also be noted that Ramoramo is about thirty-five; Kauanamo about sixty-five; and that Kauanamo is a *barau;* Ramoramo is just a layman. The question remains whether the analytical understanding of the institutions will yield the same latent meanings as the interpretations of the dreams, in which they occur. If there is a difference, a hypothesis is needed to explain that difference.

The society in which Ramoramo and Kauanamo live is matrilineal and matrilocal. Any anthropologist of the 'cultural' school would come to the conclusion that they have no Oedipus complex. The point is however that you cannot arrive at reliable conclusions regarding personality and the unconscious without analyzing dreams.

This paper is of historical significance. It shows certain initial attempts to transpose psychoanalytic technique into field research methods. The play technique if culturally adapted may be more promising than the technique as applied in the analysis of adults. Dr Róheim was concerned with culturally defined variables of the Oedipus complex. He used mainly European-made dolls for his play analyses which were modelled after Melanie Klein's concepts. As a result Róheim provides us with field observations of an unusual and provocative nature.

8

Play Analysis with Normanby Island Children[1]

GÉZA RÓHEIM

1. INTRODUCTION

In 1930 I spent nine months on Normanby Island, which belongs to the D'Entrecasteaux group, and is inhabited by a people related to the Massim of British New Guinea and to the Trobriand Islanders. Dobu is a small island between Normanby and Fergusson Island, so that Normanby Island or Duau is the same culture area as Dobu. The people live in small matrilinear village groups in monogamous families. A man sometimes has two wives but this is an exception. Brother and sister are taboo to each other only about the puberty period. They are weaned when about a year old by sending them to the grandmother or some other relative. They are taught to defecate and urinate outside and sometimes beaten if very disobedient. There is also a castration threat to prevent excessive masturbation; it may come from the father, mother or uncle; but masturbation is tolerated when the children are very small. They have a latency period and are aware of this fact. The children are not subjected to vigorous discipline, indeed, very often it is the child who tells the grown-up what to do and what not to do.

The society itself is typically matrilinear, with the father as the person who plays with the child and pets it, while authority is vested in the uncle, mother, brother. Since the child goes to live with his uncle only somewhere between his eighth and sixteenth year, this does not mean that the father does not actually discipline the child in any way. Marriage is officially matrilocal; in reality, however, it may be bi-local, and the localization is subject to individual variations.

I played with the children in our garden, introducing new toys from time to time and sometimes giving the toys names to get the role game started. I did not give them any interpretations as I

[1] This paper first appeared in *The American Journal of Orthopsychiatry*, 11 (1941).

thought the risk in doing this in a group would be greater than the possible advantage gained from a research point of view. Also, it was easier for them to overcome their shyness in a group than when alone.

2. THE CHILDREN AT PLAY

The group consists of two girls, Deororo (age about 9), Daunay (may be 8) and two boys, Ilaisa and Tobwariey (about 7). Deororo is pouting and flirting with Ilaisa. When told that she is the girl doll's 'mother' she replies with an angry negative but affirms that Ilaisa is its father. 'Well, then you two are husband and wife,' I say. Deororo's indignation knows no bounds. 'That is an enormous lie and if I am to be told things of this kind I won't come any more!' She keeps tearing the grass, is very nervous, and says she is working for her food. At the second meeting we have a big male doll, a big female doll, a small male and small female doll, two smaller red Indian dolls, a dog, a rabbit, a snake, a red and a yellow bird, and a mirror. The red bird is a *gewara* (small parrot), Deororo's totem. I give the big male doll to the girls, the female dolls to the boys. The girls protest, 'Let the boys have their brother, we want our sister'. Now Ilaisa takes the big male doll— this is Deororo's husband, the big female doll is her sister-in-law. The small male doll is Deororo's child. The doll with a feather is his (Ilaisa's) dim-dim wife (the only white woman he has seen is my wife). Says Ilaisa to Deororo, 'Your child is crying, give it milk!' Her retort, 'It is your child, it is crying because you don't carry it!' Here we have a 'custom' element, because the father is the *to-sapwara*, the 'petter' of the child. Then he declares that the smaller doll is not Deororo's child, but her husband. The big male doll is Deororo's husband, the small one is Daunay's husband. The big male doll is Deororo's husband, the small one is her lover, and now the two fight for Deororo. Ilaisa is now dramatizing the Oedipus theme, father and son are fighting for the mother. The girls say, 'Your brother is losing his *hwaraj* (pubic covering, trouser) but our sister has a good skirt.' The male doll is a bit broken on the front; Deororo was jealous and stabbed her husband's stomach with a spear. She knocked him on the head with a club and opened his stomach. Deororo's retort: 'Ilaisa is jealous, he bites his wife, she is pregnant'. Ilaisa says Deororo's husband is calling her to have intercourse. The smaller boy does not say a word, he is a *manibus* (the natives of the interior 'man in the bush'—ignorant). Deororo says the small doll is Ilaisa's son and his anus is visible. Ilaisa says the small doll is Deororo's child and has seen Deororo's anus. Deororo declares she will beat Ilaisa on the way home for this. We see the same projection of sexuality as in Central Australia[2] but everything is much more veiled or inhibited here.

25 March, 1930, we have Ilaisa, Deororo and Daunay. They start with choosing the dolls of the same sex to play with but this does not last very long. Ilaisa says, 'Your husband is crying, take him in your arms and rock him.' (Offers her the big doll and then the small one.' Deororo says, 'Your wife is crying, take her, rock her.' Ilaisa calls the big doll *tamagu*—my father. The small one, *tasigu*—my brother. Then he discovers all sorts of faults with the big doll and finally throws it at the girls, saying, 'Here is your husband, keep him!' They throw the big girl doll back saying, 'Here is your wife!' Now they start a real *lojawe* (love making) game. The big doll sticks out its tongue; he is calling the girls for *lojawe*. The big doll and the little one (father and son) go to the same girl together; they climb up the house (represented by Deororo's leg) and now he rubs the dolls in great excitement on Deororo's skirt. They both have intercourse with the same girl. Now the big and small doll are rubbed against each other as if one of them were female. 'Why standing?' I ask. 'All right, they will do it lying,' he says. 'But she must take her skirt off,' I say. Both little girls are terribly shocked at this and protest at such a break of etiquette.

Now they get terribly excited. 'Your husband cohabits with you,' Ilaisa says, and throws the father doll at the girls. 'Your wife cohabits with you' (in active role) the girls say, throwing the female doll at him. 'Undo the *dobe* (skirt),' says Deororo who a short time ago would not hear of this, 'you are a strong boy'. Now she is thoroughly excited. The three children are in a frenzy of excitement and they press and rub the dolls at each other's feet; the boy uses the male dolls, and the two girls, the female dolls. Deororo holds Ilaisa. He is now at the mercy of Daunay, she rubs the female dolls on his feet, his head and his back. 'She cohabits with his head,' the girls shout. The scene corresponds exactly to the *yausa* as described by Malinowski (referring to the Trobriand Islanders),

[2] G. Róheim, 'The Children of the Desert', *Internat. J. Psycho-Anal.*, 13 (1922), 36.

or the scene in the myth of the woman's country.[3] They declare that the little male doll is pregnant because it has a rather protruding stomach; his wife had intercourse with him and made him pregnant. Now the big male doll is cohabiting with the big female doll; I put the small doll beside them and say, 'Here is the child.' The result is unexpected; suddenly they all get gloomy and depressed. This was too much like the primal scene for them. However, the next time they came, they enjoyed the primal scene game.

I take the dolls and name them: (i) father, (ii) mother, (iii) child. They pile them all in a heap with the child in the middle; a sort of group coitus. Then they separate them and go on with the 'this is your husband' (wife) game. Then the girls play their sadistic game again; they hold Ilaisa, rub the girl doll over every part of his body, and finally press it to his nose. 'Smell the anus!' they shout. He says, 'Bloody anus.' He always aims directly at their genital and the game develops into direct sex play. Then he makes the small male doll lie on the big doll and kiss it. He also uses the snake as a substitute for either male doll. Daunay undresses the girl doll; it is pregnant and Ilaisa is the father. 28 March they go on with the 'carry your husband' game, but it gets wilder and more indiscriminate. Boys attack girls, girls attack girls. It is now more an attack of the genitalia than an imitation of coitus. A doll without legs is hailed as a pretty woman because of her hair. Ilaisa grabs all the toys he can and hangs them in a row on a tree. On 14 April the family circle is extended. The doll with the long hair is the aunt. A rubber crocodile is the uncle, the two go together. The behaviour of the girls clearly indicates that the rubber snake has ceased to be a real snake; it is now a phallic symbol. *Tomakweiro* (boy) takes the snake from the girls and puts it on the mother doll. All the toys are more or less anxiety objects. The little girl, Daunay, brings all the toys on a tray, they laugh at her and mock her, 'she is carrying her husbands', while Ilaisa suddenly gives up the technique of projection, hugs the girl doll with great pleasure and says, 'my wife'. When the others laugh at him he says, 'No, my sister'.

Projection of the sexual impulse and then gratifying it is the theme in the whole game. They throw the doll at each other, 'Your

---

[3] B. Malinowski, *The Sexual Life of Savages in Northwestern Melanesia*, London: Routledge, 1929, p. 231 (The myth of the woman's country is also known on Normanby Island).

wife (or husband)'. They disclaim the desire for intercourse and rub the doll with obvious coitus movements at the girl's vulva (or boy's penis). The boys get closer to the girls. Ilaisa slips to Deororo head foremost as if he wanted to get right into her body. She sits, he lies on his stomach with his head between her legs. She presses his head down to the ground, takes the female doll and rubs it at his nose. 'You kiss it,' she shouts. Then she takes the skirt off the girl doll and puts it on Ilaisa's head. 'If you don't kiss her, kiss her skirt.' There can be no doubt that she is excited.

A very small girl takes part in the game only in an imitative sort of way. She throws the snake at Tomakweiro, shouting, 'your wife'. 16 April, Deororo takes the big male doll and says the big female doll is Ilaisa's wife, and the smaller one is his child. Ilaisa plays with the snake, tries to shove it under Deororo's skirt, which pleases all the others immensely. They are playing the *mwanena ukahari* (you carry your spouse) game, but not as wildly this time. Deororo hugs the male doll, it is her husband. She carries the girl doll and walks up to Tomakweiro; the others shout, his lover *(rawerawe)* is coming to see him. When Tomakweiro takes the girl doll's skirt off, Deororo slaps his face with evident sadistic pleasure. 'Give me your wife's skirt,' she says. The boys shove the snake at the girl's genitals. Daunay pokes it at my feet. One of the toys is a crocodile with two black boys sitting on it; Ilaisa says they are Deororo's husbands. About two weeks later I add an elephant to the group of toys and tell them the elephant represents me.

Ilaisa starts to play. The big male doll is not the father, it is the brother-in-law. He makes the child doll bend forward—it is defecating. The mother doll standing behind it with uplifted arms. '*Sapi?*' (She is beating it?), I ask. 'No, *sapisapi*' (she is chasing the flies away), they reply. Now the dog will bite the *taubadas* (big man—myself), i.e. the elephant's right foot, right off. The *taubada* scolds the brother-in-law. *Maa* (an adult) sees eggs in our kitchen; he calls to Ilaisa 'You give your eggs (testicles) to Daunay.' One of the girl dolls is broken; they say *kaha ruadi*, 'It has two mouths,' i.e. both openings are mouth and anus. I remark that everybody has two openings (meaning mouth and anus). The little girls are terribly ashamed, they think I am talking about the vagina and the anus. The elephant is hollow, with a back that can be taken off and lollies are put into it for the children. Ilaisa is a great chief,

181

he is given a *sagari*, i.e. he distributes the lollies. His father arrives. Ilaisa tries to frighten his father with the rubber snake. There is not much novelty in their play for some time, as they repeat these and similar scenes, especially the *mwane ukahari* game. On 7 August, they play the *mwane* game in such a fashion that the existence of *coitus a tergo* is made quite clear. The boys press themselves against the back and anus of their *mwane* dolls. The explanation given by Kiwona (girl of about 4) is, 'Her husband is very small and he lies on his legs. Majowa and Kiwona play with the snake and my legs as I sit among them in the grass; *Mwata taubada ikaj* (the snake eats the master). It seems like an inversion of the paternal trauma[4] (the father 'eats' their genitalia) but I have no positive proof for this. On 13 August we have Ilaisa and Tomakweiro and three little girls, Kiowona, Nibonibobo, and Majowa. The game 'serpent eats taubada's feet' is very popular. One figure, representing a sea gull, is my wife, another (dog), her sister. Then the sea gull is my sister. Kiwona makes the two big dolls (father, mother) have intercourse with each other in the mutual fellatio position. Then the son doll kisses the mother doll; 'her husband', they say, or 'like her husband'. Majowa carries her 'husband' like a baby.

About a month later Ilaisa played with the elephant. It has been passive in a *coitus per anum* and the guts have been pulled out! Ilaisa shouts triumphantly. The phallic symbol of the snake is made quite clear by the play between Ilaisa (age 7) and our servant girl Matanogi (age 18). She is sitting in the grass as they play. Ilaisa begins to tickle her with the serpent, working upward on her leg towards her genitals. She is ashamed and goes away wiping her eyes carefully, declaring that Ilaisa had thrown the snake at her eye and she must wipe it off (this is not true).

These rather irregularly conducted play hours with the children show us certain universal and certain specific features of their psychology. Among the former I would list the Oedipus complex, the snake as the phallic symbol, lollies as excrements and food (body content fantasies) and the reaction to the primal scene. On the other hand, I think the sadistic attitude of the girls, though this may be due simply to the difference in age (Deororo is bigger and older than Ilaisa), and the specific form of the Oedipus complex,

[4] G. Róheim, *The Riddle of the Sphinx*, London: Hogarth Press, 1934, p. 162 (the father playfully biting the child's genital).

(the *mwane ukahari* game) are distinctive features of this area. It goes without saying that the content of the games is influenced by the customs of the adults; thus the shame the little girls show when I say the doll should take her skirt off reflects their courtship customs (a kind of 'cuddling' with coitus officially excluded). The father is supposed to play with his children in this culture, hence the 'carry your spouse' game applies to both sexes. Finally it is obvious that children talk about rain-magic or food distribution festivals in communities where these things are practised.

Akaripa. He is the son of Kuhua of Kebebeku village and Sine Iru of Wejoko, both of the *gewara* (small parrot totem), and is the younger brother of Ilaisa. Hisage is about 4 or 5. They had a still younger brother who was drowned recently, and their father wanted to attack his wife with an axe for her negligence, but was prevented. For some time Akaripa came alone and we played in my room. He takes a little red doll which he calls *Tasigu* (my brother) shoots it with a toy pistol and then shoots all the other dolls. Then he talks about his brother Ilaisa and declares that the big doll usually called *sinana* (mother) is *Ilaisa mwanena* (Ilaisai's wife). Ilaisa and he had a brother who was lousing their dog when he was caught by the tide. Now he is buried in the forest. It rained today. Bebe (a sorcerer) made the rain and he makes the sunshine too. They brought the skulls out at the *sagari* (festival); they brought them from the place where the dead children are. Then he shoots the elephant and calls him *Sepu* (a pig). Whose pig? The pig of the Sipupu people.

The following is a day dream. He went into the jungle with Ilaisa. They caught a big pig and the animal bit Ilaisa. If the boys fight him he kills them all with his spear. Dagujara, a Sipupu boy, beat him because he took his fish hook. Then he puts all the figures up again in a row, calls the first doll *tamagu* (my father) and shoots it. He then talks about a little brother who died, mentioning only the first syllable of his name. He says *Tua gea nuago* (enough, I don't want any more).

An interpretation is hardly necessary. His little brother's death fills him with anxiety and he is fighting against it in his day dream with his projection technique. It is not he who wishes to have his mother as a wife, but his elder brother, Ilaisa. At any rate he openly affirms the other part of the Oedipus deed by shooting his father. 'That's enough, he won't play any more.' Death is the penalty of the boys who desire their mother and kill their father.

Another time he plays with the two big dolls. Father and mother go into the house and sleep together. One of the dolls is his brother; the crocodile attacks the brother and bites his penis off. After this the popular game for some time is, coming out of the elephant's anus. All the dolls are pulled out of the elephant's anus; they are all his children. The snake and the child doll are shoved into the father doll's anus. One evening Akaripa and Ilaisa come into my room. Daunay joins them later. The elephant is a pig, it lies on the father doll and bites it. Then the father doll is Daunay's husband and they rub it on Daunay's body and skirt. When the father and mother go to sleep together and the crocodile bites the brother (i.e. himself for his desires), or when the pig bites the father because he has intercourse with mother, I think this shows sufficiently that at least in this matrilinear society, the children have an Oedipus complex.

On 24 June, he puts the small brother doll on the head of the elephant, then drops it off. 'My brother is dead,' he says. Then he puts all the figures in a pile in the box with the brother doll at the bottom, takes the father and mother doll out of the group, and makes them walk beside each other. What are they doing? They are sailing in a canoe. Then he takes the elephant, it walks, it is in a canoe. It is a pig they are taking to the *sagari* (food distribution festivals) to kill. Whose *sagari*? 'Mine,' he says. The point here is the equivalence of the parents who are sailing (going away) with the pig to be killed at his *sagari*.

3. SUMMARY

The first conclusion that follows from these play sessions with the children is that in this matrilinear society there is an Oedipus complex. It could not very well be otherwise, for in the early period of the child's life, in which the Oedipus complex is formed, his environment consists of father and mother, while the uncle has not yet appeared. We also see the specific form in which the Oedipus complex is represented. 'She carries her husband,' or 'he carries his wife,' i.e. identification of baby and spouse was the main theme. There is a strong tendency in this society towards infantilization. The beauty ideal is markedly infantile[5] and the claim that a person is only a little child is frequently made in actual life and in magic songs. The denial of being an adult is a denial of sexuality and aggression, and is explained by anxiety. The *mwanejo ukahari* (carry the spouse) game should therefore be interpreted both as the day dream of the little child (I am mother's husband or father's wife) and as the denial of incestuous desires (I am only a baby). There is a certain progression in the *mwanejo ukahari* game; starting with the infantile level (emphasis on the baby), it ends as an attack on the genitals, just as in actual life the famous and much feared sorcerer will modestly protest 'I am only a little child.'

[5] idem., 'Professional Beauties of Normanby Island', *Amer. Anthropologist*, 42 (1940), 657.

On the basis of their first overview in the field followed by four subsequent research travels, Drs Parin and Morgenthaler elaborate on particular and, to the Western observer, striking dissimilarities in the character structure of some representatives of West-African cultures. As one of the results of their original fieldwork the two investigators formulated a significant and far reaching difference in the super-ego organization and the super-ego content in contrast with the individual character structure predominant in the Western or Westernized personality. Several vignettes exemplify to us uncommon phenomena in the behaviour and attitudes of West-African natives. In accordance with a suggestion made by Freud, the investigators discovered variations in attitudes and reactions which they explain in terms of clan conscience, *a kind of collectively determined codification as compared to the more individualizing super-ego in Western civilization, perhaps due to the introjection of frustrating and controlling agencies under Western types of life conditions.*

In their further studies, mainly among the Dogon of the Republic of Mali, Drs Parin and Morgenthaler elaborated on their original findings and documented their concept of a group ego (see 'Further Reading').

9

Character Analysis Based on the Behaviour Patterns of 'Primitive' Africans[1]

PAUL PARIN and FRITZ MORGENTHALER

Ever since Frazer,[2] his contemporaries and followers turned anthropology into a psychologically useable tool, Western psychology has had much success in its efforts in studying primitive communities for apparent survivals of early stages in psychic organization.

The brilliant discoveries of Winthuis[3] about sexual ambiguity in the language of primitives, used in conjunction with Freud's interpretative and explanatory psychology, made it possible to compare the psychic processes of primitive people with those of neurotics, and to establish that the thought processes of savages obey the same laws which had been found to apply to the unconscious processes of civilized man. The animistic and magical view of the world prevalent in primitive communities matched the unconscious of healthy civilized individuals as disclosed by dream analysis; it had much in common with the symptoms of neurotics in whom the conscious processes of logical and causal thought seemed much distorted by irruptions of the unconscious.

This view of the 'archaic' nature of primitive people led to a rich scientific harvest: Freud[4] was followed by W. Reich, Malinowski, Róheim, Bonaparte and many others who made continued attempts to explore the psyche and the social and religious institutions of savages for psychological elements which could be related to basic conflicts in the psyche of children, e.g. the origin and subsequent course of the Oedipus complex. These correspondences turned out to be so fruitful and material for psychoanalysis and anthropology that modern anthropologists like Griaule[5] take magical and

[1] This paper first appeared in *Psyche*, 10 (1956/7), 311-29, and is published for the first time in English in this volume.
[2] J. G. Frazer, *The Golden Bough*, London: Macmillan, 1930.
[3] J. Winthuis, *Das Zweigeschlechterwesen*, Leipzig: Hirschfeld, 1928.
[4] S. Freud, *Totem and Taboo* (1913), *Standard Ed.*, 13. London: Hogarth Press, 1955.
[5] M. Griaule, *Dieu d'eau*, Paris, Ed. du Chêne, 1948.

sexual ambiguity in the language, myths and ideology of the Dogon as self-evident.

The Freudian school was not the only one to be concerned with archaic thought processes. C. G. Jung and his disciples, in their investigations of symbols, paid special attention to myths and religions, whereas Lévy-Bruhl[6] and other French researchers were more concerned with the thought processes among savages.

The need to find a psychological basis for sociology gave rise to a new application of psychoanalysis to anthropology which derived partly from psychoanalytic thinking about the influence of family structure and education in the formation of character. Kardiner and Linton[7] and their school were now studying entire communities, and they were no longer merely seeking fresh contents for the well-known archaic processes.

In the course of our journey across the Sudan and over British and French West Africa we tried to apply a different method of psychoanalytic investigation to the study of the psychology of 'primitive people'. We followed the views formulated by W. Reich[8] in his book *Charakteranalyse*, which are generally adopted today in any treatment of personality disturbances and have proved themselves also in coping with psychosomatic illnesses (Alexander Mitscherlich). We felt entitled to do this since the Kardiner-Linton school had demonstrated that character formation among primitives is subject to the same laws as that of healthy and sick civilized individuals.

We have, therefore, identified and isolated one particular character-trait which was frequently observable. We then studied its modifications, implications and vicissitudes, both in the same person and in other study subjects showing comparable traits. Then we used this, as well as any deviation from such typical behaviour, for a more detailed description and to check our views about the tendency isolated. Finally we correlated this isolated and observed material with the psychical factors known to us (the structural and dynamic point of view). Last of all we attempted to divine the tendency at the root of that particular character-trait.

In this we were no longer concerned with discovering neurotic

---

[6] L. Lévy-Bruhl, *La Mentalité primitive*, Paris: Presses Universitaires de France, 1922.
[7] A. Kardiner and R. Linton, *The Psychological Frontiers of Society*, New York: Columbia University Press, 1945.
[8] W. Reich, *Charakteranalyse*, Copenhagen: Verlag f. Sexualpolitik, 1933.

traits or relating character-traits with childhood experiences. From behaviour we inferred tendencies, and from these, in turn, we deduced the specific psychic processes.

In so proceeding we had obviously to bear in mind that our scheme of reference was specific and unavoidably arbitrary: the familiar psychodynamics of Western Man, including our own 'personality structure'.

We were, therefore, taking the method of 'interpretation of behaviour by means of character analysis' (i.e. a procedure that is well known and thoroughly tested in individual psychoanalysis), and applying it to a new sphere of study. The inference drawn from 'behaviour' to 'tendencies' and thence to 'specific psychic processes' may appear abrupt. But this very direct, and often seemingly brutal, procedure has demonstrated and proved its validity and effectiveness in the individual analysis of neurotics. As far as we know its application to problems of social psychology is quite new, and is still inadequately supported by the limited material we collected. The present attempt is intended to delineate the procedure: similar investigations in the future will have to show how far it may prove useful.

We want to illustrate our procedure by means of an example which sets out by observing a few character-traits typical of many 'primitive' African negroes, throws light on the nature of their super-ego and helps to a better understanding of 'primitiveness' as an expression of a particular psychic process. Admittedly by adopting this method we did not gather any new material for 'Personality and Culture', such as was collected by cultural anthropologists such as Kardiner, Linton, Ruth Benedict and Margaret Mead.[9] But we hope this approach will provide us with psychological equipment for a clearer understanding of the day-to-day activities of peoples still strange to us.

The observations used in this study concern Negroes of the following tribes: Haussa, Mossi, Fulani (Peul), Malenki, Ashanti,

[9] Following a critical remark by Prof. W. Hochheimer (to whom we are grateful for his encouragement), we should like to emphasize that a paradigmatic presentation such as ours, though it may lead to some kind of hypothesis, can never in any circumstances take the place of full-scale structural investigation or provide any convincingly evident theory.

The scope of a careful structural analysis in this field would make it impossible to publish in a periodical. An example of this would be the work which we quote by Kardiner, Linton and co-workers, or even Griaule, who for a structural analysis found they needed voluminous books or a lifework in many volumes.

Fanti and Bassari. The points we shall make were selected purely because members of these tribes, though often living far apart and belonging to very diverse cultures, again and again showed very similar patterns of behaviour. Those among them who were brought up in the Muslim tradition, or had been converted to Christianity, could be included as long as they did not differ from their non-converted relatives with respect to the character-trait under study.

With regard to our methods of research it must be said that unfortunately we did not master the various languages. To study the similarity of behaviour patterns among the members of different tribes in Africa one must either be able to speak numerous languages (more than a hundred for the area covered by our journey!), confine one's research to published material, or—as we did—rely on information from local residents in English or French and interrogation with the help of local interpreters.

For a more detailed description of our procedure we will take the example of 'native nursing staff in hospitals'. In the first of the larger clinics which we visited (Navrongo Medical Centre, run by the Mission of the White Fathers) it was the head of the Mission, who was the founder and superintendent of the clinic, who gave us a day's lecture about working conditions and the attitude towards work. This conversation was taken down in note form. The striking statement 'As soon as the doctor-in-charge is changed the trained personnel cease to be reliable' led on to an interrogation about the individual nursing staff on the subject which is discussed below in the example of the midwife. Statements analogous to these were collected, and noted down in three more clinics. A comparison was now possible, and this showed that, in about 100 persons, who although differing according to tribe and individuality were nevertheless living under similar conditions, the 'character-trait of the midwife' seemed to reveal itself, without exception, as the same in all cases. We then stayed for ten days in the third clinic, joined in the work, observed the work in operation, questioned the senior and junior staff further, wrote all this down in note-form, and followed up what were apparent or real exceptions. Individual research into motivation was undertaken only in so far as it proceeded directly from the behaviour itself. It follows that the number of those under investigation cannot be stated with any certainty. If one counts only those with whom we were personally acquainted, then the number is certainly limited; counting up the personnel in the various clinics visited we get a total of about 120. If one also takes into account the statements of a conscientious and outstanding Swiss physician, who has been acting as a medical officer in the Gold Coast for the last six years, then this figure must be doubled. A record is therefore sometimes a detailed individual description including the 'striking and predominant' character-trait; sometimes it reports a description of the behaviour of a person at second hand (viewed through a civilized 'personality structure'); sometimes it is a mere unit in a general observation. Our procedure in the case of 'Thieves', 'Religious Festivals', etc., was on the same lines.

The 'White Father' and his Native Teacher

There was an elderly French Catholic missionary belonging to the order of the 'White Fathers' who, after working for ten years in the French Sudan, had built up a good and efficient school (at both primary and secondary levels) amongst the coloured population. A few native teachers, all of whom he had at one time taught himself, were now assisting him with the work of teaching and with the administration of this boarding school. On a free afternoon the missionary was engaged in repairing the roughcast mortar on a wall of the school building. Towards evening there was still a small piece left to do for the work to be completed. But the missionary had to go in order to take part in a discussion at the local administrative council *(cercle)* in the interests of the school. One of the native teachers, who happened to be free from teaching that afternoon, chanced to pass by. The missionary said to him *'Would you mind* finishing the wall for me, before the evening rain starts? I've got to go.' The teacher replied: 'No, I don't want to.' When the missionary went on to give an explanation of the motives that led him to make this special request (i.e. he had been called away on urgent school business; the work that had already been done would be completely destroyed by the rain if left uncompleted; and so forth), he still met with the same refusal. So the 'White Father' said: *'You must* finish this work.' In fact he was not entitled to issue an order in such a case. For the working conditions and timetable of the school, which was well known to both parties, guaranteed the teacher his leisure time. But without any further opposition the African set to work on the task, and merely observed: 'You should not have asked me whether I minded doing it; you should have told me straight-away that I had to do it.'

The Good Midwife

Amongst the nursing staff of a public hospital in a small town on the Gold Coast, there was a young midwife (a girl of the Ashanti tribe). The Chief Medical Officer at the hospital, who was employed by the government and was the only white man in the organization (which employed about 60 native nursing personnel), received a report on his new employee from the school which ran a two-year course for midwives in the principal town (Accra). According to this she was very intelligent, a first-rate pupil, and certainly suitable for working independently as a midwife. Indeed this proved to be the case and after a few months the midwife was already fulfilling the expectations placed on her. She performed all her tasks with great accuracy. For example, when a maternity case was admitted to the hospital, she carried out measurement of the pelvis, took the patient's temperature, supervised the state of the birth, and throughout observed all the rules of surgical sterility. For two years the chief medical officer could count on her as a competent and reliable member of his staff. Eventually, a different medical officer came to replace him, whereupon a sudden change occurred in the working behaviour of the midwife, which was repeated among all the trained personnel at the clinic. Initially she simply began taking the measurements inaccurately, then she stopped taking them altogether, and guessed the figures which were entered on the patients' charts, until finally she even stopped doing this. By failing to pay attention to the rules of hygiene and sterility during the initial examination of her patients she managed to produce several cases of severe infection. When she became aware of this, she ceased making any examination of the maternity cases, and her statements to the physician became totally unreliable. Whereas her living conditions and usual behaviour (her moods, and in short everything except her behaviour at work) all remained exactly the same as before, there was a difference in attitude between the new medical officer and his predecessor. Here one may mention that the previous doctor bore the following important characteristics: (i) He was medically competent: his operations were in the habit of being successful, his patients recovered, and his prognoses worked out in practice. (ii) He enjoyed great respect and prestige in a wide area, both with the Africans and with white people; he had an imposing presence and voice, in short he was a 'big doctor'. (iii) Quite consciously and deliberately he 'set an example'; he never neglected any duty that fell to him (e.g. in cases of emergency at night he always came straight away). (iv) He constantly also supervised all the work of his subordinates, including that of the midwife, even after the latter had shown herself to be reliable, at least by making random checks and punishing even small offences with a scolding or penalty. (v) Although all the personnel were adequately paid by the government, they also received from this doctor, regularly each month, a considerable gift (i.e. in money), which was graded according to their rank. In addition supplementary pay was given for special services, and deductions were very seldom made—only as the severest kind of punishment in a case of neglect. The hospital workers all knew that these additional payments came out of the doctor's private means, and that all together they were being paid a considerable portion of his income.

From a medical point of view the second doctor was equally competent and successful: (i) In the first item listed above he was on a par with the first one. On the other hand he usually behaved quite differently in the hospital. (ii) He was young, and foreign to the country, and did not yet have any great prestige. (iii) He did not strive diligently 'to set an example', and often in cases of emergency he only came after he had finished his meal. (iv) He only supervised the work of those subordinates who were known to be unreliable (e.g. he did not supervise the work of the midwife). (v) He gave no private presents; but, as part of his duties, put forward the names of efficient nursing personnel for promotion into a higher salary-bracket.

We have cited these instances of behaviour on the part of the 'teacher' and the 'midwife' as modes of expression of a particular character-trait that was to be investigated. We have selected these from among many similar observations.

The 'teacher' had misunderstood the question asked him by the 'White Father'. The latter supposed that the command 'the work must be completed' would have been sufficiently bolstered up by a joint knowledge of the circumstances, by a community of interest, and by the effectiveness of his authority, to the point at which a wish would arise in the 'teacher' that would be strong enough of itself to outweigh his reluctance to work. Yet a command issued from without had to take the place of such a resolution. It may also be said that the question was wrongly phrased. Instead of addressing himself to the teacher's feelings of conscience, i.e. to his ego, and in so doing also counting on assistance from an inner voice in the teacher, the 'White Father' should have assumed straight-away that he ought to bring into operation his authoritarian command in direct opposition to the pleasure-principle in the 'teacher'. The 'teacher' seemed to agree that he had to act in accordance with the command, whereas he had apparently felt no inner imperative.

The midwife had also clearly not introjected properly the moral requirements of her profession—she had not developed any professional ethos. It is clear, moreover, that it was not simply that she and her colleagues were merely disappointed about the financial change, which was so obviously unprofitable to her, nor indeed were they disappointed with the new medical officer. There was no trace of any hostile emotion against the latter; the midwife even showed some signs of sympathy for the friendly young doctor. Such a swift act of forgetting professional knowledge cannot really be put down to a failure in work, nor can it be attributed to the view that because the doctor did not understand the procedure all the hard work would be in vain.

We believe that the inner voice, the super-ego—as regards dedication to her work[10]—was lacking in the midwife, but that the traits which we have stressed in the behaviour of the first doctor were of a kind which would induce the midwife to behave 'as if she had a super-ego'. The prestige of the doctor was such as to put a premium on any identification with him by intensifying self-esteem; this is the feature which is described in our psychology as ego-ideal-formation. The behaviour of deliberately setting an example tended to facilitate identification with a suitable model. Punishment and blame came from this model, legitimately and unavoidably, just as they would from a feeling of conscience. We can only be at peace when we have acted in accordance with our conscience. The recompense for working reliably and industriously was therefore twofold: it produced both a material and an emotional reward. The earlier medical officer took a direct and external hold upon the pleasure-pain balance of the midwife, in that he rewarded good performance with money. But as this money was his own personal property, and he was renouncing it voluntarily in favour of the recipients, the gifts constituted an expression of the doctor's affectionate feelings towards them. This doctor assured us that a small and materially insignificant reduction in the monthly salary operated as the severest kind of penalty for various offences. Just as in the upbringing of our own children when not only punishment (including withdrawal of love), but also some sort of reward must come from outside. Inner satisfaction in a duty well done proved to be no longer effective, as soon as reward and punishment disappeared. Under the authority of the second doctor the impersonal, indirect and postponed reward by means of promotion was ineffective.

As a result of these and similar interpretations we deduced that, in the case of the Africans under investigation, there was no ethos of work that existed as a continuing and effective inner structure. With regard to their working behaviour they did not seem to possess any super-ego; but seemed to operate solely on the pleasure-

---

[10] We believe that very few civilized people enjoy working. But it cannot be denied that as a rule an English, German or Swiss midwife or nurse would continue to do her work properly, even if a new doctor were appointed. Here psychoanalysis discerns the operation of an inner motivation (namely, the super-ego). It was precisely the lack of this behaviour and not mere coincidence that determined our selection.

principle, when inner satisfaction and feelings of guilt were not effective. Only such factors as a command from an external authority; imitation of, and identification with, a prestige-bearer; reward and punishment (particularly the sign or withdrawal of love) were of some efficacy. Since these factors impinged upon the person from the outside world, when they were no longer present it was just as if the person's code of professional behaviour ceased to function.

Numerous employers (both European and African) have assured us that their employees were lazy, had no sense of duty, and felt no sense of satisfaction in work well done. These statements are expressive of an economic, political and social problem, which struck us forcibly in every place where Africans came into contact with Western civilization. We shall give two more typical examples to substantiate such statements.

A road-overseer (a Frenchman) in Senegal had to maintain, with almost thirty African employees as workers, a stretch of all-weather roadway, 210 km. in length. Although these workers enjoyed a good relationship with their foreman they only worked as long as they were under supervision. When asked about this, they entirely failed to understand: 'Neither you nor your deputy were watching us! As long as one of you is there, we will work quite willingly!'

An employee in a timber-exporting business in the southern part of the Gold Coast was building with the help of about 300 workers (mostly Mossi and Ashanti) a 40 km. stretch of roadway with many wooden bridges over it. This road was to assist the export of timber and at the same time to serve as an important new link between two stretches of road already in existence. The workmen received a fortnightly payment. Only a few hundred yards were still left to be done, together with the completion of a bridge, presumably a few days' work. After the last payment of wages about 90 per cent of the workmen gave in their notice; they did not feel it worth their while to stay just for two or three days' pay. When it was pointed out that the work done by them all in common would, if left incomplete, be quite unusable, this failed to make a single workman change his mind.

When we try to bring our motives into harmony with the demands of the outside world, it is, just as in the case of the African natives, in keeping with the reality principle. The intellectual evaluation of the advantages and disadvantages of a particular type of working behaviour can be the same in equally intelligent Africans and Europeans. The differences between the often highly-differing standards of value in the two cultures can be ignored in those cases where almost the same standards of value apply, e.g. in the evaluation of remuneration (a bonus). A study of the emotional factors shows us that we usually carry out a professional task in such a way that the return for service (the bonus) only forms part of the motivation that enables the displeasure of working to be overcome. A failure to perform a duty, once undertaken, avenges itself on us in the shape of guilt-feelings. In the cases under investigation, a dereliction of duty calls down only external disadvantages.

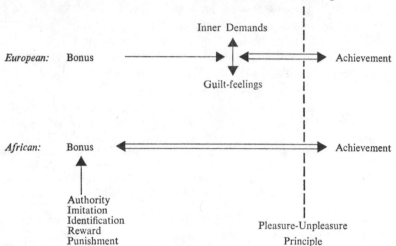

We shall now try to indicate, by means of a schema, how we represent to ourselves the effectiveness of the pleasure-principle in both a European ego and the ego of one of the 'primitive' people under discussion.[11]

The inner structure and dynamic of the African psyche, which we have illustrated by means of a single and superficially striking trait of attitude towards work, does seem to be essentially different

---

[11] It is quite deliberate when we speak synonymously of 'primitive' Africans, primitive peoples, Africans and natives (following Freud) on the one hand, and Europeans, civilized peoples, etc. on the other. By 'European' we do not, of course, mean the statistically most frequent type of European, or the 'normal person' of our civilization. Such a very generalizing expression can only be valid with reference to the equally corresponding character-trait (e.g. in work behaviour), or with reference to the similarly considered psychological factor (e.g. the super-ego). By the very nature of our material we *were bound* to renounce any statement by percentage figures. On the other hand, we *wanted* also to apply 'frequent observation and similarity' of a trait, rather than a statistical or norm concept.

from our own. Moreover this is also borne out when we come to analyze any other common mode of behaviour. Cultural anthropologists have shown by means of a number of individual investigations, that there is scarcely a single mode of behaviour which is looked upon as normal in all cultures.

We found, for example, that the cases observed by us appeared to have no barrier of disgust, though on the other hand they all revealed a strong threshold of shame. The conditions, under which people felt ashamed, tended to differ from tribe to tribe, but they were not altogether unlike our own.

From these investigations into behaviour towards work, and from similar observations in other fields (family morality, education, criminality, etc.) we deduced that *the super-ego of primitive peoples was constituted differently from our own.* We surmised the existence of another type of structure comparable to our own super-ego, though by no means absolutely identical with it.

According to Freud, our super-ego is part of an intra-psychic system which we can distinguish quite clearly from the ego and the id.

Our psychological views about the super-ego follow from a consideration of those tendencies in the personality, which appear to correspond neither to the direct requirements of the outside world, nor to the stirring of desires (in the id). We believe that the dynamic effectiveness of this 'authority' seems to stem from a consideration of the power of our conscience and, above all, from pangs of conscience or their chronic form, a sense of guilt. Feelings of guilt and conscience manifest themselves when instinctual drives that are incompatible with the demands of the super-ego gain access into the ego.

We are limited to deducing the super-ego in this indirect manner, because both its contents and its energy functions belong largely to the unconscious. By the ego-ideal, we mean those patterns or models, which have been assimilated into the ego, after it has already developed its testing functions; patterns which are retained as a more or less constant constituent, separated from the ego, and finally linked up with the earlier introjects both as to content and emotion. By conscience we denote those parts of the super-ego that are either conscious or capable of arriving in consciousness.

The most serious objection that arises here is the following: there is a probability that Africans simply have other contents in their super-ego; this would easily follow from their completely different social structure and the different circumstances of their environment and their ideals.

In fact, the Africans do have other 'contents'. But more than this, we take these to be a different category of contents. Theirs are only valid in a limited community, and are more concrete in conception. Ours are more generally valid and more abstract in conception. For example, all those we investigated remained aware, as we do, from childhood into adult life, of the command to honour father and mother and to obey them. The command to obey authorities in general, which is common to most civilized men, was nowhere in evidence.

We will not here pursue further the question of differing contents. We only wish to point out the differing dynamic factors that struck us. Above all, it was expressions of guilt-feelings, which we are accustomed to relate to an effective inner 'authority' in the ego resisting desires in the id. Further, we shall consider a few instances of striking modes of behaviour in which inner demands seemed to be expressing themselves. Lastly, we shall consider the frequent examples of anxiety observed in our subjects, with a view to discovering whether these may be regarded as pangs of conscience.

We shall use the following six examples in order to investigate how far the inner motivation of Africans is different from that of Europeans, even when behaviour appears similar. We shall not, however, include any detailed discussion of the familiar depth-psychological interpretation of the behaviour patterns of civilized men:

The Loan

A. has been friendly with B. for a long time, and in fact they were also related by marriage. B. requested a comparatively large loan from A., who was well off. A. refused this by simply saying: 'I won't give you anything, because you may not give it back.' B. acknowledged this. His friendship with A. was not in the least affected by this refusal.

In the case of Europeans, such a refusal would generally awaken aggression in B. which would be incompatible with feelings of friendship for A. and would have to be repressed. Perception of these aggressive feelings would arouse guilt-feelings in B. In an 'injured' manner he would avoid further relations with A. Or, if they did have further contact, he would not be able to behave in an open and friendly manner towards him: *viz.* mobilization of guilt-feelings, or a return of the repressed feelings of aggression.

On the other hand, A. would also have guilt-feelings on *his* side, as a result of the aggression which had been expressed in the shape of the refusal of the loan: A. would also shun B., or else would be restrained from expressing positive feelings towards B. Typical behaviour on the part of 'primitive' peoples does not exclude the possibility of B. being angry when his friend A. refused the loan. This anger is often expressed quite violently. We were unable to observe in the behaviour of either A. or of B. any sign of aggression, or any sign of guilt resulting from the reappearance of repressed aggression.

The Homicide

A man of the Fanti tribe (Gold Coast) had stabbed his brother-in-law after an argument when he was drunk. When confronted by the authorities he denied his crime, until the weight of evidence proved too much for him. After involved negotiations with the victim's family (a *palaver*) he paid the widow an agreed sum in compensation. Before the court (the death penalty was being invoked) he showed no kind of regret for what he had done, or indeed of anxiety about being executed; instead he obviously enjoyed his important role as the accused in a jury trial and all the special attention he was receiving from the authorities—in short, all the prestige which attends a capital murderer, as distinct from an ordinary criminal. The man himself was an intelligent family man of about forty.

In this case—as among most of the 'primitive' subjects—it was impossible to establish the existence of any guilt-feeling in the shape of remorse or pangs of conscience after having committed a capital offence. Reconciliation with the spirit of the victim is sought by means of some magical method (a gift to the medicine-man or Chu-chu man, for the purpose of casting a sacrificial spell). The angry relatives of the dead man are recompensed in a material form for the loss they have suffered. Thus, in the psyche of the killer there is no effective principle at all which can express itself in the shape of guilt-feelings or a fear of death. The threatened death penalty is viewed not as a form of retribution, but as an incomprehensible and unpleasant peculiarity on the part of the European authorities.

Open infringement of the strict religious commands is hampered among civilized people by an intense feeling of guilt.

Participation in a Circumcision Ceremony

The ceremony took place in a village in Upper Guinea. The dance of the lion-man was in progress, which depicts how the lion seeks out adolescent boys in order to lead them into the secret grove. Three Europeans, unknown to the natives, Malenki, of this village, came and begged to be allowed to take part in the ceremony. It is expressly forbidden for any foreigners to participate. The spirit of the lion would take its revenge for this desecration. The Europeans offered the fetish-man a gift, so that the spirit would be reconciled to the idea of unconsecrated persons taking part in the feast. The fetish-man agreed and accepted the gift. The Europeans were then able to take part in the ceremony without any more ado, and it was performed in their presence in an unperturbed way without any signs of irritation among the participants.

The demands of religion are fulfilled by means of a magical transaction. Thereafter, the behaviour of the participants is quite uninhibited, so that it is impossible to detect any feelings of guilt due to an infringement of religious customs. Instead of an inner demand in the mind of the participants, whose infringement calls forth a sense of guilt, there is an external demand of the 'spirit' (*l'ésprit du lion*), which can be assuaged in a magical manner.

There is one seeming exception to our observation that Africans do not possess anything resembling our own conscience; and this is the fact that thefts of property are extremely rare among the inhabitants of a village.

Two Thieves

At a market in a suburb of Kumasi (Gold Coast) an African, probably an Ashanti, stole a few pieces of fruit from the basket of a marketing woman, and was caught in the act. The other visitors to the market all scolded him and showed their contempt. He did not run away but wept bitterly.

On a farm at Mamou, Guinea, a young man purloined certain implements. When caught in the act, he was forced to give them back. He did not, however, attempt to run away but instead remained weeping on the ground near the spot where he had committed the theft, while the neighbours tried to drive him off with blows and insults.

The infringement of social rules (the right of property) evokes ostracism from the community. But belonging to the community often has the practical effect of being a necessity for existence. So ostracism has the effect of capital punishment. It is not the command 'Thou shalt not steal' that prevents thefts of property, but being member of a community which can expel one. Foreigners who do not belong to the community in the capacity of guests, can therefore be robbed without any compunction even by the 'most honourable' of members. In a foreign country, where one does not belong to the community, e.g. in a big town, it is possible to steal without losing one's self-respect as an honourable man.

The 'Boy'

In a household in the South of the Gold Coast, there were two male employees (a cook and a servant) from the same village in the Northern Territories. A house-servant for rough work (a 'boy') was to be employed. One man of about thirty with good references presented himself. The two other employees refused to work with him. They said: 'He will steal and will run away where no one can find him, and the suspicion will fall on us.' They said to the employer: 'Why don't you take on a "boy" from our village? He won't steal because he will not treat us as foreigners.'

From the general behaviour of Africans we already have the impression that in those analogous situations where civilized people would show signs of possessing a super-ego, three groups of phenomena emerge. The apparent exceptions to the rule which we have assumed, namely that primitive peoples do not possess a super-ego like our own, seem to reside in the same three groups of phenomena: (i) loyalty and a sense of duty towards the prestige-bearer; (ii) a sense of belonging to, or separation from, a community (clan); (iii) behaviour within the clan. The prestige-bearer is interchangeable both in theory and in practice. Loss of prestige on his part, or the emergence of a more reputable model, will make it possible for the African to surrender his previous model promptly and without conflict (i.e. 'consciencelessly'). We can easily discern that in these relationships of loyalty and duty it is bound to be a matter of identification or participation. We can also see that this is not a case of introjection, of assimilation into the personality on the pattern of earlier introjects.

Outside the clan, or any corresponding community, primitive man behaves just as if he did not have an inner voice or conscience. Within the clan and towards all members of the community he seems to obey inexorable commands. These commands are all the more inescapable since to leave the clan voluntarily would mean not only sacrificing one's means of subsistence; but would generally for inner reasons be virtually impossible for the individual even at the prospect of great material gain. Ostracism from the clan will generally be felt as deprivation of the means of subsistence, and leads to severe depression, sometimes death, even in cases where no serious practical disadvantage ensues. It may be pointed out that something similar to this also occurs with civilized people, especially if one notes that by standards of psychological effectiveness our community is very much larger than that of the Africans. In certain circumstances we, too, are accustomed to assuage our injured religious feelings by some kind of magical transaction (re-dedication of a desecrated cult site). In war we can kill, without necessarily being tormented by pangs of conscience or remorse. Foreigners (e.g. these very Africans) may be robbed and deceived by 'honourable' Europeans. In a foreign city we find it much easier to infringe sexual codes of behaviour in a way that would be impossible at home. In a 'crowd situation' civilized people can allow themselves to do things that would not be condoned by the individual super-ego.

We can say, however, that these modes of behaviour, whenever they occur with us, are considered regressive. Regarding asocial persons, in whom we assume a deficiency of conscience, we say that they place themselves *outside* the community. As for killing in war, it has been proved that this only seems to be unattended by pangs of conscience, if we are able to identify very strongly indeed with some Leader and Father, or with the Battle group.[12] Dissolution of the crowd-situation brings with it remorse and a 'sobering up' of the individuals who had been behaving regressively in the crowd.

These hints may suffice to indicate that similar factors (validity of our super-ego only within a definite community or situation, the efficacy of magic and spells in the face of inner demands and anxieties, etc.) do not rule out various differential devices of our super-ego.

Within the clan, however, strict commands obtain, known to all. These obey the well-known laws of the taboo which need not therefore be re-stated here. It can easily be observed anywhere that such unquestionable laws are not merely insignificant remnants of a tradition but are thoroughly valid rules for the social behaviour of individual primitives within the clan. We shall give two further examples of this.

Poll-tax Workers

In the area of former French West Africa the colonial administration used to require every adult villager to pay an annual tax (this is a

---

[12] W. C. Menninger, 'Modern Concept of War Neuroses', *Bull N.Y. Acad. Med.*, Jan. 1946.

poll-tax and is quite independent of property or income). This payment
was made through the head of the 'Canton' to the Receiver of Taxes,
who would act for the local administration (cercle), either once a year
or in two instalments. The head of the 'Canton' appointed by the
administration was often a man elected by the village or appointed
as village-chief by the elders of the village. In numerous villages which
have a self-sufficient economy or one in which money plays no part,
several strong men were assigned by the community to earn the tax
on behalf of the entire community by their work. The ones assigned
to this task usually made no objection when asked to leave their
family and their possessions for months at a time, or even for a whole
year, and they often had to go hundreds of kilometers to some distant
place where they would be able to find well-paid work. They would
unfailingly return on the day when they had saved up the whole sum
necessary for the entire village. No compensation awaited them. Their
families were supported in the meantime by the clan.

The Guest

A member of a tribe from the north of the Gold Coast left home
with his family and came about 1,000 km. further south, where he
earned a meagre living by working in the cocoa plantations. One day
he was visited by a member of his clan—but a man who hitherto has
been unknown to him, let us say, a distant cousin. The latter received
food and accommodation from his host, and had a claim on his host's
income. The guest liked it there, and remained months and even years.
It was not his duty to look after his own maintenance, by perhaps
taking a job in the plantations. On the contrary, it was much more the
duty of the host to support his guest. If the burden finally became too
oppressive, he could simply go away unnoticed and leave his guest
behind. But if he sent his guest away, then he himself would lose his
membership of the clan and become an outcast. This had to be
avoided at all costs; for should this happen, then the host would also
be exposed to the utmost loss of self-esteem.

We have very little to add to the views which are current on the
subject of taboo. Freud says:[13] 'It is possible, without any stretch-
ing of the sense of the terms, to speak of a taboo conscience or, after
a taboo has been violated, of a taboo sense of guilt. Taboo conscience is probably the earliest form in which the phenomenon of
conscience is met with'. And he goes on to say: 'Taboo . . . is a
command issued by conscience; any violation of it produces a
fearful sense of guilt which follows as a matter of course and of
which the origin is unknown.' Freud stresses the anxiety-character
of this guilt feeling and describes it as 'dread of conscience'. He

[13] S. Freud, *Totem and Taboo* (1913), *Standard Ed.*, 13, pp. 67-74.

notes, 'In maintaining the essential similarity between taboo prohibitions and moral prohibitions, I have not sought to dispute that
there must be a psychological difference between them.' Freud
considers that this difference lies in the fact that the taboo is 'a
social institution'. 'Only if the violation of a taboo is not automatically avenged upon the wrongdoer does a collective feeling arise
among the savages that they are all threatened by the outrage; and
they thereupon hasten to carry out the omitted punishment themselves.' On the one hand fear of the example spreading would
explain the social nature of the taboo. On the other hand an excess
of sexual urges over social impulses would explain the difference
between neurotic fear and taboo dread of conscience.

We may look upon the 'super-ego' and the 'Clan-conscience' as
products of education.[14] The energy of the partial instincts, which
have become attached to both, is directed against the desires which
have secured entrance into the ego. As a result of our earlier
observations and considerations, we can make a schematic representation of the differences between the two as follows:

Super-Ego	Clan conscience
(i) Differentiated from the ego	Less differentiated from the ego
(ii) Demands more inward	Demands more outward, or more outwardly projected (society, taboos, animistic ideas)
(iii) Valid in a wider community	Valid in a narrower community
(iv) Are to be fulfilled continually	Are to be fulfilled immediately
(v) Infringements produce more chronic pangs of conscience = guilt-feelings	Infringements produce more acute anxiety
(vi) Anxieties less accessible to mechanisms of banishing and projection	Anxieties more accessible to mechanisms of banishing and projection
(vii) Contents formulated in a more abstract manner	Contents formulated in a more concrete manner

It could be the case that the more abstract formulation of our
super-ego contents is founded on our greater capacity for abstract

[14] *Editor's note:* This statement is not in keeping with the generally
accepted psychoanalytic theory. It is rooted in the bio-psychologically
defined identification with the representatives of the child's early environment, generally the parents. This identification bears the mark of the moral
standards but is primarily conditioned by the emotional conflicts aroused
by the developmental conditions of the pre-Oedipal and phallic phase.

thought. On the other hand, it could equally well be the case that the capacity for abstract thought is derived from the further differentiation of the super-ego.

The vicissitudes of anxiety to which 'primitive' man is subjected, seem to differ from our own pangs of conscience. Primitive people do not seem to suffer from inner tensions; it is not that which drives them on. Moreover, it seems to be the case that, among our 'primitive' Africans, illnesses due to high tension only occur very rarely, whereas among the 'civilized' Negroes of America these are frequent.

It is true that the evil demons have arisen by means of projection. But they are treated throughout as if they were external enemies. This is also the opinion of Hediger,[15] when he writes:

> I know that it is difficult for us to obtain an adequate idea of the continuous possible threat to which the behaviour of an animal is subject. But anyone who has ever lived among really primitive people, as I have often on some South Seas island, can get some approximate idea. These natives of course felt little threat from wild beasts, but in an analogous fashion they did feel themselves to be continuously threatened by countless demons; and in every least action that they undertook—indeed literally at every step—they were obliged to be on their guard against evil spirits. They could not eat or spit, sit or speak, dance or hunt without taking appropriate measures to ward off the enemy— that is to say, the evil spirit.

The magical thought of primitive people and their animistic world image are characteristic of the struggle to master prevalent anxieties. Projection and undoing seem to us to be the prevalent defence mechanisms of the ego which provide a clue to character structure. The average healthy civilized adult only succeeds to a slight degree in warding off pangs of conscience in this manner. Numerous examples of these defence mechanisms have been described but deal for the most part with ritually fixed instances of projection and undoing. We would like to add a few examples from everyday life.

Most of the subjects under investigation paid anxious attention to their body functions. Bodily functions are being considered as the 'external environment' of the psyche. In particular, one matter of exceptional importance was that of excreting regularly and fre-

[15] H. Hediger, *Skizzen zu einer Tierpsychologie im Zoo und im Zirkus*, Stuttgart: Europa Verlag, 1954.

quently. Every individual seeks to aid his digestion with every conceivable kind of medicament, effective or harmful, domestic or imported. Mothers are in the habit of controlling their young children in this way, frequently resorting to the use of an enema which in most places is given by means of the mouth. Medicaments are taken everywhere even by healthy people in order to cast an effective spell on the anxieties projected into the body. The curative or prophylactic efficacy of the medicines themselves are of little concern; what is important is their source of origin (if possible from some prestige figure) and their price. In this way healthy people whom we should consider to be hypochondriacal, frequently have injections, without being in the least concerned about the pharmacological value of the fluid injected. The whole point is that hypochondriacal anxieties are undone by the use of a therapy which has its origin in the White Man. Throughout the whole territory of the Gold Coast this eagerness to secure treatment by injection led to a state of affairs where medicine men, private persons and doctors were administering injections on a large scale to private people who paid the exorbitant prices demanded, and often suffered the after-effects of drugs injected indiscriminately.[16]

After a brief survey of the possibilities of applying psychoanalysis to the study of 'primitive' peoples, we have attempted to find a different approach to the same sphere. We proceeded on the lines of 'character analysis', highlighted a number of striking modes of common behaviour among Africans and compared their probable inner motivation with analogous phenomena in Western society. We investigated a definite, frequent and striking mode of the attitude towards work from which we deduced the lack of a professional ethos as a dynamic component of an effective inner structure. In the process we discovered certain other effective psychic mechanisms and finally arrived at the assumption that in Africans the super-ego must be constituted differently from ours. In following up this distinction we arrived at the conclusion that we could observe not merely a different category of content of the super-ego, but that a different type of psychodynamic seemed to be present. We investigated this by the use of examples which made it possible to infer from guilt-feelings and anxieties the existence of unconscious processes. Modes of behaviour which often seemed to be

---

[16] *Editor's note:* This entire behaviour pattern seems more prevalent in the area of the Gold Coast than in other parts of the African culture area.

similar to our own furnished suitable examples. We recognized the importance of the clan for the behaviour of the individual African; and of the laws which govern his psychology within the community of the clan. After a brief review of the laws governing taboo, and after emphasizing their universal validity we went on to contrast the criteria of our own super-ego with those of the clan conscience. Finally, we touched briefly upon the process by which anxieties are dealt with or converted, as a further aspect important in judging psychodynamics.

The *results* of our investigation, by way of character analysis, of a peculiarity of 'primitive' Negroes in Middle and West Africa can be expressed in the following theory:

The ego of the subjects under investigation is not the arena of an inner conflict between the super-ego, on the one hand, and instinctual demands from the id on the other. Super-ego formation by introjection of a frustrating parent or other frustrating authorities evidently did not occur as it does with us. In our own case instinctual demands become attached to the introjects and ensure that commands and prohibitions are observed by the ego. The violation of inner demands is either prevented by the release of pangs of conscience or else punished by chronic guilt feelings. In the case of primitive peoples the external environment, through the exploration of reality, acts directly in facilitating and frustrating instinctual desires. In this external world personal authority plays a significant part in the behaviour of the ego—not only by reward and punishment, by the vouchsafing or refusal of love but especially by means of imitation and identification.

The fact of belonging to a clan, to a community, does indeed create within the individual a form of clan conscience of which taboo conscience has long been a familiar constituent. The difference from our own conscience consists in the greater social character of the clan conscience, for it is effective only within one particular society; and separation from this society destroys its effectiveness.

We could also say that clan conscience is only a less clearly differentiated preliminary stage of the super-ego; and that it protects certain social and magical demands, which we encounter in a more differentiated form elsewhere—as, for example, the Categorical Imperative of Kant.

What Europeans are wont to call the 'laziness and unreliability' of primitive peoples can now become explicable. External factors and interacting persons have a greater influence on the behaviour of their ego, or load the pleasure-unpleasure balance from outside, whereas in our case our behaviour is generally the result of an inner conflict between the super-ego and the id. Freud found in the psychic reactions of primitive peoples a higher degree of ambivalence than is usually to be found among cultured men alive today. The natural and infantile nature of primitive peoples has caused psychoanalysts to ascribe to the latter a higher degree of narcissism than is generally the case among civilized people.

Somewhat expanding this view, one of the authors made the following conjecture after investigating certain 'primitive' Jugoslavs:[17] 'The fact that primitive people appear to us as 'natural' and 'child-like' makes it very easy to see that, compared with their ego, their super-ego must be partly of a relatively frail structure, as well as variable and fairly undifferentiated.'

Our observations on the Africans appear to confirm both points of view. The strong ambivalence of emotions felt towards interacting persons prevents negative feelings from being fully introjected and therefore acting as external threatening demons rather than working from within. An ego that is less oppressed by a super-ego is more likely to be libidinally cathected. The narcissistic element of the libido will be large. The lack of 'inner demands' helps to contribute to the child-like character.[18]

In place of the super-ego there exists in primitive people the dynamic combination of those factors which we have described as loyalty and a sense of duty towards a prestige figure, the sense of belonging to, or being separated from, a community and the sense of clan-conscience.

Further attempts to answer problems of ethnopsychology by applying methods of character-analysis to investigations of behaviour should help to indicate how far our approach is likely to be of use. The dynamically effective factors which differentiate the psychic life of primitive peoples from that of civilized people could then be more precisely defined and deduced with greater certainty. It is very probable that other significant differences would be found. The hypothesis which we have arrived at calls for additional exploration.

[17] P. Parin, 'Die Kriegsneurose der Jugoslaven', *Schw. Arch. f. Neurologie und Psychiatrie*, 61 (1948).
[18] *Editor's note:* As viewed from our position.

Dr Devereux' paper utilizing the combined knowledge of anthropological and psychoanalytic research methods does not strictly deal with orality. It discusses derivatives such as the common practice of fellatio and reaction-formations to nursing later on in life. His material demonstrates how much information the psychoanalytically sophisticated anthropologist can extrapolate from the data potentially available. Pregenital elements in Mohave sexual life are carefully traced to early child training.

10

Mohave Orality: An Analysis of Nursing and Weaning Customs[1]

GEORGE DEVEREUX

While it is to be expected, since the Mohave Indians nurse their children for several years, that the oral stage of psycho-sexual development would be one of the most important determinants of the structure of their culture and personality, it is striking that the Mohave appear to be aware of the significance of nursing for the psychic economy of the infant.

Precisely because the culturally determined beliefs of the Mohave seem so modern and approximate so closely the findings of psychoanalysis, it is important that discussion of Mohave orality begin with a straightforward presentation of ethnological data—to avoid the appearance of forcing the data to fit psychoanalytic theory.

1. NURSING AND WEANING

As the milk does not start to flow immediately after parturition, as a rule, the baby is not nursed until the day following its birth; however, if the mother has milk available, the child is nursed after it has been bathed. The mother believes she should handle the newborn baby as little as possible, lest it have a dark complexion. Care is taken to avoid injury to the child's soft face from crushing it against the breast; during the first days of its life, the infant's face is therefore allowed to come into contact with the nipple only. No sticks are used to bring the nipple to the mouth of the child. Whether the child is carried on the mother's hip—with or without a cradle—or is sitting in its mother's lap, its head is kept above the level of the nipple and, as a result, it suckles by drawing the milk

[1] This paper first appeared in *The Psychoanalytic Quarterly*, 16 (1947).

upward. This mode of suckling is relatively rare in Western civilization.[2]

If on the second day the woman still has no milk, the child cries and becomes angry, and the Mohave institute a special treatment. The mother, or the maternal grandmother, takes two stones the size of a fist and heats them in the fire. The hot stones are placed in two shallow holes in the soil, covered with hot sand or with ashes from the hearth, and the woman lies down, placing each breast on one of the two small mounds. The heat is supposed to 'steam' the breasts and start the flow of milk. The stones and small mounds have no magic significance; the Mohave often use heat as a therapeutic agent. The breasts are also kneaded and massaged by the woman's mother or grandmother. If the flow of milk remains insufficient, the procedure may be repeated three more times. Should the milk disagree with the child, the mother is made to lie on hot ashes to 'scald' her milk and 'make it right', to stop the baby from vomiting.

The nursing of orphans and of children whose mothers have no milk presents special problems. Since the Mohave lack adequate baby foods, a substitute nurse has to be found. This is not an easy matter, as a woman who nurses her own infant will not offer to nurse a strange child.

Nettle writes:

> Should the mother die, no other woman will nurse her baby because she thinks that it will make her own baby angry, and it will die to spite her. I have seen one or two exceptions to this. Girls with young babies have tried to care for their dead mother's baby, but without exception one or the other of the children have died simply because the woman had not enough milk for two, and, as they seldom use artificial food, the weaker child succumbed. However, they will not accept this simple explanation. Twins were unlucky for the same reason. One or both died; generally both.[3]

The Mohave equate the 'spite deaths' of sucklings who have an orphaned rival for the mother's breast with the 'spite suicides' of sucklings whose pregnant mothers have to wean them. The nexus between the two ailments is made evident by the administration of

---

[2] G. Bateson and M. Mead, *Balinese Character: A Photographic Analysis*, New York: Special Publications of the New York Academy of Sciences, 2, 1942.

[3] M. A. I. Nettle, 'Mohave Women'. Unpublished MS.

identical therapies in both instances. The psychic state of the jealous infant is, they believe, one of impotent rage. Even if it be a potential shaman, it is unable at that age to harm its rival by witchcraft. Infant shamans, like any ordinary child, have to turn their aggressions inward.

Psychoanalysis has made it evident that the deflection of aggressions to one's own ego is determined by feelings of guilt, elicited through having originally directed aggressive feelings towards an object against whom aggression is prohibited. It is of interest therefore to inquire precisely how the adult Mohave came to formulate such a theory of infantile self-aggression; to discover precisely what cultural rules the child's jealous and narcissistic attitude happens to violate. In the opinion of the Mohave the jealous infant wants to deprive another Mohave of his chance to live or to be born. This constitutes a flagrant disregard of the characteristic Mohave interest in tribal continuity and solidarity.[4] Even where the jealousy is directed towards an unborn sibling, shamanistic therapy stresses only tribal solidarity, of which family solidarity is but a component. Solidarity, in turn, is rooted in the culturally prescribed —and often unconsciously resented—obligation to be generous towards everyone. In brief, the child's attitude is entirely incompatible with the central tenets of Mohave ethics.

The Mohave ascription of complete rationality, and of awareness of the difference between right and wrong, not only to infants but also to unborn children,[5] is explicit in their obstetrical practices, in their beliefs concerning twins,[6] and in the therapy of weaning difficulties. It is natural, therefore, that, implicitly at least, they should attribute feelings of guilt to the jealous child. From the psychoanalytic point of view, these beliefs are apparently cultural reformulations of infantile fantasies of destroying the mother's body, as well as oneself. In fact, these fantasies are expressed in Mohave beliefs concerning the nature and causes of the obstetrical difficulties accompanying the birth of future shamans.[7]

In view of the risks and difficulties involved in securing the

---

[4] G. Devereux, 'Mohave Culture and Personality', *Culture and Personality*, 8 (1939), 91-109; A. L. Kroeber, *Handbook of the Indians of California*, Washington D.C.: Bureau of American Ethnology Bulletin 78, 1925.
[5] G. Devereux, 'L'Envoûtement chez les Indiens Mohave', *J. de la Société des Américanistes de Paris*, N.S. 29 (1938), 405-12.
[6] idem, 'Mohave Beliefs Concerning Twins', *Amer. Anthropologist*, N.S.43 (1941), 573-92.
[7] idem, 'L'Envoûtement chez les Indiens Mohave', loc. cit.

services of a wet nurse, the Mohave attempt to induce lactation in the child's maternal grandmother, great-grandmother, or in some other older female relative of the mother, by means of the technique described above. Two shamans (one of them a specialist in 'pediatrics') and a woman informant, vouched for the efficiency of this technique even when applied to a woman 'eighty years old'.[8] These statements, denied only by Tcatc, are substantiated by the medical observations of Dr Nettle, who actually saw A.W.'s mother, one of whose daughters died, nurse her own grandchild. In this instance the treatment was omitted; the infant was simply put to the breast of its grandmother, who was well past menopause, and was suckled until the old woman began to produce milk.[9]

Children who bite or chew the nipple are either potential shamans[10] or else snake monsters. Whenever parents kill a snake during a mother's pregnancy, the child will be born deformed, i.e. with a snakelike head. Such monsters are said to be prone to bite the nipple, and their bite is believed to be poisonous. For this reason the Mohave attempt to feed them soft mush which, being an inadequate substitute, usually causes them to die. This is the best the Mohave have to offer any child whom no one can or will suckle. The bite of future shamans is not believed to be poisonous, and they are nursed like any other child.

The Mohave woman makes every effort to suckle her child as long as possible. The average child is not forcibly weaned, but permitted to wean itself. Some women suckle their children until the age of six, though children usually wean themselves spontaneously at the age of two or three years.[11] The average Mohave is an oral optimist, since usually only a new pregnancy causes an unavoidable interruption of lactation, necessitating the administration of other types of food.

Whether or not the child has to be weaned, or weans itself, it is

[8] H. Ploss and M. and P. Bartels, *Das Weib in der Natur- und Völker-kunde*, 11th ed., Berlin: Neufeld & Henius Verlag, 1927, vol. 3.

[9] M. A. I. Nettle, op. cit. The psychological and physiological basis of lactation in women who had not given birth recently is discussed in W. Briehl and E. W. Kulka, 'Lactation in a Virgin', *Psychoanal. Quart.*, 4 (1935), 484-512.

[10] G. Devereux, 'L'Envoûtement chez les Indiens Mohave', loc. cit.

[11] *Editor's note:* This custom is much more widespread and consequential than ordinarily assumed in the Western world. See also P. Parin and F. Morgenthaler's paper in this volume and J. W. M. Whiting and J. L. Child's comparative study, *Child Training and Personality*, New Haven: Yale University Press, 1953.

fed all kinds of soft food such as mush and 'gravy'. It is not given anything that has to be chewed, as its teeth are believed to be too soft for mastication. Since during the later months of pregnancy a foetus is supposed to chew and swallow its food,[12] the absence of solid foods in the diet of infants is noteworthy. Normally a child begins to feed 'at the table' between the ages of two and four, 'but if he is very much petted, only somewhat later'. Thus there exists a correlation between parental love and the age of beginning the weaning process.

The Mohave connect weaning troubles which result from a mother's pregnancy with spite, sibling rivalry and with the suckling's awareness of current intrauterine events. The imputed sequence seems to be: oral frustration, aggression (directed towards the foetus), self-aggression and suicide. Though a pregnant woman who still has some milk will not suckle an orphan if her own infant has died, she will nonetheless suckle her child as long as possible. This is due partly to mother-love and partly to the difficulties of procuring adequate substitutes. According to Mohave belief, lactation stops at the end of the sixth lunar month of pregnancy when the foetus has an immutable identity and is alleged to 'chew and swallow' its food inside the mother. It is also the age at which the foetus begins to 'dream'. Weaning is recognized to be traumatic for the baby. While some sucklings just 'give up trying' when they 'see that it is no use, that no milk will come', other children give a great deal of trouble. The following account was given by Hivsu: Tupo: ma, who specialized in this disease, as well as in the cure of certain ailments that result from being kicked by a horse.

> The suckling has the power to sense that his mother is pregnant again because the womb was once 'his own place'; the child can therefore feel that someone else is occupying it now. The ability to sense its mother's pregnancies vanishes once the child has reached the age of three [the average weaning age], and thus will no longer be hurt by something which it knows nothing about. Until that age, however, the child is likely to be jealous of the intruder. It will feel angry and hurt about its mother's new pregnancy, and will make itself sick from spite. It would not be resentful were its father to make another woman pregnant; it resents the presence of a usurper in 'its' womb, whoever the father may be. Of course, when the mother's milk flow dries up during the sixth month of her pregnancy, the child will greatly resent not being given any more

[12] G. Devereux, 'Der Begriff der Vaterschaft bei den Mohave Indianern', Ztschr. f. Ethnologie, 69 (1937), 72-8.

milk. Even if it should want to play, it will lack vigour and will soon be back, whining for milk and crying bitterly. Unable to obtain milk, it will make itself sick and fade away because it has been frustrated. Additional factors may, of course, also be involved. The child might have been scolded or 'corrected' when its parents get 'all worked up' because it is making so much fuss. [Scolding is an ancient trait, but physical punishment is due to white influences.] The sensitive child, being not only deprived of milk but also scolded or slapped, will resent it and will make itself ill. When it is thinking of the intruder it will just lie in a lethargic state with its eyes closed. Food will not agree with it, and its bowels will be loose and give trouble. The faeces will be dark green in colour, and might even contain a few streaks of blood. Though the child may not refuse a piece of candy, this will but worsen its condition, and finally the child will get really ill. It will cry and cry, and make everyone wait on it. All infants are likely to feel sufficiently hurt under these conditions to make themselves die in order to spite their parents, but twins, should they be jealous of heart, will be more affected by such 'intrusions' into the maternal womb than are other children. This does not mean, of course, that adult twins are necessarily more envious or meaner than are other adults. They are more sensitive than are other children whose souls are not immortal and do not come from heaven. Twin infants are not to be thought of as rivals for the mother's breast, however.

I must consider all the above circumstances whenever I start such a treatment. I have obtained my power to cure this and other diseases from Pahotcatc. When he made people and divided them into different groups, he explained the various diseases. Among many other ailments he also described this one. However, if the child is well taken care of and is taken in time to a competent shaman, to whom the power was given to cure this ailment, it will recover unless its parents dream of losing it. [Many Mohave dreams are regarded not as the cause but as omens of future events.] I impose no food restrictions nor any other taboo on anyone, and expect to cure the disease without singing. With my left hand I press the stomach of the child and blow my breath on its belly. I also smear some spittle on its stomach. The hand pressure will improve its bowels. I also massage the child's scalp to arouse it from its lethargy. I press its head, and blow along its eyebrows, which I also moisten with some spittle. My breath and the spittle will arouse the child from its drowsy state, as will the massage. While I do all this I sing no songs, but tell about the origin of this ailment and whatever may be connected with its cure. But this sickness is a hard one to cure. Above all, I will urge the child to have a good disposition, and tell it not to be jealous and resentful towards the new baby.

A concrete instance of this ailment is the story of Kunyii:th, of the Kunyii:th gens (the sister of two men, both of whom had committed suicide), who was married to Hamce: of the O:otc gens. They had a little daughter O:otc, three or four years old, who still suckled. This little girl became ill when her mother became pregnant. Kunyii:th thereupon called on Hivsu: Tupo:ma, asking him to treat the child. The shaman looked at the child and said: 'She acts as though she were jealous of your unborn baby. That is why she is making herself sick.' Kunyii:th denied, however, that she was pregnant, whereupon the shaman replied: 'Do not deny it or else I won't be able to cure the child entirely'. The woman kept on pretending that she was not pregnant. Eventually she gave birth to a second girl, also named O:otc. [The interpreter commented upon the 'ridiculous' habit of Mohave women—including married women—of denying they are pregnant. She described the way they tie their shawls to conceal their pregnant state, and said that the Mohave name, 'Hidden Baby', was a jocular reference to this practice.]

The manner in which the above account was obtained sheds some light upon the psychology of Mohave shamanism. The data were quite freely given, but in the third person singular. Hivsu: Tupo:ma omitted to mention that he had the power to cure this ailment. Later, when he came to know me better, he volunteered the admission of having this power, and explained that he did not wish to mention this fact to a stranger who might bewitch him for speaking of his powers. Thereupon he voluntarily repeated the account a second time, the two statements corresponding completely.

As for the technical details of the therapy, the use of the left hand indicates that the curing power was obtained from the Gods. Both the breath and the saliva are carriers of the shaman's healing and other powers.[13] According to Róheim's interpretation of data obtained from the closely related Yuma tribe,[14] pressing and rubbing are masturbatory, and the use of saliva sublimated fellatio. Róheim states that the shaman's left (curing) hand must sweat during the treatment. [Sweating and salivation sometimes coincide in certain states of tension and anxiety.] There is also a well-

[13] A. L. Kroeber, op. cit.
[14] G. Róheim, 'Psychoanalysis of Primitive Cultural Types', *Internat. J. Psycho-Anal.*, 13 (1932), 1-224.

established connection between the eyelids and sleep and states of drowsiness: children may be put to sleep by smearing their eyelids with black paint mixed with the powdered charred eyes of a little bird which goes to sleep at sunset. The Mohave believe that an overdose of this treatment in childhood can produce lifelong drowsiness and laziness.

The absence of shamanistic songs in Hivsu: Tupo:ma's therapeutic methods is noteworthy, although each shaman has his own way of doing things. The songs in themselves have no therapeutic value. Prospective shamans, when their powers begin to stir in them, learn these songs by listening to practising shamans. Anyone may memorize these songs, though if he sang them without having received appropriate shamanistic powers in dream, his singing would not merely be therapeutically worthless, but would cause a shaman specializing in the disease to whose cure these songs pertain to bewitch him for usurping shamanistic privileges. The really effective part of the songs is not their actual text, which is merely a 'decorative' verbal pattern of key words from the narrative it summarizes,[15] but the narrative content thereof, whether rendered in the above full length prose form, or in the form of brief songs.

There appear to have been songs connected with this therapy, but they have become 'lost' (forgotten) during Hivsu: Tupo:ma's own lifetime. The last one to sing them was Kuoto:va (Bat's Breast), better known as Táparnyám (Like A Clown), the latter name having been given him because he was much addicted to a certain practical joke. At gatherings he would cover his head and face with a piece of cloth, into which he had cut eyes and a mouth. [This, I believe, is the only known reference to masks in Yuman river cultures.] Thus masked, the shaman armed himself with two small sticks, and wandered through the crowd, poking both boys and girls, preferably between the legs. This behaviour parallels to a certain extent the custom which permitted old women, who had lost relatives during a raid on the enemy, to go through the crowd welcoming the returning war party, and poke stay-at-home men between the legs, calling them 'alyha:' (transvestite, coward).[16]

The infant is credited with an understanding of the causal connection between the cessation of lactation and its mother's

[15] F. Densmore, *Yuman and Yaqui Music*, Washington: Bureau of American Ethnology Bulletin 110, 1932.
[16] G. Devereux, 'Institutionalized Homosexuality of the Mohave Indians', *Human Biology*, 9 (1937), 498-527.

pregnancy. Even the therapy of difficult births presupposes the rational thinking of infants, and their perviousness to appeals to tribal responsibility and generosity. The Mohave theory of the pathogenesis of this disease, called *tàvàknyik*, rests upon the assumption that prenatal life and life in the cradle form more or less a continuum. While the child remains in the cradle it is not a true inhabitant of the house. If it dies, the house is not burned down. Its cradle however is thrown into the river since, like any other object soiled with menstrual blood or its equivalents, it must not be burned for fear of causing the mother to become barren.[17] Only when the child begins to 'move around and touch things' does the house become its true home, which must be burned down if the child dies. The Mohave, then, do not believe the cradled child to have achieved a fully extrauterine existence; as long as it suckles, it still draws upon the mother's body for its sustenance. The child, therefore, is assumed to feel that it has certain vested rights in the maternal womb, or in the maternal body.

When the child is no longer cradled, it is said to become less sensitive to true or imaginary slights, and to gradually lose its affinity with, and knowledge of, intrauterine happenings. It loses its memories of intrauterine existence, temporarily if it is to become a shaman, otherwise permanently.[18] Only after the child has left the cradle and has been weaned, is it given a personal name, thus becoming a true denizen of the world. I am indebted to the late E. M. Loeb for the information that, on the basis of data from other parts of the world, he too has reached the conclusion that no child is credited with being fully and finally born until it is given a name. Thus it would seem that just as it takes some time to turn into a ghost after death,[19] so it takes some time to become a full member of human society after birth.

It is evident from Nettle's statements that infant mortality, due to a lack of adequate substitute baby-foods, must have been considerable in aboriginal times. She did not add, however, that this mortality rate decreased considerably in recent times, chiefly because of her own ministrations which caused the Mohave to bring the sick more and more consistently to the hospital for treat-

[17] idem, 'The Social and Cultural Implications of Incest Among the Mohave Indians', *Psychoanal. Quart.*, 8 (1939), 510-33.
[18] idem, 'L'Envoûtement chez les Indiens Mohave', loc. cit.
[19] idem, 'Mohave Soul Concepts', *Amer. Anthropologist*, N.S. 39 (1937), 417-22.

ment. The Mohave theory is therefore probably partially a rationalization of this high death rate. Unable, because of conditions prevailing in aboriginal times, to do anything practical about the diet of infants, they evolved a rationalization which is far from unconvincing to the psychoanalyst. There is nothing *a priori* absurd in the view that a two- or three-year-old child can become aware of its mother's pregnancy, either through observation or from over-hearing adult conversations. It is furthermore probably not beyond the capacities of a toddler to connect pregnancy more or less consciously with the trauma of weaning. The Mohave attitude towards this form of suicide is: 'It is their nature, they cannot help acting that way'. The frustration-aggression-suicide theory of this disease may have been evolved by an adult shaman, who had not wholly repressed his own infantile memories. Indeed, a shaman is, by definition, a person who remembers intrauterine and, presumably, also early childhood experiences. It is perhaps significant that Hivsu: Tupo:ma, the shaman specializing in the cure of this ailment, was an enormously heavy eater, even for a six-foot tall and powerfully built man.

2. MOHAVE ORALITY

Oral gratification plays an important role in Mohave thought. Since the nursing of babies is part of the *reproductive* phase of sexuality, the Mohave tend to discuss lactation in a sedate manner, which contrasts with their habit of turning everything pertaining to *coitus* into a joke.[20] The infantile craving for oral gratification during lactation being insatiable, one is not surprised that even the orally optimistic Mohave should, now and then, refer in a joking and pejorative manner to the maternal breast and to lactation, although my obtaining only three examples of such jocular or insulting references suggests that humour is a relatively negligible defence against oral anxieties.

The first example concerns a man from Fort Mohave [commonly known as 'Number Nine' because he had only nine fingers] who was in the habit of saying, 'I work all the time; I have worked ever since I was born'. When anyone objected that babies do not work,

[20] idem, 'Heterosexual Behavior of the Mohave Indians', in G. Róheim (ed.), *Psychoanalysis and the Social Sciences*, 2, New York: International Universities Press; London: Hogarth Press, 1950.

he would reply, 'I did: I sucked titties'. This was considered funny, though not in good taste.

The second jocular reference to the breast was an interesting slip of the tongue. Many Mohave choose for themselves names which are slurs on the opposite sex. Allegedly incensed by the fact that a Yuma Indian assumed the name Hispan utce: ('Vagina Charcoal', a vagina darkened by constant use), a Mohave woman retaliated by changing her own name to Hama: utce: ('Testicles Charcoal', testicles darkened by constant use). When I asked her why she did not call herself outright Modhar utce: ('Penis Charcoal'), she replied, 'That would be going too far'. Shortly after she assumed this name, a Mohave man announced this amusing name at a gathering. However, instead of quoting correctly, he gave this woman's new name as Nama: utce: ('Breasts Charcoal'). This announcement was received with a great deal of laughter, because only a man or a female transvestite would adopt a name like 'Breasts Charcoal'. Some people therefore teased the woman about having become a lesbian though knowing it to be false. The following data may help to clarify some of the dynamics of this slip. Breasts are not believed to 'darken from use'; the Mohave never mentioned to me observing changes in the pigmentation of the areola, which tends to substantiate their assertion that they do not orally stimulate the mammae, although they may manipulate them to excite the woman.[21] The Mohave equate the penis with the nipple because they equate milk with the semen which they know to come from the testes. The woman about whom this anecdote was related is unusually intelligent and energetic—very different from the average gadabout Mohave woman. This may explain in part why this slip of the tongue credited her with a typically masculine, or female transvestite name, though she was quite the opposite of a lewd 'phallic' kamalo:y.[22]

The third example is a custom involving the aggressive and insulting use of the breasts. A woman may open her blouse and offer her breasts to an adult male. This gesture is sometimes accompanied by the taunt: 'Come here, little one, you must be hungry; no one has nursed you for a long time now'. This gesture has three insulting implications: that the man's mother is dead; that he can be tempted to suck the breast; that he is childish.

[21] ibid.
[22] idem, 'The Mohave Indian Kamalo:y', J. Clin. Psychopath., 9 (1948), 433-57.

'The man has no one to nurse him because his mother is dead.' Whether or not that be the case, a Mohave is insulted if anyone refers to his dead relatives,[23] or speaks of one of his living relatives as though he were dead. The Mohave Indian's sensitiveness on this score may be attributed to guilt, since death originated when Frog Woman bewitched her father, the God Matavilye, by eating his faeces.[24] This has been interpreted as oral incest with an anal penis.[25] Since witches are notoriously prone to cause the death of their own relatives, this insult also implies an accusation of witchcraft, or of death wishes against a relative.[26]

The breast of the woman being a sexual organ in the eyes of the adult Mohave male, he never touches it with his lips because of the incest taboo. The offer to nurse an adult man therefore elicits Oedipal anxieties. The Oedipal connotations also imply an accusation of witchcraft, since only witches commit incest.[27] They are, furthermore, the only ones who *deliberately* dream of sexual relations with their victims[28] which, by the way, enables the victim to exert such a lure upon the witch (witchcraft in reverse?) that the witch wishes to die and induces someone to kill him.[29]

The implicit insult, 'you are a child', may also take the curious form of a threat to 'push back the foreskin' which, according to the Mohave, is an equivalent of the offer to nurse a man. This threat the Mohave rationalizes as, 'You are so young that you are still masturbating', the obvious interpretation being that it is still another manner in which the Mohave equate the penis and the nipple. When the penis becomes erect, the foreskin usually retracts automatically; the insult therefore includes the implication that the man is impotent, and that the woman has to take the active, phallic role. The Mohave specifically state that the woman has to 'do all the work' in intercourse only when her husband is sexually inadequate. Ordinarily, the active participation of the woman in coitus is taboo, and men fiercely resent the lewd *kamalo:y* who plays a masculine role; they put down her pretensions by punitive and clitoridec-

[23] A. L. Kroeber, op. cit.
[24] J. G. Bourke, 'Notes on the Cosmogony and Theogony of the Mohave Indians of the Rio Colorado', *J. Amer. Folk-Lore*, 2 (1889), 169-89.
[25] G. Devereux, 'The Mohave Indian Kamalo:y', loc. cit.
[26] ibid.
[27] G. Devereux, 'The Social and Cultural Implications of Incest Among the Mohave Indians', loc. cit.
[28] idem, 'L'Envoûtement chez les Indiens Mohave', loc. cit.
[29] ibid., and A. L. Kroeber, op. cit.

tomizing mass-rape.[30] It is therefore of interest that the one instance known to me in which a woman actually threatened to retract a man's foreskin occurred at a *funeral*, and that in retaliation the man attempted to rape the woman. It is probable that the woman's aggressive and insulting exhibition of her breasts elicits in the man castration anxieties associated with the phallic (nursing) mother, whose imago the Mohave man needs to repress.

The interpretation of nursing Mohave women's psychology is beset with difficulties, because they are somewhat inarticulate on this subject. Their aggressive display of the breasts suggests that nursing is thought of in terms of activity: the woman who misbehaved at the funeral was disliked because of her 'phallic' personality. The aggressive aspects of nursing is also reflected in the Mohave belief that the foetus feeds partly on the mother's menstrual blood, and partly on the semen ejaculated into the pregnant woman by the father, or by some other man.[31] Only from the infantile viewpoint do the Mohave equate semen, menstrual blood, and milk. Consciously, in a purely coital context, they equate semen with the mucous secretions of the vagina.[32]

Since the Mohave woman is relegated by masculine anxiety to a passive sexual role, one is tempted to infer that the aggressive feelings which she associates with the breast and with nursing a child are compensatory and ambivalent; indeed, the failure of lactation may, in some instances, be due to a conflict over the active maternal role. Inducing lactation in older women tends to support this inference: older women sometimes become quite masculine in their behaviour. Tcatc, because of her great age, felt free to speak up in the tribal council. 'Because of her age' she was also quite ready to engage in sexual banter, obscene even by the standards of the Mohave man or of the Mohave *kamalo:y*,[33] although she had led 'a good life' in her youth.[34] The fact that the average Mohave woman is a notoriously poor cook and housekeeper, thus denying her husband oral gratification, has induced several Mohave men to desert their wives and to marry their mothers-in-law who are willing

[30] G. Devereux, 'The Mohave Indian Kamalo:y', loc. cit.
[31] G. Devereux, 'Der Begriff der Vaterschaft bei den Mohave Indianern', *Ztsch. f. Ethnologie*, 69 (1937), 72-8.
[32] idem, 'Heterosexual Behavior of the Mohave Indians', loc. cit.
[33] idem, 'The Mohave Indian Kamalo:y', loc. cit.
[34] For oral elements in obscenity cf. S. Ferenczi, *Contributions to Psychoanalysis*, Boston: Richard G. Badger, 1916, and E. Bergler, 'Obscene Words', *Psychoanal. Quart.*, 5 (1936), 226-48.

to be good housekeepers so as to conserve the affections of their relatively young husbands.[35] The flightiness and careless house-keeping of young women is adduced as the reason why men occa-sionally marry male transvestites who take pride in being good housekeepers.[36]

Women who nurse grandchildren after a daughter's death appear to experience no appreciable anxieties. They have passed the age when they are expected to be passive, and are nursing the children of men who would have been free to marry their mothers-in-law had they become dissatisfied with the housekeeping and general behaviour of their dead wives. The psychological problems of daughters who nurse siblings following the death of their mother is, however, fraught with much greater conflict. Such a girl is still required to be 'passive'. Nursing her sibling may elicit Oedipal anxieties, since she acts as an assistant wife to the father whom she is not free to marry; furthermore, she is also nursing her own child whose survival is thereby threatened. The care of an additional infant interferes, moreover, with her mobility, and with her sexual and other pleasures. The psychological problems of 'assistant mothers' have been discussed by Deutsch[37] and Riemer[38] has shown that in rural Sweden the 'assistant mother' sometimes becomes her father's concubine.

A reaction to the orally denying 'bad mother', whether real or imaginary, is frequently observed in psychoanalysis. The Mohave, though nursed for several years, still reproach their mothers for not having given them enough milk, and in adult life evolve intense reaction-formations to any suggestion of nursing. This reminds one of Freud's semihumorous remark that even native children, nursed for many years, would no doubt complain of having been orally frustrated.

One source of the Mohave Indian's belief that women are orally frustrating may be the behaviour of Mohave wives who, with few exceptions, are poor housekeepers and neglect their husbands. It is significant that Hama:Utce:, whom a slip of the tongue credited with masculine propensities, was a good housewife and a breadwinner

[35] G. Devereux, 'Primitive Psychiatry I', *Bull. Hist. Med.*, 8 (1940), 1194-1213.
[36] idem, 'Institutionalized Homosexuality of the Mohave Indians', loc. cit.
[37] H. Deutsch, *The Psychology of Women*, 2 vols., New York: Grune & Stratton, 1944 and 1945.
[38] S. Riemer, 'A Research Note on Incest', *Amer. J. Sociol.*, 45 (1940), 566-75.

as well. It is a psychoanalytic commonplace that the wife tends to be equated with the mother.[39] When seeking to discover why the sexually mature Mohave woman becomes an orally frustrating woman, one should recall that the Mohave measure the intensity of parental love by the length of the nursing period. Since the Mohave prefer boys to girls, 'because girls cannot be counted upon to settle down and take care of their old parents', it is possible that Mohave boys are nursed in preference to and longer than Mohave girls. Whether this be cause or effect, the Mohave woman behaves towards the adult members of her household as if in retaliation for her own infantile oral frustrations. The Mohave woman is also more infantile than the Mohave man, particularly in connection with unsublimated oral and anal trends. In refusing to be an active and competent housekeeper, she seems to be reducing to absurdity the passive role imposed upon her, especially during coitus. Since relatively little is known about this mechanism, this interpretation is offered tentatively. The Mohave woman's capacity to give actively is apparently overtaxed in three respects: obligatory and prolonged nursing of children; the obligation to be generous towards all and sundry;[40] the need to be aggressive sexually, often initiating sexual relations, while complying with the male demand that she be passive in the *act* of coitus. Mohave men are not the least reason for the frustrating behaviour of Mohave women: they do not particularly desire wives who remind them of the mother imago. Many a man who, disgusted with his flighty and shiftless young wife, marries her mother or a male transvestite, both of whom are good housekeepers, eventually deserts these inadequate sexual objects and takes another young wife.

The orally frustrating 'bad mother' is definitely present in the unconscious of the Mohave, who react against her with oral-sadistic fantasies and beliefs. The Mohave view erotic biting as a sign of jealousy and strongly disapprove of it. It seems probable, however, that the object of hatred in jealousy is not primarily the unfaithful sexual partner, but the real or suspected rival. What favours this assumption is the first mythical precedent for death and witchcraft

[39] S. Ferenczi, *Further Contributions to the Theory of Technique of Psychoanalysis*, London: Hogarth Press, 1926; and S. Freud, 'On the Universal Tendency to Debasement in the Sphere of Love', (1912), *Standard Ed.*, 11, London: Hogarth Press, pp. 179-90.

[40] G. Devereux, 'Mohave Culture and Personality', *Culture and Personality*, 8 (1939), 91-109.

H

which occurred when Frog Woman swallowed her father's faeces. This means that the fantasy of an anal penis is specifically present in Mohave thought, and that witchcraft consists of a symbolic ablation of the paternal penis.[41] The backward displacement of this penis (anal penis) is perhaps a result of the lateness of weaning and of toilet training among the Mohave Indians. The oral and anal stages tend to merge with the onset of the Oedipus.

Róheim suggests that among the culturally almost identical Yuma, the potentially shamanistic foetus is believed to observe parental intercourse and to have the desire to cut off the father's penis as it enters the vagina.[42] The Mohave believe that both children who have snakelike heads and shamans who remember intrauterine events and wish to kill themselves and their mothers at birth,[43] tend to bite the nipple (jealousy?). As the Mohave equate the penis with the nipple, and subject phallic women *(kamalo:y)* to castrative (clitoridectomy) mass-rape,[44] it seems probable that both the snake-headed child and the future shaman allegedly bite the nipple because they 'associate' it with the paternal penis. The Mohave specifically believe that the resentment of the infant is not directed towards the mother who yields no more milk when she is pregnant, but towards the unborn sibling now occupying her womb (child = penis).

These oral-sadistic wishes elicit fears of reprisal. A pregnant woman should not perform fellatio lest it damage the 'throat-cap' of the foetus and cause it to be born dumb. In a Yuma myth, quoted by Róheim,[45] the supernatural initiator (father), who appears to the future shaman in an 'intrauterine' dream, expresses pity for the child which cannot sing because earth is stuffed in its mouth. In the same work Róheim states his belief that coitus during pregnancy implies a wish to kill the foetus by means of the penis.

While I would not presume to express an opinion on this subject, certain facts cannot be ignored.

> Orgasm in the woman sometimes produces uterine contractions similar to those occurring during labour.

[41] idem, 'The Mohave Indian Kamalo:y', loc. cit.
[42] G. Róheim, 'Psychoanalysis of Primitive Cultural Types', *Internat. J. Psycho-Anal.*, 13 (1932), 1-224.
[43] G. Devereux, 'L'Envoûtement chez les Indiens Mohave', loc. cit.
[44] idem, 'The Mohave Indian Kamalo:y', loc. cit.
[45] G. Róheim, 'Psychoanalysis of Primitive Cultural Types', loc. cit.

The flesh of stallions—which is taboo during pregnancy because 'it would kick the child out of the womb'—is eaten by Mohave women on the eve of their confinement to accelerate delivery.

If the pregnant woman wears a necklace of beads, the cord will coil itself around the neck of the fœtus and will suffocate it.

Unwanted children, especially half-breeds and the children of deserted wives, are buried alive at birth—and always by a man.[46]

An old Mohave woman who had been abandoned by her *children*—quite an exceptional occurrence in that tribe—committed suicide by stuffing earth into her mouth. To the best of my knowledge, she was the only Mohave ever known to have killed herself in this manner.

Whether these beliefs and practices should be construed as echoes of states of suffocation during birth[47] is open to debate. It would be interesting to know whether the compression of the amniotic fluid resulting from orgastic uterine contractions, the weight of the copulating male, or perhaps some unspecified physiological processes connected with pregnancy, can bring about a temporary anoxemia of the foetus during copulation. Though I deny that my data support the thesis of prenatal consciousness,[48] the fact is that the Mohave are motivated both consciously and unconsciously by oral-sadistic impulses associated with anxieties of suffocation.

Fellatio is practised by the majority of Mohave women, whereas cunnilingus by men was universally denied. For the woman, fellatio may provide the same instinctual gratification as nursing once did: the penis is equated with the breast, semen with milk. For the man, being fellated provides a partial feminine identification (nursing) without injury to his phallic narcissism: it is active sexual behaviour, 'masculine' because the semen also feeds the foetus in the womb. This masculine 'nursing' is so literally apprehended that the male tranvestite who imitates every single other feminine reproductive function (passivity in coitus, menstruation, pregnancy, childbirth), and who calls his penis 'clitoris', his scrotum 'labia', his anus 'vagina', never pretends to suckle a child,[49] presumably

[46] G. Devereux, 'Mohave Indian Infanticide', *Psychoanal. Rev.*, 35 (1948), 126-39.

[47] S. Ferenczi, *Contributions to Psychoanalysis*, Boston: Richard G. Badger, 1916.

[48] K. A. Menninger, 'An Anthropological Note on the Theory of Prenatal Instinctual Conflict', *Internat. J. Psycho-Anal.*, 20 (1939), 439-442.

[49] G. Devereux, 'Institutionalized Homosexuality of the Mohave Indians', loc. cit.

because 'nursing' is the only reproductive function which the Mohave believe men and women have in common. Fellatio gratifies the man's hostile need to infantilize the woman whose phallic pretensions arouse in the male anxieties sufficiently intense to motivate mass-rape.[50]

This masculine nursing also has invidious and restitutive implications. The man seems to say to his orally frustrating wife, 'See how I nurse you and reward you for nursing the children?' Oral impregnation fantasies play an appreciable role. The Mohave male tranvestite acts out his pregnancy fantasy by drinking a constipating decoction of mesquite beans, and by referring to his scybalum as 'my stillborn child';[51] this is the well-known concept of the faecal child. All the evidence proves that Frog Woman did not become pregnant by Gopher, but by her father, the God Matavilye, whose faeces (anal penis) she ate.[52] According to a female informant, a Mohave man said that during fellatio he felt as though the woman were pulling his anus inward. Some of the man's pleasurable tensions connected with fellatio seem associated with the erotization of anxiety.[53] The Mohave are well aware of their biting oral sadism: their God Matavilye died when his daughter swallowed his 'anal penis'. They have strong castration anxieties: entrusting the penis to a woman's mouth (teeth) would seem to be a form of courting disaster, since the woman usually has reasons to be jealous of her husband or lover.

The hypothesis that Mohave women are relatively less fully gratified during the nursing stage than are Mohave men receives further confirmation from the prevalence of fellatio, a substitutive oral gratification in adult life. That the fellating woman is being symbolically nursed is convincingly illustrated by a case history. A woman agreed to fellatio only after the man had sulked for several days. Mohave opinion was that she was quite willing and merely pretended she did not like to do it. When the man ejaculated, the sperm 'came bubbling from her mouth'. Thereupon the *man* became known as *Namasava takavekva*, translated by the Mohave as 'white spills from the mouth', though according to Gatschet's

[50] idem, 'The Mohave Indian Kamalo:y', loc. cit.
[51] idem, 'Institutionalized Homosexuality of the Mohave Indians', loc. cit.
[52] idem, 'The Mohave Indian Kamalo:y', loc. cit.
[53] R. Laforgue, 'De L'angoisse à L'orgasme', *Rev. Française de Psa.*, 4 (1930-1), 245-58; and J. Boutonier, *L'Angoisse*, Paris: Presses Universitaires de France, 1945.

vocabulary[54] it should be translated as 'white departs' or 'white returns'. The Mohave explained to me that it looked like the bubbling of saliva and milk from the mouth of an infant. That the Mohave thought it a great joke that the semen should have spilled from her mouth[55] suggests that some women either swallow the sperm, or else, do not eject it immediately. Though I have no data to support this interpretation, the story would otherwise be pointless. That this anecdote concerns an exceptional or a unique incident is underscored by the consensus that this woman only pretended to be reluctant to perform fellatio.

The Mohave, like the culturally and linguistically almost identical Yuma, tend to associate saliva with sperm. Róheim's data from the Yuma contain references to a personage named Nemesava Kutchaer, who appeared in a shamanistic dream. Róheim's informant linked this name with a female disease. Persons afflicted with this ailment 'howled, turned round and round and foamed at the mouth'.[56] Seizures of this type are known also to the Mohave, who call the disease *kamalo:y taminyk*, and believe that it is caused by an excessive sexual drive increased by constant masturbation.[57] The culturally and linguistically related Diegueño believe the *kimilue* disease—one of whose symptoms is foaming at the mouth —to be caused by sexual frustration.[58] Jelliffe observed that schizophrenics often equate salivation with ejaculation.[59] Idiopathic epilepsy, often accompanied by foaming at the mouth, is frequently interpreted as an equivalent of orgasm. Since my Mohave informants compared the 'bubbling' of the semen mixed with saliva to milk and spittle spilling from the mouth of an overfed infant, Ferenczi's 'oral orgasm' is perhaps not as farfetched as it may sound.

There is evidence to suggest that fellatio is desirable to Mohave women as a means of assuaging their penis envy, which in one

[54] A. S. Gatschet, 'Der Yuma Sprachstamm', *Ztschr. f. Ethnologie*, 9 (1877), 365-418.
[55] G. Devereux, 'Heterosexual Behaviour of the Mohave Indians', loc. cit.
[56] G. Róheim, 'Psychoanalysis of Primitive Cultural Types', *Internat. J. Psycho-Anal.*, 13 (1932), 1-224.
[57] G. Devereux, 'The Mohave Indian Kamalo:y', loc. cit.
[58] G. Toffelmier and K. Luomala, 'Dreams and Dream Interpretation of the Dieguêno Indians of Southern California, *Psychoanal. Quart.*, 5 (1936), 195-225.
[59] S. E. Jelliffe and E. Evans, 'Psychotherapy and Tuberculosis', *Amer. Rev. Tuberculosis*, 3 (1919), 417-32; and S. E. Jelliffe, 'Somatic Pathology and Psychopathology at the Encephalitis Crossroad: A Fragment', *J. Nerv. Ment. Disease*, 61 (1925), 561-86.

instance was sufficiently intense to cause a little girl 'to break a young boy's urethra' during sexual play. Mohave women are also eager to have the penis inserted into all the orifices of their bodies. A married woman begged her lover to insert his large penis, which she admiringly contrasted with her husband's (her own?) small organ, also into her anus: 'I want to feel it in my anus too'. Curiously enough, she 'rewarded' him for his compliance with a spiteful 'anal gift', by 'unconsciously' defecating on his penis during withdrawal.[60] Accidents of this type are by no means rare, and are commemorated by the male personal name, *Porkupork*, which is an onomatopoeic anal equivalent of the name *Namasava takavekva*. It is noteworthy that the woman's vaginal moisture at the end of intercourse is believed by the Mohave to be the product of her 'ejaculation' during orgasm; hence some jealous husbands examine the genitals of their wives for traces of excessive moisture which would prove she had committed adultery in his absence. These vaginal, oral and anal ejecting mechanisms are triggered by a 'trauma of withdrawal' which is quite evident in some women's dislike of the Mohave practice of withdrawing the penis imme-diately after ejaculation, and in their contempt for the brief sexual act of the white man.[61] The convergence of genital, oral and anal reactions to withdrawal may also be explained by the protracted gratification of the partial drives past the onset of the genital and Oedipal phases of development which facilitate the fusion as well as the transformation of instincts.[62] The incorporative manifesta-tions of penis envy are probably of oral origin, at least among the Mohave, while the expulsive spite reaction is perhaps connected with the anal phase.

Unable to retain possession of the penis, the woman does retain the semen which is a phallic substitute and which, via fantasies of oral impregnation, promises to provide her with still another penis surrogate: a child. The legend that Matavilye died when his daugh-ter Frog Woman swallowed his 'anal penis' leads to the conclusion that fellatio also gratifies the woman's spitefully castrative impulses. This interpretation is supported by the association of semen with saliva which the Mohave apply to the penis before

[60] G. Devereux, 'Heterosexual Behaviour of the Mohave Indians', loc. cit.
[61] idem, 'The Mohave Indian Kamalo:y', loc. cit.
[62] S. Lorand, 'Contributions to the Problems of Vaginal Orgasm', *Internat. J. Psycho-Anal.*, 20 (1939), 432-8; and G. Zilboorg, 'Masculine and Feminine. Some Biological and Cultural Aspects', *Psychiatry*, 7 (1944), 257-96.

intercourse.[63] Saliva also playing, as it does, an important role in witchcraft, in the causation of diseases, and in shamanistic therapy,[64] its equivalence with semen gives additional confirmation to Róheim's interpretation of the sucking practice of Yuma shamans as a sublimated fellatio.[65]

The Mohave woman appears to practise fellatio without anxiety. She is permitted to gratify her oral desires because in the course of her psychosexual development she has switched love objects, and need not therefore connect fellatio too closely with murderous impulses towards the mother, and with sexual wishes for the father.

That her super-ego permits the gratification of both oral and Oedipal wishes in an almost unsublimated form may be responsible in part for the relatively greater immaturity of the Mohave woman.

Cunnilingus is denied both by Mohave women and by Mohave men. The Mohave man refrains from this act because it is connected with nursing, and also with menstruation, i.e. with drinking blood (cannibalism). The Mohave say they do not practice cunnilingus because of disagreeable olfactory sensations and (like many other warlike tribes) because the odour of human blood, and particularly menstrual blood, is nauseating to them.

A great deal of evidence suggests that cunnilingus is unconsciously equated with homosexual fellatio. According to Róheim, the dreams and fantasies of a Yuma shaman associated his mouth with his mother's vagina. The Mohave equate sperm with menstrual blood and hold that the foetus feeds on sperm. The Mohave female transvestite calls her clitoris a penis, just as the Mohave male transvestite refers to his penis as a clitoris.

The Mohave man is too fearful of passive submission to women to find pleasure in cunnilingus. The lewd phallic *kamalo:y* is clitoridectomized and sometimes deliberately killed by mass-rape. Whether regarded as an incestuous homosexual fellating of the father, or as nursing at the breast of a phallic mother, cunnilingus arouses severe anxieties in the man. A man supposedly became *blind* after some practical jokers pushed his face against the moist vulva of a drunken woman with whom the whole group was having (nonpunitive) intercourse.[66] Róheim's Yuma shaman apparently

---

[63] G. Devereux, 'Heterosexual Behaviour of the Mohave Indians', loc. cit.
[64] idem, 'L'Envoûtement chez les Indiens Mohave', loc. cit.; and A. L. Kroeber, op. cit.
[65] G. Róheim, 'Psychoanalysis of Primitive Cultural Types', loc. cit.
[66] G. Devereux, 'Heterosexual Behaviour of the Mohave Indians', loc. cit.

imagined that while he was being carried in the womb he saw the paternal penis penetrating his mother's vagina until a dust-storm arose which prevented him from seeing anything.[67]

No instance of fellatio between men, even among passive Mohave homosexuals, is known,[68] and not a single instance of homosexual incest is recorded.[69]

The women's attitude towards cunnilingus cannot be subjected to a detailed analysis because the entire subject seemed as distasteful to them as to male informants. My female informants merely stated that they were not 'civilized enough' to adopt this white man's 'vice', and that Mohave men were not 'crazy' enough to perform cunnilingus, because the vagina has a bad odour.[70] Mohave men examine the vulva visually and manually for one or more of four reasons: to determine whether or not the woman has had intercourse secretly with a lover; to humiliate her for a suspected infidelity; to ascertain whether she has venereal lesions;[71] in sexual foreplay. Mohave men 'lewd enough' to have intercourse during the woman's menses sometimes display their bloodstained penis to their friends. This is thought to be in the worst possible taste and, like vaginal examinations, is much resented by all but the most dissolute women.[72]

Cunnilingus is intolerable to Mohave males even in the form of scopophilic derivations. The long period of nursing establishes a very close relationship between oral eroticism and the nursing mother; therefore cunnilingus, homosexual fellatio, and the oral stimulation of the mammae during intercourse, arouse severe anxiety. The humorous manual *over*-stimulation of a woman's breasts is considered to be cruel.[73] The Mohave repressed oral sexuality so completely that kissing, and especially kissing the mouth, was unknown among adults in aboriginal times, and is still viewed with suspicion and disgust by the older generation.

Oral and anal traits are intimately interwoven in Mohave ideation. Both are prominent in fantasies of impregnation, and faeces and vomit tend to be equated. Whenever he had to defecate, the

---

[67] G. Róheim, 'Psychoanalysis of Primitive Cultural Types', loc. cit.
[68] G. Devereux, 'Institutionalized Homosexuality of the Mohave Indians', loc. cit.
[69] idem, 'The Social and Cultural Implications of Incest Among the Mohave Indians', *Psychoanal. Quart.*, 8 (1939), 510-33.
[70] idem, 'Heterosexual Behaviour of the Mohave Indians', loc. cit.
[71] ibid.   [72] ibid.
[73] ibid.

shaman Hivsu : Tupo : ma politely said in English, 'I am going to throw up'.

The Mohave are characterologically as a group oral optimists. Though provided with enormous appetites, they endure hunger uncomplainingly.[74] They do not worry about where the next day's meal will come from, and willingly give away their seeds, not only to the 'heaven-born twins',[75] but even to a mere starving white girl captive.[76] They labour hard and for long hours when they are interested, but do not work at all if the work bores them.[77] They prize generosity almost above any other virtue,[78] and despise habitual spongers who are not themselves generous. The oral dependent personality is rare or unknown among them. The oral sadist is more disliked than feared : a sharp-tongued and temperamental person risks being accused of witchcraft.[79] Quite capable of stolid silence in the presence of strangers, they are great talkers, fond of banter and laughter; they admire singers and orators.

The Mohave are very much aware of the oral needs of children. Infants are given strands of the inner bark of the willow to suck, chew and tear up in play. Children are free to suck their own fingers and those of adults, '. . . because they get mad and cry when they have nothing to suck at'. As befits oral optimists, they confidently anticipate oral satisfactions, and their mythology and esoteric beliefs contain no elaborate notions about nursing. By identification, they believe that hunger traumatizes the infant, and therefore attempt to alleviate such painful tensions by oral indulgences and by means of shamanistic physiotherapy and psychotherapy. Both sexes drink too much, however.

3. CONCLUSION

The Mohave Indians' awareness of the trauma of weaning and the only slightly repressed and distorted manifestations of their

[74] A. L. Kroeber, op. cit.
[75] G. Devereux, 'Mohave Beliefs Concerning Twins', *Amer. Anthropologist*, N.S. 43 (1941), 573-92.
[76] R. B. Stratton, *The Captivity of the Oatman Girls*, New York, 1857.
[77] A. L. Kroeber, op. cit.
[78] G. Devereux, 'Mohave Culture and Personality', *Culture and Personality*, 8 (1939), 91-109.
[79] idem, 'L'Envoûtement chez les Indiens Mohave', loc. cit.

orality, show an unusual degree of insight into what are obscure psychological mechanisms to most peoples in whom such id strivings are automatically repressed. This psychological intuition would be noteworthy even if it were limited to orality. In fact, a great number of Mohave beliefs are characterized by a transparent exhibition and conscious apperception of psychoanalytically revealed mechanisms that arouse interest and invite study and comment.

The Mohaves' pervasive preoccupation with dreams is surprising, because even their shamans are predominantly extroverted and active personalities. The Mohave has an adequate mastery of reality, and a well-integrated ego, capable of enduring a great deal of tension. In fact, he seeks tension and adventure: his 'exploratory reflex' is highly developed.

The Mohave Indian is extraordinarily preoccupied with fantasies and provided with theories about the psychology of prenatal and early infantile existence, which is closely associated with the idea of tribal continuity and probably also with the absence of belief in personal immortality.[80] The happiness of Mohave childhood—in which fantasies about the destruction of the maternal body, and the tendency to bite the nipple are ascribed chiefly to shamans— perhaps reinforces preoccupation with intrauterine life and with childhood, and causes the Mohave to more or less neglect life after death, which is associated neither with immortality nor with happiness.[81] These psychological beliefs, apparently based on subjective experiences and expressed in the form of tribal beliefs, tend to be in conformity with corresponding psychoanalytic interpretations.

Despite the comparative absence of early oral, anal and genital frustrations, the Mohave Indians (the women partly excepted for reasons already stated) show relatively little impairment of the ability to achieve genitality and adequate emotional, intellectual and social adaptation to the standards of their community. This is noteworthy in view of Freud's statement that without early instinctual frustration, children remain uneducable. Since many other tribes present a developmental history similar to the Mohave, the importance of frustration for the socialization of the child may

[80] idem, 'Mohave Culture and Personality', loc. cit.
[81] idem, 'Mohave Soul Concepts', *Amer. Anthropologist*, N.S. 39 (1937), 417-22. Cf. Róheim's studies about the myth of the Garden of Eden ('The Garden of Eden', *Psychoanal. Rev.*, 27 (1940), 1-26, 177-99; and 'Sublimation', *Psychoanal. Quart.*, 12 (1943), 338-52). The above correlation is predicated only for the Mohave and its opposite for Western culture. Whether it holds also for other cultures remains to be tested through further studies.

have to be reappraised. Lowie[82] and Róheim[83] are right in saying that the higher the civilization, the more cruel and frustrating is the treatment of children. Yet some civilizations prove that a high cultural development is compatible with an absence of early instinctual frustration[84] and with what Róheim calls a patchy and non-pervasive 'primitive' super-ego.[85]

[82] R. H. Lowie, *Are We Civilized?*, New York: Harcourt, Brace, 1929.

[83] G. Róheim, 'Racial Differences in the Neurosis and Psychosis', *Psychiatry*, 2 (1939), 575-90.

[84] W. LaBarre, 'Some Observations on Character Structure in the Orient. II. The Chinese', *Psychiatry*, 9 (1946), 215-37, 375-95.

[85] G. Róheim, 'A Primitiv Ember', in *A Magyarorszagi Pszichoanalitikai Egyesület Tagjai: Lélekelemzési Tanulmányok* (Ferenczi Memorial Volume), Budapest: Somló Béla, 1933.

III. Culture and Personality

In its beginnings psychoanalysis was primarily concerned with ascertaining proof of clinical findings from anthropological data. It tried to demonstrate the universality of basic fantasies, the existence of the unconscious, the connection between socialization and drive control.

This paper by Drs Hartmann, Kris and Loewenstein is the first metapsychological comment on the influence of institutionalized and non-institutionalized behaviour on personality configuration. It considers certain correlations between ego development and culture-syntonic pathways of discharge. It also draws attention to the environmentalist approach of studying mother-infant relationships with the aim of explaining stereotypes and the collective character of a given people.

11

Some Psychoanalytic Comments on 'Culture and Personality'[1]

HEINZ HARTMANN, ERNST KRIS and RUDOLPH M. LOEWENSTEIN

1. INTRODUCTORY REMARKS

The juxtaposition of culture and personality designates a vast area of research, rich in promise and stimulation. Investigators working in this area tend to point with pride to their attempts at interdisciplinary co-operation. Their views, however, differ frequently on essential points, and one may well gain the impression that we are faced with a transitory period, in which affairs are unsettled and results tentative.[2]

In view of those uncertainties one may doubt whether this is an opportune moment for the approach we here intend. One may ask what psychoanalysis can contribute to current investigations in a common field, or what these investigations have contributed and can contribute to psychoanalysis as a body of propositions; clarification in this area might then in turn be valuable to those who apply psychoanalytic propositions.

We do not question the fact that the interdisciplinary approach has proved to be highly productive, whether conducted by investigators combining training in both major disciplines, psychoanalysis and anthropology,[3] or by teams in which both these specialities were

[1] This paper first appeared in *Psychoanalysis and Culture: Essays in Honor of Géza Róheim*, ed. by G. B. Wilbur and W. Muensterberger, New York: International Universities Press, 1951, pp. 3-32.

[2] For a survey of the current discussion see C. Kluckhohn, *Mirror for Man*, New York: McGraw-Hill, 1949; C. Kluckhohn and H. Murray (eds.), *Personality in Nature, Society and Culture*, New York: Knopf, 1948; or in the Symposium *Culture and Personality*, Proceedings of an Interdisciplinary Conference held under the auspices of the Viking Fund, edited by S. Stanfeld Sargent and Marian W. Smith, New York: Viking, 1949.

[3] Our indebtedness to the work of Géza Róheim will in the following pages be stated explicitly. Suffice it to say that this essay was written in his honour and reflects the effect of his work on his friends and colleagues.

represented. Nor do we ignore the fact that in the investigating teams many skills and several professions are co-operating. Our starting point is that many psychological propositions used by workers in the field are derived from psychoanalysis. During the present phase of historical development the scientific access to problems of human conflict, and hence of personality, initiated by Freud, is exercising influence on the social sciences which previously had relied on common-sense psychology. The initial attempts to utilize psychoanalysis suggested that in order to apply the new type of psychological thinking hitherto neglected data were essential.[4] No other branch of the social sciences has taken this call for new data more seriously than anthropology. A wealth of material assembled during the best part of a generation is witness to the fruitfulness of the contact.

Under the inspiring leadership of pioneering thinkers, of whom Edward Sapir seems to have wielded incisive influence, cultural anthropology arose as a discipline[5]—a development that is not yet concluded. In the service of interdisciplinary expediency some psychoanalytic propositions have been explicitly or implicitly modified or applied incompletely. As far as the explicit modifications are concerned they are closely related to the formation of definite schools of thought or groups in psychoanalysis. If we view this phenomenon not in sociological terms it means that sets of alternate propositions have been suggested. Such alternate sets of propositions have been repeatedly formulated throughout the history of psychoanalysis as part of its development, and some of the suggested modifications and revisions have become part of the main body of psychoanalytic propositions. Few of these modifications go as far as those which Freud himself introduced, particularly during the nineteen twenties. Others found their expression in sociological organizations, i.e. in alternate teaching or research setups. Some of these alternate views were stimulated by the relation of psychoanalytic to anthropological research. This relation has been viewed in various ways. Fromm, the proponent of a considerably modified and abbreviated set of propositions, believes that the

[4] See E. Shils, *The Present State of American Sociology*, Glencoe, Ill ; Free Press, 1948.

[5] For this development and its relation to psychiatry, see C. Kluckhohn, 'The Influence of Psychiatry on Anthropology in America During the Past Hundred Years', in *One Hundred Years of American Psychiatry*, published by the American Psychiatric Association, New York: Columbia University Press, 1944.

modifications to which he refers favoured the application of psycho-analysis to social and anthropological research.[6] Thompson takes a different view: to her the modification was not the precondition but the result of this application.[7] Apart from such explicit state-ments we are faced with various elaborations and simplifications that tend to arise because either the data available do not allow for a greater complexity of viewpoints, or because the authors working in the field select out of the manifold set of psychoanalytic pro-positions some which they consider particularly revealing and well applicable, without concern for their interrelations to other data and propositions, essential in psychoanalysis as a psychological system.

Our starting point is different. We believe that the complexity of psychoanalytic propositions is not accidental but necessary. Altern-ate sets of propositions should only be accepted if their explanatory or predictive potential is equal to that of more complex proposi-tions. This, we believe, is not true of many of the modifications or abbreviations of psychoanalytic propositions frequently used when culture and personality are discussed. In what follows we select topics in the discussion of which simplifications tend to foster sweeping generalizations and are likely to lead to serious misunder-standings. We shall confront these simplifications with the relative complexity of the psychoanalytic propositional system, a system that does not exist in any codification, and has largely to be derived from the history of psychoanalysis.[8] It is mainly based on Freud's own writings, but not in a literal sense, since Freud himself did not establish a systematic synchronization of his various theories. Also, it is not limited to Freud's writings and considers the further development of psychoanalysis, particularly that of ego psychology, of developmental psychology, and of the structural concepts. We speak of a system in view of the cohesion and interlocking of pro-positions. Needless to say that we do not envisage a rigid system but one that is constantly open to modification arising out of valida-tion or invalidation of its parts. These procedures naturally require

[6] E. Fromm, 'Psychoanalytic Characterology and its Application to the Understanding of Culture', in *Culture and Personality*, cited above.
[7] Clara Thompson, *Psychoanalysis, Evolution and Development*, New York: Hermitage House, 1950.
[8] See H. Hartmann, E. Kris and R. M. Loewenstein, 'Comments on the Formation of Psychic Structure', *The Psychoanalytic Study of the Child*, 2, New York: International Universities Press; London, Hogarth, 1946, pp. 11-38.

that the propositions should be stated with due care. For this purpose the whole of psychoanalytic thinking has to be considered. It seems essential to stress this point since many of the various modifiers of psychoanalysis do not fulfil these requirements. They tend to polemize with insistence against views contained in the earlier writings of Freud and his collaborators, ignoring frequently Freud's own reformulations of the mid-twenties and particularly the development of ego psychology since that time; and yet, ego psychology may well suggest the most fruitful and pertinent propositions for inter-disciplinary co-operation. In selecting areas for the present discussion we had this possibility in mind and focused on topics around which misunderstandings frequently seem to cluster.

2. THE RANGE OF BIOLOGICAL THINKING IN PSYCHOANALYSIS

The comparative study of culture includes the question as to variant and invariant traits of 'human nature'. In this connection the view is frequently taken that Freud is 'exclusively' or 'predominantly' biologically oriented and that in his writings undue stress is laid upon invariant factors. This view implies that what is meant by the term 'biological' in psychoanalysis is limited to the innate;[9] moreover, the innate is frequently thought to be limited to instinctual drives, which in turn tend to be equated with instincts in the sense of animal psychology. We have attempted to clarify the last of these misunderstandings in previous papers. The concept of instinctual drive, we said, is not identical with the one used in animal psychology, but a construct particularly designed to describe the phenomena of conflict in a man which psychoanalysis studies.[10] It is viewed in terms of opposing psychic structures, arising out of the differentiation of id and ego from an undifferentiated state, and the id represents not less and no more a product of this differentiation than the ego. Growth, as we generally describe it,

---

[9] See, e.g., A. Kardiner (*The Psychological Frontiers of Society*, New York: Columbia University Press, 1945, p. 2) who speaks of 'biological traits, that is, inherited in the germ plasm'.

[10] H. Hartmann, 'Comments on the Psychoanalytic Theory of Instinctual Drives', *Psychoanal. Quart.*, 17 (1948); H. Hartmann, E. Kris, R. M. Loewenstein, 'Notes on the Theory of Aggression', *The Psychoanalytic Study of the Child*, 3/4, New York: International Universities Press; London: Hogarth, 1949.

is not limited to the sequence of zones of predominant erotogeneity; it includes the unfolding of ego functions, the development of thought, from an archaic phase to one in which concrete thinking is only gradually supplemented by the more and more abstract concepts, a process which is corrected by and geared to the development of reality testing; part of this sequence is the development of objectivation and even earlier that of perception and memory, upon which fantasy and thought are based; processes that presuppose certain steps in the formation of the ego and are indispensable preconditions to others. The first attempts to inhibit immediate discharge, the first nuclear conflicts between impulses and their control under the dominance of the 'reality principle' are equally part of this gradual unfolding. To put it briefly, all this is intended if we refer to the biological aspects of personality. Adjustment to reality as well as integrative functions must be viewed in the context of biological thinking. The 'biological' is neither limited to the innate nor identical with invariant traits in man.

There is obviously a vast area in which the same statements are part of both biological and sociological sets of assumptions. While the biological functions of the ego include processes of adaptation, differences in the environment act directly upon the development of ego functions.[11]

At this point it seems appropriate to introduce a terminological distinction.[12] We suggest that the term maturation be reserved for those growth processes which are relatively independent of environmental conditions, the term development for those which are more dependent on environmental conditions. To use an example of the inter-relations we refer to Freud's comment on the problems of latency, which in its brevity is representative of his views on maturation and development as here defined, and thus to at least one major aspect concerning the range of his biological thinking. 'The period of latency,' he wrote in 1935, 'is a psychological phenomenon'

[11] Compare this with Fromm's characterization of what he calls the orthodox Freudian approach '. . . Social phenomena and cultural patterns are to be explained as direct outcomes of certain libidinal trends' (loc. cit., p. 3). Freud 'saw the individual as an isolated entity endowed with certain drives rooted in the inner chemistry' (loc. cit., p. 7). One can hardly understand how it is possible to overlook the role object relations play in Freud's propositions on human development.

[12] See H. Hartmann and E. Kris, 'The Genetic Approach in Psychoanalysis', *The Psychoanalytic Study of the Child*, 1, New York: International Universities Press; London: Hogarth Press, 1945.

(i.e. a manifestation of a maturational process). 'It can, however, only give rise to a complete interruption of sexual life in cultural organizations which have made the suppression of infantile sexuality a part of their system. This is not the case with the majority of primitive peoples.'[13] The functions of the ego represent

[13] *An Autobiographical Study* (1925), *Standard Ed.*, 20, London: Hogarth Press, 1959, p. 37, f.n. 1. It might be worth recording that this statement has never been considered worth quoting by those who claim that Freud's biological orientation excluded consideration of cultural factors. The reverse, namely, the neglect for the physiological processes, is a current tendency in many theories that purport to be 'Improvements'. As an example we refer to the discussion of the anal character by Fromm (loc. cit.), who considers its description by Freud 'clinically correct and indeed one of the greatest contributions to the field of characterology'. Fromm suggests that 'what Freud called the anal character can be understood as a particular kind of relatedness to the world', describing individuals 'living in a fortified position'. Stinginess is seen as an attempt to strengthen this position, cleanliness as an attempt to ward off contact with the outside world, and orderliness as an attempt to put things in their place. Punctuality and stubbornness can be understood in a similar sense. It will be noted that what Fromm here describes are certain ego aspects of the respective attitudes. In their treatment during psychoanalytic observation it is frequently necessary to interpret the connections to which Fromm points. These attitudes may, but need not, constitute the anal character in the sense of Freud. Freud describes a specific type of relation of these attitudes to the past, i.e., to the anal phase of development; if the appropriate analytical procedure is applied such a relationship can frequently be established.

Fromm's description, however, neglects the point that characterological concepts in psychoanalysis are genetically orientated, and also that they do not only describe actual, but imply predictions of potential future behaviour. (See H. Hartmann, 'Über genetische Charakterologie', *Jahrbuch f. Charakterologie*, 6, 1929.) This neglect leads him to overlook that the behaviour syndrome he describes has only a superficial, or better, accidental, similarity to Freud's thesis: Fromm postulates a descriptive consistency of behaviour, one type of relatedness to the world. Freud's proposition refers to a triad of tendencies which in overt behaviour may manifest themselves positively or negatively, i.e., by their opposites; the individual may be either a spendthrift or stingy, particularly clean or dirty, stubborn or yielding. By limiting himself to a 'meaningful' consistency of present behaviour, Fromm has departed from the genetic frame of reference upon which Freud's finding rests.

In the case of the anal character Freud was not satisfied to conclude that 'common' experiences during childhood determined adult behaviour, but he also stated his impression that these experiences were based on a common dispositional factor. Investigations on identical twins have confirmed these impressions. Hartmann studied pairs of identical twins and found that if in one of the twins one of the character traits of the triad regularly predominated either in its positive or in its negative form. The three character traits are therefore pariavariable, i.e. they substitute for each other. ('Psychoanalytische Zwillingsstudien', *Psychiatrische Jahrbücher*, 1934.) No analysis of overt behaviour could have established a meaningful relationship between the disorderliness of the one and the obstinacy of the other.

In stating before that the behavioural syndrome to which Fromm refers may, but need not, be related to the anal character type, we had a particular aspect in mind, which might here be mentioned in order to illustrate

in this connection the bridge to the environment; in its growth there are in turn maturational factors operating most clearly, though not exclusively where the apparatus are concerned—but the decisive changes in the ego in the course of time take place under the influence of the environment. These changes are exquisitely environmental and must be examined in close contact with the environment. It is in this area that during the last decade clinical investigations have produced most encouraging results. To point to one area only: Since the early findings of Helene Deutsch on the role of infantile object relations in the etiology of schizoid behaviour[14] based on reconstructions in psychoanalysis, a large number of observers have elaborated on the various consequences of early object relations:[15] from the investigations of Durfee, Wolf, Bender, Goldfarb, Fries, Ribble, Spitz, Putnam, Rank, and others, it appears that the nature and intensity of this relationship determine a large number of features in the child's subsequent development. Moreover, in some instances it has been possible to state in detail how one particular type of conflict in the mother stimu-

the complexity of propositions required to illustrate genetic problems in analysis. The attitudes of which Fromm speaks are frequently observed surface phenomena of obsessional characters. Following Freud one was used to assume that one of the preconditions leading to such a character structure was the relative prematurity of ego development as compared to the development of other parts of the personality. Observations of children before the anal phase seem to support this point. In some cases these ego tendencies might later only be brought into relation to the development of anality and receive the imprint of this phase of instinctual development (see H. Hartmann, 'Psychoanalysis and Developmental Psychology', *The Psychoanalytic Study of the Child*, 5, New York: International Universities Press; London: Hogarth Press, 1950.) However, such connections seem not to be universal. Cases of psychotic or retarded children studied by the staff of the James Jackson Children Centre in Boston-Roxbury show characteristics of what we would tend to describe as typical obsessional behaviour in an attempt to organize a world which is bewildering since it is not sufficiently 'invested' with energy. This step functions as part of a process of readaptation and occurs as a result of therapeutic influence. One may infer that the situation is similar in cases of adults in which the obsessional façade covers schizoid trends or even a schizophrenic process. These clinical experiences reinforce the view that a satisfactory description of genetic considerations must simultaneously take into account the development of the ego, the instinctual development, and that of object relations. Only on this basis characterology becomes valuable; i.e., if we aim not only at describing present but also at predicting future behaviour.

[14] Helene Deutsch, 'Über einen Typus der Pseudoaffektivität' ('als ob'). *Internat. Z. Psychoanal.*, 20 (1934); idem, 'Some Forms of Emotional Disturbances and their Relationship to Schizophrenia', *Psychoanal. Quart.*, 11 (1942).

[15] For the following and selected bibliographical references see E. Kris, 'Notes on the Development and on Some Current Problems of Psychoanalytic Child Psychology', *The Psychoanalytic Study of the Child*, 5, New York: International Universities Press; London: Hogarth Press, 1950.

lated in the child the development of a certain pattern of defence mechanism.[16]

Investigations such as those quoted deserve to be mentioned here for two reasons: first, they are immediately relevant to the discussion of the range of biological thinking in psychoanalysis; and second, as far as methodological questions are concerned, they are to some extent similar to those which many cultural anthropologists pursue.

Freud's biological approach which characterizes human development by the length of dependence—a point of view substantiated by Bolk in his views on fetalization—implies the idea not only of the unique role of the love object in human development but also the extent to which the influence of this object determines later behaviour.[17] This is the area in which psychoanalysis can be described as a theory of learning. Research in the area of culture and personality has repeatedly been viewed in similar terms.[18]

The biological approach thus indicates a framework within which the fact that man is the social animal becomes meaningful. Once this has been clarified it becomes evident that the study of human behaviour can, and in many instances must, be viewed from both sides: we can characterize the relationship between mother and child as a biological relationship or we can characterize it as a social one; the fact that both concatenations are overlapping constitutes the human.

One might be tempted to say that the attention of the clinician, who devotes himself to the study of one particular mother and her child with the methods or the approach of psychoanalysis, is

---

[16] See E. Jackson and E. B. Klatskin, 'Rooming-In Research Project: Development of Methodology of Parent-Child Relationship Study in a Clinical Setting', *The Psychoanalytic Study of the Child*, 5, New York: International Universities Press; London: Hogarth Press, 1950.

[17] For Bolk's views see M. Levy-Suhl, 'Über die frühkindliche Sexualität des Menschen im Vergleich mit der Geschlechtsreife der Säugetiere', *Imago*, 19 (1933); G. Róheim, *The Riddle of the Sphinx*, London: Hogarth Press, 1934; H. Hartmann, 'Ichpsychologie und Anpassungsproblem', *Int. Zeitsh. f. Psa.*, 24 (1939); and recently, in a broad frame of reference, G. Róheim, *Psychoanalysis and Anthropology: Culture, Personality and the Unconscious*, New York: International Universities Press, 1950.

[18] For similar formulations see H. Hartmann and E. Kris, 'The Genetic Approach in Psychoanalysis', op. cit.; O. H. Mowrer and C. Kluckhohn, 'Dynamic Theory of Personality', in J. McV. Hunt (ed.), *Personality and the Behaviour Disorders*, 1, New York: Ronald Press, 1944; G. Devereux, 'The Logical Foundations of Culture and Personality Studies', *Trans. New York Acad. Sci.*, Series 2, Vol. 7, No. 5, March 1945; and G. Bateson 'Sex and Culture', *Annals New York Acad. Sci.*, 48 (1947), 603-64.

likely to be more interested in the biological aspects of the relationship than the anthropologist, whose interest turns to the social type. However, such a distinction would be utterly misleading. Both are interested in the same processes, but they are partly using data of different kinds; and it is to a discussion of this difference that we now turn.

3. THE NATURE OF THE DATA

The relation of psychoanalysis to anthropology is to a considerable extent determined by the difference of the data utilized and available in both. This difference may facilitate or impede interdisciplinary contact, depending on the purpose of the investigation. During the earlier part of the century the difference of the data proved highly opportune. This was the time when the validity of certain psychoanalytic findings was at stake. It then seemed relevant to prove that they described psychological events not limited to pathology or to any specific period of culture. These investigations focused on general principles and primarily attempted to demonstrate the ubiquity of certain psychological mechanisms and tendencies, mostly of what we would today characterize as 'id contents'. Under varying conditions of culture, certain mechanisms and tendencies could more easily be demonstrated than under conditions prevailing in the contemporary Western World. Rituals were studied in their affinity to symptoms and obsessional thoughts, myths in their relation to typical conflicts and to symbolism. Investigations of this kind, in part undertaken by the first pioneering generation of psychoanalysts, tend to be ignored or discarded at present. They were linked to the evolutionist trend in anthropological thinking, and to an only slightly modified version of the law of biogenesis. With the increased understanding of historical and cultural material this earlier approach has lost its interest for some students. No doubt, this is only a transitory shift of attention; but there is some danger that the rediscovery of important findings may be unduly delayed.

It is hardly necessary to emphasize that no data produced and no interpretations advanced have been able, or even seriously set out, to modify our views on the working of the psychic apparatus. Psychoanalytic assumptions on psychic structure and the interrelation of its parts, on the function of psychic energy and its

247

working, on the distinction of degrees of neutralization, of mobile and bound energies, and hence of primarily and secondary processes,[19] supply the best, or more precisely, the only set of assumptions which at present permits an explanatory approach to mental functioning. The same is true of the basic mechanisms of defence and adjustment. Assumptions concerning the differentiation which is considered responsible for the relation of the id to the ego and the tension between these two systems aim at describing the equipment of man.[20] This is true also of the instinctual drives, conceived in psychoanalysis in sharp distinction from instincts, at least in lower animals. What these assumptions describe is relatively independent of environmental conditions in the same sense as physiological processes are. That does not mean that the processes envisaged appear under all observable or conceivable conditions in the same intensity and/or frequency. We have mentioned before that clinical observations suggest that even the formation of the ego, e.g. its cathexis with neutralized energy, seems to be dependent, among other factors, on the nature of the earliest object relations, as studied recently in the vicissitudes of the mother-child relationship. There is no doubt that cultural differences may be responsible for similar variations. In fact, we expect that in the not-too-distant future anthropologists will utilize propositions in this area in describing psychological phenomena related to certain types of difference between cultures. However carefully anthropological statements are worded, they can hardly avoid some expressions which indicate distinctions of 'achievement', i.e. some of the distinctions previously described in evolutionist terms. While we do not intend to encourage any revival of evolutionist thinking or to overvalue its remnants, it seems that in speaking of 'preliterate' societies instead of 'primitive' societies one has in part substituted a different language and avoided certain connotations attached to the traditional assumption of 'primitiveness'. It is conceivable that the differences to which these expressions refer, e.g. those in degree of literateness, and other related ones, could in part—and we stress this—be viewed in terms of ego psychology. One might say that the increase

---

[19] No complete enumeration is here intended.

[20] With certain modifications these constructs might even be used in describing certain types of animal behaviour. In this sense Hartmann ('Ichpsychologie und Anpassungsproblem', loc. cit.) suggests that the tension between id and ego may exist, but less marked in higher animals than it is in man.

in automony of the ego or the super-ego organization—problems to which Freud and Hartmann have drawn attention[21]—would lend themselves for the description of such differences. In particular it might be important to study the increase in ego automony. It seems that the ability for higher mental functions is dependent on the degree to which ego activities are distant from conflict and hence autonomous, i.e. on the degree to which the ego's energy cathexis is neutralized. This will naturally depend on a large variety of factors, but cultural conditions could and should be viewed also with the question in mind which and what kind of opportunities for ego functions in a sphere free from conflict they invite or inhibit. The increase in autonomy of the ego seems to be of immediate relevance to two areas of problems. First, we may expect a diminution of the tendencies toward magical thinking, as opposed to scientific thinking; of taboos and similar restrictions, frequently, if not regularly, concomitant with magical attitudes.[22] Secondly, we also may expect that the ego's growing independence from the instinctual drives creates favourable conditions for solutions of problems of integration and adjustment and also influences the formation and elaboration of the super-ego.

The trend towards increased ego automony during the history of Western man is paralleled by the trend toward interiorization of aggression which, in its turn, contributes to the development of super-ego functions. Here, too, the problem of autonomy—i.e. in this case the independence from external pressures—deserves attention. Functions of an autonomous super-ego may be exercised in a way which may not only facilitate adaptation in a narrower sense but also the whole area of organizational functions of the ego.

Returning to our main line of thought, we restate that at the time when the demonstration of the general validity of certain psychoanalytic assumptions seemed important, the contact between

[21] H. Hartmann, 'Comments on the Psychoanalytic Theory of the Ego', *The Psychoanalytic Study of the Child*, 5, New York: International Universities Press; London: Hogarth Press, 1950.
[22] We may consider it as well established that magical thinking tends to be more frequent in areas in which we do not 'understand', i.e. in areas where our cognitive integration is poorer. From the point of view of psychoanalysis this difference is only of minor relevance. And yet we see that magical thoughts tend to retire into areas of misunderstanding and we are used to find that the removal of affective support of magical thought facilitates cognitive integration, which in turn reduces the tendency to magical thinking.

the data of psychoanalysis and anthropology proved fruitful through their difference. No explicit objections ever seem to have been raised against the assumption that the basic mental operations as described by psychoanalysis are specific of man. However, to the second set of investigations, namely those concerned with the ubiquity of certain themes in mythology, the ubiquity of symbolism, objections of many types have been voiced. One might take the view that these objections constitute an instigation to modifications of psychoanalytic propositions in their application to anthropology. The objections of which we here speak can be better evaluated if we introduce a distinction between two critical arguments. One concerns the principle by which the occurrence of this 'ubiquity' was explained by Freud and is being explained by some psychoanalysts. The second concerns the assumption of the 'ubiquity' itself.

Freud draws partly on phylogeny, and more specifically on the inheritance of acquired characteristics, which would account for phenomena such as the occurrence of sexual symbols—and—to mention only the most controversial instance—the occurrence of the Oedipal conflict. His views on this matter remain unchanged. When he became aware of the fact that biological studies had not confirmed Lamarckian assumptions (though strictly speaking they were not invalidated) he 'postulated' the phylogenetic explanation 'for psychological reasons.' Several psychoanalytic authors have voiced their doubts,[23] and suggested alternate explanations which seem fully to account for the phenomena in question. The 'ubiquity' of certain symbols, particularly of sexual symbols, seems accountable if we keep in mind how fundamentally similar every human infant's situation in the adult world is: how limited the number of meaningful situations is which the infant invests with affect; how typical and invariant the infant's anxieties are, and finally how uniform some of his basic perceptions and bodily sensations are bound to be. The fact that most sexual symbols are related to parts of the body and their function has repeatedly been pointed out. These functions are familiar from a large number of

---

[23] See e.g. E. Jones, 'Review of S. Freud, *Moses and Monotheism*', *Internat. J. Psycho-Anal.*, 21 (1940), 230-40; G. Róheim, *The Origin and Function of Culture*, New York: Nerv. Ment. Dis. Mon. No. 69, 1943; R. M. Loewenstein, 'Historical and Cultural Roots of Anti-Semitism', in G. Róheim (ed.), *Psychoanalysis and the Social Sciences*, 1, New York: International Universities Press; London: Hogarth Press, 1947; H. Hartmann and E. Kris, 'The Genetic Approach in Psychoanalysis', loc. cit.

experiences of the child and these experiences themselves are organized in the image of the body, one of the apparatus of the ego.[24] However far the differentiation of human behaviour by environmental influences may go, the basic relationship of percepts to parts of the body, of movements to the impulses to caress or hurt, to eliminate or to include, to receive or to retain—at least to these—not only form the basis for the formation of symbols but are equally the basis for the universality of nonverbal communication. The posture of the body is expressive without comments (Schilder). The differentiated part of posture, i.e. gesture, is highly modified by the ego; and yet in certain fundamentals the language of the body is universal. The limits of the universality, the degree to which gesture replaces expression by posture, might well be examined in each specific instance. One might expect that the language of the body will prove to be not culturally specific if close to the id.[25] This does not exclude that certain ego functions find equally general modes of expression. What universality of symbols there is in the meaning of psychoanalysis can be viewed in similar terms and might well be investigated with an analogous intention. However, the case seems more complex; not only the body is 'human'; the fact that the personality is structured, that verbalization is part of the function of the apparatus of all men, that the transitions from primary to secondary processes in the child's development, etc., are universal, is bound to influence the formation of symbols. A detailed study of the ontogenesis of symbol formation would be highly desirable in order to clarify these problems. This investigation could then be related to our expectations concerning symbols in different cultures. We expect to find 'limits' of ubiquity and cultural variations and superimposed symbolic meanings around an ubiquitous core. But here as elsewhere in this area no reliable data exist; work has not even been seriously initiated.

Propositions dealing with the Oedipus complex imply similar assumptions: The fetalization of the human and the extraordinary dependence of the infant on adult (maternal) care and protection, the development of impulses of a genital order at a time when the child lives among adults, is attached to them and at the same time

[24] See P. Schilder, *The Image and Appearance of the Human Body*, New York: International Universities Press, 1950.
[25] See E. Kris, 'Laughter as an Expressive Process', *Internat. J. Psycho-Anal.*, 21 (1940).

still totally dependent on them, is the nucleus of a conflict situation which we believe to be universal.[26] We know from clinical experience a large variety of manifestations of the Oedipus complex, but we do not assume that all that exist, or could conceivably exist, have been described. We are aware of differences caused, e.g. by the nature of the family constellation, or have detailed information about the differences in reaction of male and female children. We have come to view the development of the Oedipal conflict in its relation to the phases of the development of the ego and its synthetic function, and have certain impressions on its possible relationship to presence or absence of one of the parents, on severity or indulgence of the atmosphere and other factors—however, we do not yet find it possible to make statements on the frequency or infrequency of one or the other type of Oedipal constellation under any given environmental situation: here, too, the relevant data seem not yet available.

Statements concerning the absence of the Oedipus complex under given social situations seems frequently due to the fact that observers have too simple or too narrow a view of what is meant by Oedipal conflict. This may concern some of the more differentiated manifestations of the Oedipal conflict, e.g. the occurrence of day-dreams and fantasies varying the theme of the family romance.[27] Margaret Mead considers this fantasy as typical of the American cultural background with its 'family whittled down to father and mother' who are 'all the anchors' the child 'has in the world which is otherwise vague and shifting. And so the fantasy of adoption develops, the fear which grips so many children's hearts that they are adopted, that they don't really belong anywhere at all'.[28] It seems obviously necessary to investigate whether or not and to what extent the 'American' fantasies vary the widespread pattern described in analytical literature. The variations, if any, due to the American scene, the size of the family, and the frequency of adoption in American culture, would only become meaningful if seen against the background of the universal pattern. Similarly, the fact

[26] This point has repeatedly been emphasized by Géza Róheim.

[27] See S. Freud, 'Family Romances' (1909), *Standard Ed.*, 9, London: Hogarth Press, 1959. For an experimental confirmation of Freud's findings (not recorded in the literature of experimental validation of psychoanalytic hypotheses) see E. S. Conklin, 'The Foster-Child Fantasy', *Amer. J. Psychol.*, 31, (1920).

[28] *And Keep Your Powder Dry*, New York: William Morrow, 1942, pp. 85-7.

that the negative Oedipus complex in the little boy is a regular part of the typical conflict situation tends to be ignored; hence the statements that under conditions of primitive society in which pregnancy is openly discussed and carried with pride the boy may develop an envy of the female genitalia,[29] seems not to take into account that the wish to bear a child in the male needs no particularly extravagant conditions to arise. We assume that it is present in every male child at one time or another, but have developed further hypotheses which state under what conditions it is likely to reach an intensity leading to pathological consequences.[30] It would be important to learn, whether under different cultural conditions manifestations of the negative Oedipus complex are likely to change and in which directions.

If we are informed that anthropological data collected in any given society do not reveal the existence of an Oedipal conflict, we are inclined to raise the question what such statements mean. They assume obviously that the Oedipus complex can be seen by outside observers. If this was true why did it need psychoanalysis to advance the view that there was in Western civilization a stage in child development in which the conflict is typical? Or is it that once this has been stated we can now assume that, with open eyes, we won't fail to see what was previously missed? If half a century after the initial formulation we are asked to state the criteria by which one can recognize the absence or presence of the conflict in a given child of our own environment by outside observation, we have to refer to a large number of very specific clues, which reach from symbolic expression to mood changes in the child. We find it hard to believe that so intimate a familiarity exists between anthropological observers and their subjects. We naturally assume readily—and here Malinowski's formulations on the subject and Ernest Jones' reply to them have gratefully to be mentioned—that cultural conditions produce variations of behaviour during the conflict situation. We are particularly inclined to believe in the wide range of these variations since, contrary to Freud's view, we do not find it necessary to stress as much as he the hereditary elements in the formation of the Oedipus complex. We also believe that many features that suggested to Freud a phylo-

[29] See M. Mead, *Male and Female,* New York: William Morrow, 1949.
[30] See e.g. E. Jacobson, 'Development of the Wish for a Child in Boys', *The Psychoanalytic Study of the Child,* 5, New York: International Universities Press; London: Hogarth Press, 1950.

genetic explanation can be accounted for by ontogenetic factors. The earliest needs of the child—partly no doubt inherited, but partly due to individual experience—and the environment's reactions to them form already the basis of the intensity of the Oedipal conflict and the pattern it may develop.

Manifestations of the castration complex in men and of penis envy in women are likely to be subject to similar variations. The idea that in speaking of penis envy one only uses an established metaphor for the prevailing hostility between woman and man, since in fact penis envy is a cultural phenomenon of patriarchal civilization, while breast envy might well be one of matriarchal society (the view of Thompson)[31] need not be discussed here. What we should like to mention is that clinical impressions seem to support the view that decrease of status difference between man and woman in our society seems not to have reduced penis envy. The misunderstanding of the complexity of the problems of penis envy seems to indicate not only a preference for cultural instead of 'biological' explanations—based on the misconception that the two are mutually exclusive—but mainly the vanishing understanding for the ontogenetic approach in psychoanalysis, i.e. for the life of the individual seen in the context of his life history.

In speaking of penis envy in the adult woman of our civilization we may refer to a variety of phenomena, which are ontogenetically connected with the repressed wish of the little girl to be able to equal the phallic (urinary) performances of her male playmate, at a time when her behaviour as a female was not yet 'institutionalized'. The adult behaviour, however, may, or may not, have an overt relationship to rivalry with the male; it can express itself as rivalry with women, as dissatisfaction with the self, or in a variety of other manifestations. Data on the variations which cultural conditions produce in these manifestations would be particularly valuable.[32]

In the preceding discussion we have already touched upon the problems in the treatment of which the difference of data used in psychoanalysis and in anthropology no longer facilitates interdisciplinary contact but may impede it. This danger, however, exists only if the difference is neglected and the data are treated as if they were equivalent; once the specificity of each set of data is

---

[31] 'Penis Envy in Women', *Psychiatry*, 6 (1943).
[32] See in this connection E. P. Hayward, 'Types of Female Castration Reactions', *Psychoanal. Quart.*, 12 (1943).

acknowledged, common ground can readily be established and common interests pursued.

Since the development of ego psychology new vistas have opened up. The study of id impulses and their derivatives was likely to offer a more uniform picture than that of the defence mechanisms, which are part of the ego's equipment. The further extension of ego psychology to the study of other ego functions is likely to reinforce this trend in the distribution of interest. Supported from other sources, particularly the development of psychoanalytic technique, the ever more detailed study of the reality to which adjustment took place became imperative and—particularly in psychoanalytic child psychology—an environmentalist approach was more emphasized than before.[33] These trends brought the viewpoint of psychoanalysis closer to that of anthropologists, who in their turn had abandoned the interest in the ubiquity of psychological events, as they had been relevant to an evolutionist theory of culture, and turned to the investigation of different cultures in their specificity and that of different cultural phenomena in their functional interdependence. The problems arising in interdisciplinary contact at this point may be introduced by an example. In describing and comparing behaviour of subcultures within the Western world, anthropologists describe concordant and discordant traits. Their description deals with material which is within general awareness. 'Every nation has images of other nations with whom it has or has had contact of some kind,'[34] and tends to condense these images into stereotypes. Each cultural contact since Herodotus or Tacitus has produced such stereotypes. Apart from true characteristics these stereotypes tend to express attitudes and preferences of those who hold them and are, therefore, likely to give rise to misleading expectations. The anthropologist who studies this problem will tend to account for clusters of concordant habits through the study of the history of the people, their customs, specific traditions, and social conditions. He is likely to attempt to organize these traits into an image of the typical characteristics, i.e. in an image of the 'national character',[35] which is presumably no longer tinged by pre-

[33] See E. Kris, 'Notes on the Development and on Some Current Problems of Psychoanalytic Child Psychology', loc. cit.

[34] E. Kris and H. Speier, *German Radio Propaganda*, New York: Oxford University Press, 1944.

[35] For a critical evaluation see O. Klineberg, 'A Science of National Character', *J. Soc. Psychol.*, 19 (1944); G. Devereux, loc. cit. and recently M. L. Faber, 'The Problem of National Character', *J. Psychol.*, 30 (1950).

ference statements or preferential attitudes of the observer. This organization of data is frequently based on certain general expectations, derived from psychology. In certain instances this framework was derived predominantly from Gestalt psychology; in many others, probably in the majority, it is derived from psychoanalysis. It is only to these studies that we refer. The question may now be raised how do these differences appear to the psychoanalyst. In the case of the subcultures in the Western world comparative data from analytical treatment are known. We are, however, not aware of investigations that would have attempted to present pertinent psychoanalytic data in a systematic fashion, and before we discuss what the scope of such presentations might be, we should like to state generally that the analyst is likely to be less impressed by the facts and the range of differences in everyday behaviour than the anthropologist.

It is not only the focus of attention that seems to make differences less important. Analysts too are aware of differences of behaviour caused by cultural conditions; they are not devoid of that common sense which has always stressed these differences, but their impact on the analytical observer tends to decrease as work progresses and as available data move from the periphery to the centre, that is from manifest behaviour to data, part of which is accessible only to an analytical investigation. What is central in this sense is frequently also of paramount value to an explanatory approach.

Statements on what are, in this context, often termed 'psychological regularities' usually are highly ambiguous, for a number of reasons. Here, we only point to certain aspects of this complex problem, which make it necessary to break down the concept of 'psychological regularities' in order to facilitate the formulation of fruitful hypotheses. We only want to mention that such regularities obviously also include those general characteristics of the human which we have briefly discussed before. (On the other hand, it should hardly be necessary to mention that differences, too, may be 'biological' in origin.) What we wish to stress is the fact, well known to every analyst, that the psychological significance of very similar behaviour may differ widely; its psychological significance can, in the field in question, only be ascertained relative to the environment to which the behaviour relates—about which more will be said below. Thus, even if reliable and critical studies on the distribution of behaviour forms or details in the various sub-groups of Western civilization were already available, questions most relevant to the study of culture and personality would still remain unanswered.

We said that differences of behaviour which are likely to strike the outside observer may be less relevant to purposes of explanation. An anthropologist studying the sexual habits in certain urban areas in the U.S. today might well be impressed by the comparative frequency with which answers from individuals interviewed emphasize the ubiquity of masturbation, its complete harmlessness, and the fact that no guilt is attached to its performance. But such individuals, on the analyst's couch, may sooner or later come to realize their previously unconscious masturbation guilt, and sometimes even the fact that the very symptoms which led them to seek the help of psychoanalysis are closely connected with it. Similarly, what could be ascertained by anthropological methods about sex education in the families of 'modern-minded' parents will often be contradicted by their actual behaviour as seen in the analysis of their children.

The development of the doctor-patient relationship during analytical work may illustrate another aspect of the point we want to make. There is little doubt that the way in which the initial contact between the Frenchman, the Englishman, the New Yorker, the Bostonian and the psychoanalyst is established covers a wide range, e.g. from curiosity to restraint, familiarity to suspicion; certain of these attitudes are more frequent in one group than in another. However, as soon as this superficial and initial contact develops into transference, the differences appear to be much more limited: they concern the way in which the patient reacts pre-consciously to his experience of transference, to the modes of verbal expression or rationalization, but according to our clinical experience no significant difference exists in the formation of transference—positive or negative—or in its intensity, structure or essential manifestations.

We should like to introduce here a consideration of method. We know from analysis, and it has been mentioned before, that differences in dynamically or structurally central aspects may have a low probability of behavioural manifestation. Confronted with the same reality situation, individuals of widely varying personality types or character structures may in certain areas behave very much alike.[36] On the other hand, the fact that different conditions often find similar reflection in the behaviour of the same individual, or in the behaviour of individuals who dynamically or structurally belong to the same character type, is a matter of common knowledge. However, it has so far not been sufficiently investigated—though many isolated clinical data on the subject no doubt exist—in what areas and to what extent such replacements of one attitude by another take place. We would suggest observing how one type of personality reacts under different cultural conditions, i.e. the variety of ways in which the same central personality factors are, according to the cultural environment, expressed in various types of behaviour accessible to the anthropological approach. We assume that in each environment certain predominant pathways of discharge, sublimation, etc., are more or less accessible and therefore certain patterns of behaviour facilitated and others impeded. Their psychological meaning in terms of a psychology of personality, or in terms of their indicative value for the establishment of character types—individual or national—can only be ascertained on the basis of such a law of cultural substitution. We are here speaking of adults. Cultural modifiability is different in the child, and so is cultural substitution in the sense just outlined. We shall later refer to one aspect of this problem.

Investigations of the kind here suggested would have advantages, since much of what is at present formulated on the level of however suggestive impressions could to some extent be documented by an empirical approach, based on comparable events. However, it would for obvious reasons remain limited. We have up to this point dealt with the cross section of behaviour and purposely avoided the historical aspect.

Psychoanalytic propositions are dynamic and genetic; if only dynamic ones are being taken into account, their predictive value is considerably reduced. Anthropologists have become aware of this and when we mentioned that new data were assembled in order to approximate those which psychoanalysis had shown to be relevant, we had in mind particularly the manifold recent anthropological reports on child care and child rearing.[37] They constitute the most

[36] See T. Parsons, 'Psychoanalysis and the Social Structure', and H. Hartmann, 'The Application of Psychoanalytic Concepts to Social Science', both in *Psychoanal. Quart.*, 19 (1950).

[37] For a comprehensive bibliography, see M. Mead, 'Research on Primitive Children', in L. Carmichael, *Manual of Child Psychology*, New York: John Wiley, 1946.

fruitful and the most suggestive contact between psychoanalysis and anthropology, and it is the discussion of problems arising in this area to which we now turn.

Let us assume that in a given culture certain procedures of child rearing, of mother-child relationships have been observed; they refer not to one but to several steps; they describe a sequence of indulgence in one area, deprivation in another; oral indulgence, for instance, versus restriction of motility and expression. There is no doubt that these sequences and patterns may influence the structure of personality. How can this influence be described and what are its limitations?

The methodological questions have been discussed in considerable detail by N. Leites, to whose paper we refer.[38] The methodological foundations upon which the studies discussed by Leites rest can be evaluated to some extent in our own environment. Obviously few conclusions on what happens later to a child can be drawn if we rely on single events of childhood, be they observed while they take place or reported later, unless they occur in the context of analytical material. Similar experiences in childhood tend to produce the most varied results or symptomatologies. The very large number of superseding factors, each in turn determined by others, constitutes the net of interlocking events, tendencies, etc., with which psychoanalysis deals. Attempts to study mother-child relationships from the outside are being undertaken at present in a variety of clinical setups. These studies produce a wealth of detail; however, it is doubtful whether any of the setups devised, any of the observational conditions alone, permit definite conclusions on the relevance of the factors to which the data of observation refer. The only source from which such indications can be gained is psychoanalytic observation, i.e. the *reconstructive* study of life histories. While it is true that reconstructing studies remain inconclusive in certain areas and the tendency to supplement them by

[38] 'Psychocultural Hypotheses', *World Politics*, 1 (1948). In his opinion, most psycho-cultural hypotheses are stated with an awareness of the fact that data sufficient either to verify or invalidate them, has not yet been collected, although the gap between available and required evidence may not always be clearly indicated. Without discussing it in detail here, we want to emphasize the relevance of Leites' paper to our subject. The author, though a proponent of psycho-cultural research shows a succinct awareness of, and points with unusual clarity to, its many inherent difficulties. One gets the impression that very few, if any, psycho-cultural hypotheses advanced so far would measure up to the methodological aspirations formulated in his paper.

observational data is fully justified, observations without reference to reconstructive studies tend to produce a blind mass of data.

The close correlation of psychoanalytic data with those gained in child observation which is at present developing (Denver, New York, Boston, Roxbury, New Haven) may well supply further insight, which might be applied to the interdisciplinary contact of psychoanalysts and anthropologists. As far as the study of Western civilization is concerned such contact seems to offer obvious advantages which have so far not been used in the anthropologists' study of culture and personality. An anthropologist's statement on the nature of the Oedipal ties among one of the Western European nations might well have been compared to data attained by analysts. From our own contact with analysands of the country in question and reports from analysts from the same country no similar statement seemed to be warranted. The contact of both psychoanalyst and anthropologist might be extended to non-Western countries and there is little doubt that it might produce more precise data than those gained by methods hitherto used.[39]

One of the problems frequently raised in this connection concerns the range of the analyst's work outside his own culture, a specialized case in the quest for optimal cultural distance between observer and subject. The analyst is in various ways in a privileged position. His particular equipment should reduce the danger that what is recognized as nonfamiliar should also be experienced as totally alien—a tendency in the human observer, to which Franz Boas has drawn attention.[40] The difficulty which the observer meets in a strange cultural environment, and the task which the distance from the own cultural experience imposes, have been discussed by others, e.g. Herskovits, with the implication that, while one understands one's own culture, one has to learn to understand an alien culture.[41] However, on the level on which understanding becomes relevant in psychoanalysis, the understanding of individual behaviour even in a familiar environment is limited indeed without special training. It seems, therefore, appropriate briefly to review the problem of cultural distance from the specific viewpoint of the psychoanalyst.

Psychoanalytic experiences of analysts of Western cultures with

[39] Other aspects of this problem will be briefly discussed in the next sections.
[40] F. Boas, *The Mind of Primitive Man*, New York: Macmillan, 1948.
[41] M. J. Herskovits, *Man And His Works*, New York: Knopf, 1948.

non-Western analysands have not been reported in sufficiently great detail. Impressions gained from various sources—e.g. from supervisory work with an Indian colleague treating white patients— seem to indicate that the analytical situation is setting conditions in which the cultural difference tends to be minimized, provided that the analyst is familiar enough with the cultural surroundings of his patients, in order to be able to understand, for instance, the details of reality involvements and ego interests.[42] That such know- ledge cannot overcome every kind of limitation is clear, and in order to establish limits, cases like the analysis of a native South African medicine man reported by W. Sachs might well be studied in detail.[43] Sachs's case at any rate will hardly meet all require- ments which one might have in mind. However, it lends itself to a discussion of the question to what extent the cultural distance between analyst and patient affects the latter. Here too there are clearly cases in which the distance may be viewed as 'too great'. No similar experience plays a relevant part in analyses carried out in Western countries by members of other subcultures. The cultural difference between analyst and patient obviously remains an important factor—but it can be handled by the rules of analytical procedure. The patient's reaction to cultural difference is in prin- ciple not unlike his reaction to cultural sharing. Of Western culture, at least, it seems to be true that of the various factors in the analyst's personality which are bound to influence his work with any given patient, his cultural background is of comparatively minor relevance.

At this point a question poses itself. To what extent and by what procedures can data obtainable through psychoanalytic observation be replaced by other data, and what is the relationship of these data to each other? It is obviously a complex question and one not limited to the relation of psychoanalysis to anthropology. We referred to it briefly in discussing the study of child develop- ment—but then, too, we only mentioned one of its various aspects.

[42] This naturally includes the guarantee that institutionalized behaviour is recognized as such, lest 'we may ascribe to some known "accident" of the individual's life history a trait which he actually shares' with all mem- bers of his group who 'have not been subjected to that event at all'. C. Kluckhohn, 'Personal Documents in Anthropological Science', in *The Use of Personal Documents in History, Anthropology and Sociology*, by L. Gottschalk, C. Kluckhohn, R. Angell, Social Science Research Council, Bulletin, 53, 1945, p. 144.
[43] W. Sachs, *Black Hamlet, the Mind of an African Negro Revealed by Psychoanalysis*, London: Geoffrey Bles, 1937.

Wherever we compare data collected in psychiatric or social-service interviews or those obtained by the use of projective testing with those obtained in psychoanalysis, an analogous question is bound to arise. Its importance can best be characterized if we mention that much uncertainty prevailing at the present time in several areas of psychiatric diagnosis and—partly in consequence of this—the lack of unambiguous criteria that beset the problem of indication for each one of the various psycho-therapeutic methods (including psychoanalysis) is rooted here.

Since no systematic study of these problems has yet been attempted, and even the variety of impressions which force themselves upon the psychoanalyst as analytical work follows the exploratory contact with his patient have never been studied in a comprehensive way,[44] it seems obvious that as far as the context of this study is concerned we have to limit ourselves to general impressions only. The problem has as far as anthropology is concerned gained in importance since the study of individual life histories has begun to attract attention and various types of biographical material have been accumulated in order to facilitate the study of the 'individual in culture'. Studies of this kind have been surveyed by C. Kluckhohn in a most competent monograph, in which the view is taken that until anthropologists can deal rigorously with the 'subjective factors' in the life of the individuals they study, 'their work will be flat and insubstantial'. However, it seems that Kluckhohn does not sufficiently stress the fact that the dilemma which faces the anthropologist in interpreting his sources is akin to the difficulties which face any investigator in the study of man who tries to evaluate only documentary and observational data, and that the study of life histories in psychoanalysis has a unique contribution to make:

> It is not only a method which provides relevant data otherwise not obtainable, it is not only, at least frequently, the one way to establish relevance of experience in the child's life but it is also the method to show how various phases of the past were inter-related: to see the life history as a whole, as it is organized by the personality and has organized the personality. But this factor in itself establishes its limitations.[45]

[44] Research along these lines has recently been initiated at the Treatment Center of the New York Psychoanalytic Institute under H. Hartmann's direction.
[45] E. Kris, 'Notes on the Development and on Some Current Problems of Psychoanalysis and Psychology', loc. cit.

In the context of systematic study of behaviour the psychoanalytic approach and the approach from the outside might well be said to supplement each other.

4. PATHWAYS OF DISCHARGE

In the preceding discussion we have taken it for granted that certain types of behaviour shared by many individuals in a given group may be related to common practices in child care and education. We do not look upon these practices as the only causative factor, but rather as initial links in a chain of influences acting upon the individual. We are aware of the multiplicity of these influences: they include naturally economic, social, and ideological factors of many kinds. Out of the same or similar early imprints various types of adult behaviour may develop, depending on the later course of upbringing and many types of subsequent experiences. Also, similar adult behaviour may be manifested by individuals whose early experiences were different—if later common experiences followed. Other cautions can briefly be stated: even within one group, adult behaviour is differentiated according to specific regional, economic or social patterns, and is subject to historical change.[46] In this sense adult behaviour has to be viewed in relation to its antecedents and to the rate of change to which it is exposed.[47]

Within the area of these hypotheses we are concerned with the question of how far the phenomena hitherto studied as shared, supply clues to an understanding of behaviour which we would consider as dynamically relevant. It is our impression that little certain and not too much plausible knowledge exists, if we use the term dynamic in the sense in which it is used in psychoanalysis. Before we indicate some of the reasons for this view we shall choose a term to designate the shared behaviour within a group. We shall adopt none of the terms currently used such as basic character structure (Kardiner, and Linton while collaborating with Kardiner) national character (Benedict, Gorer, Mead, and others) or social

---

[46] Obviously we find also within each group diversified types of behaviour and similar personality types in different cultures.
[47] For some similar cautions in the formulation of psycho-social propositions, see Leites, loc. cit., particularly pp. 110ff.

character (Fromm)[48] though they refer in part to the same or related phenomena; to each of these terms definite connotations are attached in regard to theoretical assumptions and expectations, which only to a limited extent coincide with our own. We prefer to adopt a terminology which involves no commitments of this kind, and we shall distinguish between behaviour that has become typified in a given environment by its institutional regulation and behaviour that is less subject to such regulation. We use 'institutional regulation' in a very wide sense; any group preferences, any conventions that may be pertinent, should be included. Practices of child care as they are current in a given society are, therefore, part of what in an abbreviated formulation we shall call institutionalized behaviour.

The point we should like to make is concerned with the difference between institutionalized and non-institutionalized behaviour. Psychoanalytic observation suggests that from a dynamic point of view they may differ considerably and in various ways. The differences seem most relevant as far as problems of motivation and of discharge are concerned.[49] We will not forget that behaviour which is institutionalized must also be described as to its place in the total pattern of motivations. Institutions affect different individuals in different degrees and in different directions. The same institution may, in some persons, appeal most effectively to their ids; in others, to their super-egos; in a third group, it may be used predominantly by their ego interests, etc. The influence of institu-

[48] Fromm defines social character as the nucleus of character structure which is shared by most members of the same culture in contradistinction to the individual character in which people belonging to the same culture differ from each other. Quite aside from what Bertrand Russell has to say about the vicious circle inherent in statements of this kind it will hardly be necessary to state explicitly where our views in spite of partial convergence differ from Fromm's.
[49] Views in this section are to some extent similar to those of Hanks (see H. L. Hanks, Jr., 'The Locus of Individual Differences in Certain Primitive Cultures', in *Culture and Personality*, pp. 107-26). His starting point is the difference in accounts by anthropologists and psychologists. However, he is impressed by the fact that the biological accounts recently collected by anthropologists resemble strikingly case histories reported by psychiatrists concerning individuals of Western civilization and reaches the conclusion that the anthropological accounts to which he refers deal with behaviour which is to a considerable extent socially inconsequential, and that behaviour that is more variable is also less institutionalized. He suggests a spectrum of behaviour arranged according to the degree of institutionalization. Individual behaviour differences will tend to concentrate at the less institutionalized end of the spectrum.

tions may relate to various developmental levels. It may affect personality formation. It may be set apart as the 'institutional' part from the 'private' part of the personality, etc.

We choose an example that has been pointed up by recent research experiences and we refer again to observations concerning child care, made by a number of independent investigators in various areas of the field. Some of these investigators expected to produce relevant changes in the effects of child care on infants by advocating the replacement of rigid scheduling by self-regulation, i.e. by a less exacting distribution of indulgence and deprivation in the child's life. Experts in the field of child psychiatry, pediatrics and education advocating this change of régime found that the type of régime adopted was less relevant to the effects of early experiences than thought before. A decisive point had been insufficiently taken into account: the mother's personal attitude, extending through all ranges of awareness, but particularly her unconscious attitude not only towards all her children but to any given child. The new programme in itself had been chosen by some mothers in order to overcome apprehensions or as a defence against hostile attitudes. No briefing, and no approach except individual therapy could modify this behaviour.[50]

We use this example in spite of the fact that it deals with a recent modification of institutionalized behaviour—i.e. practices of child care—since we have reason to believe that even in the study of established and stable typified behaviour analogous observations impose themselves. Wherever the closer study of the mother-child relationship has been undertaken, similar facts have been discovered, and a group of clinical investigators has undertaken a comprehensive study of these relations, in which the part played by the mother's unconscious fantasies concerning her child seems to be the key concept.[51] Observations indicating the importance of modes of handling the child, which are not determined by institutionalized practices of child care, are familiar to anthropologists.

[50] For this problem, see E. Jackson and E. B. Klatskin, loc. cit.
[51] See B. Rank, M. C. Putman and Rochling, 'The Significance of Emotional Climate in Early Feeding Difficulties', *Psychosomatic Medicine*, 10 (1948); B. Rank, 'Aggression', *The Psychoanalytic Study of the Child*, 3/4, New York: International Universities Press; London: Hogarth Press, 1949; and B. Rank and D. MacNaughton, 'A Clinical Contribution to Early Ego Development', *The Psychoanalytic Study of the Child*, 5, New York: International Universities Press; London: Hogarth Press, 1950.

It seems, however, that they have not always drawn the necessary conclusions.[52]

Thus Fromm (loc. cit.) stresses the importance of emotional factors in child care—with the implication that this constitutes an improvement compared to Freud's views—but sees these attitudes only as part of the 'social character'. It seems to us that such a view avoids to take into account what our clinical data and more detailed studies in fact indicate, namely, the margin left to the non-institutionalized behaviour. We assume that not only with mothers in any one of the Western subcultures, but probably also with mothers in 'preliterate' societies, the problem of a gradation in devotion to the child exists; that even there a child may represent the self, the sibling, the own mother, etc., and mobilize unconscious impulses of various kinds. We therefore suggest the formulation that non-institutionalized behaviour may serve an important function of discharge. In the examples given what is discharged are unconscious tendencies. In further generalizing we should like to stress that while institutionalized behaviour offers many important pathways for discharge, the quantity of energy to be discharged may in many other instances, be reduced by the fact that it is institutionalized. The study of its motivation tends, in this case, to lead to the area of rationalization rather than into that of deeper motivational connections.

This generalization takes into account what psychoanalytic observations suggest in the area of motivation attached to institutional behaviour. In this connection it seems appropriate to stress that no short-cuts from institutionalized behaviour to an individual attitude or tendency are psychologically warranted. The American who follows the behaviour pattern of his group may impress Englishmen as boisterous, the Englishman who follows his own tradition may impress Americans as arrogant—but applied to the individual we can obviously make no statement as to the boisterousness of any given American, or the arrogance of any given Englishman.[53] The behaviour of both may have its own meaning for each

[52] For an approach partly similar to ours see M. Mead's discussion of R. Benedict's paper, 'Child Rearing in Certain European Countries', *Amer. J. Orthopsychiat.*, 19 (1949), 349.
[53] C. Kluckhohn (1945, loc. cit., p. 144) discusses this problem in terms which we find highly illustrative: 'Clarity and consistency in such discriminations are essential to sound work in the "culture and personality" field. Otherwise we shall continually run the danger of interpreting a person's behaviour in a given situation as reflecting certain trends in his

of them. In taking as indicator the institutionalized behaviour, the habit, one would behave as if in the example used before, not the mother's attitude to her child, but only the routine she follows was decisive.

This is in fact what anthropologists are tempted to do; they tend to draw conclusions from observed behaviour to underlying motivations and neglect frequently, paradoxically enough, to take into account that in different environments similar impulses may find different expressions. The exhibitionism of the Englishman may manifest itself not as boisterousness but as a preference for understatements. It is at this point, then, that a criticism sometimes levelled by anthropologists against psychoanalysis might well be reversed: psychoanalysis, one used to say, underrates reality factors. One might answer that what reality means to the individual, what opportunity for direct discharge processes it offers, and which defences it encourages, has to be taken into account when we refer to environment or reality in a context in which psychodynamic hypotheses are being used.[54]

"core personality" (idiosyncratic component) when he is only conforming, very acceptably, to social expectations of performance of that role. Only after careful scrutiny can behaviour be taken at its face value as providing clues to the idiosyncratic variant of socially approved norms, which any human organism's actions represent'.

[54] This is an explicit formulation of views which Freud held through the best part of his development. Already in *Psychopathology of Everyday Life* he points out that 'the self-inflicted injury which does tend towards self-annihilation . . . has no other choice in our present civilization than to hide itself behind the accidental or to break through in a simulation of spontaneous illness. Formerly it was a customary sign of mourning: at other times, it expressed itself in ideas of piety and renunciation of the world'. (A. A. Brill (ed.), *The Basic Writings of Sigmund Freud*, New York: Modern Library, 1938, p. 123). The idea that certain manifestations of mental illness are related to cultural conditions had been current during Freud's youth, when he became familiar with G. M. Beard's views on neurasthenia, the 'Morbus Americanus'. It is well known how critically he reacted to this simplification (see H. A. Bunker, 'Symposium on Neurasthenia. From Beard to Freud. A Brief History of the Concepts of Neurasthenia', *Medical Review of Reviews*, 36, 1930). Later Freud undertook at least one detailed attempt to demonstrate the relationship between psychopathology and culture. In 'A Seventeenth Century Demonological Neurosis', (*Standard Ed.*, 19, London: Hogarth Press, 1961) he described a specific pathological condition in its time-bound 'demonological shape'. See for further formulations in this area of problems: H. Hartmann: 'Psychoanalysis and Sociology', in Sandor Lorand (ed.), *Psychoanalysis Today*, New York: International Universities Press, 1944; Henry Loewenfeld, 'Some Aspects of a Compulsion Neurosis in a Changing Civilization', *Psychoanal. Quart.*, 13 (1944); and W. Muensterberger, 'Ethnologie und Ichforschung', in P. Federn and H. Meng (eds.), *Die Psychohygiene*, Berne: Hans Huber Verlag, 1949.

Psychoanalytic experience indicates abundantly that the same institutionally regulated behaviour may be used for the expression of a large number of even contradictory tendencies and represent for any given individual a large variety of things. Success, one of the key concepts in recent analyses of the American National Character, appears in analytical observation in its relation to id tendencies—e.g. the gratification of aggressive strivings; to ego functions, e.g. in relation to ego interests; or to super-ego functions, e.g. in relation to self-esteem (as God's beloved child); and in each individual case we have reason to differentiate between the relative importance of each of these aspects.

This simplified example is briefly mentioned in order to indicate that the distinction of institutionalized and non-institutionalized behaviour suggests a large number of empirical investigations. It will be obviously important to assess how far in each culture institutionalized and how far non-institutionalized behaviour is utilized in discharge processes. On the other hand, it might be significant in the study of individuals to assess to what extent they use the most commonly accepted patterns of institutionalized behaviour as main pathways of discharge.

The importance of this distinction seems particularly great since the comparative study of culture has attracted attention to many types of institutionalized behaviour and comparatively less attention to the great variety of its psychological significance. We feel in no position to decide to what extent the recent increase in biographical studies as part of anthropological field work is likely to modify this distribution of interest, nor do we wish to decide whether any other method except psychoanalytic observation can at present produce reliable data in this area.

The distinction between institutionalized and non-institutionalized behaviour leads at this point back to the difference of data with which anthropologists and psychoanalysts work. In stating that social science neglects unique and divergent, psychoanalysis convergent events, Bateson and Ruesch have stated a dichotomy which the distinction here suggested tries to eliminate.[55] We refer to the empirical question of discharge processes as they actually occur; in order to establish these occurrences data collected by anthro-

---

[55] See J. Ruesch and G. Bateson, 'Structure and Process in Social Relations', *Psychiatry*, 12 (1949); for a somewhat similar dichotomy see G. Devereux, loc. cit., p. 127.

pological field work and psychoanalytic observation will have to be combined. Few similar investigations are available. To illustrate their advantages we point to a few remarks of Greenacre's, on the relationship of a certain type of woman, the child wife, to a specific culture.[56] Greenacre does not claim that the type is limited to the American South but that it occurs there as a socially accepted feminine ideal, probably inherited from the days of slavery; she also considers how the existence of a mother of this type supplemented by the proverbial Negro mammy affects both male and female children and creates conditions favourable for the survival of the child-mother type. In the data used by Greenacre both institutionalized and non-institutionalized behaviour are considered and the relation of the child-mother to her own children is seen as determined by the unconscious factors of her desire to have a child. It arises out of a 'narcissistic body competitiveness first as solution for penis envy and second, as competitiveness with other women'.

In using data of the kind Greenacre has utilized, starting from the clinical impression and following the distribution of a nosological picture or of a characterological type into cultural areas in which they are more or less frequent, psychoanalysis makes its own contribution to the problem of culture and personality. One may inquire into the experiences of the Indian and Japanese analysts, working in their own environment and organize the collection of data as the training of psychiatrists in psychoanalysis expands to other lands. This may open the way for deeper insight into the fields of comparative psychiatry.

The psychoanalytic contributions to the problem of culture and personality might well be able to sharpen our view on the degree to which traits of human nature are variable. At the present state of our knowledge much remains unsettled. The question, however, may be asked which view is likely to give rise to more misunderstanding at this time, the exaggerated stress on variable or invariable traits. It is our impression that under the impact of cultural anthropology the question how man behaves under any given set of circumstances tends to be neglected in favour of the question how a member of a specific culture behaves. In this connection it is, we believe, the privilege of the analyst to recall that

[56] P. Greenacre, 'Child Wife as Ideal: Sociological Considerations', *Amer. J. Orthopsychiat.*, 17 (1947).

the historical function of analysis was a definite one. The question in what respect groups of human beings—races, nations, classes, etc.—differ from each other, in what respect they are linked to each other by the fact of their being human, is age old. It has been answered at various times and in various cultures with different emphasis and different aims in mind. As far as Western tradition is concerned, the shift from ethnocentricity to a universalist approach was inherent in that part of Hellenistic thinking which entered Christianity. Other approaches, which stressed the unity of men, can, we believe, be recognized as secularization of this religious, or as a revival of the pre-Christian, classical and post-classical, tradition. As far as we can see, only analytical psychology has come into being comparatively independent of those trends, and is not based on preference statements of any kind but on a system of scientific propositions. This system, by virtue of its existence, may in turn strengthen existing preferences, i.e. humanism in the modern world.

To put it concretely: insight based on psychoanalytic psychology tends to enlarge the cultural area or the number of groups to which one feels linked and towards which one feels responsible; an attitude which can well be characterized by its opposite. To interpret one's own actions predominantly in terms of national character seems to contradict the lesson implicit in psychoanalytic psychology.

This paper takes issue with the cultural anthropologists' field method in applying it to the study of heterogeneous cultures. It points out that the methodological procedures as used by anthropologists presupposes an organic unity of the culture. Conditions in complex cultures do not favour the sampling method and cannot reliably reflect the variations of character types or the assumed uniformity of defence systems. The effects of the complex environment upon character formation cannot be deduced from general codes of conduct. One cannot presume that heterogeneous societies mould the individual into an easily identifiable cultural personality.

12

Comments on Anthropology and the Study of Complex Cultures[1]

SIDNEY AXELRAD

Within recent years, anthropologists have undertaken the study of complex cultures. This extension of the scope of anthropology is probably neither minor nor transitory; it is still, however, a movement of individuals rather than of the discipline as a whole. *Anthropology Today* does not include an inventory paper on the topic of the anthropological analysis of complex cultures, although Margaret Mead[2] and Robert Redfield[3] allude to it in their papers. Although the movement had begun earlier with the work of the Lynds[4] and of Warner[5] and his group, the last war and world developments since then have given a decided impetus to it. During the war, anthropologists were drawn into government service to aid the policy makers and to 'crack cultures'. Another determinant of major importance is the shrinking of the world; the penetration of hitherto untouched cultures by Western civilization.

Such changes of interest are not confined to anthropology. Even within the past fifteen years, similar trends have been observed in the two fields most closely related to anthropology: psychology and sociology. The major shift in psychology has been towards areas formerly reserved for psychiatry: diagnosis and therapy. Sociology, which since Durkheim was rather proud that it could disregard the individual and everything related to his psychology, has contributed heavily, at least in numbers, to social psychology

---

[1] This paper first appeared in *Psychoanalysis and the Social Sciences*, 4, ed. by W. Muensterberger and S. Axelrad, New York: International Universities Press, 1955.

[2] M. Mead, 'National Character', in A. Kroeber (ed.), *Anthropology Today*, Chicago: University of Chicago Press, 1953.

[3] R. Redfield, 'Relations of Anthropology to the Social Sciences and to the Humanities', ibid.

[4] R. S. and H. M. Lynd, *Middletown*, New York: Harcourt Brace; London: Constable, 1929, idem, *Middletown in Transition*, New York: Harcourt Brace; London: Constable, 1937.

[5] W. L. Warner and P. S. Lunt, *The Social Life of a Modern Community*, New Haven: Yale University Press, 1941.

and to the study of personality. And as part of these waves of invasion and succession, anthropology and anthropologists now contribute to the study of complex civilizations, an area formerly reserved for the sociologist. If the anthropologist who studies complex culture becomes a sociologist, the transition need only be described. If, however, he remains an anthropologist, then the problem lies in how his approach will differ from that of the sociologist.

In this paper the logic of the application of certain anthropological concepts and methods to the study of complex civilizations will be explored. An attempt will be made to define and delimit those spheres in which the anthropologist may be most successful in his research, to evaluate his present tools, and to suggest new ones that may be of use to him in the field that he has so recently entered.

Considering only the anthropologist and the sociologist, complex culture has traditionally been the sphere of the latter. A point of distinction between anthropologists and sociologists is that the former study culture while the latter study society. This at first sight seems to be a distinction between descriptions of learned shared behaviour, i.e. culture, and descriptions of forms of interaction, i.e. society. In practice, the distinction is extraordinarily difficult to make. It is almost impossible to describe the forms of interaction without an explanation of the patterns of interaction by which it is carried. Since traditionally sociologists have worked within familiar cultures, it has not been necessary for them to describe the patterns of behaviour. They have been able to focus on developing the laws of interaction. The anthropologists, who by definition have worked with peoples whose ways are not their own, have found themselves concerned with describing how people lived; theory has lagged far behind. Obviously, the techniques developed in the two fields have differed greatly.

There are certain sociological researches in which an anthropological approach has been used; in general, whenever the sociologist was dealing with an unfamiliar subculture within the sphere of complex civilization itself. For instance, the work of Thomas and Znaniecki[6] is, in its delineation of the culture patterns of the Poles in Poland and in America, a forerunner of much later work, since it included some of the techniques represented by the

---

[6] W. I. Thomas and F. Znaniecki, *The Polish Peasant in Europe and America*, New York: Knopf, 1927.

'culture at a distance' school.[7] In particular, it placed reliance upon personal documents and presented a thematic analysis of the culture. Thomas[8] was a pioneer worker in the field of culture and personality, and an early and unappreciated functionalist. Under his influence, some of the early Chicago ecologists investigated American subcultures: the delinquent and the criminal, ethnic groups, and urban groups.[9] More recently, the *culture* of the factory and of other small groups has been investigated (e.g. by Whyte[10]). However, in these studies, the sociologist was concerned as much with patterns of interaction and with formal methodological problems such as sampling, standardization of the methods of investigation, and quantification of findings, as with the substantive aspects of the culture. In general, the sociologists in these studies, except for Thomas, avoided the problem of the relation of culture to personality and sought generalizations that would be applicable to boys' gangs wherever found, rather than descriptions of the intrinsic aspects of some specific culture. Again, except for Thomas, both the older and the newer studies have been conspicuous for a reliance upon an extreme form of environmentalism, a bland lack of concern about unconscious factors, and a deterministic scheme based on a rather primitive form of learning theory.

These quasi-anthropological studies of complex cultures have employed, in the main, sociological techniques. If the anthropologist who now studies complex culture does not develop techniques that differ from those of the sociologist, or if he does not set aside some particular sector of complex civilization as his domain, anthropology may become merely an adjunct of sociology. Is then the entire field of complex culture or some specific sector of it particularly amenable to the methods and conceptualizations of the anthropologist?

The application of anthropological concepts to the study of complex cultures seems to involve an ideational contradiction. It is generally agreed that the special province of cultural anthropology is the study of primitive societies. A culture is called primitive if

[7] M. Mead and R. Metraux (eds.), *The Study of Culture at a Distance*, Chicago: University of Chicago Press, 1953.

[8] W. I. Thomas, *The Unadjusted Girl*, Boston: Little, Brown, 1923.

[9] F. M. Thrasher, *The Gang*, Chicago: University of Chicago Press, 1927; C. Shaw, *The Jackroller*, Chicago: University of Chicago Press, 1929; and H. W. Zorbaugh, *The Gold Coast and the Slum*, Chicago: University of Chicago Press, 1929.

[10] W. F. Whyte, *Street Corner Society*, Chicago: University of Chicago Press, 1943.

it is not literate; if its social structure is organized on the basis of small local groupings and kinship; if its technology is simple, and if there is in general little economic specialization.[11] The typical approach to the study of culture is to see it as a whole—to see that 'every aspect of the culture is related to every other aspect', that culture functions as an integrated whole and that all culture serves human needs.[12] This is obviously the viewpoint of Malinowski and his school. Although some anthropologists will not agree with one or another detail, this set of concepts represents a fairly typical anthropological approach. Except for those studies in which acculturation or diffusion was the central problem, the anthropologist has viewed culture as static and unchanging. When his interests turned to the dynamic processes of socialization, he saw them as operating within a fixed culture. In the field as a whole, there has been a loss of interest in cultural evolution and almost an abhorrence, until quite recently, of the study of universal psychic elements.

Although complex cultures differ basically and radically in structure from primitive ones, it may be that some of the concepts and methods applied in the study of the latter will prove useful in the study of the former. While the anthropological study of complex civilization does not consist of treating them as though they were primitive, the anthropologists engaged in the study of complex culture have retained three marks of their former interests: an attempt to see each culture as a whole, an assumption of the homogeneity of the culture, and an interest in the interrelatedness of culture and personality.

[11] R. Piddington, An Introduction to Social Anthropology, Edinburgh: Oliver & Boyd, 1950.
[12] Cf. S. F. Nadel (The Foundations of Social Anthropology, Glencoe: The Free Press; London: Cohen & West, 1951). This definition of primitive culture needs qualification. For instance, anthropologists have studied cultures with large populations, e.g. the Inca and certain African cultures. But there are three overriding elements in all definitions of primitive culture: isolation from the main streams of Eastern or Western civilization, simple technology, and non-literateness. (One is tempted to speculate whether the absence of writing, and thus complete reliance upon oral tradition and the spoken word does not create an overemphasis upon the importance of words in themselves. This could lead to a mutually reinforcing effect between the absence of writing and certain aspects of the primary process: the apparently greater reliance of all primitives upon imagery, concretistic thinking, and magic. This relationship should be equally true of illiterate or largely illiterate subcultures or groups in literate societies. Clinical data about children with reading disabilities suggests a change in type of thought process, once the ability to read and write is acquired.)

Each of these elements warrants discussion in order to arrive at some estimate of the status of the anthropologists' research in the field of complex culture.

In a complex society, it is apparently impossible to see the culture as a whole if one thinks of scientific vision, not only because of the dynamic nature and heterogeneity of the culture, its multiplicity of groups, the difficulties produced by demographic factors, the often hidden nature of the relationships between the material and the non-material culture, but also because of the limited usefulness of the concepts derived from the functional approach, which was, as we have said, developed for problems of a different order. The anthropologist who persists in seeing modern culture as an organic unity does not add to our knowledge. Yet the functional approach, with its emphasis on organic unity, has most often been present in the work of the anthropologists who studied complex cultures, for instance in the work of Zborowski and Herzog.[13]

The logic of the organic unity of culture or of reciprocity, is itself open to serious question. The very notion of reciprocity represents what Merton[14] has called an *approach*. It states no hypothesis. It is of the nature of a philosophical or metaphysical proposition rather than a set of logically interrelated propositions usable for prediction. Isolated functional hypotheses do not, in themselves, specify the interrelatedness of the culture, nor do they clarify how culture is to be conceptualized in such a way as to relate it as a whole to man's needs. If these hypotheses are useful at all, they are most appropriate for cultures that are stable, where integration and consensus in all areas of life are palpable. Almost all modern cultures are characterized by tensions, cultural lags, and great deviations from any conceptual norms.

Analyses of complex cultures on a functional basis must be on a low level of generalization; they can do little more than detail a multiplicity of culture patterns. In *Middletown*, the more narrowly functional of their books, the Lynds,[15] using almost no theoretical framework, did not do much more than describe living in Middletown.

The anthropologist, if he retains two of the three marks of his

[13] M. Zborowski and E. Herzog, *Life is With People*, New York: International Universities Press, 1952.
[14] R. K. Merton, *Social Theory and Social Structure*, Glencoe: The Free Press, 1949; London: Collier-Macmillan (rev. ed.), 1957.
[15] R. S. and H. M. Lynd, *Middletown*.

former interest—that of seeing culture as a whole and that of its homogeneity—will not be successful in his study of complex culture. If he does not retain these points of view and carries on research in the general field of complex culture, there will be nothing to distinguish him from the sociologist, whose theory and method he will be forced to employ. That the anthropologist working in what was once exclusively the sphere of the sociologist becomes a sociologist is at once apparent, for instance in the anthropological studies of southern American communities and in the work of Warner and his associates in Yankee City. In the latter, which spells out the operation of social classes within an American city, a classic sociological problem, the approach in a number of areas was even historical.[16] The basic method of allocating class and of discovering the number of classes was quantitative. Steward,[17] although an anthropologist, when he wrote on certain problems in the study of complex culture areas, developed a theory and a method that placed great emphasis on formal institutions, history, complex economic organizations, patterns of interaction, and upon quantification and sampling. But these are the hallmarks of the sociological study of a community or a society.

In later work, a number of the concepts utilized, such as the folk-urban, bear a startling resemblance to standard sociological concepts, such as *Gemeinschaft* and *Gesellschaft*, or sacred and profane. This convergence is not to be deplored. But there would be less time lost and energy wasted, and perhaps fewer discoveries of old concepts under new names, if the anthropologist would start out with a mastery of relevant sociological theory.[18] Both Max Weber and Parsons have provided concepts that can be used to describe and analyse types of societies. It might be more economical for the anthropologist to test the utility of these types than to rediscover them. Parsons'[19] analytical framework should be particularly congenial to the anthropologist since it includes propositions

[16] There is, of course, a strong historical tradition in cultural anthropology. Much of the work of the classic American anthropologists, for instance, Wissler and Kroeber, is historical. But this movement seems to have lost some momentum, and is not typical of those whose major interests are the anthropological study of complex culture, and culture and personality.
[17] J. H. Steward, *Area Research: Theory and Practice*, New York: Social Science Research Council Bulletin 63, 1950.
[18] R. L. Beals, 'Urbanism, Urbanization, and Acculturation', *Amer. Anthropologist*, 53 (1951), 1-10.
[19] T. Parsons, *The Social System*, Glencoe: The Free Press, 1951; London: Routledge, 1952.

that involve the relation of the individual to society and the relation between social role and personality. But the anthropologist who uses these concepts and quantitative methods will no longer be an anthropologist but a sociologist. There is no way for the anthropologist to do a rigorous study of contemporary civilization and remain an anthropologist.

If the functional theory of the anthropologist is not adequate for the study of complex culture, one may question whether the standard methods of the anthropologist, based upon the assumption of the homogeneity of a culture, will be adequate. Briefly stated, this method involves direct observation, participant observation, and inquiry of one informant or of a few.

To see a culture whole and to see it true has been extraordinarily difficult, even in the case of cultures and societies that were relatively homogenous, shared by few, and limited territorially, for even among them the problems of sampling existed. However, there was a universe of such an order (usually) that the investigator could check the statements of his informants by direct inspection. These conditions do not exist in complex cultures, in which problems of sampling are greatly increased by the multiplicity of subcultures, by the number and diversity of roles available to the individual, and by the increase in the size of the universe itself.

In studying primitive cultures the anthropologist's concern is with process, since he either assumes that homogeneity is present, is not interested in variations, or can establish that homogeneity is actually present. Logically, this is the only basis for the anthropologist's reliance on few informants. But in complex cultures the lack of homogeneity is immediately apparent. The investigator must be concerned with distribution and with variations, since there are many subcultures, which are themselves of considerable heterogeneity, or because there is differentially shared behaviour. Under these circumstances rigorous quantitative methods are essential. The only alternative would be to continue research that does not go beyond hypothesis-making and that is impressive for its ingenuity rather than as a contribution to science. The objection is not to the construction of hypotheses as such, but to their lack of specificity and to the impossibility of disproving, and hence of proving them.[20]

[20] e.g. G. Gorer, *The American People*, New York: Norton; London: Cresset Press, 1948; and G. Gorer and J. Rickman, *The People of Great Russia*, New York: Chanticleer Press, 1950; London: Cresset Press, 1949.

Margaret Mead has recently formulated 'a sampling assumption' for use in studies of complex culture:

> Any member of a group, provided that his position within that group is properly specified, is a perfect sample of the group-wide pattern on which he is acting as an informant. So a twenty-one-year-old boy born of Chinese American parents in a small up-state New York town who has just graduated *summa cum laude* from Harvard and a tenth-generation Boston-born deaf-mute of United Kingdom stock are equally perfect examples of American national character, *provided that their individual position and individual characteristics are taken fully into account.*[21]

This statement is obviously not an assumption, since it is capable of verification. It is also partially incorrect; and where correct, it calls for the application of extremely complicated sampling techniques which, to my knowledge, have not yet been employed by anthropologists engaged in the study of complex cultures.

The error lies in the assumption that patterns, which are of interest and importance in the anthropological study of complex cultures, are equally distributed among all members of a group and that, if they are so distributed, they are discernible either through the introspection of the informant or through the observation by the anthropologist of any single member of the group. Mead's sampling assumption obviously rests on the premise that the patterns are so distributed and that they can be elicited in the ways mentioned above.

While it is still theoretically possible that these hypotheses are correct, they have not been verified. There has been, to my knowledge, no attempt to verify them. The nature of the pattern being investigated and upon which the individual is acting as informant is of course crucial to this discussion. The more superficial the patterns and the greater their distance from personality, the more accurate their description will be. The more the patterns are formal, institutionalized and behavioural, the more hypotheses about them will tend to conform to reality. But the more the process has been affected by dynamic unconscious determinants for its current expression and on non-institutionalized and non-institutionalizable relationships for its transmission, the greater is the error contained in Mead's assumption.

The most vulnerable propositions are those that have to do with the effects of childhood training upon adult personality and

[21] M. Mead, 'National Character', loc. cit., p. 648.

behaviour. No matter what the formal patterns of child rearing are, they are so sharply affected by the unconscious conflicts of the individual parents and by other non-institutionalized elements, that any assumption that one individual constitutes a perfect sample, must be in error unless both the institutional and non-institutional factors are stated.

Mead's escape clause, '. . . *provided their individual position and individual characteristics are taken into account*', is either an expression of good will or, if it is really intended for practice, calls for such expression of knowledge of the universe and of the individual that both sampling procedures and a formal study are rendered superfluous; or it increases the number of universes to the number of individuals. The difficulty actually lies in the fact that a prior knowledge of the effects of the '. . . *individual position and individual characteristics . . .*' upon the informant is needed, but in order to obtain this knowledge the patterns themselves must be established, and in order to do this, the problem of obtaining as representative a sample as possible must first be solved.

There is no special virtue in the sociologist's concern about sampling problems. He samples because of his concern about problems of distribution. By employing large samples he reduces the risk that his findings will be vitiated by the multiplicity of factors encompassed by the term bias. And he does all this when the subject of study is typically a fragmented aspect of public opinion— a relatively simple problem in contrast to those which the anthropologist who studies complex culture sets himself.

Another problem, closely linked to that of sampling, which if unsolved renders even the best sample useless, relates to the accuracy of the informant's statement. Obviously, the more the statements are to be capable of verification, the more limited in scope the questions must be. But much of the work of the anthropologist in complex cultures deals with an order of events that is either not verifiable—for instance, child-rearing practices of a generation ago—or not verified.

It has been demonstrated that responses are affected by the interviewer, to say nothing of the form in which the questions are asked. For instance, members of one social class respond in one way to interviewers of the same social class and in another way to those of a higher social stratum. There are more subtle factors at work when questions of greater psychological significance than those typically contained in the poll or survey are being studied. It is indisputable that even the best-intentioned informant distorts, and that he does so in a way that is not discernible to the interviewer. *A priori*, in studies where there is a long and intensive contact between the interviewer and the informant, there is little reason to doubt that a type of transference and countertransference develops, and that distortion takes place on both sides. It does not matter that the relationship between the informant and the interviewer is not of a therapeutic nature, so long as the subject matter is such that it touches unconscious conflicts in one or both. I do not refer to conscious distortion or suppression, but to the acting out in the interview situation of unconscious impulses and defences. At some risk of being misunderstood, I must point out that both the willingness to be an informant and the need to be a student of human life must stem, at least in part, from unconscious conflicts; and that these tend to result not only in greater perceptivity, but also in distortion. This danger is greatest in the study of child-rearing practices and of behaviour related to sexuality and aggression. An interesting example of this is the case of the rather shrewd observer of child-rearing practices who was rather badly deceived when he took for fact certain seeming irregularities of practice that were actually the fantasies of his informants. The informants believed that the occurrences in their fantasies had taken place.[22]

Modern society is heterogeneous, stratified, and impossible to see as a whole. Any attempt to use one informant as a representative of the whole is doomed to failure and any attempt to use the single informant as a representative of his unique group does not go far towards reducing the complexity of the problem, since the picture that it gives us is as complex as culture itself.

We are left then with the third mark of the anthropologist; the assumption of the interrelatedness of culture and personality. There is then the possibility that if the whole field of complex culture is not suited to the training, methodology and conceptual framework of the anthropologist, one specific area may be.

It is in the study of culture and personality that the functional approach of the anthropologist is not found wanting. The anthropologist looks for the functional relation between man's needs including the biological, and man's culture. His next step is to dis-

[22] E. Jones, *The Life and Work of Sigmund Freud* (3 vols.), New York: Basic Books; London: Hogarth Press, 1953-7.

cover the reciprocal relationship between the individual and culture. The anthropologist would be the first to see the relationship because of his exposure to different cultures, different ways of behaving, and because of his relative objectivity. And there is no question that the anthropologists have made contributions to the solution of this problem in primitive cultures. Thus it is probably not accidental that many of those trained as anthropologists have turned to the study of culture and personality. There is no longer any need to demonstrate that culture and personality are related, nor that there is a casual relationship between the two. Instead, attention must focus on how they are related. There is general agreement that the learned, the culturally imposed, patterns of child rearing influence adult personality, although there may be violent disagreement as to the extent.

Freud saw the relationship between culture and personality as a complex one. He was explicit in stating[23] that the object relations both preceding and following the primal crime are the factors responsible for culture and that the Oedipus complex (and all that it means in the development of human personality) can exist only under certain cultural and biological conditions: those in which the child can identify the parent figures and in which he is dependent on them for care during infancy and childhood.

The working definition of personality found in most anthropological writings on culture and personality is a minimal one: personality and *intrapsychic life* are synonymous terms. Intrapsychic life is a term which on closer examination is either more or less complicated than at first sight. It is used to refer to part of the personality or to the total personality; it can mean structure, content, or both. There is apparently little agreement between anthropologists as to its meaning.

Some studies in culture and personality have been successful because they tapped only the most superficial levels of intrapsychic life, i.e. the most superficial levels of the emotional and ideational content of human life. Considering that culture is learned, and that for the individual much of what is learned is, in the strictest sense of the term, intrapsychic (i.e. in his head), and that he can verbalize much of what is intrapsychic, it is not surprising to find certain correlations between culture and personality. For example, the

[23] S. Freud, *Totem and Taboo* (1913), *Standard Ed.*, 13, London: Hogarth Press, 1955.

relationship between suspiciousness, anxiety and sorcery, or that between the blocking of the channels for the overt expression of hostility and the high incidence of displacement, can be stated almost without reference to personality. These are equations in which the terms on both sides are cultural.[24]

The scientific worth of studies in culture and personality depends on the personality theory used, the accuracy of the methods of observing both culture and personality, and the meaningfulness of the problems. I shall comment briefly on the first two.

The intrapsychic life of man can be conceptualized in a variety of ways. There are three fairly well-delineated views: learning theory, perception theory, and Freudian psychoanalysis. Hullian learning theory is logical since it is by nature deductive. I am not, however, impressed by its applicability to the significant dimensions of human psychological life. Personality theory based on perception is largely subsumed under part of psychoanalytic ego psychology, namely, the mechanisms of defence, or is an almost banal variation of learning theory. If it is the latter, it does little more than reiterate that the situation is defined as the individual learns, through culture, to perceive it. This is surely correct, but it seems that we always knew that pork is seen differently by the Moslem and the Christian. I shall discuss only the last, not only because I believe it to be the most useful and accurate, but also because it contains the most logically interrelated set of propositions that are applicable to human psychology. In limiting myself to a discussion of Freudian psychoanalytic theory as applied to the study of personality and culture, I have also taken into account the fact that most studies of personality and culture have been based either on psychoanalytic propositions or upon modifications of them.

To spell out the psychoanalytic theory that ought to be employed is beyond the scope of this paper.[25] I shall discuss some of the difficulties in culture and personality study: the consideration of infantile experience as the sole determinant of later personality, the use of isolated fragments of psychoanalytic theory, the disregard of ego psychology in general, and of the psychology of character formation and character dynamics specifically.

[24] Substantially the same point is made by E. Shils in *The Present State of American Sociology*, Glencoe: The Free Press, 1948.
[25] There is a detailed and exact discussion of this by H. Hartmann, E. Kris and R. M. Loewenstein, 'Some Psychoanalytic Comments on "Culture and Personality" ', now in this volume.

Although much work in culture and personality attempts to explain some phase of adult behaviour or personality by reference to some aspect of the child-rearing practices of the people in question, often the explanations arrived at are based on outmoded or incomplete models of psychoanalytic theory.

Some investigators operate with the belief that according to psychoanalysis, the experiences of infancy and earliest childhood should be sufficient to determine major aspects of adult personality. Thus, Leighton and Kluckhohn confront the anxiety, moodiness and suspiciousness of the adult Navaho with 'self-demand' nursing, the great permissiveness of childhood discipline, and the affection with which children are regarded, and claim that this is a refutation of the beliefs of certain psychoanalysts (who are unnamed) about the importance of infancy. They say:

> Infantile indulgence probably does constitute the firmest foundation upon which, if later circumstances are reasonably favourable, a secure and confident adult personality can be developed. But it affords only a possible basis. . . . The high degree of tension observed among adult Navahos may be traced partly to the exceedingly grave pressures to which Navaho society is at present subject, and also the conflicts caused by weaning, other experiences of later childhood, and beliefs about supernatural forces.[26]

Certainly psychoanalytic theory does not predict that infantile indulgence can prevent real anxiety. Whatever his infantile experience has been, the Navaho adult faces an extremely difficult life. The death rate is high. There is great poverty; hunger is often endemic. The anxiety is probably exacerbated by the knowledge of the Navahos that these circumstances need not exist. The details of Navaho infancy and childhood from the Kluckhohn and Leighton material indicate both a less idyllic state of the infant and child and some explanation of the mood swings, the tension and the anxiety of the adult. Until the end of the first year of life, Navaho infants are bound tightly to a cradle board. There is maximum feeding of the infant, whenever it whimpers, and aside from the restraints imposed by the cradle board, minimum frustration of the infant and toddler. Children are nursed for a long period. Mothers often masturbate the genitals of the children while they nurse. Weaning, although gradual, seems to be most commonly

---

[26] D. Leighton and C. Kluckhohn, *Children of the People*, Cambridge: Harvard University Press, 1947, p. 110.

occasioned by the next pregnancy of the mother. At the time of weaning, toilet training is imposed. The child is no longer permitted to sleep with the mother, but must sleep with older siblings. Temper tantrums are frequent. There is intense sibling rivalry. The family itself is rather unstable, because of the high death rate, the frequency of separation, and the subsequent formation of other unions. Unfortunately, Kluckhohn and Leighton have made few attempts to relate systematically Navaho adult personality and culture to the factors mentioned above. Yet, these experiences can be fitted into psychoanalytic personality theory and then related to the national character of the Navaho, to Navaho culture, and the use made of the culture for the solution of unconscious conflicts.

Other writers overlook the distinction between dynamic and genetic propositions.[27] Applied to the field of culture and personality, dynamic propositions are those that deal with cross-sectional inter-relationships between the culture and the individual, with the conflict of forces within the psychic structure at any given maturational level, and with the relationship of these conflicts to the culture. Genetic propositions are those concerned with the history of these conflicts, with the relationship between current personality structure, defences, and conflicts and the developmental history of the individual. To be complete, statements about the effects of child-rearing practices must include both the dynamic and the genetic aspects. It should be noted that in order to do this, a knowledge not only of the id content, but also of the defensive structure, i.e. of the ego, is required.

Many workers in the field of culture and personality, particularly those concerned with child-rearing practices, appear to have been completely oblivious to the discovery of the ego. Two exceptions are Erikson[28] and Róheim,[29] both of whom had training in psychoanalysis as well as in one of the social sciences. That the

[27] For a discussion of this aspect see H. Hartmann and E. Kris, 'The Genetic Approach in Psychoanalysis', *The Psychoanalytic Study of the Child*, 1, New York: International Universities Press; London: Hogarth Press, 1945, pp. 11-30; and S. Axelrad and L. Maury, 'Identification as a Mechanism of Adaptation', *Psychoanalysis and Culture*, New York: International Universities Press, 1951, pp. 168-84.

[28] E. H. Erikson, *Childhood and Society*, New York: Norton, 1930; London: Hogarth Press (rev. ed.), 1964.

[29] G. Róheim, 'Psychoanalysis and Anthropology', *Psychoanalysis and the Social Sciences*, 1, New York: International Universities Press; London: Hogarth Press, 1947, pp. 9-33.

same behaviour can represent two opposite unconscious constellations is a much neglected fact. Anthropological treatments of Balinese, German, Japanese, and Russian national character are cases in point.

I am aware of Leites'[30] specification of the hypotheses of psycho-cultural theory and of Mead's[31] defence of Gorer. I would, however, go further than the view of Hartmann, Kris, and Loewenstein,[32] who say that much of the work does not come up to the methodological specifications that Leites posits. It does not seem to me that there has been any attempt to meet these specifications in many of the researches in this field. And Mead's statement, *'From an analysis of the way Russians swaddle infants, it is possible to build a model of Russian character formation which enables us to relate what we know about human behaviour and what we know about Russian culture in such a way that Russian behaviour becomes more understandable'*,[33] indicates that there is too great a reliance upon one aspect of infantile experience. The theory is too simple.

On the one hand, the effects of swaddling are the central theme of Gorer's analysis, and on the other, the swaddling experience and its effects seem to be completely irrelevant for Gorer's conclusions.[34] In dovetailing swaddling with Great Russian culture, Gorer uses Kleinian psychoalanytic theory. That Gorer makes use of that variant of psychoanalytic theory developed by Melanie Klein is surprising. The theory is questionable as a valid body of psycho-analytic propositions. Glover[35] demonstrates that this theory attributes very complex psychic functions and institutions to the infant of six months or less. It assigns one factor, which occurs between the third and the sixth month, as the cause of all neurosis. Of all the variants of psychoanalytic theory, Kleinian theory allows the least room for the effects of the environment. This school specifies

[30] N. Leites, 'Psycho-Cultural Hypotheses about Political Acts', *World Politics*, 1, New Haven: Yale University Press, 1948, p. 102.
[31] M. Mead, 'The Swaddling Hypothesis: Its Reception', *Amer. Anthropologist*, 3 (1954), 395-403.
[32] H. Hartmann, R. M. Loewenstein and E. Kris, 'Some Psychoanalytic Comments on "Culture and Personality" ', now in this volume.
[33] M. Mead, 'The Swaddling Hypothesis: Its Reception', loc. cit., pp. 401-2 (Mead's italics).
[34] G. Gorer and J. Rickman, *The People of Great Russia*, pp. 190-3.
[35] E. Glover, 'Examination of the Kleinian System of Child Psychology', *The Psychoanalytic Study of the Child*, 1, New York: International Universities Press; London: Hogarth Press, 1945.

as rigid and inborn just those elements of general psychoanalytic theory which as is shown below, Gorer believes to lack universal validity. Seemingly, Gorer is able to make use of Kleinian psychoanalysis because, like many of the other workers in the field of national character, he uses isolated concepts or fragments of the totally, interrelated set of psychoanalytic propositions. However, as Hartmann, Kris and Loewenstein have shown,[36] psychoanalytic theory cannot be used in this fashion. Assuming that the swaddling experience is of great importance to the Great Russion infant, we would expect it to influence the behaviour of the Great Russian adult. However, we can understand its effects only if we have a knowledge of the current psychological conflicts of the Great Russian adults, and if we are able to perceive how the swaddling experiences of infancy are used in the service of these conflicts.

Gorer, said by Mead[37] to be the person 'who has done more than any other anthropologist to develop the study of national character', writing on its theory and practice, says:

> The term 'national character' would appear to carry three connotations which are partly complementary and partly contrasting:
> 1. National character isolates and analyses the principal motives or predispositions which can be deduced from the behaviour of the personnel of a society at a given time and place.
> 2. National character describes the means by which these motives and predispositions are elicited and maintained in the majority of the new members who are added to the society by birth, so that a society continues its culture longer than a single generation.
> 3. National character also refers to the ideal image of themselves in the light of which individuals assess and pass judgment upon themselves and their neighbours, and on the basis of which they reward and punish their children, for the manifestation or non-manifestation of given traits and attitudes.[38]

The problem in this formulation is the level of the 'motives or predispositions'. Gorer implies that this level is both conscious and unconscious, but this question is never explicitly handled. There appears to be no systematic statement, except that 'statements about

[36] H. Hartmann, R. M. Loewenstein and E. Kris, loc. cit.
[37] M. Mead, 'National Character', in A. Kroeber (ed.), *Anthropology Today*, Chicago: University of Chicago Press, 1953, p. 8.
[38] G. Gorer, 'National Character: Theory and Practice', *The Study of Culture at a Distance*, Chicago: University of Chicago Press, 1953, pp. 57-63.

national character try to define and isolate those attitudes and pre-dispositions which are manifested by the most representative and approved of members of the society, the manifestations of which in others is criticized or punished'. The outcome of the study of national character is the formulation of a type. These statements by Gorer imply that relationship can be stated between behaviour, or culture, unconscious motivations which are discharged through culture, methods of child rearing, and perfectly conscious images of how children and adults should behave, on the basis of which children are reared. At first sight, it would seem that little objection should be taken. Certainly, whatever their adaptive or rational functions, it is known that culture and institutions have discharge functions, and are related to unconscious conflict. That the level of interaction is not stated is unfortunate, since these relations will have economic, dynamic and structural components. As a general rule, we would expect that there would be some causal linkage between methods of child rearing and later unconscious conflict. There is, however, unfortunately an overemphasis on the influence of the 'ideal image'. But the point is that the motives or predisposi-tions cannot be stated in terms of child rearing practices as they affect the child at the age or phase at which they are applied, but rather as they are operative in terms of current conflicts: that is, the typology must refer to the ego and its defensive operations, as well as to the infantile conflict. As defined by Gorer, studies of national character cannot utilize the body of psychoanalytic theory and can result only in fragmentary, point-to-point correlations.

Further evidence of this may be seen in Gorer's[39] account of the psychological concepts which he believes to lack universal validity. He assumes that the super-ego is not universal, that the Oedipus complex is probably either not universal or that there are societies where it is completely resolved, that castration anxiety and penis envy are culturally determined, and that sadism and masochism are probably not biologically based. How Gorer could know, with-out having either psychoanalyzed or without having access to the analytical treatment of representative individuals from the societies where the Oedipus is resolved, is questionable. But the major point should be clear; these propositions which Gorer rejects are the basic and interrelated propositions of psychoanalytic theory. It will not be possible either to integrate psychoanalytic theory with this

[39] ibid., pp. 71-3.

work in national character, nor will the results of studies made on the basis of these assumptions be useful in the development of psychoanalytic anthropology.

Since so much of the work of the anthropologist in the field of culture and personality takes the form of statements about *character*, we express the hope that a reasonably complete theory about character will be developed and utilized. By definition, character traits are ego-syntonic. In psychoanalytic parlance, 'character' refers to certain constant attitudes that the ego takes toward the id, the super-ego, and reality. The oral, anal, urethral, phallic, and genital character typology implies an extremely complicated set of relationships between instinctual impulses, their vicissitudes, and the relative strength of the psychic institutions.[40] Each character type, with the exception of the genital, may comprise either a neurotic constellation in which the unsuccessful defences (chiefly reaction formations) against the instinctual impulses predominate, or each character type (including the genital) may comprise a normal constellation in which sublimations predominate. Any statement of national character, or any attempt to relate cultural phenomena to personality, must go beyond a description of the phase of libidinal organization represented by the character type. No statement about character is complete unless we know how the Oedipal conflict has been resolved, and what the effects of a specific child-rearing practice are on the resolution of this conflict. A complete formulation of national character requires a knowledge of the personality changes that take place during adolescence. It is probable that adolescence is as crucial a period of personality development as earlier ones. Very few of the investigations of national character meet these criteria. Character tends to mean anything at all that can be subsumed under personality.

In most cases there are great gaps between the descriptions of the early phases of libidinal organization and the descriptions of the adult personality. In most anthropological accounts of child rearing much data are included on the pre-Oedipal phases, which are in gross form more easily observed than the resolution of the Oedipal conflict. This conflict is, after all, resolved through repression. The manner of its resolution, and the extent and quality of its subsequent effects on character and personality are not accessible

[40] O. Fenichel, *The Psychoanalytic Theory of Neurosis*, New York: Norton, 1945; London: Routledge, 1946.

through observation. The only adequate way of obtaining these data is through the psychoanalytic interview.

With this, we come to the problem of the methods and techniques desirable in studies of culture and personality. Here I am concerned only with those studies in which there is direct access to the people involved. There are two areas of technique: the description of the child-rearing practices and the description of personality. As far as the study of child-rearing practices is concerned, there are two dangers that beset the investigator: description that is primarily intuitive and qualitative, and description that is primarily objective (factual).

The qualitative and intuitive account of child-rearing practice is inadequate for the study of both process and distribution. In any complex culture, there are a great variety of character types and an even greater variety of child-rearing practices. Simple observation results in impressions which, it may be predicted, will present a picture of a non-existent homogeneity. Quantitative analysis of the mother-infant interaction, in one study conducted in a mid-Western city of the United States, indicated that both qualitative impressions and objective categorizations, for example, in terms of breast and bottle feeding, gave only shallow and misleading results. When the quality of the interaction between mother and infant in a number of activities was scaled and analysed, a number of types emerged. These types cut across such categories as self-demand and scheduled feeding, breast and bottle feeding. These types, based on the mother's sensitivity to the cues of the infant, are free of cultural bias and are applicable for cross-cultural study.[41]

No matter how accurately the standard methods of child rearing in any culture are described, they have differential results in practice. The adult personality of any individual is partially dependent on the unconscious fantasies of the person who administered the method. It is sometimes forgotten that although the culture may set the standard, it is the parent and not the culture who rears the child. The culturally set standard is always mediated through individuals.

The unconscious attitudes of the person who cares for the child become part of the practice. The infant or child is apt to be as sensitive to attitudes as to behaviour. He may even be more aware

[41] S. Brody, *Patterns of Mothering*, New York: International Universities Press, 1956.

of the unconscious attitudes than of the actual practice, and certainly he will be more aware of both of these than of the culturally set standard of parental behaviour. The adult, while aware of what the culture prescribes, is usually not aware of what his own attitudes are, and thus he is unaware of the totality of his behaviour. For this reason both observation and interview are insufficient. Some method which can take account of the unconscious fantasies is needed, since there is no reason to believe that the fantasies will cancel each other out.

It seems to be the standard procedure for one, or at most two, projective tests to be used in psycho-cultural studies.[42] Often these tests are administered by one who has not had the training to interpret them. In our own culture, when for purposes of diagnosis a description of personality is needed—a description often much less elaborate than those sought in studies of personality and culture—a complete battery of tests is used. To these an elaborate social and psychiatric history is added. On the basis of all this, then, a diagnosis is formulated. Since the diagnostic problem is probably even more complicated with so-called 'normal' people, who should of course be the subject of any psycho-cultural inquiry, these tests that make up the standard test battery of the diagnostician should be employed as a minimum. Even these may not suffice. Probably the best tool would be the psychoanalysis of representative cultural specimens. A statement of the correlations between culture and the type of personality could be drawn from this.

To my knowledge the best pieces of work in this field are Rudolph M. Loewenstein's study of anti-Semitism, *Christians and Jews*,[43] and the Adorno, Frenkel-Brunswik, Levinson, and Sanford study of *The Authoritarian Personality*.[44] Loewenstein drew heavily on his experience as a psychoanalyst in two cultures. In *The Authoritarian Personality* the basic hypotheses were drawn from psychoanalytic theory. The study was really an attempt to verify certain deductions drawn from this theory about a specific kind of child-rearing practice: specific unconscious conflicts in the adult, the way they are defended against, and attitudes toward outgroups.

[42] J. Henry and M. E. Spiro, 'Psychological Techniques: Projective Tests in Field Work', in *Anthropology Today*.

[43] R. M. Loewenstein, *Christians and Jews*, New York: International Universities Press, 1951.

[44] T. W. Adorno, E. Frenkel-Brunswik, D. J. Levinson and R. N. Sanford, *The Authoritarian Personality*, New York: Harper, 1950.

Both studies relate psycho-cultural phenomena to the resolution of the Oedipal conflict. Both utilize ego psychology, and both employ techniques that are specific for an understanding of the defences.

If one translates these techniques of investigation into essential skills, then the investigator in the field of culture and personality will need some of the knowledge that is standard for the anthropologist, and almost all of the knowledge of the practising analyst. The pioneer work in the field, Lasswell's *Psychopathology and Politics* exemplifies this need.[45]

How the expert in culture and personality is to acquire adequate training is a grave problem, for which no solution is at hand.

At the same time, it should be mentioned that the verification of the universality of certain analytic propositions and of the way in which culture varies the form of the resolution of the Oedipus complex, can only come from the psychoanalysis of individuals in diverse cultures. That is, the development of culture and personality study is important for the growth of psychoanalysis itself.

A prediction may be made. Culture and personality is at this time a field of multidisciplinary study, and one that is interstitial to several disciplines: anthropology, sociology and psychology. If the history of science is any guide, a new science will emerge, with unique problems, unique methods, and as a unique field of inquiry. Much of the confusion inherent in the field is the symptom of intellectual growing pains. The field of culture and personality seems to call for a unity of work and of theory between specialists in culture and specialists in personality. But the best kind of unification of science is that which takes place in the head of the individual investigator. In all likelihood, this investigator will be a social scientist, with sufficient mastery of psychological techniques to permit him to investigate personality as an independent operator. As culture becomes more complex, social roles become more diversified. Even the social sciences cannot be an exception.

[45] H. Lasswell, *Psychopathology and Politics*, Chicago: Chicago University Press, 1930.

In the last thirty years our knowledge of factors responsible for character development has increased to a considerable extent. Due to ego-psychological observations, facts regarding differentiation and functioning have become accessible to us which help us understand the critical influence of socio-cultural expectations and habits· The following study of the Southern Chinese modal personality has benefited from previous works but has combined it more specifically with diagnostic criteria based on repeated interviews with representative individuals from that area.

Rather than commenting on his own paper, the editor will quote from a critical review by Sarlin (Charles N. Sarlin, 'Identity, Culture, and Psychosexual Development' in American Imago, *24, 1967, pp. 211 f.) '. . . the influence of the [Chinese] culture on the development of the characteristics of masculinity and femininity becomes quite clear. Both the men and the women, by virtue of their infantile mechanisms of identification with oral-sadistic aggressors characteristic of the oral phase, develop complementary character structures consistent with that primitive level of development. As a result, both autonomy and psychic separation are impaired.'*

13

Orality and Dependence: Characteristics of Southern Chinese[1]

WARNER MUENSTERBERGER

The purpose of this study is to arrive at a closer understanding from a psychoanalytic point of view, of certain characteristic features we have observed among a group of Southern Chinese. These observations were made in the field, namely in the Chinese quarters of New York and San Francisco, i.e. among immigrants and visitors to the United States. Most of them come from the southern part of China and, in particular, from a semi-rural area in the Kwang-tung province, the Toy Shan district. It is a comparatively poor area, and the economic condition requires that its inhabitants earn their money elsewhere. No doubt this economic situation intrudes in the life pattern we are trying to understand psychoanalytically.

Personal contact was limited to a continuous series of interviews

[1] This paper first published in *Psychoanalysis and the Social Sciences*, 3, ed. by G. Róheim, New York: International Universities Press, 1951, is based on work done as a member of the Chinese group of Research in Contemporary Cultures, a project of Columbia University, inaugurated by the late Ruth Benedict, under a grant from the Office of Naval Research, and according to the terms of the contract, reproduction in whole or in part is permitted for any purpose of the U.S. Government.

Research in Contemporary Cultures was designed to apply to the study of modern cultures the standard methods of cultural anthropology and some methods drawn from clinical psychology and psychoanalysis, thus the project was both interdisciplinary and cross-cultural.

The Chinese section was organized in June 1947 and continued to function as a group until June 1949. During this period individual members conducted intensive studies on various levels, and met in biweekly seminars to discuss their data, methods and results. All materials, such as records of interviews, analyses of literature, etc. were available to all members of the group. In these seminars many of the ideas and insights in the following paper were developed.

In this paper I have drawn upon the work of the following colleagues: Dr R. Bunzel, Dr T. M. Abel, Miss Gitel Poznanski, Mr J. Weakland, Dr E. H. Hellersberg, Dr. H. C. Hu, Mr S. Schwartz, Dr W. Chen, Mrs C. H. Liu, Miss J. Belo, Miss V. Heyer, Mrs E. Lee. I have arrived at the psychoanalytic interpretations and conclusions in this paper independent of the other members of the Chinese section. Documents referred to in the following pages are Documents of Research in Contemporary Cultures and are on file at Columbia University.

with fifteen men between the ages of twenty and thirty-five and six women of the same age group. The selection of these informants was dictated only by the attempt to gather psychological data from Southern Chinese, regardless of their social and economic position or individual history. Among these people were waiters and artists, laundrymen and physicians, salesmen and students. The interviewed women without exception belonged to the intellectual group. In several cases we made use of the psychoanalytic technique of interviewing, employing free associations and dreams. These interviews were conducted for a period of more than two years. Records of other interviews collected by co-members of the research team, were used extensively. In addition, projective material such as folk-tales, legends, films, tests, modern literature, and field reports provided us with supplementary information.

The language used in our conversations was English. But occasionally Chinese words, expressions and proverbs were cited and translated literally. For example: one of the Chinese words for 'prostitute' literally translated, is 'animal spirit' and as such may have different connotations. Our word is associated with feelings of contempt, while this Chinese expression is extended to imply uneasiness or anxiety. More than once I felt the limitations, necessarily dictated by this fact. The Chinese language is richer than ours; only very few of my informants had mastered English well enough to express themselves fluently. This, too, may have at times influenced our impressions.

Our method of collecting data does not permit us to make general statements about *the* Chinese. Nor does it seem justified to form conclusions about the Chinese in their own environment in their homeland. We dealt with people who had already made certain adjustments to the American environment and the American behaviour patterns which in many respects make conflicting demands on their behaviour and reactions. The modifications of the environment, language, habits and inter-personal relations necessarily alter the attitude of the informant. Potentialities which had to be repressed or substituted in the environment at home could be brought into play in the new and different American society. And, on the other hand, what might be considered objectionable among Americans, could be accepted, or even demanded in a Chinese milieu. In Western Europe and North America, there is much more permissiveness in the relationships between age groups.

The restraint to which he was accustomed in China, gave the Chinese male a feeling of security, while the American pattern might give rise to feelings of insecurity. In China he knew his proper status, in the New World he does not. Because of these changes in strains and stresses I do not feel permitted to draw definite conclusions about Chinese characteristics in the more balanced society at home. So when I speak of 'the Chinese' or 'China' it only refers to those persons or that part of the country which my informants represent.

But the cultural differences have even deeper manifestations and a methodological question arises in connection with the problem of the variations in the ego and super-ego formation in different cultural settings. The infant takes over orders, ideas, regulations, prohibitions and permissions of the parental authority. Identification with parents and individuals in the environment, object relationships, rules and codes are of far-reaching importance. The controlling and regulating agency, which we call the super-ego is created out of this relation to the external world. But what happens when the authoritative image changes? What was prohibited or uncustomary in China, may be easily accepted in the Western world. What might be called a pathological symptom among Americans, is demanded from the Chinese in their homeland.[2] The cultural condition influences the super-ego at this point. At least with regard to these problems we can speak of the development of a 'double super-ego' which may at times distort our view or cause us to jump to conclusions. In observing and interpreting behaviour then, we have to be aware of the presence of two psychic agencies operating separately.[3] Only the comparison of a number of analytical case

[2] In a general discussion on methods and techniques, Otto Klineberg made the following remark: 'Some years ago a group of Chinese psychologists applied a number of the standard inventories like the Bernreuter, Thurnstone and others to Chinese students and arrived at the sad conclusion that the Chinese students were very neurotic. One of the investigators closed with a plea for more mental hygiene in the Chinese universities to overcome this unfortunate situation. What has happened, of course, was that the specific items in the inventory *were interpreted quite differently* by the Chinese. One question went like this: "Do you allow others to push ahead of you in line?" Of course all the Chinese said "yes", which apparently is marked on the neurotic side. Well there are no such lines in China; they all gather around together. So everybody turned out to be neurotic.' *Culture and Personality*, Proceedings of an Interdisciplinary Conference held under the auspices of the Viking Fund, New York, 1949, p. 103 (my italics).
[3] The expression 'double super-ego' was formulated in a personal conversation with Bertram D. Lewin.

histories of patients of different ethnic backgrounds, combined with more extensive material gathered from other fields of study, will help us overcome this dilemma. As we add to our knowledge, we may have to reject many of our present ideas and conclusions, but what we have gained from such a preliminary study is a starting point and a direction in which to seek the much needed information.

1. THE MATERIAL

For many generations the Western world has clung to images of China and the Chinese which in many respects are stereotyped misconceptions. The Chinese society was pictured as a completely patriarchal one, incorporating a strong belief in immortality, ancestor worship, and an erudite philosophy embraced by even the most lowly peasant.

It is true that Chinese society is officially organized along patriarchal lines. But what the official social organization of a society demands, is often quite different from reality. In the China described by my informants, we find the women holding a much stronger and more powerful position than one would gather from the stereotype descriptions. 'In theory the father of the family is supreme in his authority. In practice, however, the mother is the centre of the domestic life.'[4] To me, this reversal of our expectations concerning the relative position of male and female was most striking. Even today many usually well-informed people think of the Chinese woman as a meek, docile, loving servant to the authoritarian, powerful and all-wise man. But those who know the Chinese at close range tell a different story. They report that although the Chinese woman suffers under many restrictions, she plays a more influential role within her family than does the man; and the man, potentially at least, lives in a state of uncertainty and insecurity.

Superficially, at any rate, I have found this conspicuous contrast to exist among the Chinese males and females whom I have known personally. Most of the men were quiet, co-operative, interested, sociable, and usually willing to establish some sort of positive

[4] Y. K. Leong and L. K. Tao, *Village and Town Life in China*, London: Allen & Unwin, 1924, quoted by F. Van Heek, *Westersche Techniek en Maatschappelijk Leven in China*, Enschede: M. J. van der Leoff, 1935, p. 113.

relationship. They were friendly and exceedingly polite. Generally, the women who were very reserved at first, became freer and more talkative, at times even quite aggressive.

Of course, this picture is broad and generalized, but these sharp contrasts were found in all other areas of our study as well as in the personal contacts with our informants.

The projective material, and the literature into which we delved, corroborate this scheme. The differences between the sexes were found to be clear enough, so that we can speak of the situation qualitatively, if not quantitatively. And when we investigate the childhood of the Southern Chinese, the pattern is not at all surprising. In view of our findings, we could hardly expect any other kind of inter-individual relationship to have developed between man and woman.

Everybody in China wants sons: the father because a son guarantees the continuation of the generations and because he will venerate him after his death at the ancestral shrine; the mother because the son, as a new representative of the family, raises her status, and gives her influence in surroundings in which, until a son was born, she had no place.

To have a child is one of the highest qualifications which life can offer to the poor as well as to the rich. So the Chinese pay much attention to pre-natal care, and have developed all sorts of measures to guarantee positive results at childbirth. As soon as they find that they are pregnant, many expectant mothers discontinue sexual intercourse, sleep in their own rooms or at least use an individual covering in the family bed *(kang)*, thereby tabooing sexual intercourse. Some informants mentioned the fourth month of pregnancy as the proper time for the separation. A pregnant woman must not quarrel or lift heavy objects or go out late at night. She ought not eat sausages. Salty food is good for her. Sewing or tying knots might adversely affect a smooth delivery. She must not personally prepare anything for the delivery because the child, in that case, might be stillborn.

It is believed by many that one can predict whether the newly born will be a boy or a girl by the shape of the abdomen of the mother. If it is round she will have a girl; if it is pointed she can look forward to a son.

If a girl is born one does not openly resent her. A Shanghai informant mentioned that most families even prefer having a girl as the oldest child: 'First the flower, then the fruit,' is a proverb. But while boys are always welcome, there are certain times during which it would be better if girls were not born. For example, the fifteenth of the month is generally not favoured for the birth of a girl. It is an indication that the family will eventually be poverty-stricken. A girl, born in Tiger years, may become wild and unruly, and will make her family unhappy.

The wish to bear boys expresses itself in the pursuit of magic influences. Into each receptacle in the bridal room, the jars, cups, pots, wash basins and toilet bowls are put several kinds of seeds. The word for seeds *(tze)* and for sons is identical.

No matter what the sex, there are elaborate ceremonies and celebrations for the first-born, probably because even if a girl is born, the mother has given proof of her fertility. (The father's fertility was not in question.) And then, the next child might be a son.

The birth of a son at any time, is an exciting event which calls for colourful festivities. People congratulate the parents and grand-parents who, for instance, may send red-coloured eggs to relatives, friends, neighbours as a symbol of luck and good fortune. The attitude is quite different when a second girl is born. One does not congratulate the parents to the same extent. Most neighbours and relatives studiously ignore the situation, and some console the parents by saying: 'It is not so bad.' The birth of a girl is not openly lamented, but it seems as if she is not to be considered as an asset. Of course there are economic reasons for this. Girls are costly. They have to be fed and educated and finally leave their parents' house in order to join their husband's family. If the mother is unlucky and gives birth only to girls, she will very likely lose prestige.[5] If her husband can afford to, he will take a concubine to provide him with a son so that he is assured of the familial chain.

To the mother, the birth of a son is the source of great happiness. He represents a kind of haven in her life. Having a male child enables her to assert herself, more or less, for the first time. As a daughter, the woman is generally trained in household duties at an

---

[5] The Chinese have a significant proverb: 'A thief will not enter a house with five girls'—parents with many daughters are considered poor because the dowry demands much of their property.

early age. Traditionally, any education other than this was not considered necessary or wise since sooner or later she was to leave the house of her parents and join her husband's family, where her mother-in-law would be running the household.[6] There she was often ill-treated. The attitude of her husband's family was often described to us as cold and noncommittal or even hostile. The constant tension between mother-in-law and daughter-in-law was one of the themes stressed by my female informants.

From a Western point of view, the neonate experiences much indulgence. We hear that the baby sleeps in the parents' bed, often usurping the place of the father. Everybody is anxious for the child's well-being. To quiet a crying child, the grandmother, mother or an older sister may masturbate him, or place his penis in their mouths.

Eating, in South China, is a matter of great concern, and the fact of its importance can be seen in earliest childhood. Whether the infant is a boy or a girl, whenever it demands food by crying or otherwise fussing, it is fed. But when the hungry one is a male child we find time and again that special attention is given him. The paternal grandmother, upon hearing his loud demands, often seizes the opportunity to reproach her daughter-in-law for not having fed her grandson.

The length of the nursing period for both girls and boys depends much upon the economic level of the family, and differs, in South China in rural and urban surroundings. Those who can afford a wet nurse will employ one, so that the little child can be breast-fed for a long time. But the period during which the child is actually nursed, seems to vary considerably. There seems to be a minimum of about six weeks. Even as early as the second month, the infant may get some supplementary food, in the form of rice mush. But this is apparently not the prevalent Chinese custom. In the so-called overseas villages, most of the young married men go off to America or Southeast Asia after the first or second child is born, leaving their wives behind. It does not seem that the women object to the separation. 'Different morality,' an informant explained. 'The women there like it. *They* want to bring up the son. Americans cannot understand that.'[7] The children, and in particular

[6] Since the revolution of 1912, education has been extended for girls of the upper and middle classes.
[7] Cf. Research in Contemporary Cultures, Document CH 318, p. 2, line 11. My italics.

301

the young ones, are under the constant care and guard of the women, the mother, an older sibling or the grandmother. Frequently the women work in the fields and return to their customary occupation some days after the delivery. But even then the baby is never alone. He is taken to the field, to visits, to ceremonies and parties. A female informant described to me how she brought her baby brother to the fields where mother was working and where she would feed him.

There is always milk for the newborn baby. The neonate does not get the first 'suck' from mother's breast, but from another healthy woman who had a child of the opposite sex. From then on mother nurses the baby, and if she does not have enough milk, someone else will supply it. 'You can get a suck from a neighbour,' a Fukien woman told me. Ida Pruitt, in the autobiography of a Chinese working woman, which she transcribed, says, in speaking of a woman and her daughter, who had children at the same time, 'my daughter and I arranged between us. At night and in the morning, I nursed the two babies, and in the day she [her daughter] nursed them both.'[8]

Boys are fondled more, and carried longer than girls, while girl babies are swaddled longer than boys. Boys are given preference in the important matter of food. A Chekiang informant had a sister who died several days after she bore a female baby. This child was given to an orphanage because it was a girl and nobody was found to take care of her. We were assured that if this child had been a boy, a foster home would have been found. Even the father of the child did not want to be bothered with her.[9]

This attitude seems atypical to me, but it has its foundation in the generally accepted, differentiated reaction towards male and female neonates.

Most of the informants agree that boy infants often continue nursing at the breast longer than the girls. 'Usually the mother has enough milk for quite some time,' a Chinese physician told me, 'for about a year or even longer.' When there is a shortage, it is the boy who is favoured at the expense of his sister. In case the mother has no milk and engages a wet nurse, this woman is let go earlier

[8] Ida Pruitt, *A Daughter of Han*, New Haven: Yale University Press, 1945, p. 166.
[9] Cf. Research in Contemporary Cultures, Document C.S. 16, p. 2, line 26 to p. 3, line 4.

when the infant is a girl. 'But if it is a boy,' my female informant stressed, 'you would try your best to keep her longer, to feed him longer.'[10]

In spite of the fact that the child may be given solid food at an early age, nursing continues to be a matter of importance throughout infancy. The child should be fed as much as possible. Under normal conditions he learns to wean himself through the alternation of supplementary solid food with mother's milk. Many children are still nursed after the loss of the milk teeth. Generally speaking, one can state that children are breast-fed until the milk gives out or mother's menstruation commences or the mother is again pregnant. People believe that the milk of menstruating women is no longer nutritious, while the milk of pregnant women is even poisonous. These ideas make it quite clear that there is some ambivalence with regard to prolonged nursing.

After weaning, male children are given strengthening medicines. They receive the better part of the meal. We were told about a certain beef soup which is considered to be especially nutritious. However, the meat out of which it is made, is dry and stringy. The boys get the soup. 'We girls get the rest,' my informant said. And then she added. 'When a boy is ill, he will receive much more attention than his equally sick sister will.' The conscious rationale is that boys are believed to be harder to bring up than girls.

In swaddling the infant, his hands are tied to his sides with tape, his legs are straightened and his knee joints bound in such a way that the mobility of the legs is greatly reduced. Boys are usually swaddled for a month. Girls are even further constrained and for a somewhat longer period. This, the older people say, is to prevent the child from becoming too mischievous. In later years, if the child misbehaves and steals, people remark: 'Didn't your mother tie your hands when you were born?' Later in life the boy, upon greeting persons who are his social superiors, will assume a position similar to the one in which he was swaddled. A student from South China showed me how he was taught by his paternal grandfather to put his arms to his sides and to press his knees and heels together when he was greeting people of higher status. The restraint of the infant's movements seems to be preparing him for situations

[10] Interview with Chinese informant, 28.12.1948, p. 3.

in later life which will require strong self-control. While we find comparative indulgence in the matter of food and with regard to body functions, the freedom of movement is restricted. As so many things in China seem compulsively structured—poems, calligraphy, houses, furniture, art objects—so the locomotion seems to be confined to a pattern which is gradually relaxed as the individual grows older.

Almost all the Chinese I talked to stressed the 'don'ts' of their early childhood, in connection with touching objects. These 'don'ts' and the non-doing of his later years are closely interrelated. The child has few toys, so that he concentrates either on looking or on himself, unless people play or fuss with him. But even during this period he is already told and playfully shown how to behave towards people of higher status.

Small children urinate and evacuate whenever and wherever they please. In order to facilitate this they wear trousers with open crotches. An infant's faeces are never considered disgusting. Any soiling or breaking of wind is accepted without comment, and the baby's stool is called 'ten thousand ounces of yellow gold'. Visitors may take up a baby, smell its body and poke it (except for the head and abdomen) with their fingers. This is apparently the equivalent of the Western habit of kissing.

The infants are washed and kept clean, although bathing does not occur too frequently because it is believed that it would take away the essence of life. Cleanliness and sphincter control are felt to be two different problems at this early age. The Southern Chinese believe that since the little child is unable to understand demands for sphincter control it is useless to explain or to insist upon it.

For urination and defecation the infant is held out at arm's length, at opportune moments, in order to suggest to the child the voluntary character of those functions. The regulation of emissions soon becomes a matter of communication between mother and child. At first, it is the duty of the mother to sense the infant's urge and to begin teaching him how to behave. A child of eleven or twelve months is said to be able to withhold urine. He is supposed to understand at the walking and talking stage. Little children may do wrong but there is no scolding connected with soiling or defecation or breaking wind. The odour of faeces is evidently felt to be less disgusting than it is in Anglo-Saxon countries.

When another baby is born, the usual arrangement is for the previous child to leave the bed of the mother or the parents with whom he had been sleeping since birth. From then on, the child will sleep with his grandmother or with an older sibling, but never alone. Mother paying more attention to the younger one, becomes less lenient, and, as informants have often stressed, is more inconsistent in her disciplinary methods. However, it is quite conceivable to the Chinese that very young children do not know how to behave, so they naturally make mistakes and should be taught with much care and gentleness until they are at least five. Adults show much concern about this kind of learning process in the child. He first learns to sit, then to stand and then to walk towards the outstretched arms of his mother or grandmother or somebody else in the family.

Around the latency period, a more purposeful attempt is made to discipline the child. At this time he is met with a rather sudden change in the attitude of his parents, grandparents and those outside his immediate family environment. I was told time and time again that with the 'age of understanding' there is a break in the leniency with which the child was treated before. In the country the children go naked until this age. But from now on the little girl is reminded that her lower parts are 'dirty' and have to be covered. The water she uses for washing the lower part of her body should not be used for the upper ones.

This is the time when the young Chinese boy starts to learn that his very existence involves an obligation to others. He has to obey his parents, his grandparents, older siblings and, if he goes to school, his teachers. He has to observe those amenities which society demands of him. It is mainly the male child who is expected to understand the ethical and religious concepts of the outer world. He is often reminded that he does not belong to himself but to the family, to the preceding and succeeding generations. What, during the previous years, was taken for granted and permitted, is suddenly forbidden. A male informant described how until he was eight, he slept in one bed with his mother and sister. Before this age, his mother loved him 'too much', he said. She forbade him to go anywhere, which he considered an expression of love, not of chastisement, 'because to go outside that's danger'. Until he was ten his mother always woke him up in the morning—she 'dressed me, put on my coat, my clothes and then I woke up. If she did not dress me or ask to get up, I didn't get up. . . . She treated me like a baby until I was ten. But after ten I started my different life.'[11]

It is generally understood that boys during the latency period behave rather aggressively. A female informant said: 'Seven to ten is the age when boys are "stinky", undesirable to adult society.' We see that when the boy is about ten, he starts to become a more responsible member of the group, understanding more and more the restrictions put upon him. Not only must he learn to assume responsibility for himself emotionally and intellectually, but he must learn to care for himself physically, as well. It seems to me that this kind of physical control which was imposed upon the child during his early infancy in the form of swaddling, is gradually transferred to other areas. I have already mentioned the fact that children are repeatedly reminded not to touch objects; that they have comparatively few toys and are, so to say, forced to concentrate on themselves, their own body—playing with the penis is not forbidden—and to watch others. By the age of three or four they are taught to be careful not to hurt themselves. When the boy reaches the age of six he should know that he is vulnerable and should be cautious. He is warned not to be reckless and to avoid injury. He has to be careful with his own body, as this is his obligation to the generations. When the boy does hurt himself he is severely punished, since in case of severe injury, he might deprive his father of his male descendants. He would offend posterity.

Even today, under the changing conditions, Chinese culture keeps this precept. A modern film made use of the same theme: A young man, the son of a commanding general, had voluntarily fought in the civil war. He was killed. When the father returned home, his wife and daughter tried to conceal the young man's death from the father. When the father learned what had happened he became angry, destroyed the picture of his son with a walking stick, and then broke down.

At times, the mother takes a major part in discipline, especially with younger children. A Fukien informant told: 'Some mothers use rods . . . spanking rods, on the palms and on the buttocks. . . . You are not supposed to cry, but you cry anyway. Then people remark: "If you cry again, I will beat you again." Then you don't

[11] Research in Contemporary Cultures, Document CH 231, p. 11, line 18 to p. 12, line 7. *Author's comment (1969):* Conditions like these indicate the powerful super-ego force which ultimately dominates the capacity for renunciation.

cry so much. If you run away you get more beating. You are caught anyway.' Another informant, from Toy Shan, lived with his mother, maternal grandmother and little sister. His father was overseas. Mother administered all the discipline. When he was to be spanked, she first tied his hands behind his back: 'Mother always beat me when I did wrong.'

When the boy is sent to school, the tutor is often asked by the grandfather or father to administer punishment (generally a spanking) whenever it seems justified. Even small villages in the Toy Shan district have their own tutor, or share a tutor with a few other communities, and he takes over this function. Because of this, and because of the very nature of the Chinese school itself, his entrance in school is one of the first marks of this sudden change in a boy's life.[12] Philosophy of religion and morals used to be more important in China than the study of language and mathematics. Learning still involves the understanding of the basic concepts of ethics, conduct and morality. The work is difficult. The school regimen is severe. From an easy-going life, free of responsibility and harsh discipline, the boy is thrust into a demanding situation, where any breach of conduct is punished by spanking, which is sanctioned and often demanded by the father who tries to keep out of the disciplinary picture. The boy knows that the mother also condones the beatings, in addition to taking a more active part herself. All my male informants described the severe corporal punishment to which they were subjected by their tutors.

Just as the family home is a sheltering place, so is the school cold and hostile, except for the friendship of the boys for one another. Male informants made mention of heavy masturbation, single and mutual, during those years. Sometimes older boys may tell them not to overdo it.

During the school years the contact between father and son diminishes. Officially, the father remains the authority throughout the man's life.

Gradually, after the age of six, a noticeable distance between father and son is built up. The son will not talk to his father unless the father first approaches him. He will avoid looking directly at his father. 'You act like two persons, when you talk to mother,

[12] I am merely referring to the old tutorial school, not to the Westernized type of school where the subject matter is not restricted to morals and philosophy.

when you talk to father. With mother you say automatically what you want. With father you don't know what he wants,' a young man explained to me. Often father and son are described as two strangers to one another. 'With their fathers they can never dare to be themselves.'[13] I never heard about a close and confidential relationship between the two. It is the worst insult to be called 'son' by anybody but one's parent. It is humiliating and offending and implies that the speaker has had intimate relations with the mother. The same holds true for one of the strongest epithets: 'I slept with your mother,' because this too implies that the speaker took the father's position. Even tutors or teachers who often administer corporal punishment, are not supposed to call their pupils 'son'.

The Chinese have the fundamental commandment of filial piety which regulates particular attitudes towards certain relatives with reference to the specific status of each person. For many centuries, the *Twenty Four Examples of Filial Piety* laid down their main directives for the proper education of children. Obedience and respect are demanded for all those older than oneself. As an example of filial piety, Lao Lai-tze, when he was seventy, put on a child's dress and played with toys to amuse his parents; Mr Mang let himself be eaten by mosquitoes in order to keep them away from his parents. The boy is beaten when he hurts himself, since his body is not his, but belongs to the family, to the generations. A well-brought up young man is subservient to his parents. The obedient son remains a child although he is seventy and a grand-father himself. The well-educated son never approaches a girl unless the parents have arranged their marriage. 'The mores denoted by the term filial piety fix the obligations, duties, and responsibilities towards others in the bloodgroup. Conversely it also determines the range and nature of obligations of others towards oneself.'[14] But while the father-son relationship is 'tinged with hostility', as Hu points out, the filial piety for the mother is expressed chiefly in devotion. In spite of the positive attitude towards having children, the child has to exhibit this servile conduct. The son, wanted by both parents, is part of themselves. With a son you are a man, without a son you do not exist. If you have no son, others will

[13] Cf. Research in Contemporary Cultures, Document CH. Hsein-chin Hu, 'Chinese Folk Literature and the Chinese Child', pp. 25-6.
[14] Daniel Harrison Kulp, *Country Life in South China, Phenix Village, Kwantung*, New York Teacher's College, 1925, pp. 135f.

laugh at you.[15] A man is ridiculed or perhaps pitied if he does not beget sons. In Chinese newspapers, at home and abroad, are many graphic advertisements for aphrodisiacs which promise the man, afraid of impotence, new virility. Having a son assures a man social dignity and status.

While the son's relationship with his father is burdened with so many restrictions and inhibitions, the contact between father and daughter seems to be freer and closer. Girls, for example, are not beaten so often and when they are, the beating is administered by their mothers. There is a saying: 'Girls have a greater sense of shame and their skin is thinner.'

No wonder, the informants agree that the years between six and ten are, for boys, the most difficult in Chinese life. The same period, for girls, is less difficult. (Under the old system, before the revolution of 1912, foot-binding represented for the girls the same stage as entering school does for boys). They do not have to cope with the problems of school, because, even if they attend classes, schooling is not regarded with the same seriousness for girls. Although girls may be spanked, they are more often scolded with threats of what will befall them under the domain of their future mother-in-law and the new unknown family of their husband. Usually more allowances are made for the daughter, particularly after she enters puberty. But she is expected to stay 'within the gates' of the parental home.

The beginnings of married life for the young people of Toy Shan seem strange to the occidental observer. There are about thirty thousand Chinese in New York City. One tenth of them are women —wives and daughters of the immigrants. This leaves a large number of men who are either unmarried or who have their wives in China. Like situations exist wherever the Chinese settle and form colonies.[16] This pattern is true not only of immigrants, but is also found among the Toy Shan Chinese in their home country. Often the young husband, after his wife has given birth to one or two children, leaves for one of the Chinese settlements abroad. Or if

[15] Cf. Francis L. K. Hsu, *Under the Ancestors' Shadow*, New York: Columbia University Press, 1948, p. 76.
[16] A similar pattern was found in the Chinese community in Holland. In 1934-5 there were approximately twelve hundred Chinese men living in Katendrecht, near Rotterdam, but only one woman. Cf. F. van Heek, *Chineesche Immigranten in Nederland*, Amsterdam: J. Emmering, 1936.

he stays within China, he may join the army, take a government post, or find a job in one of the larger cities. From then on he visits his home infrequently

After working hard—sometimes sixteen hours a day, and often at strenuous tasks—for many years, during which time he usually sends a great part of his earnings home, he returns to his family. And when another few children are born, he leaves again, this time taking his eldest son along. After a while, if the son is not married, he returns to his home village where his mother has found a suitable wife for him. One of my Toy Shan informants told me that he might find a Chinese girl, suitable for him, in the United States. It would cost him a certain amount of money. For an equal amount he could make a trip to China, ask his mother to find a wife for him and marry her over there. He added that, honestly, he would prefer the second way. 'If mother likes her, I like her.' (After considerable conflict this informant married an American girl. But this fact was withheld from his interviewers for many months).

Even when the young man remains at home, his marriage is generally arranged by a matchmaker, at the behest of his mother (although the father is officially supposed to be the initiator of such action). If both sets of parents approve, the marriage can take place. The wife, who is often several years older than her husband, usually moves into the home of his family.

As a new bride, it is customary for the woman to behave in an extremely shy manner. One Toy Shan informant mentioned that the young bride should be so shy that she does not permit her husband to penetrate her for the first three nights to consummate the marriage. Several other informants, from the same neighbour-hood, however, did not agree. In the Kwangtung province it is even customary to demand the tokens of virginity on the morning after the wedding. The bedclothes are taken to the girl's home, often accompanied by a pig for a present, and the son-in-law makes a sacrifice at her ancestral shrine if she is a virgin. If she is not a virgin she can be returned to her family.

We know that the new daughter-in-law has a menial position in the household. This is how an informant described the situation: 'As I was the eldest daughter I did a lot of work in the house. . . . We have to lead the cows to the pasture and then come home to take care of the younger brothers and sisters. After the children are fed and washed, we have to feed the pigs. After the household chores are done, it is time for us to take care of bringing the cows home again. . . . Nothing like it is here. Of course, my husband's family is better off economically than our family, but because I was the youngest daughter-in-law in the family I had to work as hard. He has four brothers and the youngest in the family is a sister. He is the third one. I had the sisters-in-law and the young sister to deal with so it was not an easy life, but it was all right.'

The role of the young husband is not too clearly defined. Several times we were told that if the daughter-in-law quarrels with her husband's mother, the husband will support the latter.

Both husband and wife seem to fear contact with any notion of romance. In a modern Chinese novel, the hero, Lao Lee, 'considered his wife his parents' daughter-in-law, and his children his parents' grand-children. He had not realized that he was the husband and the father'. As the couple matures, the woman's position and influence in the home increases while the man's active participation diminishes. Once he has fathered sons, the most important task of a man's life is done. If he is ambitious and still wants his family to expand, or if there are daughters, he has to build up his fortune in order to prepare dowries. But he spends a great deal of his leisure time outside the house—in the tea house, joking and gambling with other men. If the family lives in the country, he often goes to the city, spending weeks or even months away from it.

Ideally when the children marry and the man becomes a grandfather, he will retire from most of his activities and from immediate family responsibilities. The young man frequently pictures himself in just this situation, withdrawn from the daily activities into a life of comfort and contemplation; a life which the Westerner would call passive. But to the Chinese, thinking is not passive, and is in fact considered an active experience. The wife usually takes care of the home, the children, the money. If more complicated problems arise, the older members of the family are called in to help solve them.

To rely on someone for help in financial problems, in making a decision, in settling a dispute, is taken as a matter of course. If a marriage has to be planned, it is the matchmaker who brings the two parties together. If two people quarrel, a go-between will be sought (or will present himself) to settle it. If a business transaction has to be arranged, a negotiator will discuss the matter with those involved. There are numerous instances in which the mediator is considered indispensable. Very often a friend or a relative will act as the go-between. For these people, the use of a go-between is a cultural institution. If a favour is asked of a family member, it must not be refused. Families have been financially ruined through the squandering of their money by their weaker relatives.

Abroad, important problems which arise are handled by the so-called 'family associations' which take care of persons belonging to the same village or the same surname group. This is a kinship organization *(tsu)* which in China was vested with a kind of judicial power and which played an important role with regard to handling community affairs. The *tsu* as well as the family associations are organizations for mutual help and benefit,[17] and have influenced the pattern of expansion and emigration. When a Chinese immi- grant comes to New York, one of the first steps he takes is to go to his particular family (surname) association for help and advice. A young man, whom I met, was given one hundred dollars on two separate occasions, by his fifth cousin. He had never seen this man before and approached him with only a letter of introduction. He was highly insulted when his third request for financial help was delicately refused. Several students whom I had interviewed repeatedly asked me to furnish them with introductions to other persons who might be of service to them. But they were reluctant to approach the same persons directly. They counted on the aid of a go-between or mediator. It was frequently mentioned that in South China asking for this kind of help of a 'cousin'—i.e. a member of his *tsu* or a good friend who would definitely give his assistance— is taken for granted. It seems that the idea of independence is a concept foreign to the Southern Chinese.

Just as retiring into the lethargic bliss of grandfatherhood is the ideal for an old man, for a young man the ideal is to be a student or a scholar. To be studious is to be virtuous. The scholar, in the Chinese sense, is not a man of science. The socio-economic struc- ture gave much power to the learned man, and the fact of having studied the ethical codes often opened the gate to important posi- tions in the government. Nevertheless, the philosopher who is well acquainted with traditional thinking and ethics, or the poet who produces verses according to age-old schemes, assume a significant

[17] Cf. Hsien-Chin Hu, *The Common Descent Group in China and Its Functions*, New York: Viking Fund Publications No. 10, 1948, pp. 9-10.

role in the ideal formation of young boys: 'The one whose hand is never without a book and whose feet never step out of the gate.' Several of my male informants mentioned this significant saying.

The scholar plays an eminent role in Chinese life and might be considered as belonging to a special class, since knowledge lifts the social status.

The man who does not leave the gate is idealized. So the learned man figures as the hero of a great number of legends and folk tales. There, he appears isolated except for his books and scripts; or he lives alone with his mother who takes care of his worldly needs.

A very well-known story begins as follows:

'At Lo-Tien, in the state of Chu, lived a youth named Wang Tse-fu who at a tender age lost his father. He was a clever lad, and when fourteen years old took his first degree (as a scholar or official). His mother idolized him and would not allow him to wander as far as the outskirts of the village. His betrothed, a daughter of the Siao family, had died before the wedding, and he was still unmarried. . . .'[18]

The male heroes of many Chinese folk tales are not strong or dominant characters. They are artists and scholars or merchants, young or old. Very often these men do not show an immediate interest in profane matters.

In the story of Ying Ning, the young scholar Wang took a walk with his cousin Wu one day. On their walk they came upon an extremely beautiful girl with whom the shy Wang immediately fell in love. When he returned to his home he lay down and became seriously ill, as a result of his longing for the girl. Nobody could help him until he confessed to his cousin the real cause of his sickness. The cousin promised to find the girl for him and to arrange, if possible, the marriage. After several adventures, he found and married her and brought her home to his mother. Wang then learned from his cousin Wu that an uncle of his had married a fox-woman and subsequently died. This fox-woman had a daughter named Ying-Ning, which was the name of Wang's wife. Ying-Ning was a loving wife to Wang, and a good daughter-in-law to his mother. One day, however, the neighbour's son saw her in the garden. He was fascinated by her beauty, seized and raped her.

'But on the instant a stabbing pain pierced to his very heart, and, shrieking, he fell to the ground. On looking closely, he saw it was not Ying-Ning but an old tree trunk leaning against the wall. . . . Hear-

[18] Cf. P'u Sung-ling, *Chinese Ghost and Love Stories*, translated by Rose Quong. See 'Ying Ning, The Laughing Girl.' New York: Pantheon Books, 1946; London: Dobson, 1947. Also Richard Wilhelm, *Chinesische Volksmärchen*, Jena: Diederichs, 1917, pp. 307 ff.

ing his cries, his father rushed out, but to his questions the son gave no reply; when his wife came, however, he told her everything. They brought out a torch, and, searching the hole, discovered a *scorpion* the size of a small crab. The father hewed asunder a tree trunk and killed the scorpion. He carried his son into the house, and at midnight he died."[19]

Another story with a similar theme is that of the Beautiful Giauna.

A young scholar, Kung, descendant of Confucius, met a lad who asked him to become his teacher. Young Kung agreed, and the two became very close friends. After a while Kung became very sick; a large swelling grew out of his chest and everybody expected him to die. Then his friend's sister, an exceedingly beautiful girl, appeared upon the scene. Although she was only fourteen or fifteen years old, she was the only one who knew how to cure Kung. Her brother begged her: 'This is my best friend whom I love like a brother. So sister, I implore you to cure his illness.' Then Giauna, the sister, took a fine knife out of her girdle and cut off his swelling, taking away all the bad blood. She stopped the flood of blood with a small red ball. At the same moment, young Kung began to feel much better, and he realized that he loved Giauna very much. But his friend explained to him that the girl was much too young to marry, and suggested that he had better take her cousin. A few days later there appeared the cousin who looked precisely like Giauna. Kung married her and returned with his good friend's supernatural help to his home district. Many years later he met a woman and a man whom he recognized as his old friends, Giauna and her brother. This time the brother needed Kung's help—he revealed that he and his sister were foxes and not human beings. A thunderstorm, deadly for all foxes, was coming up. Kung tried to protect his friends by holding a sword up against a monster who had appeared upon the scene. The monster seized Giauna, and Kung tried to kill it, but at the same moment he succumbed and died. Meanwhile the storm had blown over and Kung's wife, Giauna and her brother, saw that their protector was dead. Now, again, Giauna took her small red ball out of her mouth and put it on Kung's mouth who immediately came to life.[20]

'In the Province of Kwangsi lived a scholar of repute, by name Sun Tse-chu.' This man was born with six fingers. He wanted to marry a beautiful girl, Ah-pao, whom he had never seen but about whose beauty he had heard. Not taking his wish too seriously, the girl sent a message that he cut off his sixth finger as a proof of his love and devotion. So he took a chopper and lopped off the extra finger. The

[19] Cf. *Chinese Ghost and Love Stories*, pp. 113ff. My italics.
[20] R. Wilhelm, op. cit., pp. 298 ff.

314

pain pierced to his very heart, and blood flowed in such a stream that he was brought to the brink of death. As he was known as a fool, the girl now demanded that he cut out his foolishness. When he heard this, he tried to forget about her. One day, many months later, he took a walk and saw her for the first time. He was struck by her beauty. Sun fell into a kind of trance. His friends brought him home where he lay on his bed. His spirit meanwhile had left for Ah-pao. When the girl heard about Sun's feelings for her, she was deeply impressed. After some time Sun tried again to see the girl, and once more he became ill and lay unconscious. At that time, a parrot, belonging to his family, died. Sun wished to be the bird in order to fly to his beloved's house. As soon as this thought entered his mind, the parrot came back to life and flew to the girl. There he revealed his identity: 'Only to be near your fragrant self is all that I desire.'[21]

There are many similar stories. All the stories which I read or heard were checked with my informants, in order to establish the degree of familiarity to the young generation. All the men and women we questioned were well acquainted with them. The figures of fox maidens and fox ghosts appear as beautiful and desirous girls, mainly to men who are considered weak. 'Foxes bring upon those whom they bewitch sickness whereof they die, that's why they are so much feared.'[22] Other stories tell of highly dangerous women with teeth or tusks like swords and hair like fire, who eat the raw flesh of captured animals. Other women appear as men, or *poison* those who fall in love with them.[23]

In what is probably the best-known children's story *Monkey*, the hero accompanies the holy monk Tripitaka, who spends his time begging for food. In one chapter, the monk is described as being led into a compound by seven beautiful girls. These girls are the seven spider spirits who try to seduce Tripitaka. But when the monk resists the temptation, they hang him up and close the entrance to the compound with threads emanating from their navels.[24]

These themes appear, too, in present-day versions and show the danger which is believed to be the essential quality of beautiful women.

In several instances, Ning Lao T'ai-T'ai, the woman whose autobiography was told to Ida Pruitt, expresses her belief in castrating

[21] Cf. *Chinese Ghost and Love Stories*, pp. 17 ff.
[22] ibid, p. 30.
[23] Cf. R. Wilhelm, op. cit., pp. 217 ff.
[24] Cf. Hsien-chin Hu, 'Chinese Folk Literature and the Chinese Child', Research in Contemporary Cultures Manuscript, pp. 18f.

315

females. She remembered a young man who was working for his official examinations. 'One night he dreamed that a tiger, walking by, struck him on the chest. And he awoke very happy, feeling it to be a good omen that the king of the beasts had touched him. When fully awake he saw that his wife's hand was on his chest. He threw it off angrily and announced to the family that he was not going to take the examinations. His brother demanded to know why. The younger brother then told the story of the dream and ended up by saying, "And when I awoke I found that it was that thing's hand upon my chest." ' [25]

Modern Chinese authors make use of the same theme, acceptable for the twentieth-century reader. In a striking novel *Rickshaw Boy*, the well-known Chinese writer, Lau Shaw, describes at length the development of a young strong country boy 'Happy Boy', who comes to the city and becomes a rickshaw puller. This novel is noteworthy in more than one respect because it shows a number of the same attitudes which we observe in the Toy Shan immigrants. [26]

The first point which should be mentioned is Happy Boy's intense wish for independence. He works very hard, suffering insults and humiliation in order to achieve his dream . . . his own rickshaw. His wish is fulfilled after many disappointments. But shortly after he becomes the owner of a rickshaw he loses it again through no fault of his own. He ends up as a poor, worn-out, starving man. Parallel with this development runs his entangled relationship with a woman whom the author significantly names Tiger Girl. 'She was the same as a man in everything; even when it came to cursing a person, she was just as fluent and sometimes had more ways of expressing herself.' (p. 48). 'But no matter how much he hated her, how much he despised her, Tiger Girl seemed always to have her claws in his heart; the more he wanted to stop thinking of her, the more likely she was suddenly to leap up from his heart, all naked and bare, to bring to him at one time all her ugliness and whatever beauty and good there was in her, to give it all to him . . . he was like a little bug caught in a spider web . . .' (p. 80). The woman was older than he, and had seduced him. He hated her and she was at the root of his failure. But out of anxiety, insecurity, longing for a home and food, and out of the need for contact with some human being, he finally married her. 'It was no proper wife who awaited him there, but an old bitch possessed of the spirit of the she-wolf who steals at night into the darkened chambers of lonely men and sucks them empty of semen, drinking so deep into their manhood that the well runs dry, and

---

[25] I. Pruitt, op. cit., p. 118.
[26] Lau Shaw, *Rickshaw Boy*, New York: Reynal, 1945.

they wander through the rest of their time staring vacantly at the world about them and mumbling to themselves' (pp. 242 f). This woman 'was avid for every last drop of strength she could wring from his loins, and night after night she was after him, drinking away his substance even after he was too weary to move. There was no way he could drive her off. . . . Happy Boy was finished' (p. 282).

Right from the beginning, Happy Boy feels his inadequacy, and after several disappointing events he foresees a lonely future. In a tea house for rickshaw pullers he sees hungry and sick old men, and at this moment he decides to marry Tiger Girl: 'He had the choice between accepting destruction or being destroyed' (p. 132). The woman lured him with food and perhaps, a home. And the need for these was stronger than his aversion for her.

This concept of the male-female relationship in literature is certainly not the exclusive one. But the quantity, distribution and popularity of such stories, permits us the use of these stories as projective material. The conception of the Chinese woman depicted in these legends, modern stories and films is that of a demanding, aggressive, destructive person. Even the language mirrors the deep suspicion: the element 'woman' appears in the words for jealous, treacherous, false, uncanny.[27] Psychoanalytically, we speak of the castrating woman. Considering the indulgence the infant experiences during his early years, it certainly seems surprising to find men creating this configuration.

2. ANALYSIS

The adult Southern Chinese male apparently does not give up his early instinctual demands, his longing for dependence and passivity. What appears manifestly as passive mastery of reality through abstinence, idealization of rest and retreat, and submission is essentially connected with indulgence during early childhood. In applying psychoanalytic concepts to the cultural and environmental modification of characteristics, we find on the basis of our material, the determining infantile situation.

The emotional development of the Southern Chinese male, which originates in the first oral phase, is decisively influenced by the very special attention paid to features of oral satisfaction. Few children

[27] H. A. Giles in *The Encyclopaedia Brittannica*, vols. V and VI, 13th ed., London and New York, 1926, p. 219.

are fed and treated with so much permissiveness. As far as we can ascertain, oral deprivation does not occur during this early period. Experience with hunger is avoided, by feeding the child upon hearing him cry. In addition, the objective world is introduced to him during this time, as a continuity of the protective mother-child relationship. There is always somebody around, and the child is never left alone. It is easier, then, for the family or the group to substitute for the mother.

One would expect from this pattern that the indulgence and the resulting pleasure of receptivity, which the infant experiences in this initial phase of life, would give him a continuous feeling of security. But oral satisfaction is given so freely and frequently and over so great a period of time, that the individual does not easily learn oral renunciation. The oral indulgence, the very mechanism designed to make him strong and powerful, serves to weaken the boy's masculinity. The constant availability of a mother or a mother substitute (grandmother, older sibling, the family) does not give him the chance to build up the strong mechanisms which would enable him to overcome his oral preoccupation and the related longing for passive-receptive mastery.

The same emotional tendency is enhanced by still another means. When the child shows the first signs of physical motor functions, he is inhibited in regard to locomotion. By so disciplining the child, at this point, he is forced to seek refuge in earlier more passive pursuits. The child experiences active motor expression as an aggression, whereas receptivity as a result of overprotection and overindulgence is tolerated. However, the effect of both is to de-autonomize his ego functions. His helplessness and prolonged dependence become a 'cultural trait configuration' (Erikson). In this way, orality and its derivatives create a regressive as well as a defensive reaction throughout life.

One of the manifestations of this distinctive reaction is the adult Chinese's preoccupation with matters of food. When two Chinese greet each other, their first question for well-being is: 'Have you eaten your rice?'[28] Visits, meetings, invitations inevitably include eating. The great importance given to a simple bowl of rice, and

---

[28] Weston LaBarre, 'Some Observations on Character Structure in the Orient', 11. The Chinese', *Psychiatry*, 9 (1946), 215. LaBarre noticed the oral tendency in comparison to our 'How do you *do*?', emphasizing anal functions.

the time spent at it, seem foreign to the Western observer. The dinner party is the proper occasion for building up a personal atmosphere. Almost always, during the first or second interview, my male informants preferred a dinner invitation, stressing the pleasure of having a meal and an hour of leisure together. The parties are carefully arranged. The meals are prepared so that everything is cut into tiny pieces—just a step away from food prechewed for the baby. People who have settled a dispute will get together for dinner when the agreement is effected. Friends who meet after a long separation will go, first of all, to an eating house. Food is the principal link between people, just as it once established the first relationship between the neonate and the external world.

There are many other aspects of Chinese life which fundamentally spring from the same childhood experience, and which have their basis in the longing to remain sheltered and passive. One of the most prominent of these is the institution of rest *(hsiu-hsi)*. In an article, 'The Edge of Outer Darkness', Christopher Rand reports:

> In Chinese life, a remarkably high value is set on the idea of rest. The phrase *hsiu-hsi* is indispensable in Chinese discourse at any level of society. In association with Chinese of the leisure class, one is constantly invited to *hsiu-hsi* (which usually takes the form of drinking tea and exchanging polite conversation) even though there is nothing to *hsiu-hsi* from. Fundamentally, *hsiu-hsi* connotes a cessation of effort, and it is the phrase chair coolies aways use when they stop for opium.[29]

The regressive tendencies become apparent in other addictions. Nearly every male informant of mine admitted that he had gambled at times, and American gamblers are impressed with the passion and foolhardiness which the Chinese show at games of chance. From a small community in the Kwangtung province we get the following description:

> Gambling is not for the purpose of recreation. . . . One member of the village who realized the extent to which he was controlled by the habit, so that he cut off the fingers of his left hand to keep himself from the allurements of the game. But when the New Year holidays came around again, he was found playing with cards by holding them between the stump of his hand and his knee.[30]

[29] *The New Yorker*, 20.5.1950, pp. 90 f.
[30] D. H. Kulp, op. cit., pp. 325 f.

The gambler in his fantasies is asking fate (i.e. mother) to protect and care for him. Compulsive motives lead to this peculiar form of intoxication, closely related to drug addiction and homosexuality. The strong oral fixation paves the way for the widespread 'sucking' addiction to opium in China.[31]

Through gambling and addiction, the oral Chinese regresses to the sadomasochistic experience of the pregenital level. Reality cannot be overpowered, so reality overpowers him and chases him back into a state of dependence on fate and fantasy. The smoker in his leisure who is not supposed to raise himself up on his elbow, regresses to the infantile pleasure of resting (hsiu-hsi) and sucking. Like the gambler, he is enjoying the same infantile feeling of omnipotence at mother's breast. If a gambler is lucky it is a sign that mother cares for him. If he loses, he yields to his masochism and wish to be castrated—as in the case of the man who mutilated himself in order to become helpless, thereby regressing to his unconscious infantile ego ideal. This masochistic attitude is a well-known attempt to force the external world to pay attention and give love.

We see here how the effect of the early mother-child relationship lays the groundwork for pathogenic defences in the adult Chinese male—pathogenic from the point of view of Western observers. That the behaviour of the Chinese is marked by a strong reliance upon the family and friends, is still another indication of his wish to remain in the state of dependence. The Chinese find it easy and necessary to create a mother out of the surroundings. Just as little children are never left alone, always having somebody available, so the adult Chinese, in his interpersonal activities, makes use of the 'go-between'. Interpersonal activities of any importance are negotiated, not by the participants themselves, but by a go-between. He is a buffer between an individual and the dangerous outside (i.e.

---

[31] I do not discuss the opium addict in this paper because I did not receive much information about it. In the above-mentioned report by Christopher Rand in *The New Yorker* we find the following observation (p. 90): 'An opium smoker generally avails himself of the assistance of a friend, because a great deal of fiddling with the pipe and the lamp is necessary, and *the smoker should not be subjected to such distractions.* Smoking is an intimate occupation, and a relaxed one. *A smoker is not supposed even to raise himself up on an elbow; he must lie back, head on pillow, in flat repose. The mood induced is one of profound harmony and inactivity.*' (My italics). Cf. E. Bergler, 'The Gambler: A Misunderstood Neurotic', *J. Crim. Psychopath.*, 4 (1943), 379-93. Bergler observed similar unconscious tendencies among his Euro-American patients.

reality) situation and, as such, supplants the helpful mother. By using the mediator, one does not lay oneself open to danger. What in his infancy was achieved by the boy's protecting environment, in his later years is partly affected by the go-between, represented by the immediate family circle, relatives of the same surname group, a professional matchmaker, or a few friends, and overseas, the influential family association. With them, one is not alone. The individual feels protected, becomes part of the group, and satisfies his longing to be sheltered.

Our reference to passivity in the Southern Chinese male, is not at all in contradiction to his hard and intensive work habits which are observed among the students as well as among laundrymen, salesmen and waiters. A sixteen-hour workday is not exceptional for these people in an American city.[32] Work gives a man an opportunity to hide himself in a kind of pseudo activity which only keeps him away from more dangerous involvements and encounters with the external world. He rationalizes with the thought of building up a reservoir of property so that he may retire as soon as possible. Then he will be relieved of his worldly obligations, his activity and responsibilities. It is this idealized passive mastery of life which explains why so many folk tales, novels and sagas describe the scholar, the poet and the artist and philosopher as their hero, and not the warrior, the conqueror and the experienced lover.

In studying the characteristics of Southern Chinese women we find a corresponding emphasis on orality and its derivatives. But in the case of the woman orality is coupled with an active-demanding and offensive rather than a defensive attitude.

A China-born unmarried woman of about twenty, the daughter of an emancipated family, had the following train of free associations in a psychoanalytically conducted series of interviews:

> My mother taught us everything, my sister and myself. She [mother] is a biologist. She taught us how to dissect fish, animals, even a cat. She did it when we were little. So to us it is nothing to use scissors. I would not hesitate—any time. I could do it to anybody. If somebody was cruel to you, it would be a pleasure to use scissors.
>
> Emotions—I don't know. We are very generous, we are very proud in our family. We resent it very much when somebody—

---

[32] The Chinese in Southeast Asia show the same pattern.

not criticize but I hate when somebody doesn't know anything and criticizes. For instance that old woman. I didn't ask her for advice. She is an older woman, she is an old woman. She thinks she is intelligent. Oh, she is so stupid. I told her I did not like her. One day I came home with apples and she was offended when I didn't offer her. I don't want anything from her so she mustn't want anything from me. . . . My boy-friend, I like to be seen with him because he is so good-looking. He is tall. All the girls envy me. I don't love him. It sounds very mean, I know. He is very intelligent. He is a very good student. I wish I had an apartment. The first day I had my room I took J. [boy-friend]. I like to have people in my room. She [the old woman, landlady] won't let me. Where shall I take him? The only place I take him is the elevator. That crazy woman won't let me. I spoke to a boy from X. He has the same kind of a landlady. One day he took another boy. He told me we should push her out of the window. She is an old woman. We should put on the gas. No one would know. I would do it, believe me. It is not so hard.

This girl is not representative of the typical South Chinese woman. She is rather the prototype of the aggressive, castrating and dominating woman, generally symbolized in Chinese literature. There is a certain affinity between this young informant and the type of woman described in *Rickshaw Boy*, the scorpion girl, and the spider woman or the fox maiden.

On a more general level, recent Rorschach protocols reveal a 'greater flexibility' in the China-born woman (living in or visiting the United States) than in the men. 'In accepting their less challenging role,' Abel and Hsu state, 'they [the women] have found a way of life. . . . They have a less rigid status role to maintain; they are not as responsible as the male. . . .'[33]

The gradual development of this difference in behaviour structure between male and female can be observed from infancy on. Mother being 'only' a woman has in her lifetime felt the deprivations of her sex. Just as the little boy apparently enjoys the rewards and importance accorded his sex, so the little girl must feel the rejection resulting from the lower esteem in which she is held. I am not referring to conscious reactions, but to unconscious ones. The need of the infant for closeness to the mother is, as psychoanalytic studies have shown, so intense, that in its early emotional

[33] Theodora M. Abel and Francis L. K. Hsu, 'Some Aspects of Personality of Chinese as Revealed by the Rorschach Test', *J. Project. Techn.*, 13 (1949), p. 299.

dependence it senses the unconscious feelings of the mother. I have mentioned some of the differences in the treatment of male and female infants.

We do not have any statistically valid material about the infant's development during the first year in South China, but from what we have gathered during our conferences, the preference for the male child carries with it a more overt, ambivalent feeling towards the girl. Adults may not always be consciously aware of this fact. But there are, no doubt, certain nuances in the manner in which the infants are handled and treated. The quality of these attitudes is both individually and culturally determined. Recent research has shown how the mother's emotional attitude moulds the child's reaction and development; how in nursing it may influence the baby not only directly, but also indirectly, especially because it affects the flow of breast milk.[34]

There is no conclusive evidence as to whether or not swaddling is an anxiety-producing factor in the infant, but there seems to be a negative effect. As I pointed out, the limbs of the baby are straightened, and even in hot weather the body is wrapped in warm cloth. The infant's condition is expressed in a typical saying which I learned from a female informant: 'There is no June for a baby.' Girls are swaddled longer than boys are.

The boy's well-being is of greater importance to the family than is the girl's. This strong desire and religiously rationalized need for boys can be easily sensed by the growing girls. From the time a girl starts walking she, too, is restrained from running, jumping and climbing, and, if possible, protected from injuries. She is also reminded not to hurt herself—a disfiguring scar makes her marriage a difficult problem. (It would be more difficult and more expensive to find a suitable husband for her.) But although the boy is warned not to hurt himself, the implications are that he must take care of himself so that the family will not lose him. He is precious. The girl on the other hand must be careful, so that the family can successfully lead her into marriage.

As a consequence of these attitudes in the formative years, we can presume a difference in the beginning state of the mother-daughter and the mother-son relationship. Since the girl child is

[34] Margaret E. Fries, 'The Child's Ego Development and the Training of Adults in his Environment', in *The Psychoanalytic Study of the Child*, 2, New York: International Universities Press; London: Hogarth, 1946, p. 93.

less wanted and under certain conditions even a liability, this culturally and economically defined phenomenon may very well modulate her psychic requirements and structure.

The fact that Chinese culture and tradition have placed such a premium on being a male, stimulates the need for self-esteem and security in the female. Since in her early years when she experiences rejection, the woman is expected to observe a certain amount of restraint, she overreacts with considerable ambition, aggressiveness or even rivalry. These women, then appear threatening, dangerous and castrating. In contrast to the Chinese conscious ideal of a woman, it is the aggressive one whom we come across time and again. It is the woman with a strong penis wish and penis envy. Through the Rorschach tests, Abel and Hsu have confirmed the 'greater flexibility' in the women which is one of the consequences of the social and psychological difference of male and female.

In her rivalry with her brothers and other male contemporaries, the woman finds her chief, socially acceptable gratification in becoming the mother of a son. So that, in addition to its biological function, childbearing to a woman, serves the cause of self-assertion. The woman then is characterized by her ambivalent strivings to become, on the one hand, an overprotective mother and, on the other hand, a demanding and prohibiting one—wish-fulfilling and vindictive.

In view of these factors, we arrive at a closer understanding of the inner development of the relationship between mother and son. Ning Lao T'ai T'ai, Pruitt's informant, said: 'My old man was now fifty-four and he was not strong. For a month he was ill and then he died. In these later years he had been good. But I did not miss him when he was gone. *I had my son and I was happy. My house was established.*'[35]

The early deprivation and submissiveness which as a young girl and a young daughter-in-law, a woman has to observe, can be gradually given up after she has born a son. The woman's deep need to overcome her frustrating position is largely met by her becoming the mother of a boy child. This changes her strategic position. Her narcissistic desire for reparation and her ego ideal demand that this son be virile, but she uses him at the same time as her instrument. Here her unconscious ambivalence towards the male breaks through. She has the need to establish her superiority.

[35] I. Pruitt, op. cit., p. 166. My italics.

So with her feeling of maternal love, coexist feelings of envy and retaliation. Her son is a highly esteemed extension of herself, a narcissistic tool. She has produced a penis, so that her penis wish is partially fulfilled. It seems to me that in this particular cultural configuration the birth of a male child engenders transformations in the ego structure of the mother.

Time and again we find the strong desire of the woman to be in a controlling position and to dominate. Historical reports are full of descriptions of these energetic and influential women. In a recent novel a wife talking about her husband, says: 'He doesn't even dare to frown at me. That's how I have trained him.' While, in the same book, it is the opinion of the man that, 'if a woman makes up her mind to destroy you, she will do it completely and thoroughly.'[36]

Now, it is obvious that the oral-sadistic tendencies, ascribed to these women, are maintained and reinforced by the complementary emotions of the Chinese male.[37] They are often prompted by the projections of men who fear or try to avoid genital contact with the mother substitute.

Psychoanalysis of Euro-American children has shown that parental leniency makes the super-ego more forbidding. As Ruth Mack Brunswick pointed out:

> The [child-mother] relationship is dominated not by the usual active oedipal love but by an attachment which is to a large extent preoedipal and passive. Because of the primitive nature of this passive, tenacious attachment to the mother, an intensely ambivalent relationship between the man and his mother substitute results.[38]

As a general idealization, a Toy Shan informant in his early thirties explained the universal ideal for a beautiful woman was that she be shy and gentle. But for men these characteristics have a sadistic connotation. In stories and descriptions by men we hear about those women who *suck* the life out of their lover's body.

---

[36] The author of this novel is a man. Lau Shaw, *The Quest for Love of Lao Lee*, New York: Harcourt, 1948, pp. 181, 143.

[37] In a personal conversation, the sinologist Dr Karl A. Wittfogel wittily commented upon this trait: 'If he [the Chinese] cannot eat, he sublimates by fornicating'.

[38] Cf. R. Brunswick, 'The Pre-Oedipal Phase of the Libido Development', *Psychoanal. Quart.*, 9 (1940), 293 ff. Reprinted in Robert Fliess (ed.), *The Psychoanalytic Reader*, New York: International Universities Press; London: Hogarth Press, 1948, pp. 261 ff.

I mentioned the folk tales which describe young women as attractive and beautiful, but at the same time castrating, murderous or destructive.[39] The stories indicate that most of the depicted men suffer castration fear. And it is usually the men who perpetrate these tales. The Chinese male uses his castration fear as an instrument to defend himself against his own unconscious, aggressive and incestuous impulses for the mother. It is self-protection against his Oedipal aggressiveness and the danger of being castrated. We find that regression is used both as a means of re-creating the pleasurable experiences of the oral phase, and as a defence against his genitality, his desire for the mother as a love object. This hypothesis is attested to by the fact that many Southern Chinese men, even several among my more advanced informants, who have intimate relations with women, try to abstain from experiencing emission. The rationalization is that in orgasm one loses the essence of life. Many men who do have an orgasm perform coitus interruptus. And there is no or little initial love-making. In addition to this kind of oral regression the Chinese male uses another method of avoiding the contact with the woman (i.e. the mother substitute). Chinese culture lays emphasis upon filial piety, upon obedience and the maintenance of a certain amount of distance between father and son. The moral institution of filial piety, based on Confucian principles, is more than a cultural convention. It is a method by which one tries to avoid the conflict between the generations. We can say that we find an external (educational) and an internal (oral-regressive) device to circumvent and, if possible, to escape from the conflict with the father.

The two following dreams of informants of mine exemplify the situation:

1. *Initial explanation:* 'I slept between my father and my mother, and one time I was so sick that I was delirious.'
   Dream: 'I dreamed of four horsemen. The horses were charging toward me.'

[39] O. Fenichel writes: 'Oral-sadistic tendencies are often vampirelike in character. Persons of this type request and demand a great deal, will not relinquish their object and affix themselves by "suction"', *The Psychoanalytic Theory of Neurosis*, New York: Norton; London, Routledge, 1945, pp. 488 ff. See also J. Riviere, 'Womanliness as a Masquerade', *Internat. J. Psycho-Anal.*, 10 (1929); S. Rado, 'Fear of Castration in Women', *Psychoanal. Quart.*, 2 (1933), 425-75; F. Wittels, 'Kindweib, die grosse Mode', *Almanach der Psychoanalyse*, Vienna, 1930, pp. 133 ff; S. Blanton, 'Phallic Women', *Psychoanal. Quart.*, 16 (1947), 214 ff.

Associations: 'I had been to many shows but I can only recall the time when I sneaked into the theatre through the back door. I was especially fond of one actress, but many years later I heard she was a prostitute, paid on occasion by rich merchants. My mother used to have meals ready for us and I recall that I used to race upstairs after hearing my mother calling me and have a few gulps of rice and then race downstairs again. At that time we went back to China. . . . During the train transfer at Y. I was run over by a luggage dolley. It crushed my left little toe. On arrival at S. I was walking again. In S. we went to a show and I still remember the big and crispy apple I ate.'
Interpretation: I wanted to sleep with my mother but father was there and prevented it. It was he who slept with her, I saw them together in bed having intercourse (theatre). Mother is a prostitute because she has sexual relations with father. My wishes for her are forbidden. Father would castrate me (four horsemen; crushed little toe during the train transfer). Instead, I return to the mother of my infancy, remain passive and get oral satisfaction, on her breast (crispy apple).[40]

This is a dream of an unmarried young Toy Shan Chinese who was, at the time of our contact, jobless and indulged successfully in gambling. The next dream is that of an intellectual man in his early thirties, China-born, unmarried.

2. *Initial explanation:* 'There are about a hundred houses in my village. All of them belong to the K-family (same surname). Our house is in the middle. The front door opens to a wide street, the back door to the backyard. Between our house and the houses to the left and to the right is a narrow alley.'
Dream: 'At my family's house in the village, I am in the street and walk to the left corner of our house. Then I hesitate whether to go home through the alley or not. I am thinking of going to the opposite house. I am afraid of father because I was outside to play.'
Associations: 'In the opposite house was a girl. I played with her. Her mother took care of my boy cousin. We are not supposed to play together (the girl and I). They are much poorer; she much older than I. Once I asked her to take off her clothes in the outhouse and she did.
Father—I am the oldest child. No affection. [During our second session this man had already stressed his dislike for his father.] He was very severe. You [interviewer] looked at the bill when I invited you for a meal.'
Interpretation: I should like to oppose father and have sex

[40] I did not receive any associations about the *four* horsemen.

327

with my mother (going through the alley; the older girl in the opposite house). But this is forbidden (forbidden to play) and father would punish (castrate, kill) me. He is observing me anyway and does not permit me to take over the father role (playing outside has also a cultural connotation because Chinese men spend much time 'outside', in teahouses and gambling halls; looking at the bill).

Basically the instinctual claims of these two Chinese men do not differ from those of Western men of Euro-American background. The differences lie, perhaps, in the channelization of impulses which is in part culturally determined. In both cases we find the genital demands of the son for the mother or her substitute and the fear of conflict with the father. In the first case we notice the active and passive desires which the young man has for his mother. His do-nothingness, however, is not solely an attempt to avoid retaliation, but also to regain the oral satisfaction and pleasure of his early childhood.[41] The second dream does not indicate oral regression, but the dreamer decides to give up his wishes for his mother in order to save himself from conflict with the father.

It is quite evident that the rigid system of obligations serves not only to control the son's Oedipal wishes, but also the father's unconscious hostility against his son. Since Chinese tradition and belief demand from the man that he becomes the father of sons in order to be venerated after his death, the father is to some extent dependent on his son. His feeling of security is more or less based on the fact that through his son, his line and life will continue. It seems to me that this dependence on the son is partially responsible for the manifold restrictions imposed on the father-son relationship. The measures prescribed by the rules of filial piety suggest that both father and son have to control their ambivalence for each other.

Two of the most popular Chinese novels, *The Dream of the Red Chamber* and the *Three Kingdoms* describe events concerning the Oedipal situation. There are several stories concerning discords aroused by the love for the same woman: the father takes a younger attractive concubine, approximately of his son's age. The son, then, tries to approach father's new wife. In *Monkey*, the most famous popular story for children, the aggression or aggressive fantasies of

---

[41] 'Eating the apple' can be interpreted as an oral-sadistic compensation, so that the passivity could be questioned.

the young boy are clearly depicted. Boys can easily identify with Monkey. This fairy-tale figure has an enormous desire for power, rebellion and mastery of the world. With the other little monkeys he fights the hordes of animal spirits, but when he comes into conflict with the paternal authority that reigns over the universe, he cannot cope with it. This authority is represented by three different father images: Buddha Tathagata, the supreme ruler, the Jade Emperor and the monk Tripitaka. 'Since the culture demands that the child inhibit his natural urge for activity, self-assertion, experimentation, and exploration,' Miss Hu writes, 'it is understandable that Chinese children should find in the restless, nimble antics of Monkey and in his reckless, fearless behaviour, a source of unending delight.'[42]

The culturally prescribed alienation between father and son, of necessity, leads to a greater closeness between mother and son. But I believe I have shown how psychological mechanisms take care of the quality of their relationship, and, what is more, of the 'libidinal blend' of the Chinese male: his passive longings serve to counteract his aggressive demands.[43]

3. CONCLUSIONS

The Southern Chinese chooses ways of channelization and sublimation of drives which appear, on first sight, strange to us. To a greater extent than among Westerners, his pregenital impulses and fantasy systems continue to find expression directly together with his reality adjustments. In avoidance of Oedipal conflicts it is culturally permitted to resolve inhibitions and tensions in daydreams, ideals, hallucinations, and pseudo activity. The dependence on each other is a culturally determined defence mechanism against instinctual demands. As a result of this psychic constellation the Chinese have created their art and philosophy and contribute so much to human civilization.

[42] H. Hu, op. cit., p. 8, lines 25-8.
[43] Following Freud's suggestion, the Chinese would belong to the obsessional-erotic type. Cf. 'Libidinal Types', *Standard Ed.*, 21, Hogarth Press; London, 1961, pp. 217-20.

This study focuses on the Jones-Malinowski debate regarding the universality of the Oedipus complex. Other papers in this volume (Freeman, Róheim, Muensterberger) discuss the problem from various points of view. This highly significant and exemplary contribution puts the entire question into a clear perspective: it emphasizes the culture-specific qualifications and variables of an instinctual condition. It was Malinowski's contention that among the natives of the Trobriand Islands the Oedipal reaction followed a different pattern in that the hostility of the little boy is directed against mother's brother rather than against his biological father while his incestuous desires concern his sister and not his mother. In this paper Dr Parsons shows variations of the same theme as manifested among Southern Italians. The male's devotion to his mother is expressed in the adoration of the Holy Virgin while his sexual impulses are diverted towards prostitutes. The father-daughter relationship is hardly desexualized.

14

Is the Oedipus Complex Universal?
The Jones-Malinowski Debate Revisited and a South Italian 'Nuclear Complex'[1]

ANNE PARSONS

1. INTRODUCTORY REMARKS

In the nineteen twenties a famous debate took place between Ernest Jones and Bronislaw Malinowski which set forth some outlines of theoretical differences between psychoanalysis and anthropology which are still unresolved today.[2] On the basis of field work in the matrilineal Trobriand Islands, Malinowski drew the conclusion that the Oedipus complex as formulated by Freud is only one among a series of possible 'nuclear complexes', each of which patterns primary family affects in a way characteristic of the culture in which it occurs. In this perspective, Freud's formulation of the Oedipus complex as based on a triangular relationship between father, mother, and son appears as that particular nuclear complex which characterizes a patriarchal society in which the most significant family unit consists of mother, father, and child. The alternative nuclear complex which he postulated for the Trobriand Islands consisted of a triangular relationship between brother, sister, and sister's son, this in function of the nature of matrilineal social structure in which a boy becomes a member of his mother's kin group

---

[1] This paper first appeared in *The Psychoanalytic Study of Society*, 3, ed. by W. Muensterberger and Sidney Axelrad, New York: International Universities Press, 1964, pp. 278-328.

[2] E. Jones in a paper read before the British Psycho-Analytical Society ('Mother-Right and Sexual Ignorance of Savages' (1924) now in *Essays in Applied Psychoanalysis*, 2, New York: International Universities Press, 1964, pp. 145-73) first discussed three prior publications by B. Malinowski: 'Baloma: The Spirits of the Dead in the Trobriand Islands' (*J. Roy. Anthropol. Inst.*, 46 (1916), 353-430) and two articles which were later published together as the first two sections of *Sex and Repression in Savage Society* (London: Routledge, 1953). The last two sections of this latter work were written in response to Jones's paper. For the most complete summary of the Trobriand field data, see B. Malinowski, *The Sexual Life of Savages*, London: Routledge, 1929.

and is subject to the authority of his maternal uncle rather than the biological father. One of his most important observations was that in the Trobriand Islands ambivalent feelings very similar to those described by Freud with respect to father and son can be observed between mother's brother and sister's son. Relations between father and son, on the other hand, are much more close and affectionate; however, Malinowski felt that the father should not be considered as a figure in the kinship structure since the Trobrianders do not recognize the existence of biological paternity. The child is seen as conceived by a spirit which enters the mother's womb and later the father appears to him as the unrelated mother's husband.

In addition, Malinowski noted that the Trobrianders give a very special importance to the brother-sister relationship. While the brother has formal authority over the sister and is responsible for her support, their actual relationship is one of extreme avoidance, to the point that an object may be handed from one to the other by means of an intermediary. He characterized the brother-sister incest taboo as 'the supreme taboo' from the Trobriand standpoint; while incest with other primary biological relatives and within the matrilineal kin group at greater biological distance is also forbidden, in no instance are the taboos as strict or surrounded by intense affects as in the brother-sister case. He also discerned, with his acute clinical eye, many evidences of the real temptations underlying the avoidance pattern, for example, in that while no Trobriander would admit to having such an incest dream, the questioning itself aroused a great deal of anxiety and often the assertion that 'well, other people have such dreams, but certainly not me'. He noted brother-sister incest to be a primary theme in Trobriand mythology, for example, in that love magic is seen as originating in a situation in which brother and sister actually commit incest and died as a result of it. He considered these variations from the European pattern of sufficient significance to uphold the view that the Oedipus complex is not universal.

Jones, in his 1924 paper, upheld with considerable vehemence the classical psychoanalytic point of view that it is. Thus while he felt that Malinowski's field data were in themselves interesting, he came to the conclusion that they did not point to the need for any important theoretical revisions in the psychoanalytic framework. For the data on the Trobriand failure to recognize the biological relationship between father and son, he provided an alternative explanation, namely, that the non-recognition was a form of denial covering affects originating in the Oedipus situation.[3] Much to Malinowski's dismay, this argument was carried to the point of the assertion that matrilineal social organization can itself be seen as a defence against the father-son ambivalence universally characteristic of the Oedipus situation. He also pointed out that Malinowski's observations of ambivalence between mother's brother and sister's son concerned adolescent and adult life, so that, theoretically, it is possible to see it as a secondary displacement in that there is an initial Oedipal rivalry between father and son, but that in adult life the hostile feelings are displaced to the mother's brother. He also commented that similar patterns can be observed in Europe, for example, in that the hostile father figure may later be an occupational superior or rival, while the actual father remains a positive figure.

A re-examination of the debate in a contemporary perspective indicates that actually there are a number of intertwined issues. In the first place, it is characterized by a highly polemic character related to the newness and consequent defensiveness of both fields: for Jones 'the' Oedipus complex appears as a kind of point of honour upon whose invariance psychoanalysis would stand or fall, and exactly the same is true of some elements of Malinowski's argument, in particular those which touch on the resemblance between Jones's views and those of the older evolutionary anthropology which he himself did so much to overthrow. Thus, concerning the question of whether matrilineal social organization can be seen as a defence against Oedipal affects, it seems difficult now to see how a complex social pattern could be based on the 'denial' of an affect which occurs in the individual. But on the other hand, one can regret that Malinowski, in his rebuttal, went into a tirade against the evolutionary implications of this view rather than attempting to answer Jones's much more cogent point, namely, that Freud's concepts concern infantile life, and in this perspective it is quite possible that the hostility towards the mother's brother observed in adolescent and adult Trobrianders might be displaced from hostility initially experienced towards the father. What is perhaps most regrettable of all, given his status with regard to the psychoanalytic

---

[3] Not all anthropologists have accepted Malinowski's observations on this at face value; however, the data he presents indicate that the Trobrianders had formulated a reasonably coherent and intelligent picture of the facts of biology for a people lacking in any scientific framework.

theory of symbolism, is that Jones never discussed in detail Malinowski's observations concerning the special importance of the Trobriand brother-sister relationship and the integrally related material concerning dreams and mythology.

When we look at the present state of theoretical knowledge, we might come to the conclusion that the question of whether or not the Oedipus complex is universal is one which should not be asked in such a way as to create the impression that there is a yes or no answer. In the first place, the theoretical assumption that there are infantile sexual wishes is one which has proved so useful, and has brought together such a variety of clinical facts, that it seems simply foolish to abandon the general Freudian scheme until such a point when we have an alternative that appears scientifically more valuable. In retrospect, one might say that the major point that Jones wished to maintain was simply the idea that there is an infantile sexual life. Secondly, the main point which Malinowski was supporting is now also so well established that we need not any longer be defensive about it—that human societies do structure family patterns in different ways according to laws of kinship, or particular phrasings of the incest taboo, that by no means can be derived directly from the biological facts of mating and reproduction. These latter simply cannot explain facts such as the extreme significance given to the brother-sister incest taboo by the Trobrianders in comparison to ourselves.

Taking these two points for granted, we might then proceed to ask again the same questions which were asked by Jones and Malinowski and to re-evaluate some of the major points made by each in the light of contemporary psychoanalytic and anthropological knowledge. It is this task which we have set ourselves in this paper. After some general theoretical considerations, we will discuss a particular case with respect to the possibility of formulating a third distinctive 'nuclear family complex' differing both from Freud's patriarchal one and from the Trobriand matrilineal case.

2. THEORETICAL POINTS

Much of the Jones-Malinowski argument centred on the evidence presented by Malinowski to the effect that Trobriand Islanders are unaware of the facts of physiological paternity. The main importance of this material to Malinowski lay in its value for demonstrating the independence of social from biological kinship; certainly one of the major points which troubled him and has troubled many other anthropologists since about psychoanalytic theory is the implication that these two must overlap. However, while Jones's formulation leaves itself open to just this objection, one might now wonder whether in fact psychoanalytic theory does presuppose such an equivalence. One of the fundamental tenets of instinct theory is that an instinct is displaceable according to source, aim, and object; but if we use the term 'object' in a social sense, referring to either an external person who is the focus of a drive or to an internalized representation of a person, we might then say that the possibility of variant family structures is built into even Freud's earliest formulations. Moreover, Freud's theory, while it anchors affects and fantasies in biological concepts of instinct, might also better be seen as a psychological than a biological one; so that to the extent that it postulates universals, we should also see these psychologically rather than biologically.

Contemporary concepts of object relations and object representations[4] make it possible to bring this point out more clearly than was done by Jones. Any clinician can cite from immediate experience a great many instances in which the object focus of Oedipal affects has been a person other than the biological mother or father—an adopted parent, a more distant relative, or as in many cases today, a child therapist. Actually, Freud himself was very much concerned with the role played by domestics in the early sexual life of the Victorian upper status child. We might then say that the question of the Oedipus complex has two sides to it, the first related to instinct and fantasy, and the second to identification and object choice. But it is hard to believe that the latter processes are not in some way directly dependent on social structure and social norms, or the available possibilities for object choice and object representation.

[4] See E. Jacobson, 'The Self and the Object World: Vicissitudes of their Infantile Cathexes and their Influence on Ideational and Affective Development'. In R. S. Eissler et al (eds.), The Psychoanalytic Study of the Child, 9, New York. International Universities Press; London: Hogarth, 1954, pp. 75-127; T. Parsons, 'Social Structure and the Development of Personality: Freud's Contribution to the Integration of Psychology and Sociology', Psychiatry, 21 (1958), 321-40; and A. H. Stanton, 'Propositions Concerning Object Choices in L. Bellak (ed.), Conceptual and Methodological Problems in Psychoanalysis, 76 (1959), New York: Annals of the New York Academy of Sciences, pp. 1010-1037.

In this perspective, the idea of the distinctive nuclear complex for each society becomes much more compatible with the psychoanalytic idea that there is an invariant series of developmental phrases which is rooted in instinct; the social factor need only influence the object side. Using this assumption, we might interpret Jones's displacement hypothesis as saying that the passing of the Oedipus complex in the Trobriand Islands is equivalent to assimilating the polar distinction between two socially represented figures, the mother's brother and the mother's husband. Each of these then comes to have a differing or contrasting affective valence and one can even say that the boy identifies with both, but that each identification represents a different social function or aspect of personality. According to this view,[5] it is the social distinction which lies at the basis of the conscious representation, which could not even arise without the mediating effect of social exchange; if there were none, the biological drives would presumably arise nevertheless, but they would not give rise to a personality. Such a formulation seems much simpler and less awkward than to say that first the Trobriand child goes through an Oedipus phase centred on the father, somehow acquiring a knowledge of biological paternity which adults in his society do not possess, then represses this knowledge and displaces the affects to the mother's brother. What we are saying is rather that conscious representation of objects by definition depends on collective representation, though their affective charge or valence may be rooted in unconscious or instinct-based constellations which are prior to culture.

This formulation would permit us to say that it does not make much difference whether the relevant figure is father or mother's brother; psychoanalytic theory requires only that the small boy has some available figure for masculine identification. However, a second aspect of the Oedipus theory raises a more difficult problem. This is that, according to Freud, the boy's hostility to the father arises from the fact that the latter has sexual relations with his mother; in other words, the Oedipus complex is rooted in sexual jealousy. However, in the Trobriand Islands, it is the biological father, and not the mother's brother who has sexual relations with the mother. In fact, though it is not impossible that the mother may

---

[5] Which utilizes Durkheim's concept of collective representations. See E. Durkheim, *The Elementary Forms of the Religious Life*, Glencoe, Ill.: Free Press, 1958.

have other sexual involvements as well, the one person who could not be a sexual object for her is precisely the maternal uncle, since he is, of course, her brother.

Here it seems that we have reached an insoluble impasse; either we must abandon the Malinowski attempt to isolate distinctive nuclear complexes, saying that the initial Oedipal object must always be the father since he is the actual sexual rival, or we must take the more empiricist 'culturalist' viewpoint which abandons the idea of infantile sexuality altogether and says simply that various role patterns are learned in direct relation to social inter-action. But since neither solution seems satisfactory (the second because it does not utilize instinct theory), we might do better to look further. Perhaps in reconsidering some of the various possible phrasings of psychoanalytic theory, we may find that some are more compatible with Malinowski's attempt than others.

It is well known that Freud's thinking contains many, not always compatible, interwoven strands. One of his earliest conceptionaliza-tions was the trauma theory; this is the one which most directly influenced Malinowski and, moreover, most of the early workers in the field of culture and personality. According to the trauma theory, specific sexual events or observations take place in childhood which then have crucial consequences for adult personality and attitudes. In much of Freud's writing about infantile sexuality (before he reached his more general structure and dynamic formu-lations), he acts as if he were taking the trauma theory for granted, for example, when he portrays the Oedipus crisis as the point when the child observes or becomes aware of the 'primal scene', asks questions about sexuality and comes to some conclusions about this matter and his own future sex role. This formulation presupposes a highly rationalistic child and a very direct relationship between environmental factors and psycho-sexual development. However, over the course of psychoanalytic history, the trauma theory has gradually slipped into the background; much of it today might well be given the status of myth. The main reason for this may well be that it simply has not worked; we certainly cannot try to predict today, nor does anyone, complex adult personality patterns from specific and limited kinds of infantile events. Applied in the anthropological field, however, the trauma theory very readily lent itself to the view that almost any kind of cultural difference could give rise to variations in the nature of the Oedipal situation, and many of Malinowski's own convictions, like those of the later culture and personality theorists, were certainly derived from this kind of rough empirical evidence.

However, here we are concerned with the question of global structures rather than with specific items of socialization of other kinds of cultural behaviour. With respect to family structure, trauma theory would lead us to believe that if it is in fact the father who has sexual relationships with the mother, then he should be the object of Oedipal jealousy. However, in a somewhat different framework we could also reach the conclusion that this need not be so. It is often said that psychoanalysis began precisely at the moment when Freud abandoned the trauma theory, i.e. when he began to consider the verbal productions of his hysterical patients as fantasies. At this critical point he became much less concerned with the environmental question of whether or not his patients actually had been seduced in childhood and much more concerned with the questions which were formulated and reformulated throughout his later life: what are the instinctual roots of fantasy, and what are the inhibiting factors which can prevent instinct discharge on the biological plane and how do they operate? The work on hysteria, of course, led Freud right into the problem of the incest taboo, since his explanation of the genital inhibition associated with it precisely that later objects may represent tabooed incestuous ones; moreover, he, at this point began to interpret the relevant genetic sequences and drive constellations retroactively from fantasy and symbolic productions, rather than to postulate environmental events *ad hoc*. This shift went along with very close attention paid to the actual mental content of patients in all its details. In this perspective, we might come to the conclusion that if the brother-sister-sister's son triangle is most emphasized by the Trobrianders themselves in mythology and dreams, that this one indeed has a primary unconscious significance in Trobriand culture. Jones's main methodological mistake would then be that he did not pay sufficient attention to Malinowski's clinical detail and rather postulated a paternal trauma on the basis of theory alone. On this level, his formulation is logical, but it is as if he had tried to apply the genetic theory of hysteria to a schizophrenic patient without having tried to modify it to fit what the patient actually had to say.

But if we abandon trauma theory, it might be possible to postulate a distinctive genetic sequence that does not depend on the actual sexual relationships of which the child may be aware. Lacking the necessary material, we can only make a hypothesis, but to do this we might begin by summing up the three major facets of the brother-sister-sister's son triangle as it operates in adult life. First, it is very evident from the dream and myth material that even though there is a strict taboo, or just because there is one, brother and sister are to each other very highly cathected libidinal objects. Second, not only is the expression of any wishes for sexuality or intimacy forbidden, but also the relationship is one of respect, so that the expression of aggression is inhibited as well; the sister must show deference to her brother as an authority figure, and he, in turn, owes certain responsibilities to her. Third, the sister's son comes into this relationship in that he owes respect to the mother's brother; and for social continuity to be preserved, he must identify with him; for in time, of course, he will become a mother's brother with respect to his own sister's son.

Translating this into the genetic perspective, two difficulties arise. First, although this is not true in some other societies, the mother and father do share a habitation which is independent from that of the mother's brother. Second, as Jones points out, it may be difficult to conceive of the sister as a primary object (for example she may be younger and not present or an infant at the Oedipal crisis), and later feelings about her may be displaced from the mother. In any event, one would expect the mother to form a part of the Oedipus triangle in almost any society since Oedipal affects arise from the body closeness which is experienced in early infancy.

However, we can include the mother as a primary object and also make the mother's brother into the primary focus of masculine identification if we presuppose that much of the boy's early feelings about him derive from the special place which the uncle, as her brother, occupies in his mother's eye. Presumably, at a very early age the small boy becomes aware of the special importance which he has to her, both as an authority figure and as a primary object in her fantasy life. In this perspective the idea of sexual jealousy can be built into the triangular situation involving mother, brother, and son in that we might say that, by some process which is not yet fully understood, the boy becomes aware of the strong affective importance which the brother has for his mother; and when his jealousy and anger are awakened, he deals with them by identification. The mother's brother then becomes the primary rival. Moreover, assuming that the passing of the Oedipus complex is equivalent to an assimilation of social representations of objects in the child's mind, we could also assume that much of his perception of his own mother is based on her role as sister, linked to the maternal uncle in the kin group to which he belongs. Having made this supposition, we could then suppose that the representations of the brother-sister relationship which are assimilated, in which the boy identifies with the brother role, then become transferred to the actual brother-sister relationship, within which the taboos are taught in the home very early in childhood. Such a formulation presupposes that identity and jealousy can both be transmitted through symbolic processes alone, without depending on particular observations or knowledge of parental sexual relations, but it would bring in the mother as a primary object, the distinctive aspect of the complex lying in the inclusion of her brother and the emphasis on her role as sister rather than father's wife.

Much of this is, of course, speculative since our knowledge of the possible range of perceptions of the Oedipal child still has many gaps. However, such a formulation could reconcile the two assumptions with which we began, and moreover, could place the Oedipus complex in a more dynamic and wider social perspective, in that it would link up psychological knowledge with anthropological knowledge of kinship structure, given that we already know that this triangular relationship has a crucial status in the functioning of the matrilineal kinship system.

In a more general perspective, it should also be possible to say that each culture imposes restrictions on primary drives according to a particular pattern, and from the pattern of restrictions it should be possible to predict much of the cultural content from the assumption that symbols arise when a primary impulse is denied gratification. Such a possibility is found in the concept of repression, but perhaps comes out more clearly if we use the recent formulation of David Rapaport,[6] according to whom it is the fact of delay in drive expression which gives rise to the symbol, than in at least one facet of Jones's[7] summary of the psychoanalytic theory of symbolism according to which there are biologically given types of primary symbolic content.

[6] D. Rapaport, 'The Structure of Psychoanalytic Theory', *Psychological Issues*, Monograph 6, New York: International Universities Press, 1960.
[7] E. Jones, 'The Theory of Symbolism' (1912), *Papers on Psychoanalysis*, Boston: Beacon Press, 1961, pp. 87-145.

Returning to the Trobriand example, we could then say that the model for delay, or the elaboration and maintenance of complex cultural productions, is provided by the brother-sister relationship. This latter would then be seen as the key relationship in a distinctive nuclear complex which can be used or interpreted on a number of levels: it is manifested directly in the myths of which brother-sister incest is the theme; it appears integral to matrilineal social structure; it presumably has genetic roots; and if we look to the actual experience of childhood and adolescence, we can see that quite concretely the brother-sister relationship is presented as the symbol of delay, for example, in that while infantile sexual games are generally rather freely permitted, this is not the case between brother and sister, just as later in adolescence rather casual affairs are the rule, but between brother and sister the taboo is very strict. In other words, for the Trobriand Islanders the brother-sister relationship has a special place on the borderline between instinct and culture; but it should also be possible to isolate such specially important relationships for other cultures as well.

3. SOME SOUTH ITALIAN CULTURAL COMPLEXES

At this point, I should like to attempt the description of a third nuclear complex, resembling neither the matrilineal one of the Trobriand Islands nor the patriarchal one described by Freud. The material concerns Southern Italy, but descriptions by other researchers indicate the existence of similar patterns throughout the Latin world and possibly even in pre-Reformation Europe. My own concrete observations were made primarily in the city of Naples where I carried out a study of working-class families; however, the basic pattern does not seem fundamentally different in other areas of Southern Italy or in other social class groups, though, of course, there are many variations in details. What I shall try to do is to bring together a number of facts from quite diverse areas—general cultural patterns, intrafamily behaviour, and projective test material—in a way which depends on the framework sketched above.

The South Italian family system, similar in this respect not only to other Latin countries, but also to much of the Mediterranean world, is in a certain sense intermediate between the kind of lineage system found in the Trobriand Islands and the discontinuous nuclear family characteristic of the industrial world. As we have seen in the Trobriand Islands, it is quite possible that units other than the biologically based mother-father-child one serve as the key axis of social structure; this is very often true of primitive societies where the latter unit is usually enclosed in some wider kinship unit which in turn defines patterns of social organization for the society as a whole. In industrial societies, on the other hand, it is often said that since there is such an elaboration of alternative nonkinship social structures (religious bodies, bureaucratic organizations, governments, etc.) the functions of the family have contracted to an irreducible minimum, i.e. the satisfaction of intimacy needs and the caring for small children. The family is discontinuous in the sense that it lasts only as long as particular individuals are alive; as children grow up they gradually move into a wider society and eventually form new families on their own rather than acquiring adult roles in a continuing social group. The world outside the family is seen in this perspective as a locus of positive achievement.

The South Italian family is an intermediate form in two senses. First, although there is no corporate lineage, since religious, economic, and political functions are handled by nonkinship organizations just as in any complex society, there is a rather loosely organized body of extended kin, the *parenti* which has some significance; one's *parenti*, or relatives in a generic sense (usually meaning siblings of parents and their offspring), form the most immediate field of social relations and in theory at least are the persons on whom one can best count for aid in time of trouble. Second, while the family unit is the immediate biological one (with monogamous marriage, no legal divorce, and co-residence of husband, wife and minor children) this latter tends to be centripetal rather than centrifugal. In other words, parents, or in particular the mother, bring up children in such a way as to strengthen loyalties towards themselves rather than to move increasingly into a wider social context. This latter tendency is in turn associated with a definition of the world outside the family as hostile and threatening and very often as a source of temptations towards sexual or other forms of delinquency and dishonesty.

We can begin on the level of global culture patterns by examining a key complex of attitudes, namely, those surrounding the Madonna. The importance of the Madonna complex, throughout the Latin world is evident to even the most casual observation; in the South Italian villages she stands in every church and along with the saints may be carried through the streets in procession, and in even the poorest quarters of the city of Naples she is likely to occupy some niche or other, decorated with the flowers or even gold chains brought by her children grateful for her favours. Moreover, every home has a private shrine, in which pictures or statues of the Madonna appear along with photographs of deceased relatives illuminated by a candle or lamp.

As a figure in Roman Catholic theology, the Madonna, of course, is only one element in a much wider religious complex. However, popular religion in Southern Italy does not always conform to theological doctrine, for example, in that it has a considerable mixture of magical beliefs and in that the Madonna and the saints are conceived of more as persons of whom one can ask a favour (Italian *grazia*, or a grace) than as ideal figures in a moralistic sense. The Madonna may also be seen in characteristic folk manner as a quite familiar figure who is very much part of daily life. One older woman has said, 'The Madonna must have had a hard time when she was carrying the Saviour, because people couldn't have known about the Holy Ghost and they always gossip about such things'. Religion in general is seen in this concrete and living way, and religious vocabulary as exclamations, for example, *Madonna mia* and *Santa Maria*, are very much part of daily conversation.

The most important characteristic of the Madonna is that her love and tenderness are always available; no matter how unhappy or sinful the supplicant, she will respond if she is addressed in time of need. Acts of penitence may be carried out for her, for example, pilgrimage or even licking the steps of the church one by one and proceeding to the altar (today only in the most traditional rural areas). Even such Acts of Penitence, however, are apt to be conceived of as means of showing one's devotion in order to secure a favour, such as the recovery of a sick child. In this sense, the Madonna complex is based on an ethic of suffering rather than sin; the devotee seeks comfort for the wrongs imposed by fate rather than a guide for changing it.

The Madonna is quite obviously the ideal mother figure, and the relationship of the supplicant to her is conceived of as that of a child. The other family figures in the Christian pantheon are, of course, not lacking, that is, the father and the son. However, God the Father is usually conceived of as being so distant that he is unapproachable except through the intermediary of the Madonna or a saint; in Naples, the first cause theory of creation is very common, according to which God set the world in motion and then let it run according to its own devices. Christ, on the other hand, is perceived not as in many Protestant denominations as a representative of moral individuality, or even as an alternative comforting figure, but rather either as the good son who is truly and continually penitent or else in the context of suffering; as dramatized in Lenten rituals, the Madonna weeps when he dies *martyred* by a hostile world. Of the three figures, it is the Madonna who has by far the greatest concreteness in the popular eye. Moreover, of all her characteristics one of the clearest is her asexuality: she conceived without sin and so became mother without being a wife.

Not only is the most apparent deity a feminine one, but also religion is defined as a primarily feminine sphere. Thus, while small boys may attend mass regularly in the company of women, as they approach puberty most of them are teased out of this by their male peers or relatives. The level of participation in religious functions (except for those touching on the secular such as fiestas) is in general very low for adult males; but at every Sunday mass one can observe crowds of young men waiting outside the door. The reason they themselves give for being there is that the girls are inside; thus, at the courtship phase religious participation becomes an opportunity for escaping surveillance, but with the difference that the girl's overt devotion increases and the reverse is true for the boy. Moreover, Southern Italy is noted for its anticlericalism, but, along with some socioeconomic aspects, a major feature of this anti-clericalism is a joking pattern whose main consequence is to raise doubts concerning the ideals of purity which religion represents. This joking pattern is an important part of interaction in the male peer group which crystallizes around adolescence. It thus seems as if religion and adult male sexuality are conceived of as incompatible with each other.

The oppositional or sceptical trend which is represented by anti-clerical joking is seen in a number of other cultural patterns as well; first, in swearing and obscenity which are extremely widespread. The particular expressions used can be divided into four groups: those wishing evil on someone else (e.g. 'may you spit up blood,' from the extreme anxiety evoked by the idea of tuberculosis); those reflecting on the dead ('curse the dead in your family'); those reversing religious values (the most common oath being 'curse the Madonna'); and those reversing the values of feminine purity. The latter group includes graphic expressions for a variety of possible incestuous relationships with mother or sister, anal as well as genital, and can also be linked with the horn gesture (index and little finger extended) implying infidelity of the wife. Cursing may be engaged in by women as well as men, but it is far more characteristic of the latter, particularly in the last two types.[8]

The context and seriousness of insult and obscenity is extremely variable; one may curse the Madonna on the occasion of stubbing one's toe, but raising the possibility of the 'horns' or using the incestuous expressions with enough seriousness may also lead to murder. It is this subtle distinction of style and context which differentiates Neapolitan patterns from those found in association with lineage systems where there are more formalized distinctions between those kin relationships which permit joking or obscenity, and those which do not because they are based on respect.[9] But the essential point is that the frequency of obscenity as used by men is such that one might talk of any positive rule as reversible into a potential negative one; the reversibility relation is in turn confirmed by the particular content choices.

A second index of the same oppositional or sceptical trend is found in the style of masculine behaviour and in social interaction within the male peer group. From adolescence on, an important segment of male life takes place on the street corner, at the bar, or in the club setting which at least psychologically is quite separate from either the home or the church. But in this setting in contrast to the other two, it is masculine values which predominate over feminine ones. Not only are swearing and anticlerical joking characteristic, but most social interaction has a particular style

[8] Women may in quarrelling with each other call each other prostitutes, but without reference to incest. They may also substitute euphemisms for actual curse words, such as *mannaggia alla marina*, literally, 'curse the seashore' for 'curse the Madonna'.

[9] See A. R. Radcliffe-Brown, *Structure and Function in Primitive Society*, Glencoe, Ill.: Free Press; London: Cohen and West, 1952, pp. 90-116. For the Trobriand Islands obscene jokes are freely exchanged with the father's sisters but not with the mother's brother, and there are obscene expressions referring to mother, sister, and wife. Of these the most serious insult refers to sexual relations with the wife, a fact which is not quite congruent with the emphasis we have placed on the brother-sister taboo (See B. Malinowski, *Sex and Repression in Savage Society*, pp. 104-8).

which is partly humorous and partly cynical in quality; many features of both language and gesture point in the direction of scepticism. Moreover, attitudes towards all forms of higher authority, secular as well as religious, are far more negative than positive in emphasis. Much of this style has a ritualized quality to it, but again we have a further index of the reversibility in the masculine setting of values defined as positive in the feminine context. In addition, many male peer group patterns, in particular the emphasis on gambling and risk, are such that they provide a kind of counterpoint to the extreme emphasis on protection and security found in the Madonna complex.[10]

The second cultural complex which we will describe centres on courtship. Courtship is highly dramatized, and in the very important tradition of Neapolitan drama one can find over and over again the same plot: girl meets boy, this is kept secret from the family, or in particular from the father, father finds out (by catching them or by gossip from others), there is a big fight in which the girl or the financé stands up for the couple's rights against the father, father gives in at last, and here the play ends. Sometimes there are attempts on the part of the parents to marry a daughter to an old and ugly man for reasons of *interesse* or financial gain, but they are apt to be frustrated and never go without protest from the daughter. Says Rita in the early nineteenth-century play *Anella* when her father tries to marry her off to a rich but effeminate rag dealer:[11]

> You can cut me up piece by piece, but that Master Cianno, I'll never take him. Poor me! Even if I had found him while Vesuvius was erupting, I wouldn't have gone near him. If I weren't your daughter but your worst enemy, even then I wouldn't think of marrying that sort of man. What sort of life would it be?

The same play also serves to point up the very high degree with which courtship is romanticized and the particularly humble and supplicative position attributed to the young man. The following

---

[10] See R. Vaillant, *The Law*, New York: Knopf; London: Cape, 1958; W. F. Whyte, *Street Corner Society: Social Structure of an Italian Slum*, Chicago: University of Chicago Press, 1943; and I. K. Zola, 'Observations of Gambling in a Lower Class Setting', *Soc. Problems*, 10 (1963), 353-61 for descriptions of relevant patterns.

[11] Gennaro Davino, *Anella: Tavernara A Portacapuana*, in G. Trevisanai (ed.), *Teatro Napoletano dalle origini* (2 vols.), Bologna: Tip. Mareggiani, 1957.

dialogue is addressed to Anella, standing in the balcony, by her suitor, Meniello: [12]

> What sleep, what rest! What sleep, what rest can I have if I am in love, and the man in love is worse off than the man who is hanging on a rope and as soon as he gets a bit jealous, then the cord tightens. What sleep, the minute I close my eyes from exhaustion, jealousy makes me see my Anella up on her balcony surrounded by a crowd of lovers all looking up at her from below . . . what sort of sleep can you look for. And the worst of all is that I haven't even any hope of getting out of torment, because I can't even ask her mother to give her to me as a wife because my dog's destiny made it happen that just to make a baker's dozen her mother is in love with me, too. You see what terrible things can happen in this world to torment a poor man in love!
>
> ANELLA *appears*: Oh, Menie, is that you?
> MENIELLO: Oh, beautiful one of my heart!
> ANELLA: What on earth is wrong? I haven't even dressed yet, and you are up already. Why on earth are you up so early?

The dialogue continues between Meniello's supplications and Anella's much more self-assured and often more mundane reassurances against his jealousy.

Courtship is not only a theme of popular drama; it is also one of the major topics of conversation and joking in everyday life. In one sense, the social norms surrounding it are very strict, in that there are patterns of chaperonage, parents have many active rights of control, and the whole area is surrounded with an aura of taboo. Above all, it is considered highly important that the young girl keeps her virginity until she is able to stand in church in the white veil which symbolizes it. Thus, there is a very sharp polar distinction between the good woman and the bad woman, the virgin and the prostitute. The assumptions underlying courtship are linked up in turn with a metaphorical image from which one can derive many specific customs and sayings: in a similar bipolar fashion, the home is defined as safe, feminine, and sexual, and freely accessible only to men. Thus, a woman of the streets is one who had violated the taboos and in a sense has taken over masculine prerogatives. Coming into the girl's home is a very crucial step in legitimate courtship (popular terminology distinguishes between the often quite casual 'so-so engaged' or 'engaged in secret', and the formalized 'engaged in the house', i.e. with parental knowledge and approval) and the

---

[12] ibid., pp. 118-19.

doorway occupies a particularly strategic intermediary position. Young girls usually become very excitable and giggly when they have the occasion for a promenade, and street phobias are a very common neurotic symptom in Italian women.

But a second aspect of the courtship complex is that in spite of the apparent strictness violations continually occur nevertheless, and the whole topic is treated with a particular kind of humorous ambiguity. Thus, while sexual matters are never referred to in serious or 'objective' ways in everyday conversation, in a teasing or joking way they are an almost continuous focus of social exchange. The actual atmosphere or attitudes created by the strictness are far from puritan; it is rather as if the mothers and aunts and cousins who watch over the young girl with terrible threats about what will happen if she is 'bad' are at the same time very much enjoying the possibility with her. One might by analogy to the many primitive societies in which there is a polar distinction between social relationships based on teasing or joking and those which are based on seriousness or formal respect, distinguish along the same lines between the Madonna complex and the courtship complex. For this reason, the distinction between the good woman and the bad woman is not as absolute as it might seem; often these may be alternative asexual and sexual images for the same woman, as when a father in anger calls his daughter a prostitute because she has come in late.

However, there is one point at which the sacred and the profane come together, and this is at the point of marriage, which almost without exception is symbolized by a church ceremony. Thus, while courtship is a secular process and while the idea of violation of chaperonage norms is often treated with humour, its more serious aim is nevertheless that it should end up in church with the young girl being able to stand 'in front of the Madonna' in the white veil.[13] At the same time, marriage for the man symbolizes a kind of capitulation to the feminine religious complex, whose importance is denied in the male peer group setting by the pattern of sarcasm and secularization. In contrast to the girl, whatever prior sexual entanglements he has had lack significance. Thus, while at least in peasant areas even today the girl's 'honour' may be verified by relatives after the wedding night, the whole question is seen as

[13] Voluntary abstention from public church ceremony sometimes occurs when wearing the veil would be a shame in front of the Madonna.

simply irrelevant on the sexual plane as far as men are concerned: said one informant, 'How would anyone ever know if a man had it or not?'

There is, nevertheless, a sense in which the idea of honour is relevant to masculine identity as well as feminine. This is that the task of chaperonage is seen by the father (or brother) as a matter of maintaining his personal honour as well as the collective honour of the family. Thus, if a girl falls into disgrace, it will be said that the family honour has been lost, or that her father is also a *disgraziato* or lacking in grace. Moreover, whenever insults are cast at female kin, as in the oaths which reflect on the purity of mother, sister, daughter, or wife, the man is expected to consider this as a violation of his own personal integrity and to immediately come to their defence—in some instances with a knife. There are areas where the violation of the honour of a daughter or sister can lead to socially approved homicide, necessary to the defence of the family honour. This pattern is particularly characteristic of Sicily, where the brother's role is more important than in Naples. In eighteenth and nineteenth-century Naples the task of protecting the honour of slum women was taken over by the Camorra, the most highly organized form reached by the Neapolitan underworld, which was not averse to using knives in order to force a reluctant man who had violated virginity into marriage.

We can now try to sum up some of the respective implications of the courtship complex and the Madonna complex as two contrasting sides of a global cultural pattern. One of these we have seen as a joking pattern and the other as a pattern of serious respect and desexualization, although the two meet and cross each other both in the male peer group rebellion against the Madonna and in the culmination of legitimate courtship in the church wedding. The symbol that unites them is that of virginity, or an initial asexual image of femininity that can only be violated in the appropriate social circumstances. These contrasting but interdependent patterns in themselves give us some of the elements of a distinctive nuclear complex; the two most important elements are that of the sublimated respect of children for the ideal mother and that of the game in which erotic temptations continually come into clash with this image of feminine purity. In the latter context, the most important actors, as Neapolitan drama would suggest, are the girl, her father, and the prospective son-in-law. The key value is that of virginity or honour, and the father seeks to preserve it against all comers; it is here that we can look for a distinctive triangular situation.

4. FAMILY STRUCTURE

At this point, we can turn to the more direct consideration of the family. We noted earlier that the primary unit is the nuclear family but that it is embedded in a larger kin group, and there is a high degree of continuity to the mother-child tie. The family is close in a certain sense, at least in that family ties and obligations outweigh all others, but family life is also characterized by a great deal of aggression and conflict. One way in which conflict is handled is by various patterns for the separation of roles, a result of which is the extrafamilial male peer group. After marriage, as well as before, many of the man's needs for comradeship and mutuality continue to be filled by the male peer group and much of the time he is out of the home. The woman, on the other hand, continues in close daily exchange with her natal family (perhaps less in the city than in the villages, and neighbours may also be important) so that many needs for mutual sympathy are fulfilled by mother and sisters or by other women. The division of the sexes is such that the marriage relationship is not often a focus of continuous intimate or reciprocal affective exchange. After the courtship phase and the honeymoon, it more often than not becomes very conflictual, principally because of the emotional ties which both partners retain to the natal family.

In actual fact, of course, there are a great many varied families as well as the noted regional variations; however, many of the observable norms and patterns can be interpreted from the above structural givens. For example, there is a variety of possible balances to the husband-wife versus primary family conflict. For Naples, the most common type of residence is in the vicinity of the wife's family, but the husband as an individual is likely to maintain important contacts with his own. Sometimes the couple together becomes assimilated into one family or another; women, for example, who have had particularly unfavourable relations with their own families, or who have lost a mother by death, are more likely to accept the mother-in-law as a mother surrogate, thus achieving a better relationship with her than is generally expected.

350

The same may happen in the case of the man who marries into a fatherless family or one consisting of girls alone who may take over male roles in that family with relative success. This is unlikely if there are competing figures. Quarrels concerning where the couple should reside are very common, and they are accompanied by a great deal of mutual projection; thus, a man may complain that his wife is much too dependent on her mother and pays little attention to him, and then suggest as a solution to the problem that they move to the house next door to his mother. In extreme cases the two families may end up with quite violent feelings about each other; in studying schizophrenic patients, we found this to be common, and many marriages, while maintained in form, actually dissolved with each partner returning to his own home. The uncertainties of the conflict are intensified by the fact that in contrast to many simpler societies, there are no fixed rules of choice or subordination. A result of this uncertainty is that in situations of choice and conflict, it is more often the feminine point of view than the masculine one which prevails, since it is the woman who in daily life is most concerned with and most emotionally involved in matters pertaining to the family.

It is also the mother who is the primary personage in maintaining family unity, and many results of this can be observed; for example, ties with father or siblings are very likely to break up or become more distant on the death of the mother. Another consequence is seen in differential attitudes towards the remarriage of widows and in differing consequences of the death of parents. If a man is left without a wife, it is taken for granted that he will need a woman, and whether or not he has children, he is likely to find one, though often outside of legal sanction. Thus, many persons who have widower fathers simply state that they have drifted off somewhere, and the ties are no longer very real. On the other hand, a widow or a woman deserted by her husband may be condemned if she seeks alternate sexual attachments before her children marry; it is assumed that her primary loyalty is to them. Marriage, which in Naples is likely to take place either in the late teens or not until the late twenties or thirties, often in this latter instance follows very closely on the death of the parents. Remarriages when both partners have children are often conflictual on the grounds that each prefers his own offspring, and the stepmother is seen as in the Cinderella legend. She may do her best by the children, but even then the tie is never the same; the best possible solution to the loss of a mother is seen to be adoption by the mother's sister, who, because related by blood, will come much closer to fulfilling the maternal role. Marriage to the deceased wife's sister is not uncommon in the case of widowers, though practised more in rural than in urban areas.

The importance of the mother-child tie as the axis of family structure is seen in some additional patterns characteristic of lower-class Naples. Where illegitimacy occurs, the child is legally recognized and brought up by the mother in about 50 per cent of the cases; such status is not formally approved but it does occur.[14] Fathers very rarely recognize illegitimate children, but there are, on the other hand, certain forms of semi-institutionalized polygamy according to which a father may have two distinctive families, one of which is legal while the other is not. In contrast to the pattern of the affair where it is assumed that if the relationship is not socially sanctioned, precautions will be taken to avoid reproduction, it seems that aside from prostitution it is usually assumed that children are the necessary and wanted consequence of any sexual relationship; thus, the rapid multiplication which often characterizes monogamous families also characterizes polygamous ones.

The major requirement for a husband is that he be able to feed and support his family. However, in the urban working class, it very often happens that he is not able to fulfil this task; thus, one common source of arguments is that the husband has not brought in any money. It is also the case in urban areas where the married woman often works in her own right; for example, women may be street vendors, artisans, domestics, etc. At the lower socio-economic levels it is often the woman who has a better opportunity of earning money than the man. She is more motivated to work since she more willingly accepts a low-prestige or low-reward position because of concern for children, while for the man, peer group relationships or a kind of pseudo identification with the higher status groups offers a more immediate rewarding proof of masculinity. One of the primary symbols of peer groups belongingness in Naples is the ability to offer food or drink to others, so that the man is faced with

---

[14] Of the illegitimate children born in Naples in 1956, 51 per cent were legally recognized by their mother alone, as compared with 9 per cent by the father alone, 10 per cent by both parents, and 29 per cent remaining unrecognized. See *Annuario Statistico del Commune di Napoli: Anno 1956*, Naples: Stabilimento Tipografico Francesco Giannini & Figli, 1959, p. 22.

an inherent conflict in that what he spends to gain status in relation to other men is bread lost out of his children's mouths. Thus, a vicious circle may be set in motion in which the wife accuses the husband of irresponsibility, and the husband in turn goes off in anger and tries to recapture his self-esteem by taking risks at cards or by treating his friends to coffee. It is, moreover, the way of dealing with this situation which differentiates male relationships with wives and mothers; the mother, if she has anything at all, will give it to her son, but the wife expects the husband to hand everything over to her in the interests of the children. Thus, financial conflicts are one factor which can push a married man back to ask for support at home.

A second factor is the degree to which intrafamily behaviour is characterized by rivalry between husband and children for the attention of the mother in her food-giving role. One symbolization of the difference between South Italian society and the more truly patriarchal Victorian one can be found in the nature of eating patterns and their relation to family social structure; in contrast to the regular ritualized mealtimes of the Victorian epoch, with father taking a commanding position at the head of the table, there is a highly irregular eating pattern (since space often makes a regular dinner table impossible) in which each member of the family may eat according to his own preference at his own time, but in which the mother is almost continually involved in the process of feeding. In this structure the superior position of the father, and of sons as they grow up, is symbolized by the right to demand what they want and the right to complain if not pleased. When a man complains, a woman will try to do what she can, and as long as she has anything at all, she will give it; but the pattern also puts the husband on an equal subordinate basis with his children.

Thus, the ties to the primary family, the high significance of the maternal role, and the very great difficulties in making a living which characterize most of the working-class groups are such that in spite of appearances the husband and father does not actually enjoy much prestige or authority in the home. From this standpoint the male peer group can be seen as an escape; the man who gets totally 'fed up' always has the possibility of leaving. Likewise, many of the male rage reactions, which give the impression that the Italian family is patriarchal, though much more stylized, have the quality of the child who throws his plate on the floor when he has had

M

enough. Moreover, many of the status-gaining activities of the peer group can be seen as identifications with the feminine feeding role, for example, the high importance attributed to offering food or coffee. However, a second aspect of the masculine role in the home and its relations to sex segregation should not be neglected. This is that male rage may be seen as truly terrifying to women, so that kicking men out becomes necessary; and this goes with an image of masculinity as a kind of threatening force which is a disruptive factor in the feminine circle; images used in daily conversation clearly suggest the idea of phallic intrusion.

A few details on socialization can serve to round out the picture of family life. Children become a centre of attention as soon as they are born and receive a great deal of physical handling which does not undergo systematic interruption; moreover, as they are weaned, substitute gratifications are provided so that there is no significant discontinuity ending the oral phase of development. However, it would be a mistake to conclude from this that they simply receive that much more of the 'security' and maternal warmth which are currently so highly valued in the United States. In the first place, the mother may give little attention to any individual child, being busy and often having many; moreover, maternal behaviour (in the sense of giving food and physical caresses) is so widespread that in actual social reality the maternal attachment is far from being exclusive. Rather, one might say, that the circle of maternal objects progressively widens to include the family as a whole and in many respects strangers; along with this goes the learning of certain kinds of politeness and formality having to do with eating and giving.

In the second, handling of children is often very rough and unsubtle and includes a very high aggressive component.[15] As physical motility appears, it can be systematically frustrated by anxious adults who immediately bring back the wandering or assertive child to thrust a cookie into his mouth; one can see here the beginning of the forced feeding pattern which characterizes moments of tension in the family throughout life. An illustrative example concerns a three-year-old son of a gardener who picked

[15] It is roughest among the poorest and here also may be quite erotically stimulating as well. I am indebted to Vincenzo Petrullo for the suggestion that this latter may be the case because when the children have to go hungry, erotic stimulation may be a means of maintaining their interest in life.

up his father's tools and was immediately called back by mother with the tacit support of father. Children at this age may show considerable diffuse aggressivity and put on an unnatural amount of weight. Later, most of them learn to 'talk back' with verbal rhetoric and gesture; these important components of South Italian culture might be seen as developed in counterreaction to muscular inhibition in that they become a major means for expressing individuality. A second relevant example concerns an eighteen-month-old girl who seemed hardly interested in learning to walk and was not yet able to talk; yet, held by her father she was able to perform fairly complex symbolic operations with her hands, such as snapping her fingers ten times when asked to count to ten.

For these early phases there seems to be little difference between the handling of the small girl and of the small boy, with the single exception that the small boy is more likely to go unclothed from the waist down and to have his penis singled out for teasing admiration.[16] This open phallic admiration is characteristic of the behaviour of mothers to sons, and in teasing intrafamily behaviour the genital organs may be poked or referred to with provocative gestural indications. Children may also share beds with their parents or with each other even at advanced ages (crowding often makes this necessary)[17] though precautions are taken to prevent their observing parental intercourse. One young man was asked what he would do if he saw this; the answer was 'I would kill them'. Except for small children, modesty taboos are very strict, and while physical proximity within the family is very close with respect to anything except genital activity, this latter is surrounded with some secrecy.

There are, however, two crucial points at which sex difference is more prominent. The first is in the ritual of First Communion which ideally takes place at the age of six or seven. Around this age the growing attractiveness of the little girl is the focus of considerable teasing admiration from father or older brothers, uncles, etc. One Neapolitan informant, for example, told me how his seven-year-old daughter had taken to getting into bed with him in such

[16] This pattern is even more characteristic of Puerto Rico (See K. R. Wolf, 'Growing Up and its Price in Three Puerto Rican Sub-Cultures', *Psychiatry*, 15, 1952, 401-33) where sex differences in modesty rules are also sharper.
[17] I know of examples of mothers sharing beds with adult sons, and also of a case of a mother who lost a child in infancy whereupon she asked a thirteen-year-old son to take the milk from her breast; he, however, refused on the grounds that 'she was my mother and I was ashamed.'

a seductive way that he finally had to slap her and kick her out. It did not surprise him in the least when I said that a famous Viennese doctor had made quite a bit out of this sort of thing. However, once the small girl's Oedipal affects had been excited to this degree, it is also necessary that the culture find a resolution for them which it does in the ritual of First Communion; the small girl is dressed as a miniature bride, and at this point it must be impressed on her fantasy that she must delay fulfilment of her wishes until such a time as she can again appear in church in a white veil. Thus, a particularly elaborate cultural symbolization is provided for feminine Oedipal wishes.

For the boy, on the other hand, there is much less in the way of such elaboration of the Oedipus crisis, nor for that matter is there any ritual symbolization of masculine status at adolescence, as there is in many other cultures where socialization at earlier stages is so exclusively in the hands of women. First Communion does take place, but masculine emphasis and degree of symbolization is simply less. Moreover, in many ways the boy's position at home is much more passive than that of the girl; the beautiful warm-eyed docility which one can observe in many boys in the Neapolitan slums might make for the envy of the American mother in the Hopalong Cassidy phase. The same degree of aggressive tension does not appear to be present, nor for that matter is there as much elaboration of the phallic 'I want to be when I grow up' type of fantasy. What does differentiate the small boy from the girl is, first, the open admiration which may be shown for his purely sexual masculine attributes, and second, the fact that he has much less in the way of home responsibility and is in many ways favoured by his mother; but since the father is so often out of the home, his socialization is placed in feminine hands almost as much as that of the girl.

In other words, while cultural ritual can be seen as providing a complex symbolic framework for feminine Oedipal wishes, this is not true in the case of the boy, who may receive special privileges and an open acknowledgement of his physical masculinity, but no such elaborate social symbolization of it. Presumably, this should result in much stronger motivation for the delay in sexual wishes in girls than in boys. This kind of differential in turn becomes extremely important in adolescence, at which point the pattern of sex differentiation becomes a much sharper one, for it is then that chaperonage rules begin to apply to the girl, and the boy in turn acquires a special freedom to move out into the inherently dangerous and sexualized world of the street.[18] It is at this latter point that the prerogative of adult masculinity crystallizes, especially with respect to the quasi taboo on feminine inquisitions concerning masculine activities which take place outside the home.

5. PROJECTIVE TEST MATERIAL

One of our initial assumptions was that culture appears in the individual in the form of object representations which crystallize in the conscious mind at the time of the passing of the Oedipus complex. In this perspective, the norms of intrafamily behaviour should be reflected on the psychological plane in the form of more or less uniform representations of the significant family figures in relation to the self. This dimension is one which can be measured through the use of projective tests. Such material will be presented as a supplement to the cultural and social observations which we have already made.

In two separate studies, a number of cards from the Murray TAT were presented to working-class informants in Naples. Four cards (6GF, 6BM, 7BM, 7GF) will be discussed here. They were presented to the informants with the specific directive that they represent family scenes (mother-daughter, father-son, father-daughter, and mother-son), and they were to describe the scene as it appeared to them. Though few very elaborate stories were given, the subjects saw the cards in an amazingly vivid way with a high degree of sensitivity to the immediate perceptual and gestural details of the figures.[19] The high degree of uniformity of response is in itself a proof of the psychological reality of culture. This uniformity was greatest for the mother-son and father-daughter scenes.

A. *Mother-Daughter Card*

The mother-daughter card was presented to twenty-six female

---

[18] Boys are, of course, outside earlier too, the actual age and amount of time depending on the specific social milieu. The street gang in the slums may include girls and in some groups much of the family income may come from small boys. The important fact is the lack of any very formalized masculine authority over the boy.

[19] 'Stories' more often took the form of 'well, from the way his eyes are you can tell that . . . ', followed by a conclusion about motivation or feeling.

informants with a specific directive: 'The mother is advising the daughter, what do you think she is telling her?' Additional questions such as 'How does the daughter feel about it?' were also asked. Thus, we purposely biased the situation in the direction of emphasis on maternal authority. However, only to a certain extent was this the major theme; rather, the responses fell into three distinct groups, of which the first is most directly relevant to the question of authority as such.

For eleven subjects, the mother appeared as giving some very definite form of censure or advice. In only one such instance is the reaction of the daughter to this seen as wholly positive; in one other instance the reaction of the daughter is openly rebellious, and in the remaining nine, the daughter accepts the advice as 'for her own good', but with expressed resentment; however, the mother is finally vindicated since 'things don't turn out well in the long run':

> The mother is giving good advice to the daughter; the mother tells the daughter to behave well, not to go out much, to pay more attention to things at home. She has to help her mother to do the housework. The picture is beautiful because there is nothing bad in it.

> The mother is yelling at the daughter because with the excuse of the child who is her little brother she goes out walking and comes in late. The daughter talks back to her mother saying 'What do you want with me? You made this baby and now you go around finding out bad things about me.'

> The mother is moralizing. The daughter is a bit fed up with the mother's words. . . .

> The mother tells the little girl that she has to do housework and the daughter is not looking at the mother as if she had not heard and did not want to do this work. . . . Things won't go very well because the daughter won't listen to the mother.

The first reaction is particularly interesting in that by implication it so clearly brings out the asexual nature of the home in contrast to the outside world where there may always be 'something bad'. The second is equally interesting in that where there is open rebellion on the part of the daughter the mother is also portrayed as a sexual being. The remaining responses show a very classic pattern of internalized but ambivalently accepted authority; the mother is clearly a super-ego figure, but considerable rebellion and resentment are experienced towards her.

For the next group of subjects, the card itself provided a particular difficulty. The Murray card shows a girl in the latency period being read to by her mother and holding what could be either a doll or a live baby. The situation of a mother reading to the daughter is, of course, somewhat out of the ordinary in this group, but in addition a number of informants were led to comment from the girl's age that this could not actually be an authority situation since 'the girl is too young to be given the most important advice'.

Thus, these responses were limited to fairly factual and emotionally neutral kinds of advice ('the mother is telling the daughter how to bring up her little brother'), and more crucial attitudes of mother and daughter were not made clear. The responses are important principally for their value in pointing up just how crucial the courtship situation is as compared to any other area of performance with respect to the question of authority in general.

For the third group of three respondents this was true as well, but they simply ignored the age of the girl on the card and perceived the situation as involving a mother, her daughter, and the latter's illegitimate child:

> The mother talks with the daughter that is married and has a child, no, I mean the daughter is not married. The mother tries to help her and get her married, the mother is good and does not throw her out of the house.

> The girl is not married and it seems to me that her mother gives her advice on how to bring up the child. It seems that the mother has forgiven her and tells her to treat the child well. The mother gives advice to the daughter about how to behave and how not to fall a second time. Because the mother is understanding she says to the daughter to be careful because the mother should try not to say to the daughter that she is guilty because the girl could do something to hurt herself, she could commit suicide or fall into the same error again thinking that she doesn't have anyone who cares.

This, of course, is a crucial and dramatic situation where norms have actually been violated. The responses make clear that fear of loss of maternal love is a major threat preventing more frequent violations; but also in the actual crisis situation the mother may not really kick the girl out of the house. Another evidence of the internalized nature of maternal authority is seen in the respondent who conceived of suicide as a possibility in the event that such forgiveness did not take place.[20]

B. *Father-Son Card*

The father-son card was presented to ten men and ten women in a second study. No specific directives were given beyond the statement that the scene involved a father and a son. Authority, however, turned out to be the most important theme, found in the responses of seven men and three women, but in contrast to the mother-daughter responses the specific content of the advice or censure given by the father to the son was left indeterminate. However, there is no doubt that fathers were seen by the majority of men as censuring figures:

> . . . the father reproaches the son . . . the son is a delinquent, you can see from his face that he is not a nice person and I think he will not listen to the father's advice. . . .

> The son is bitter and the father displeased because the son would like to talk about something and doesn't. During the family life, the father asks the son what trade he would like to have while the son takes the matter unhappily. He would like to be a chauffeur and the father makes him learn carpentry and the result is that he practises his trade against his own will and cannot succeed in it. After a few years he begins to hate the father and so he remains without any trade at all. The son on his side would like to be a chauffeur. As a result the father and son fight, the son curses the father, the father says 'you ought to listen to me'.

The second response was stated to be an autobiographical one; the respondent was the son of an artisan and, as the result of having gambled away his youth and refusing to learn a trade, was at the time I saw him a very despondent man, father of eight children whom he tried to support as a street vendor. Moreover, while all the male respondents were themselves fathers with children, they seemed not to take the perspective of the father. The exceptions to the rule that both were seen negatively were only partial ones; one respondent did unconvincingly portray the father as affable

---

[20] Low suicide rates are often taken as evidence of the lack of internalized super-egos. However, material from Southern Italy, including the fact that depressive symptoms are not at all rare, might suggest that instead there are secondary social mechanisms (i.e. the possibility of forgiveness) which alleviate guilt whose subjective intensity may nevertheless be very great. The high suicide rates found in modern industrial countries may result then from the lack of these, or what Durkheim calls anomie (see *Suicide*, London: Routledge, 1952, Glencoe, Ill., Free Press, 1951).

while another (particularly intelligent and outward seeking) was the only respondent to think of the possibility of positive rather than negative assertion against the father.

> The son is affable and absolutely convinced of the father's counsels.

> The father is decided and authoritarian, ugly. The son *might* be bad, he has an independent spirit and does not want to listen to the father. The son follows something else, as if the father's wisdom were something annoying, not very important for him.

Two of the remaining three men saw the situation as one of shared sorrow for the death of a woman and the third presented an alternative comradely view of their relationship:

> There is a close friendship between the father and son, they confide in each other.

But for women it was themes of common sorrow and depression which took precedence over those concerning authority. Thus, three saw authority themes and three a common sorrow over death; but the remaining four show the two as sharing a common sense of helplessness with respect to the (primarily economic) external reality:

> They are desperate [for money]—they worry. Nothing more.

> They are worrying about something, the office, work, because they are melancholy.

> What a shame, the father is completely blind! Don't you see he has his eyes completely closed and an absent expression? The son is as if he were listening to something, it must be a radio, but the father has the look really of a blind man. [Don't they say anything to each other?] No, the father minds his own business, really with the look of a blind man, and the son on the other hand is listening, he must be listening to the radio.

In this the women seem to be able to portray a socially very real aspect of their relationship, that it is hard for a man to be an effective authority when he cannot provide anything for his son, which the men themselves have to deny.

The most striking features of the responses to the father-son card are, thus, the lack of a clear social agreement concerning the nature of this relationship, and for the men the lack of effective internaliza-

361

tion of paternal authority. By the latter, we mean that sons are simply seen as 'bad' or 'delinquent' in relation to the father, without, as was the case in the mother-daughter situation, there being a view of how the son ought to accept the authority for his own good, etc. One might say that this provides further evidence that the society is not patriarchal, and masculinity is defined more in terms of rebellion than positive identification. In simplest terms, the conflict is that portrayed by one informant who says, 'They seem against each other'.

C. *Father-Daughter Card*

For a contrast with responses to the father-son scene, we might again quote the street vendor, who turned to this card with con- siderable relief and pleasure:

> This case here defines a father, he is sociable. Here it is no longer a job problem, the girl must know a man and he knew from the information that he has been a delinquent. He says 'look for another path, there are millions of men.' The father wants happiness for his daughter, he wants her to marry someone who will give her something to eat. (Q) The daughter answers 'it's my business', no daughter ever listens to her father. (Q) They get bitter but then they make peace after a child is born.

Unfortunately, we do not have enough male answers to this card to analyse quantitatively; however, this one indicates that while the father does have authority over the daughter, its overthrow is to be expected even by the father himself and while they may 'get bitter', the bitterness is nothing like the real hostility of the father- son antagonism. The same card was administered to thirty-two female respondents, and it was among these that the highest degree of uniformity was found. Twenty saw the situation as conflict between father and daughter related to courtship:

> The father does not want the daughter to get engaged to a man he knows and he does not want this man to marry his daughter. The father is making her ashamed. The father seems bad to me. He is jealous of the daughter and does not want her to get engaged. The daughter is a beautiful girl. She cares a lot about this man that her father doesn't want to give her to and she wants to get married at any price.

> The father is mortifying the daughter. The father is having it out with the daughter because other people have told him some-

thing. He makes her ashamed and she remains surprised and amazed. The father wants to know the story of his daughter's engagement. She does not want to tell about her affairs and probably the father heard about this engagement from other people. The father wants to know if it is a good marriage for his daughter.

The daughter seems like an actress. The father is reasoning with the daughter. They are probably talking about the daughter's fiancé; the father wants to know how things are going in her engagement. The father is happy and the daughter is a bit fed up because her father wants to know many facts about her relationship with the fiancé. For this reason she is not answering spontaneously.

Nine of the remaining twelve respondents gave generally very inhibited answers or denied that the scene could actually be father and daughter in such a way as to suggest some neurotic inhibition.

I don't know how to say anything about this picture. The father is mad and the daughter is calm. They are talking about not very important problems that have to do with family life.

[Informant says that the test seems a bit complicated here.] The father is upset because the daughter didn't do something in the house; she should have done some errand and didn't do it. The father says to the girl, 'You got dressed up to go out and didn't do errands.' The father doesn't let her go out but the relations between father and daughter aren't bad.

And finally three informants saw the scene as one in which the father was making seductive advances towards the daughter.

The father is looking at the daughter in a strange way, that is more like a man than like a father. She looks at him perplexed and almost struck dumb. The father will not succeed because the daughter has understood his intention, she will control herself unless he attacks her. The father is not behaving very well; he has gone astray . . . maybe because the girl is attractive.

All three saw the girl as able to control the situation. An additional two among the above nine, while denying that the scene could be father and daughter, saw, respectively, a husband and wife, and an older Don Juan boss seducing a secretary.

As far as we know the incest responses were not given by seriously disturbed women and they show fewer signs of inhibition than the respondents who did not perceive any shame or conflict between father and daughter at all.

For the first group there was not a single informant who failed to perceive the situation as a conflictual one in which the conflict lay between the father's censure or possessiveness and the daughter's wish to have a boyfriend. Moreover, the card typically evoked a complex of affects which included pleasure (blushing and giggling), shame, and embarrassment. When we look for the outcome of the conflict, we find one element in common with the father-son card, namely, the tendency is in the direction of expected rebellion rather than internalized acceptance of paternal authority. In ten out of twenty instances the daughter is specifically stated to win the battle with father, while in only three does she concede; in the remaining cases the fact of conflict is simply stated. In other words, the TAT responses repeat the same dramatic pattern which we have already seen in the play *Anella* in which the courtship situation is a triangular relation between father, daughter, and prospective son-in-law, and the expected outcome is the ritual termination of the father's possessive relation to the daughter.

D. *Mother-Son Card*

The most important characteristic of these responses is the extent to which they show a close correspondence to the Madonna complex, just as the father-daughter card corresponds to the courtship one. One theme occurs over and over again, more frequent among male than female respondents, namely, that of the penitent son who is returning to the mother:

> . . . the son is asking forgiveness of the mother, repenting of the evil he has done. . . .

> The mother pushes the young man away and he asks for something insistently. Or maybe he did something very serious, probably he went away, and so now he has come back to ask her forgiveness and the mother no longer wants to receive him.

> The mother has a son she has not seen for many years . . . he returns after having done many bad things, stealing and other things. He returns to the family to ask forgiveness. Who knows whether or not the mother will give it to him but I think she will.

> The son is asking forgiveness for something . . . a mother would always forgive her son, even if he were an assassin, even if he were Chessman.

> The penitent son who returns to the mother and the mother cannot or does not know how to forgive him.

In comparison to the responses concerning the father, what is most striking is the extent to which the son places the burden of guilt upon himself, in that asking for forgiveness implies an internalized sense of wrongdoing.

There was some variation among the respondents as to whether the mother was seen as certain to provide forgiveness or not; the fact that some expressed doubt or uncertainty is evidence that maternal love is not conceived of as wholly unconditional. In two instances informants were known to have marked difficulties in their actual relationships with the mother. One of these is the informant who states that 'the mother cannot or does not know how to forgive'—but he portrays the son as the saint who forgives the mother unable to forgive. The second, recently kicked out of home, is the only one who saw the mother as acting aggressively ('The mother pushes the young man away'), etc., but after in a sense blaming the mother, he changes pattern and like the others puts the burden of guilt on the son.

For ten male and ten female respondents, what we call the penitence response was given by seven men and four women. Among the other responses, three portrayed simple sadness ('The mother is sad because the son will leave'), and three anger. All of the anger responses were given by women, who, on the whole, presented a less romanticized view of the relationship. One response given by a beggar is particularly interesting in that it shows a relation between psychic abnormality and open anger and sexual deviance on the part of the mother:

> As if he [she?] were all upset. You can see the son is arguing with the mother, he has turned his back, maybe they had a family fight. [About what?] Mama and son because the mama you can see made a lot of scandals and the son wants to find out something, who knows what, and so mama and son are arguing . . . because you can see that the mother is a bit off in the head because she turns her back on the son. [Yes, you can see that she is a bit angry. But how does the son feel about it?] The son has an enraged face, he has his nerves out of place too. [In response to further questions, she shifts subject.]

In many instances the fact that the American card portrays a mother looking away from her son was sensed as disturbing but that it could imply psychic distance was denied. Thus, while it may be perceived by women, there seems to be a taboo on perceiving anger in the mother-son relationship by men. In this respect there is a very clear contrast with respect to the father-son relationship.

6. CONCLUSIONS

We began, with reference to the Jones-Malinowski debate, by considering the possibility that each culture is characterized by a distinctive nuclear complex whose roots lie in its family structure. Our subsequent task has been to pull together various orders of data concerning South Italy in such a way as to portray such a nuclear complex which differs both from the brother-sister-sister's son triangle characteristic of the Trobriand Islands and from the patriarchal complex isolated by Freud. In the South Italian data we have found that two cultural complexes, the sacred one centred on respect for the feminine Madonna figure and the secular joking pattern surrounding courtship and embodied in popular drama, also have their reflections in the actual patterning of family life and childhood experience and in the intrapsychic life of the individual as seen in projective tests. It is this continuity which has led us to the conclusion that it is possible to define a single global complex which can be perceived simultaneously either as intrapsychic or as collective, the representations which are passed on from generation to generation on the social level coming to be internalized in the individual in the form of representations of the self in relation to objects. The task which remains is the more precise summary of the outlines of the South Italian nuclear complex, comparing it with Freud's patriarchal one, and the drawing out of some more general implications with respect to research methodology and application.

Our principal supposition is that the two most significant among the biologically given family relationships are those between mother and son and between father and daughter. In the former instance the son occupies a subordinate position in the sense that authority stemming from the mother is fully internalized, and violations of it are subjectively sensed as inducing guilt, in comparison to the father-son relation where the son may openly express hostility or rebellion in such a way as to put the father in a negative light. In other words, respect for the mother is much stronger than respect for the father. We do not mean by this to say that women dominate in any simple sense, since it is evident that many other taboos, such as the barring of feminine interference in areas of activity defined as masculine ones, act against this result, not to mention the open admiration and permissiveness which women usually show towards the masculinity of their sons. However, in many ways the mother-son relationship is qualitatively different from that of our own society or that of Freud, most notably in the continuation throughout life of what might be referred to as an oral dependent tie, i.e. a continual expectation of maternal solace and giving rather than a gradual or sudden emancipation from it.

It is this fact that might lead an American observer to speak of an 'oral' culture, or one based on feeding as the dominant mode of libidinal interaction, in contrast to a hypothetical 'anal' or 'phallic' based one. However, this type of formulation we would consider quite inadequate both with respect to theory and the empirical facts. It is evident that types of interaction based on the exchange of gifts and food do have an extremely important role, though these result in very complex types of adult interaction which can by no means be derived directly from infantile roots. More important, however, is the theoretical postulate which would lead us to believe that the phallic phase of development nevertheless occurs. In other words, although he may not give up oral types of gratification, the boy nevertheless passes through a phase at which the wishes he experiences towards the mother are sexual and masculine in nature, and that, moreover, this phase will be associated with aggressive reactions against the subordinate feeding position. We can then trace some of the implications of these postulates rather than simply stopping with the 'oral culture' formulation.

In this perspective we can better see some of the more general consequences of the fact that the masculine role is so little emphasized within the home and that cultural values centre on the feminine image. From the genetic standpoint, we might say that while oral gratifications do not have to be renounced (although they do come to take more complex social forms), this is not true with respect to phallic and aggressive wishes towards the mother; these in fact must systematically undergo repression as they arise. In fact, to characterize the relation to the mother as one based on respect, in social language, is exactly the same thing as to say in psychodynamic language that sexual and aggressive wishes cannot be expressed directly. We then can ask what happens to these wishes, assuming that in some form they persist, and arrive at three kinds of formulation, each of which is relevant to the understanding of culture patterns. Through all of them the important contrast with Freud's formulation lies in the greater continuity of the relationship with the mother and the lesser continuity of that with the father.

First, referring back to the concept of the symbol as arising in precisely those areas where a culture both exploits (by actual affective closeness) and inhibits (by imposing of taboos) primary drives, we can say that the erotic wishes of the son towards the mother come to be sublimated, and it is precisely this fact which gives rise to the representation of the Madonna figure. Moreover, in her characteristics, we can see both derivatives of the actual cultural reality, e.g. in that the dependent relationship of the penitent to the maternal figure is preserved, and some unrealizable aspects of fantasy, e.g. in that the Madonna became a mother without being a wife. This latter is, moreover, the characteristic which in itself represents Oedipal repression, in that the Madonna is perceived as an asexual maternal figure. But in addition, in contrast to the 'oral culture' view which might say simply that mothers are more permissive, the Madonna is a 'super-ego' figure; she could not be forgiving if she did not have a concept of sins which have to be forgiven. In this perspective we can say that Oedipal wishes are repressed in such a way as to give rise to an internalized representation of the tabooed object, who then comes to play the role of conscience. However, the complication in this case is that the internalized subject is in the case of men a feminine one; it is this which we mean by speaking of a matriarchal rather than a patriarchal 'super-ego'. What it leads to then is a masculine identification with a set of cultural values identifiable as feminine, or even as very concretely perceived according to a feminine body image. The most important of these is the respect for virginity, shared by men and women alike and manifested in the courtship taboos on entering the home of the girl who is sought before the relation is formalized. The identification of the girl who is legitimately courted with the idealized mother is seen in the similar submissive relation adopted by the male; the infantile wishes underlying the image of the pure woman are also seen in a sometimes extreme degree of defensiveness concerning the issue of whether or not the purity is real and to be believed.

368

Second, however, impulses which are repressed can also be dealt with by displacement. It is in this respect that the significance of the masculine peer group and the definition of the sphere of life outside of the home, i.e. the sum total of masculinity as defined by the rebellion pattern which we have discussed, become apparent. Many of the patterns of the outside peer group are distinctively phallic in nature. Moreover, in many more concrete senses one can conceive of the outside world as the focus for aggressive and phallic wishes which must be displaced outside the home, e.g. the common situation of the male in anger who simply picks up and leaves, or the great importance of cursing. Thus, aggression which arises within the home may be dealt with by displacement outside it. One characteristic of the Madonna is that she is an ideal figure; ordinary mothers of course rarely approach her, in that they may not forgive, they may very often get angry or impatient, or they may in fact dominate in a very aggressively matriarchal way and in this event the recourse of the male is the privilege of exit. Women in turn support this form of expression of masculinity by respecting taboo on interference and often by direct admiration and encouragement of even delinquent extrafamilial activities. In addition, anger which arises in a mother-son relationship conceived of as exclusive in fantasy may also be dealt with in a complex series of intrafamilial rivalries and jealousies within which the affective consequence of reality frustration *vis-à-vis* the mother may be expressed with respect to other family objects. Thus, displacement both within and outside the family is used to deal with aggressive impulses whose direct expression towards the mother is tabooed.

Third, erotic wishes may be displaced as well as aggressive ones, and it is here that we can find the source of the bipolar distinction between the good woman and the bad woman. The contrary image to the Madonna is, of course, that of the prostitute, and the close intertwining of the two images is seen at a great many points, e.g. in the obscenity patterns that reverse the values of feminine purity and in the family quarrels where even closely associated women may be accused of promiscuous impulses. The persistence of the early sublimations in later life is manifested in two crucial assumptions: first, that the sexualized woman may be appreciated in a naturalistic way, but she is always perceived as on a lower spiritual plane than the pure one; and second, the idea of sexuality is almost inevitably associated with the possibility of betrayal and pluralization of the relationship, i.e. that wives, sweethearts, and mistresses are continually suspected by men of wanting other partners than themselves as soon as the idea of sexuality comes into play.

It is facts such as these which lead us to postulate an underlying and persistent fantasy of an exclusive maternal object as a theoretical assumption. Because of repression, we cannot, of course, acquire direct information concerning the sexual aspect in most cases. One particularly important area of research, however, is found in schizophrenic cases where one may see gross breakdowns of cultural sublimations. One of two South Italian schizophrenic men whom I have seen intensively showed the sexual aspect of the mother-son relationship and the associated Madonna complex in a very transparent form: having many religious delusions; while praying to the Madonna he had open and bizarre erotic experiences and he was unable to distinguish consistently between maternal and erotic objects. The early history was probably one in which prolonged nursing merged into the awakening of genital feelings. However, the second case points up the need for care in separating local and individual variations from global patterns. Coming from a mountainous area where patriarchal patterns and a lack of sentimentality are more typical, the patient showed a much more autistic form of pathology of which the most conspicuous elements were warded-off homosexuality and an extremely submissive identification with the father. He rejected the breast of a wet nurse at an early age, and a crucial traumatic experience was a childhood seduction by an older brother.

One consequence of such a relationship, which fits many of the data we have concerning the South Italian family, is that it acts against social mobility in the broadest sense of the term by making for a very strong centripetal tendency. In other words, if a key axis of family structure is the relationship between mother and son, and if this relationship tends to maintain itself by the preservation of an infantile fantasy which is then dealt with by a complex series of social sublimations and displacements, rather than by attenuating its significance by dispersal or replacement by other objects, then we should have no theoretical basis for explaining the formation of new families. Rather we should expect each mother-son combination to simply continue until the death of the mother; the incest taboo alone does not seem sufficient for explaining the process of change, since nothing in South Italian norms prevents the adult son from obtaining immediate sexual gratification outside while continuing to occupy the emotionally more important position of son. It is at this point that we might turn to the examination of the father-daughter relationship, which can be seen as complementary to the mother-son one in defining a total structure.

The most important difference between these two lies in the dimension of continuity. The father is not continually and lovingly interested in his daughter as the mother is in her son, but rather his interest becomes particularly important at two points in the daughter's life history: the Oedipal phase and the courtship phase. At both of these points the father is highly sensitive to the daughter's femininity, and the daughter is given considerable scope for exploiting this sensitivity in what is often a very active way. Moreover, while the taboo on incest between mother and son is as in all societies a very deep-lying one, it is very easy to come to the conclusion that the desexualization of the father-daughter relationship is not nearly as complete. Thus, in particular in instances where the mother has died, father-daughter incest is not an unheard of phenomenon and the possibility may be referred to even rather casually, as in the many stories about 'that case in our village' that go around. We noted this on the TAT responses. In an American setting an openly incestuous perception might be taken as an indication of serious pathology, but we have no reason to believe this was the case for our informants. Their counterpart in the normal case where the taboo is preserved is found in the teasing behaviour or embarrassed avoidance which characterizes the relation between the father and the sexually more mature daughter or in the giggling embarrassment which women associate with the idea of being found out in their love relationships.

In other words, the incestuous impulses in the father-daughter relationship are quite close to the surface, in such a way that we might speak of a lesser degree of repression than is implied in Freud's concept of the Oedipus complex. There is of course a taboo but one might well speak of a persistence of the incestuous impulses on a preconscious level in such a way that they are openly expressed in cultural idiom as in the frequent use of the word jealousy to describe the father's feelings about the daughter's suitors, and transformed into a joking pattern which is characteristic of the courtship complex.

The major significance of the triangle involving father, daughter, and prospective son-in-law, moreover, lies in the fact that it is to a much greater extent with respect to the daughter than to the wife or mother that the man plays an active role. When he himself is courting, he has to beg at the balcony for a well-protected woman whose virginity he has to respect, but in the case of his own daughter it is he who does the protecting and whose consent has to be sought by the prospective suitor. Thus, the most fully institutionalized masculine role in Southern Italy, one which is defined positively and not by rebellion, is that of the protection of the honour of the woman who are tabooed. In turn, if the sexual affects felt towards these are quite close to the surface, considerable fantasy satisfaction must take place in a way which is active and masculine in contrast to the mother-son relationship, which in so many ways spreads into the marital one, where the male role is passive.

But in addition it is in the father-daughter relationship that we can find a mechanism of change which acts against the centrifugal family tendency. The courtship situation not only gives the father an active role but also has a particular affective style, namely, that of a sudden explosion in which erotic impulses break out with a dramatic intensity which suggests some underlying dynamic force. Moreover, in spite of the chaperonage norms, the behaviour of young women at this point is not such as to suggest much innocence or ignorance of sexuality; they just as well as the young men seem propelled to rebel against the taboos, and they are very often teasers. We have also commented at length on the ambivalent nature of the taboos themselves, in that while violations may be severely condemned explicitly, it often seems as if they were just as much encouraged. It almost seems as if the entire pattern of restriction and parental control were a kind of cultural fiction whose actual purpose is to cover something else; this is what we mean in characterizing it as a joking pattern.

In this perspective it is not at all difficult to postulate that much of the actual source of tension lies in the socially exploited incestuous tie between father and daughter. Thus, the South Italian girl does not appear as inhibited or naïve for precisely the reason that even though carefully kept away from outside men, she has in a great many indirect ways been treated as a sexual object by father (and brothers or other male relatives) both at puberty and during the Oedipal crisis. Within the family the incestuous tension may be handled by joking (or avoidance[21]), but to the extent that the wishes generated seek a biological outlet, the daughter has to seek an object outside the family—and the father has to rid himself of a woman whom he perceives as very desirable but cannot possess. We would then say that it is the strength of the incestuous wishes which accounts for the dramatic and explosive quality of the courtship situation; and the father-daughter relation, by accentuating incestuous tension and at the same time by imposing a taboo, acts as a kind of spring mechanism which running counter to the strong centripetal forces inherent in the mother-son tie has sufficient force as to cause the family unit to fly apart, resulting in the creation of a new one. In this context the insufficiency of the oral culture view again becomes apparent.

One can then see the father's role in defending the honour of the daughter as the masculine counterpart of the Madonna identification; the father's incestuous impulses are sublimated in the active role which he plays towards the daughter in competition with her suitor. Since the sexual wishes cannot be fulfilled, the symbolic assertion of authority is much more important than the actual outcome, a consideration which can explain the ritualized nature of the father's control over courtship and the gracefulness with which he eventually backs down. As the street vendor stated, his real wish is for his daughter's happiness, but in order to show that he is a man he has to be able to demonstrate the power he has over her, and over the still subordinate prospective son-in-law. The principle means he has at his disposal for doing this is by being obstinate in such a way as to increase the excitement of the drama—of which one could say the most important member of the audience for him is the daughter. Likewise, the complementary wishes of the daughter are sublimated in the pleasure which she experiences over the fact of being controlled, a pleasure which is evident in the courtship descriptions of women, however much they may verbally express resentment or rebellion. Moreover, just as the Madonna fantasy provides a feminine identity for men, so the courtship complex provides masculine modes of expression for women, in that in participating in an active teasing pattern the daughter may also identify with the father, as seen in the great importance which

[21] Casual joking and teasing between men and women within the family is characteristic of urban areas; in some country ones (where courtship taboos may be taken more seriously), there is more likely to be embarrassed avoidance, or *vergogna* (shame), between father and daughter.

women attribute to their own capacity to make a stand in front of him which demonstrates that they really want a suitor.

In other words, while the mother-son tie acts primarily as a centrifugal one; in that it maintains itself in such a way as to make for an unbroken continuity in the primary family, the father-daughter tie acts in the inverse sense in that the incestuous tension, being much closer to the surface, has to seek an external outlet so that a kind of spring mechanism is generated. The two together make up a viable structure which can be differentiated from our own on two counts: first, it emphasizes the romantic cross-sex ties within the family far more than same-sex identifications, and second, it preserves incestuous fantasies, in such a way that they may never be fully replaced by the actually sexual husband-wife relationship. Thus, though courtship is based on the idea of individual romantic love, this latter does not appear as a prelude to an intimate emotional interdependence between husband and wife, but rather as a temporary suspension of an equilibrium in which intergenerational ties are in the long run more significant. One might say that after the wedding the supplicant suitor returns in fantasy to his own mother, and at the same time comes increasingly to resent the maternal aspects of his wife in such a way that he is again driven outside, much as in adolescence.

The wife on the other hand may experience a parallel disillusion when she discovers that the husband is not the father of fantasy, and she comes increasingly to transfer her own affective needs to her son, and so the pattern repeats itself. The husband will, of course, have a reawakened interest in the family later, namely, when he has a daughter.[22] Thus, on both sides, it is having children, and in particular children of the opposite sex, which provides the principal effective source of commitment to the family.

[22] The importance of the father-daughter relationship becomes particularly apparent when we contrast South Italian patterns with those seen in other cultural groups where the rule is the matrifocal family, in which there is no stable husband-wife attachment and the only constant relation is between mother and child. The matrifocal family (found throughout the Caribbean and among working-class American negroes) seems regularly to appear where masculine identity cannot be easily maintained on the basis of some real occupational achievement. The same conditions hold in Southern Italy and should be seen as underlying the matriarchal trends which we have described; however, with a few exceptions the monogamous family is nevertheless maintained. But the active role which the father has vis-à-vis the daughter must be one of the primary reasons for this, a view which should be considered by social agencies that often too readily seek to save daughters from fathers whom they see as acting solely from cruelty.

We have up to this point given little systematic attention to the mother-daughter and father-son relationships, which we have conceived of as having a lesser cultural significance than the cross-sex pairs. This is, of course, not to say that they are inexistent or unimportant; but what we mean by a lesser cultural significance might come out more clearly if we draw a few brief contrasts with our own society and with the Oedipus complex as formulated by Freud.

The TAT responses for the mother-daughter card indicate a pattern that is quite classic in that the daughter appears to internalize maternal authority, but she does so in an ambivalent way—contrasting with the romantic internalization found in the case of the son. Moreover, the actual mother-daughter relationship corresponds to that found in most societies; it is the mother who teaches the daughter the routine techniques of daily life. However, an additional feature of the TAT responses was that the informants themselves often stated that 'these counsels are not very important', implicitly by comparison with those given during the courtship phase. But this comment gives us the possibility of tying together one global feature of South Italian values with the family nuclear complex; utilitarian accomplishments, notably in contrast to Protestant value systems, simply do not receive much emphasis. As our society sees the Oedipus complex, its outcome is that the child gives up the sexual fantasies centred on the parent of the opposite sex and then identifies with the parent of the same sex, whom he or she takes over as an ego ideal. Thus, the small girl wants to grow up to be a woman like her mother, and fantasies that when she is, then she too will have a husband, this depending on how well she learns to carry out womanly tasks. But in small girls or young women in Southern Italy there is remarkably little in the way of ego ideal, or the superior person one hopes to emulate. The necessary tasks are taken for granted, but the effectively more important matter is not becoming something one is not yet but rather guarding something one has already, namely, virginity. This in turn can be related back to the fact that the infantile wish is dealt with to a greater extent by symbolic replacement (the First Communion enactment of the role of the bride) of the cross-sex fantasy than by identification with the same-sex parent. In other ways the mother-daughter relationship acts as a centrifugal force in much the same way as that between mother and son, and the two go together in defining a somewhat static social tendency rather than an active accomplishing one.

The father-son relationship on the other hand seems to constitute an unresolved cultural problem, a fact which may have roots in economic conditions which make continuity of identity from father to son through occupational or social achievement very difficult to attain, though the nature of the family may in turn help to create such conditions. It is in examining father-son relationship that the contrast between South Italian patterns and those described by Freud becomes clearest. The TAT responses do indicate that the father may be perceived by the son as a judging or condemning figure. However, when we have said that this does not give rise to an internalized paternal super-ego figure, what we meant was that on the whole our male informants did not present any social values going beyond their immediate relationship which the father represents, e.g. according to a pattern of 'well he was tough but he did it to teach me to act like a man'. Moreover, although they were adult men, they identified with the son figure far more than the father, and they saw the outcome as a simple mutual antagonism in which the father accuses the son of delinquency but the son justifies himself and his own rebellion, rather than channelling the rebellious forces into any kind of sublimated form.

In other words, father-son hostility simply leads to fights and antagonism rather than being restrained in the interest of higher social goals or symbols. The clearest case in this respect was that of the street vendor, who very explicitly relates the kind of decreasing social energy with respect to occupation—for which he is one of a great many representatives—to a failure to solve the problem of antagonism with the father in any creative way. But for Freud, of course, the exact opposite is true: in perceiving the great importance which hostile wishes against the father on the part of the sons may have in psychodynamics, he also provides a cultural resolution in his view of repressed father-son rivalry, and its many derivatives in adult life, as a dynamic which can underlie superior creative achievements—including his own creation of psychoanalysis which resulted from his reactions to the death of his father and the contemporaneous intellectual competition with Wilhelm Fliess.

In this perspective it is possible to look at Freud's formulation of the Oedipus complex in its wider cultural context in such a way as to bring out some of the contrasts with the South Italian complex.

First we might sum up some of the essential characteristics of the latter in such a way as to make a comparison possible. We have seen the mother-son relationship as the primary axis of family continuity and emphasized the degree to which the son maintains a dependent position *vis-à-vis* the mother, dealing with sexual and aggressive feelings in a variety of ways among the most important of which is an identification with the feminine values of purity; we have also brought out the extent to which the father-daughter relationship provides a counter-point pattern by a failure to repress the incestuous element. We have also noted that cross-sex relationships are emphasized more than same-sex ones and have suggested that this may build both romantic and conservative elements into the social structure, in that the strength of intergenerational ties wins out over individually formed ones and in that the cross-sex emphasis acts against the creation of ego ideals which the individual seeks to achieve. Both the conservative and feminine elements are summed up in the importance given to virginity as a social symbol: virginity is something which is given and not acquired and it is given to women and not to men.[23]

But in discussing the Oedipus complex Freud is quite explicit about the fact that the Oedipal wishes are given up in such a way as to be replaced by identifications with the same-sex parent; where this does not take place the resulting phenomena are seen as pathological. Moreover, his formulations start from the assumption that the primary factor is rivalry between father and son; these two struggle with each other for the possession of a woman whose background position is taken for granted, just as is that of Sarah who waited until the age of ninety-nine for a son with only one outbreak of sceptical laughter and then did not complain when Abraham took Isaac off as a sacrifice to a patriarchal God. And finally he assumes a very high degree of capacity for delay or sublimation which takes the form of an ability, based on identifications, to turn instinctual impulses into future-oriented creative achievement. This in turn in his own thinking primarily takes the form of masculine imagery, e.g. penetrating reality in the interests of scientific conquest

[23] At least from the South Italian perspective, where the body referent is very clear: as a humorous response to the assertion that Freud defines femininity in terms of a lack of masculinity, we could again refer to the Neapolitan informant who when questioned about the double standard replied 'But how could you ever tell if a man had lost it or not?'

and overcoming resistance, whether in patients or in any other facet of reality.

What differentiates his view of the father-son relationship is then the very high degree of sublimation which he assumes to characterize the conflict: identification with the father, in his view and in his own life, even if ambivalent, does not result in the kind of open hostility and decreasing social energy which we saw in the case of the street vendor, but rather in a complex identification with a continuing tradition. As opposed to the South Italian view, it is the feminine sphere which is the lower and more naturalistic one, while father-son conflict gives rise to the most complex social sublimations, e.g. the many intellectual ties based on a patriarchal model which characterize Freud's life. This is not to say that he was insensitive to other human possibilities—the work on hysteria, and in particular the paper on transference-love, bear witness to a kind of paternalistic but subtly seductive appreciation of women, in many ways a more sophisticated variant of the South Italian father-daughter pattern; and of course his fantasy view of Rome as a romantic opposite to the active competition of his Viennese life is well known. But it is hard to doubt that Freud was a patriarch with a patriarchal view of man.

The sources of his patriarchal bias can be seen as twofold: the first in the Hebraic tradition which, as discussed in *Moses and Monotheism*,[24] was of considerably symbolic importance to him, and the second in elements common to Western society since the Reformation. From both perspectives one can see ways in which the Oedipus complex formulation ties in with broader cultural features. The historical importance of Moses lies in his having organized what was initially a series of patrilineal kin groups into a larger collectivity. The Old Testament makes many of the specific taboos and perceptions of the patrilineal kin group very clear: in the image of the thundering patriarchal God (which we can think of as arising when demands for respect taboo the expression of aggression against the father), in the emphasis on rivalry between brothers, in the tracing of lines of descent solely through men, and in the strong taboo against homosexuality (as seen in the story of Ham who was cursed for looking on his father's nakedness, and perhaps in the extreme anxiety which surrounds the idea of seeing

---

[24] S. Freud, *Moses and Monotheism* (1939), *Standard Ed.*, 23, London: Hogarth Press, 1964.

God). From the second point of view, Freud does nothing more than reinforce and deepen our genetic understanding of values of active accomplishment and mastery of external reality, which in the degree of emphasis contrast post-Reformation Western Society with many others and which can be thought of as masculine in style. In this perspective, moreover, the continuity between Freud's society and that of contemporary United States becomes apparent—the common elements being the emphasis on active mastery, the delay of gratification for future rewards by means of identification and ego ideals, and the emphasis on separation from early feminine attachments.

However, questioning of some of Freud's more narrowly patriarchal bias has been characteristic in this country and has had many reflections in psychoanalytic thinking, for example, in the much greater emphasis given to the mother-child relationship. This must certainly be related to the more egalitarian concept of the family, and one might say that psychoanalysis itself has been crucially involved in the elaboration of some new cultural values and images which are feminine in quality: the terms 'warmth', 'security', and 'support', with all of their psychological and social ramifications, are evidence of this, and they in turn serve in the definition of norms for intimate relationships, for example, that the mother should send the child into the outside world, but not in such a sudden or traumatic way that he loses the sense of support of security.[25] In the same way, the ideal wife furthers her husband's extrafamilial activities by giving her support, in a way which may imply far more submissiveness than the Italian image of an intruding male presence which may on occasion be kicked out, and this goes with the positive rather than negative definition of the extrafamilial world. In addition, family patterns may in many ways make for lack of differentiation between maternal and erotic aspects of love, in that the latter are not defined as 'bad' or forbidden in themselves, but rather, in current American morality, tend to be legitimized precisely to the extent that they are assimilated to qualities such as 'warmth' or 'security'. Thus, in contrast to many societies, we perceive no inherent conflict between family continuity and the sexual instinct. The details of this pattern and its cultural ramifications have yet to be described, but while it certainly

[25] Cf. the harsh separation characterizing early school life both in the Puritan and Orthodox Jewish traditions.

involves major changes from nineteenth-century ideals of discipline and control or emphasis on masculine authority in the direction of a higher cultural valuation of the feminine role, it also seems likely that values such as warmth and security will nevertheless remain subordinate to the primary social goal of mastery; we would not see these changes as working in the long run in the direction of matriarchy.[26]

In conclusion, we should like to say a few words on the subject of research methodology. Psychoanalysts who have continued to base their work on Freud's theory of instinct have often commented that work based on the concepts of culture is likely to deal with motivation in a way which is behaviouristic or even superficial. That many of the potentialities of Freud's theory were overlooked in much of the early work on culture and personality is, we believe, quite true. Among the reasons for this is a too-hasty attempt to take over the trauma theory in such a way as to postulate uncertain and often mechanical relationships between specific features of child training and adult personality or culture patterns, e.g. culture X is oral because it has a long nursing period, and culture Y is anal because toilet training is surrounded with anxiety. At the same time, in particular where it has not hesitated to deal with cultural patterns of meaning as expressed in symbolic form—for example, Mead and Bateson's[27] attempt in *Balinese Character* to relate an entire ritual sequence to infantile experience—the field of culture and personality has also produced some quite new modes of thought. Similarly, beginning with Malinowski's work, the use of the psychoanalytic concept of affect and the emphasis on the more intimate dynamics of the family have added an entirely new dimension to the comparative study of kinship, the field which makes up the most solidly founded and scientifically based area of social

[26] Grete Bibring has commented on some differences between European and American family patterns as reflected in comparative analytical case material. While noting important matriarchal trends in the latter setting, she comments that these are nevertheless not congruent with the total social context and may become pathogenic for this reason. One could add that matriarchalism in the sense of uncompensated female dominance in the family may be quite common as the result of various processes of social change, but that in the long run compensating social mechanisms should appear. (See G. L. Bibring, 'On the "Passing of the Oedipus Complex" in a Matriarchal Family Setting', in R. M. Loewenstein (ed.), *Drives, Affects, Behaviour*, New York: International Universities Press, 1953, pp. 278-85).

[27] M. Mead and G. Bateson, *Balinese Character: A Photographic Analysis*, New York: Special Publication of the New York Academy of Sciences, 1942.

anthropology. In contrast to the field of culture and personality, this latter is almost completely unknown in psychoanalytic circles, a fact which can lead one to believe that the assertion that the 'culturalist' approach is a superficial one is as much based on attitudes concerning differences on theory and technique which have arisen within the psychoanalytic movement as it is on serious study of the actual work of anthropology.

Moreover, at the present time psychoanalysis is facing a crisis as the result of increasing pressures both from without and from within for more careful scientific demonstration and elaboration of its conceptual apparatus. One of the potential dangers of this situation is that psychoanalytic research will itself take an increasingly behaviouristic direction, i.e. attempt to reduce concepts whose initial originality derived from their immediate perception of meaningful or symbolic phenomena to a form which is quantifiable or experimentally testable in a way which is independent of the interpretive sensitivity of the observer. But this latter, for the anthropologist just as much as for the clinically oriented psychoanalyst, is a factor which cannot or should not be left out of any attempt to create a truly human science of human behaviour, however sophisticated we may become concerning the inevitable emotional or normative bias of individual observations. In this perspective the moment when Malinowski, alone in the Trobriand Islands, had to turn to the Trobrianders themselves for companionship—because in his isolation he had lost interest in the questions concerning evolution and the nature of primitive man which he had so heatedly debated with his colleagues in London—is to modern anthropology what Freud's discovery of transference is to psychoanalysis: both make the observer's sensitivity to what is happening around him a primary instrument of research, and both focus research on living human situations rather than artificially created ones.

But today one might say that the initial supposition of Malinowski and numerous other anthropologists that comparative work provides a particularly important means of testing and elaborating psychoanalytic concepts is not less relevant than it was a generation ago, both in that the variety of living cultures provides a natural laboratory setting and in that participant observation, or the attempt to at least hypothetically adapt the framework of a culture different from one's own, may provide an antidote for that part of observer bias that stems from the taking for granted of particular cultural suppositions, i.e. normative bias. In the latter respect, in fact, one might say that comparative work is perhaps all the more necessary now that psychoanalysis, rather than being an isolated and badly misunderstood field of endeavour, has in itself become a source of social norms. One of the dangers of the latter situation is that personality attributes favouring psychoanalytic investigation may be postulated as components of an ideal 'human nature' and in turn may be built into a theoretical apparatus. Many qualities common in Southern Italy, for example, may well appear as 'ego weakness' from the standpoint of a therapist, but if we look at them in their own setting we may find ways in which they are adaptive and in turn use such observations to enlarge our concepts of the ego and adaptation.[28] A great variety of concepts and postulates also takes on new meaning or leads to new questions if they are applied in the comparative framework.

This paper in itself, moreover, raises many theoretical questions which we have not even tried to answer; for example, can one really say that some kinds of incest wishes are closer to consciousness in one society than in another, and if so, what does this imply for the concept of repression? Or, what are the theoretical consequences for concepts concerning psychopathology and delinquency of what we have called the lesser internalization of paternal authority in Southern Italy and its related social consequences such as the importance of negativism in the peer group setting? It is clear that failure to show a positive masculine identification in the occupational sphere cannot in itself be taken as an indication of psychopathic personality, if by the latter we mean the lack of any super-ego restraint, because it is by no means incompatible with a fully internalized respect for women and family norms: witness the affirmative role played by the Neapolitan underworld in the protection of virgins. But such facts should in turn lead us to seek a more careful definition of the super-ego, which, if it is indeed a universally found psychic apparatus laid down in early infancy, should be definable independently of variations in norms relevant to adults.

In other words, in a great many areas more careful and self-conscious comparative thinking might help us to tighten up some

[28] See A. Parsons, 'A Schizophrenic Episode in a Neapolitan Slum', *Psychiatry*, 24 (1961), 109-21.

of our theoretical concepts and in particular to separate that which refers to early infantile life from that which defines normative expectations for the adult. Such attempts can in turn have immediate clinical implications for matters such as diagnosis and prognosis. Many social scientists have pointed out the ways in which normative bias may appear in diagnostic judgment when there are social differences between psychiatrist and patient; moreover, such biases follow some fairly consistent and predictable patterns. Thus, diagnoses such as 'character disorder' and 'psychopathic personality' are certainly overused for Italian male patients; when the neurotic acts out his difficulties outside the family, or even within it (as in the common example of the depressed and despondent man who beats his wife), he quite often gets into trouble with the law. Similarly for women, 'oral' elements are commonly overemphasized (in the sense that significant areas of competence or of genital focus in intrapsychic conflict are overlooked) in the light of the greater restriction of life to the family setting. It would be our view that in this group one can individualize the major genetically rooted personality structures predictable from psychoanalytic theory (schizoid, depressive or cyclic, obsessional, and hysteric), but that the overt differences in phenomenology can be such that even the experienced diagnostician may have difficulty if he does not know the cultural expectations. Such difficulties in turn may have important implications for the evaluation of the depth of pathology or for treatment decisions.

In summary, we believe that comparative research has a potentially very important contribution to make in the light of the current need for further testing and elaboration of psychoanalytic concepts with respect to a variety of materials. Moreover, this is the case both for general social or cultural formulations and for more specific studies of psychopathology in ways which are relevant to the understanding of personality dynamics and which can have immediate applications for diagnosis and treatment. For the original question of whether the Oedipus complex is universal or not, we would sum up by saying that it is no longer very meaningful in that particular form. The more important contemporary questions would rather be: what is the possible range within which culture can utilize and elaborate the instinctually given human potentialities, and what are the psychologically given limits of this range? Or in slightly different terms: what more can we learn about what Claude Lévi-

Strauss[29] has characterized as the 'transition from nature to culture'? To answer fully questions such as these will require the equal and collaborative efforts of psychoanalysis and anthropology.

[29] See C. Lévi-Strauss, *Les Structures Elementaires de la Paranté*, Paris: Presses Universitaires de France, 1949; and idem, 'L'Analyse structurale en linguistique et en anthropologie', *Word*, I (1949), 35-53.

Further Reading

ABRAHAM, K., 'Dreams and Myths: a Study in Folk-Psychology', in *Clinical Papers and Essays on Psycho-Analysis*, London: Hogarth Press, 1955, pp. 151-209.

AXELRAD, S., 'Infant Care and Personality Reconsidered: A Rejoinder to Orlansky', in *The Psychoanalytic Study of Society*, 2, New York: International Universities Press, 1962, pp. 75-132.

BATESON, G., and MEAD M., *Balinese Character. A Photographic Analysis*, New York: Academy of Sciences, 1942.

BOYER, L. B., 'Psychological Problems of a Group of Apaches: Alcoholic Hallucinosis and Latent Homosexuality', in *The Psychoanalytic Study of Society*, 3, New York: International Universities Press, 1964, pp. 203-77.

CARSTAIRS, G. M., *The Twice-Born*, Bloomington: Indiana University Press; London: Hogarth Press, 1957.

CAUDILL, W., 'Anthropology and Psychoanalysis: Some Theoretical Issues', in Gladwin, T. and Sturtevant, W. C. (eds.), *Anthropology and Human Behavior*, Washington: The Anthropological Society of Washington, pp. 174-214.

DUNDES, A., 'Earth-Diver: Creation of the Mythopoeic Male', *American Anthropologist*, vol. 64, no. 5, 1962, pp. 1032-51.

ERIKSON, E. H., *Observations on the Yurok: Childhood and World Image*, University of California Publications in American Archaeology and Ethnology, vol. 35, no. 10, 1943, Berkeley: University of California Press.

ERIKSON, E. H., 'Childhood and Tradition in Two American Indian Tribes', in *The Psychoanalytic Study of the Child*, 1, New York: International Universities Press; London: Hogarth Press, 1945, pp. 319-50.

ERIKSON, E. H., *Childhood and Society*, New York: Norton, 1950; Harmondsworth: Penguin Books, 1965.

EVANS, W. N., 'The Passing of the Gentleman', in *The Psychoanalytic Quarterly*, vol. 18, 1949, pp. 19-43.

FLUGEL, J. C., *Man, Morals and Society. A Psycho-Analytical Study*, New York: International Universities Press, 1955; London: Duckworth, 1945.

FOX, R., 'In the Beginning: Aspects of Hominid Behavioral Evolution', *Man*, vol. 2, no. 3, 1967, pp. 415-33.

HALLOWELL, A. I., *Culture and Experience*, Publications of the Philadelphia Anthropological Society, vol. 4, Philadelphia: University of Philadelphia Press, 1955.

HARTMANN, H., 'The Application of Psychoanalytic Concepts to Social Science', in *The Psychoanalytic Quarterly*, vol. 19, 1950, pp. 385-92. (See also PARSONS, T., below.) For Hartmann's papers see now H. Hartmann, *Essays in Ego Psychology*, New York: International Universities Press, 1964.

JACKSON, S. W. (reporter), 'Aspects of Culture in Psychoanalytic Theory and Practice' (Fall Meeting of the American Psychoanalytic Association, New York, 1967) in *Journal of the American Psychoanalytic Association*, vol. 16, no. 3, 1968, pp. 651-70.

JAQUES, E., 'Social Systems as a Defense against Persecutory and Depressive Anxiety, a Contribution to the Psycho-Analytical Study of Social Process', in *New Directions in Psycho-Analysis*, edited by M. Klein, P. Heimann, and R. Money-Kyrle, London: Tavistock, 1955, pp. 478-98.

JONES, E., *Essays in Applied Psycho-Analysis, Vol. II, Essays in Folklore, Anthropology, and Religion*, London: Hogarth Press, 1951.

KLUCKHOHN, C., 'Some Aspects of Navaho Infancy and Childhood', in *The Psychoanalytic Study of Society*, I, New York: International Universities Press, 1944, pp. 37-86.

LaBARRE, W., *The Human Animal*, Chicago: University of Chicago Press, 1954.

LEIGHTON, A. H., LAMBO, T. A., HUGHES, Ch. C., LEIGHTON, D. C., MURPHY, J. M., and MACKLIN, O. B., *Psychiatric Disorders Among the Yoruba*, Ithaca: Cornell University Press, 1963.

LEWIN, B. D., Review of G. Bateson's and M. Mead's *Balinese Character* (see above), in *The Psychoanalytic Study of the Child*, 1, New York: International Universities Press; London: Hogarth Press, 1945.

MILNER, M., 'Aspects of Symbolism in Comprehension of the not-self', *International Journal of Psycho-Analysis*, vol. 33, 1952.

MONEY-KYRLE, R., *The Meaning of Sacrifice, International Psycho-Analytical Library*, no. 16, London: Hogarth Press, 1930.

MONEY-KYRLE, R., *Superstition and Society*, London: Hogarth Press, 1939.

MORGENTHALER, F., and PARIN, P., 'Typical Forms of Transference Among West Africans', in *International Journal of Psycho-Analysis*, vol. 45, 1964, pp. 446-9.

MUENSTERBERGER, W., 'Psyche and Environment: Sociocultural Variations in Separation and Individuation', *The Psychoanalytic Quarterly*, vol. 38, April 1969.

NICHOLS, C., *The Evolution of Social Theory and a Metapsychology of Culture in the Writings of Géza Róheim* (mimeographed), Waltham: Brandeis University, 1967.

ORTIGUES, M., and E., *Oedipe Africain*, Paris: Librairie Plon, 1966.

PARIN, P., MORGENTHALER, F., and PARIN-MATTHÈY, G., *Die Weissen Denken Zuviel*, Zurich: Atlantis Verlag, 1963.

PARSONS, T., 'Psychoanalysis and the Social Structure', in *The Psychoanalytic Quarterly*, vol. 19, 1950, pp. 371-84 (see also HARTMANN, H. above).

RÓHEIM, G., *The Origin and Function of Culture, Nervous and Mental Diseases Monographs*, New York, 1943.

RÓHEIM, G., *War, Crime and the Covenant. Journal of Clinical Psychopathology, Monograph Series*, I, Monticello, N.Y.: Medical Journal Press, 1945.

RÓHEIM, G., *Psychoanalysis and Anthropology: Culture, Personality and the Unconscious*, New York: International Universities Press, 1950.

RÓHEIM, G., *Magic and Schizophrenia* (Posthumously edited by W. Muensterberger), New York: International Universities Press, 1955.

SARLIN, C. N., 'Identity, Culture and Psychosexual Development', in *American Imago*, vol. 24, no. 3, 1967, pp. 181-247.

SAVAGE, C., and PRINCE, R., 'Depression Among the Yoruba', *The Psychoanalytic Study of Society*, 4, New York: International Universities Press, 1967, pp. 83-98.

SIMENAUER, E. 'Oedipus-Konflikt und Neurosebedingungen bei den Bantu Ostafrikas' in *Jahrbuch der Psychoanalyse*, vol. 2, Koeln and Opladen: Westdeutscher Verlag, 1961/2, pp. 41-62.

STEPHENS, W. N., *'The Oedipus Complex. Cross-Cultural Evidence*, New York: The Free Press of Glencoe, 1962.

Works Cited

An Outline of Psycho-Analysis (S. Freud), 11
An Autobiographical Study (S. Freud), 67
The Authoritarian Personality (W. Adorno et al.), 297
Balinese Character (M. Mead and G. Bateson), 380
Charakteranalyse (W. Reich), 188
Christians and Jews (R. M. Loewenstein), 292
Civilization and its Discontents (S. Freud), 11
The Ego and the Id (S. Freud), 14
The Interpretation of Dreams (S. Freud), 71, 72, 73
Moses and Monotheism (S. Freud), 74, 378
Psychopathology and Politics (H. Lasswell), 293
The Psychopathology of Everyday Life (S. Freud), 72, 73
The Religion of the Semites (R. Smith), 60
The Riddle of the Sphinx (G. Róheim), 82
Sex and Repression in Savage Society (B. Malinowski), 88
Studies on Hysteria (S. Freud and J. Breuer), 13
Three Essays on the Theory of Sexuality (S. Freud), 98
Totem and Taboo (S. Freud), 11, 31, 32, 53, 54, 55, 63, 64, 68, 69, 85,
   88
The Twenty-four Examples of Filial Piety, 93

Author Index

Subject Index

Girls,
attitudes among Chinese to birth of, 300
Go-between,
as cultural institution, 312
as replacing mother, among South Chinese, 320-1
'Good father', and increase of guilt feelings, 174
Growth,
as including unfolding of ego functions, 243
as peculiar to man, 21
Guilt,
as diminished by belief in primitive origins, 68
and internalization of conscience, 20
at surpassing father (Freud), 72
as traceable to remote progenitors, 68
Guilt feelings,
and access to ego of incompatible instinctual drives, 197
among Africans and non-Africans, 198
and feelings of aggression toward prohibited object, 213
in relation to capital offence, 199

Health,
as broader concept than normalcy, 109
as not equivalent to adaptation, 109
Hebraic tradition, and Freud's patriarchal view of man, 378
Helplessness,
as inability to bear frustration, 39
and super-ego development, 82
and superiority among humans (Thomas), 81
Hostility, between father and son, among South Italians, 376
Human behaviour,
as based on biological and social relations, 246
basis in hypothetical event in primeval times, 26
Human development,
as determined by phylogenetically based steps, 14
and mediation between givens and modes of adaptation, 14
multiplicity of forces governing, 18
Human nature,
and conservation of infantile situation, 38
and human institutions, 47
variant and invariant traits of, 24